Making the Net Work

Deploying a Secure Portal on Sun Systems

Robert L. Baker

Sun Microsystems Press
A Prentice Hall Title

Prentice Hall PTR offers excellent discounts on this book when ordered in quantity for bulk purchases or special sales. For more information, please contact: U.S. Corporate and Government Sales, 1-800-382-3419, corpsales@pearsontechgroup.com. For sales outside of the U.S., please contact: International Sales, 1-317-581-3793, international@pearsontechgroup.com.

Executive Editor: *Gregory G. Doench*
Cover Design Director: *Jerry Votta*
Cover Designer: *Kavish & Kavish Digital Publishing and Design*
Manufacturing Manager: *Alexis R. Heydt-Long*
Marketing Manager: *Christopher Guzikowski*

Sun Microsystems Press:
Publisher: *Myrna Rivera*

First Printing
Text printed on recycled paper

ISBN 0-13-148338-2

Sun Microsystems Press
A Prentice Hall Title

Acknowledgments

This book is made possible through the generous support of many individuals. I sincerely appreciate the time and effort that everyone donated to bring this book to publication.

Special thanks to the following people for sharing their invaluable technical expertise and support, which contributed to the technical quality and completeness of this book:

Divya Jain	Thor Mitchell	Christian Candia
Russ Petruzzelli	Nagendra Kumar	Dean Polla
Rick Evans	Swaminathan Seetharamen	

Thanks also to the following people that provided technical assistance, which contributed to the technical quality of this book:

Neelabhra Haldar	Vinay T	Noble Paul
Amlan Chatterjee	Rakesh Nayak	Jeff Sokolov
Vinod Seraphin	Jack Ciejek	Mark Oslowski

I would like to express my gratitude to those people who contributed to this book through their proficiencies in management and book development:

Jerry Sadin	Lucy Ruble	Barb Jugo
Sue Blumenberg	Diana Lins	Vicky Hardman
Danesh Forouhari	Billie Markim	Cathleen Nielsen

Many thanks are owed to family members who provided encouragement and understanding when most needed. Thank you Wendi Baker, and Chris Ruble.

Finally, I want to thank the many readers of my online articles. It was those readers who provided the inspiration and motivation for this book.

Contents

Preface

This Sun BluePrints™ book describes how to get the most out of the Sun's portal server secure remote access (SRA) product. The best practice suggestions contained in this book evolved from real-world implementations, proof-of-concept exercises, and presales support, all related to deploying and managing a secure portal on Sun systems.

Sun BluePrints Program

The mission of the Sun BluePrints program is to empower Sun customers with the technical knowledge required to implement reliable, extensible, and secure information systems within the data center using Sun products. This program provides a framework to identify, develop, and distribute best practices information that applies across the Sun product lines. Technical subject matter experts contribute to the program.

The Sun BluePrints program includes books, guides, and online articles. Through these vehicles, Sun can provide guidance, installation and implementation experiences, real-life scenarios, and late-breaking technical information.

The monthly electronic magazine, Sun BluePrints OnLine, is located on the Web at `http://www.wun.com/blueprints`.

Purpose

The primary purpose of this book is to provide the reader with the technical know-how to take advantage of the latest portal technologies from Sun and to deploy a portal for secure remote access using the Sun portal server SRA software as a foundation.

This book delves into issues related to the integration of third-party products, diagnosis of problems related to sizing and performance, management of application access, and problem isolation. This book also makes suggestions for handling specialized deployment scenarios.

Most of the content in this book originates from the author's experience as a sustaining and backline support engineer for the Sun portal server software. Topics concentrate on some of the best practices developed over the past several years of the portal server software life cycle for existing customers running real-world, large-scale, secure portal deployments. This book represents a manifestation of support cases, calls, technical notes, README files, release notes, escalations, and the author's personal interaction with the product.

Who Should Read This Book

This book is intended for portal server administrators, portal content developers, Sun and OEM sales forces, professional services and integrators, CIOs, solution architects, Internet service providers, and third-party software developers.

The skill requirements vary based on the reader. For instance, a CIO may only need to understand fundamental portal server terminology for comparing and contrasting the Sun portal server software with other products, while an integrator requires a wide-ranging technical skill set to apply the information put forth in certain sections in this book.

Before You Read This Book

This book is not intended to be a general how-to guide on installing and using Sun server products, or to supersede the product documentation. This book complements, and at times refers to product documentation, BluePrint articles, and the *Sun ONE™ Portal Server 6.0 Deployment Guide* for specific step-by-step instructions related to administrative tasks, or higher-level overviews such as end-to-end deployment architectures.

You can access the product documentation that pertains to the version of Sun portal server software that you are using at: http://docs.sun.com.

How This Book Is Organized

The main chapters of this book describe the components of the Sun portal server software product using a repetitive arrangement as follows:

- What it is
- Why use it
- How it works
- How to deploy it
- Deployment scenarios
- Tips from the trenches
- The latest features

You can use this predictable organization to quickly access the information that pertains to what you want to know from the following chapters:

Chapter 1 introduces the Sun portal server software and lays the foundation needed to understand the chapters that follow. It also provides information on product evolution, how to get it, and patching information.

Chapter 2 describes the Netlet component of the Sun portal server secure remote access (SRA) software product. The Netlet is used to provision internal applications to authenticated end-users securely over the Internet.

Chapter 3 presents information on the NetFile component of the Sun portal server SRA software product. NetFile is a file management application that enables end users to access and control remote file systems over the Internet.

Chapter 4 explains the Rewriter component of the Sun portal server SRA software product. The Rewriter enables remote end users to access the Intranet by rewriting URLs so they can be proxied in a secure environment.

Chapter 5 discusses the Gateway technology in the Sun portal server SRA software. The Gateway is used to direct traffic from remote users to the other portal server components and internal resources, and enforce access policies to these resources.

Appendix A provides instructions about how to integrate Microsoft Exchange and Lotus iNotes with the portal server software.

Appendix B provides information about the problems you might encounter using the `deploy` command, and offers suggestions for avoiding them.

Glossary is a list of words and phrases and their definitions.

Obtaining Downloadable Files for This Book

A variety of files are available for use with this book. The files provide scripts and full code listings that are used in examples. These downloadable files are available to you free of charge, and by obtaining them, you'll be able to perform many of the best practices described in this book without having to reinvent the code.

We've made every attempt to provide code that is trouble free; however, because every compute environment is different, you should test the code thoroughly before using it in a production environment. As with most freely distributed code, these scripts and tools are provided to you with no support commitment on the part of Sun Microsystems, Inc.

To obtain any of the downloadable files for this book, first download the compressed file from the Sun Download Center and unzip the it (instructions below). See TABLE P-1 for a list of files that you will have after unzipping the file.

▼ To Download and Unzip the File

1. **Go to the Sun BluePrints Scripts and Tools download Web site:**

   `http://www.sun.com/solutions/blueprints/tools/index.html`

2. **Select the link titled Deploying a Secure Portal.**

   Note – Not all software listed at this site pertains to this book.
   ---

3. **If you are not already registered at the Sun Download Center, register now.**

   You must be registered at the Sun Download Center before you can download the scripts and tools. If this is your first visit, select *Register now*. You only have to register once, and it's free. Whenever you come back to the Download Center, just enter your user name and password to log in.

4. **Log in to the Sun Download Center.**

5. **Accept the License Agreement.**

6. **Select the link titled Deploying a Secure Portal (downloadable file), English.**

   Perform the download according to the download procedures presented by your browser.

7. **In the directory where you downloaded the file, unzip the it:**

```
# unzip 817-5024-SDLC*.zip
```

8. **Using a browser, view the following file:**

```
./download_directory/817-5024-SDLC1/index.html
```

The information in the `index.html` file is similar to what is described in TABLE P-1.

What You Get

TABLE P-1 lists the subdirectories and some of the files that you will have after unzipping the downloadable file. It is possible that the downloadable files will be updated over time, and those changes might not be listed in this book. In such cases, any changes will be described in a `README` file. Read any `README` files (if present) after unzipping the downloadable file.

TABLE P-1   Downloaded Subdirectories and Files

Subdirectory/File Name	Description
`./desktop`	A subdirectory that contains the code for the custom desktop type that is shown in FIGURE 2-20.
	This directory also contains Citrix channel JSP code listing and the embedded Netlet pop-up window described in CODE EXAMPLE 2-15.
	Files in this subdirectory:
	• `./sunone/Bookmark/display.template.OWA` – Bookmark provider template used to make sure that the link to launch OWA is not rewritten for the purpose of the Netlet/Exchange Integration.
	• `./sunone/SampleJSP/citrix.jsp` – The Citrix channel created from the SampleJSP provider that ships with the portal server software.
`./exchange2ksp3-int`	A subdirectory that contains the scripts you ned to perform the Exchange 2000 SP3 integration through the Rewriter as documented in "Microsoft Exchange Integrations" on page 360. The files in this subdirectory are described in "Downloadable Scripts and Files For This Integration" on page 361.

TABLE P-1   Downloaded Subdirectories and Files *(Continued)*

Subdirectory/File Name	Description
`./misc`	A subdirectory that contains miscellaneous code examples from several file listings given in the book:
	`PACTest.java` – Boilerplate code to perform automatic proxy configuration file debugging for the Netlet. The code is similar to what is shown in CODE EXAMPLE 2-5.
	`url_auth_display.template` – Bookmark provider boilerplate code to enable the channel to support authentication URLs. See CODE EXAMPLE 4-16.
`./perf`	A subdirectory that contains script listings and some files that are helpful in performing load tests as described in "Baselining Gateway Performance" on page 338. Key files are:
	• `login-only.js` – A full file listing for the Web Load script described in the maximum load testing section of Chapter 5. See CODE EXAMPLE 5-1.
	• `reliability.js` – A full file listing for the Web Load script described in the reliability testing section of Chapter 5. See CODE EXAMPLE 5-2.
`./rulesets`	A subdirectory that contains rulesets for some third-party application integrations through the Rewriter:
	• `exchange_2003_owa_ruleset.xml` – Ruleset supplied in portal server 6.2PC4 for Exchange 2003 Outlook Web Access integration.
	• `owa_sp3_ruleset.xml` – Ruleset discussed in the Microsoft Exchange integration for Exchange 2000 SP3.
	• `iDA_ruleset.xml` – Ruleset used to integrate the iPlanet Delegated Administrator software through the Gateway.

Shell Prompts

Shell	Prompt
C shell	*machine-name*%
C shell superuser	*machine-name*#
Bourne shell and Korn shell	$
Bourne shell and Korn shell superuser	#

Typographic Conventions

Typeface or Symbol[*]	Meaning	Examples
`AaBbCc123`	The names of commands, files, and directories; on-screen computer output	Edit your `.login` file. Use `ls -a` to list all files. `% You have mail.`
`AaBbCc123`	What you type, when contrasted with on-screen computer output	`% `**`su`** `Password:`
AaBbCc123	Book titles, new words or terms, words to be emphasized. Replace command-line variables with real names or values.	Read Chapter 6 in the *User's Guide*. These are called *class* options. You *must* be superuser to do this. To delete a file, type `rm` *filename*.
⊘	Marks examples of what not to do.	

[*] The settings on your browser might differ from these settings.

Accessing Sun Documentation

You can view, print, or purchase a broad selection of Sun documentation, including localized versions, at:

http://www.sun.com/documentation

Sun Welcomes Your Comments

Sun is interested in improving its documentation and welcomes your comments and suggestions. You can submit your comments by going to:

http://www.sun.com/hwdocs/feedback

Please include the title and part number of your document with your feedback:

Making the Net Work: Deploying a Secure Portal on Sun Systems,
part number 817-5024-10

Bibliography

Note – Sun is not responsible for the availability of third-party Web sites mentioned in this document. Sun does not endorse and is not responsible or liable for any content, advertising, products, or other materials that are available on or through such sites or resources. Sun is not responsible or liable for any actual or alleged damage or loss caused by or in connection with the use of or reliance on any such content, goods, or services that are available on or through such sites or resources.

Shearer, Dan "Configuring Samba (smb.conf)" from:
`http://us1.samba.org/samba/docs/man/install.html#id2873230`
Samba-HOWTO-Collection

Minasi, Mark "Linux's Smbclient Command" from:
`http://www.winnetmag.com/Articles/ArticleID/8897/pg/2/2.html`
Windows & .NET Magazine, Summer 2000

"Microsoft Exchange 2000 Server: Customizing Microsoft Outlook Web Access White Paper" from:
`http://www.microsoft.com/downloads/details.aspx?displaylang=`
`en&FamilyID=6532E454-073E-4974-A800-1490A7CB35BF`

Dallas Semiconductor "iButton Overview" from:
`http://www.ibutton.com`

## CHAPTER 1

Introduction

This chapter introduces the portal server secure remote access software, and lays the foundation needed to understand the chapters that follow. It also provides information on product evolution, patching information, and describes how to obtain the downloadable files that are available for this book.

The chapter is organized into the following sections:

Portal Introduction

Web portals are almost as old as the Web itself. The original portals were static information repositories that seemed to fade into obscurity when new push technologies were developed. Today, portals are everywhere, consisting of a variety of media, uses, and purposes. There are many factors contributing to this recent portal resurgence, and the rapid and global adaptation of information technology plays no small part. Flexible mobile work forces, the exponentially growing size of the World Wide Web, and the emergence of Web services, have all created a need for singular points of content aggregation, online communities, and network entry points.

Some portals such as the eBAY auction site fill niche markets with a single purpose in mind. Other portals like Yahoo create personalized entry points to the Web and offer special free and paid services to create what's commonly referred to as *stickiness*—having enough interesting content to keep users on their site; satisfying advertisers, business partners, and end users alike.

There are almost as many types of portals as there are portals, but the majority fall into one of the following categories:

- Business to Business (B2B) portals offer businesses the ability to maintain a unique partnered relationship over a public network. A B2B portal might include a parts-ordering interface for an original equipment manufacturer and a parts supplier.

- Business to Employee (B2E) portals offer remote access for employees to back-end resources on the corporate network. They may also aggregate employee-accessible applications in a single location.

- Business to Consumer (B2C) portals offer public-facing portals to the Web community, creating interesting starting and destination points, community outreach, and Web commerce.

There are also portals tailored for specific devices, such as wireless portals that offer varied content depending on how the portal is accessed. A B2C Web site that sells ring tones for a variety of cellular phones is a good example of a device-specific portal.

In general, the term *portal* describes a single point of content aggregation. Even so, the term is somewhat ambiguous and people have differing opinions and ideas about what constitutes a portal. Many of the larger portals have some common components. For instance, MyYahoo, MyNetscape, and MySun portals all contain authentication, individual channels, channel controls, customizeable content layouts, themes, and a selectable subset of available content to display on the *portal server desktop*. Some channels, such as stock channels, allow the content inside of the channel to be controlled by storing personal preferences about which stocks to show or how they should be displayed. User preferences are typically stored in a user profile associated with a user ID so that when a particular user returns to the portal and re-authenticates, their channel preferences and layout are the same as when they last logged out. Some example channels taken from the three sites mentioned above are shown in FIGURE 1-1.

FIGURE 1-1   Second Generation Portal Channels

These channels exemplify a subtle contrast from early-generation portals and push technologies that flooded desktop space with an overwhelming amount of content—both wanted and unwanted. Early-generation portals also treated users with an equal level of anonymity. Besides the small amount of information which could be stored in a persistent cookie, they did little to offer users a way to change, customize, personalize, and organize the content.

Content aggregation is often used to describe one of the primary functions of any portal, the process of taking a significant amount of disparate content and assimilating it into a single interface. The single interface is consistent, making it easier to navigate, and presents the most recent and relevant content that a user might be interested in from the multitude of originating sources. To achieve this, the portal needs to know a bit about the user. This is done through the generation of an *identity*—an extension to the user profile that can include more specific organizational data such as the user's role within the company, or the group or business unit to which the user belongs. A user's profile can contain additional information, including personal details like a user ID, email address, and favorite color scheme.

As the amount of data used to describe the average portal user grows, it must be stored in a place where it can be easily and quickly retrieved. For a transaction-based portal such as an e-commerce site, this data is sometimes stored in a relational database because of the write-intensive nature of portal users' interactions with the site. Informational portals tend to use Lightweight Directory Access Protocol (LDAP) instead, because the user preferences are not updated as often and the content is usually not written into the directory store.

It is impractical to merge disparate Web pages into a single Web page, so portals often employ the use of *channels*. Channels can provide many functions, such as Web clipping, scraping data from other Web sites, book marking important sites, providing application launch spaces, performing data extraction, running Web services, and executing embedded applications written to the browser or Java™ platform.

Without identity management, there is no way to designate policies governing which users have access to which applications, or how to provide the most appropriate portal experience which fits the user's role, responsibilities, and interests. FIGURE 1-2 shows an example of how content can be aggregated from a multitude of resources through the use of a portal.

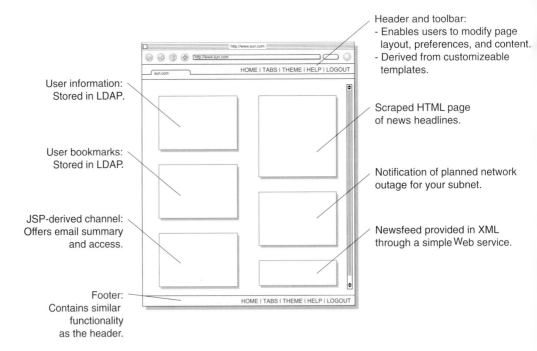

FIGURE 1-2 Portal Content Aggregation

Of particular interest in the deployment of B2B, B2E, and identity portals is the issue of security. In addition to the usual challenges with OS hardening, network security precautions and the like, the network administrator must also figure out the safest way to provide secure remote access to internal applications and information. In the case of identity provisioning portals, the user should also have control over who has access to what personal information—even if the information itself is not stored on their own computer. Ideally, a portal solution should not be invasive or require modification to an existing security infrastructure to provide portal access.

For instance, a human resources (HR) company outsourcing for a bank cannot dictate security modifications to the banking network so that bank employees can access their HR resources. Additionally, the HR company would probably not be able to force all of the banking employees to install a client application locally before they were able to access their HR information. This client footprint is one reason virtual private networks (VPNs) are usually not a good fit in these kinds of situations. Another reason is that without policy enforcement, VPNs allow open-ended access to the network once a user has authenticated. Thus, the HR tool would have to be isolated from the rest of the internal network.

Often B2B and B2E portals must access applications that run natively on different machine architectures, or need a downloadable client such as an applet which communicates over TCP/IP to interact with a back-end application (such as Internet Message Access Protocol (IMAP) tunneling). Securing this data, and providing the flexibility for a wide variety of user types and applications, are the primary functions of a secure remote access portal.

Creating in-house solutions in the portal space that include this level of flexibility, manageability, personalization, and security is a major undertaking, to say the least. There will be significant requirements for stability, availability, and scalability because the portal is the major entry point for users accessing the network. Productivity, stickiness, and user satisfaction can be adversely affected by the availability as well as the quality of content presented.

Portals can be accessed from anywhere using a multitude of devices, client user agents, and locales. This access must be provided in a manner that does not compromise security of the data being accessed, while maintaining a high level of availability. The demand for niche applications and end-to-end solutions in the portal space has created a frenzy among independent software venders (ISVs) and major software vendors. Some, like Tarantella and Citrix, have partnered with portal infrastructure providers like Sun to provide end-to-end solutions that enable portal users to securely access native desktop applications through a Web browser.

Sun Portal Product Evolution

This section describes the evolution and product naming changes for Sun's portal server product. This information is included so that you can understand the products as they are mentioned throughout the book. The changing marketing designations represent Sun's ongoing commitment to openness in computer networks and network applications. For convenience, TABLE 1-1 summarizes the product names.

The portal server software originated from a small company called iPlanet that Sun acquired. The product was called Secure Remote Passage, and it shipped on an iPlanet hardware device designated as the Gateway. Later, the Remote Passage designation was changed to Sun Web Top and carried a 2.0 major release number. This was a software-only solution that no longer required the iPlanet hardware. Sun deployed this version of the product as a company-wide secure remote access solution. Many Sun customers also deployed it to support their needs.

Once the Sun|Netscape Alliance was forged, iPlanet™ was chosen as the marketing designator for Sun's entire suite of e-commerce products. Though the secure remote access software was not considered an e-commerce product like the rest of the X line of Netscape™ products, it was nonetheless developed alongside the e-commerce products.

iPlanet™ Portal Server 3.0 software was the first version of the product to include more portal-like features, and the release focused less on secure remote access, and more on the infrastructure presentation layer for applications. Portal Server 3.x software shipped in the form of Service Packs, Hot Patches, or one-off patches. Portal *Service Packs* (SPs) were full product distributions that could be installed from scratch, or used to upgrade existing installations. *Hot Patches* (HPs) were cumulative patches created by the Sun Portal Sustaining organization to consolidate fixes between minor releases. *One-off patches* were created in special situations, and for critical fixes.

The secure remote access capability of the portal server 3.x software was sold as a separate product for licensing purposes. It was called the iPlanet Portal Server Secure Remote Access Pack (SRAP).

When the Sun|Netscape Alliance dissolved, most of the server products were tagged with the new marketing designation: Sun™ Open Network Environment (Sun™ ONE). The portal server 6.0 version was the first version that carried the new marketing designation, becoming the Sun™ ONE Portal Server 6.0 software. This version separated out the policy engine and the user and session management into a separate product called Directory Server Access Management Edition (DSAME). The portal server software retained its presentation layer functionality, adding different kinds of application containers including Java Server Pages™ (JSP™) technology,

Simple Object Access Protocol (SOAP) Web services, and Extensible Markup Language (XML). Additional desktop features were added, including tabbing and themes.

The secure remote access functionality was sold as the Sun ONE Portal Server 6.0 Remote Access software, a separate product also containing both the Sun ONE Portal Server and DSAME software. Sun ONE Portal Server 6.0 Secure Remote Access software was modified to include better administration of rulesets for the Rewriter, an internationally compliant NetFile component, and Netlet enhancements.

A short time after the Sun ONE Portal Server 6.0 software was delivered, Sun ONE Portal Server 6.1 software was released. Version 6.1 contained mostly customer fixes and features that had been added to iPlanet Portal Server 3.0 Service Pack 5 (SP5) and were not included in the Sun ONE Portal Server 6.0 Secure Remote Access software. Version 6.1 also shipped with a new version of DSAME, now called Identity Server. To date, there is one patch consolidation for the portal server 6.1 release, called Portal Server 6.1 Patch Consolidation 1 (PS6.1PC1). For information about patches, see "Patching the Portal Server Software" on page 10. Around the time of the version 6.1 release, Sun announced that all Sun server software would henceforth be released on a single release train called the Sun Java™ Enterprise System.

The portal server 6.2 software is the first version that carries the recent Java Enterprise System designation. The Java Enterprise System Portal Server 6.2 software has been reunited with the Secure Remote Access software, and can be installed from the unified Java Enterprise System installation media.

While this book is intended to mainly cover the Sun ONE Portal Server 6.x and the Java Enterprise System releases, many of the portal server versions and variations, including patch levels, are referred to throughout this book. Consult the product documentation for your specific release for enhancements and other changes.

TABLE 1-1 summarizes the portal server product names for the products that are referenced in this book.

TABLE 1-1   Portal Server Product Name Summary

Product Name	Comments
iPlanet Portal Server 3.0	Requires the addition of the Secure Remote Access Pack for SRA features
iPlanet Portal Server 3.0SP1	SP stands for Service Pack
iPlanet Portal Server 3.0SP2	HP Stands for Hot Patch
iPlanet Portal Server 3.0SP2HP1	All service packs and hot patches provide fixes and functionality for the Portal Server and the Secure Remote Access Pack (SRAP)
iPlanet Portal Server 3.0SP2HP3	
iPlanet Portal Server 3.0SP2HP4	
iPlanet Portal Server 3.0SP2HP5	
iPlanet Portal Server 3.0SP3	
iPlanet Portal Server 3.0SP3HP1	
iPlanet Portal Server 3.0SP3HP2	
iPlanet Portal Server 3.0SP3HP3	
iPlanet Portal Server 3.0SP3HP4	
iPlanet Portal Server 3.0SP4HP1	
iPlanet Portal Server 3.0SP4HP2	
iPlanet Portal Server 3.0SP4HP3	
iPlanet Portal Server 3.0SP5	
Sun ONE Portal Server 6.0	Requires Secure Remote Access software for SRA features
Sun ONE Portal Server 6.1 6.1PC1	Requires Secure Remote Access software for SRA features PC stands for Patch Consolidation
Sun Java™ Enterprise System Portal Server 6.2	Includes Secure Remote Access features

A full portal server deployment requires the installation and configuration of a variety of software. The following list provides an example:

- Sun ONE Portal Server (core) software

- Sun™ ONE Directory Server software

- Sun™ ONE Identity Server (formerly the iPlanet™ Directory Server Access Management Edition) software

- Sun™ ONE Web Server software, or an application server, such as Sun™ ONE Application Server, BEA WebLogic, or IBM WebSphere Advanced Edition software

- Sun ONE Portal Server, Secure Remote Access software

In this book, the term *portal server* refers to the Sun's portal server software with the Secure Remote Access software unless specified otherwise. *Portal server node* and *portal platform node* refer to the portal server core product.

Purchasing Portal Server Software

The Sun Java Enterprise System software is available from a number of resources. The following URL provides a good starting point:

`http://www.sun.com/sales/`

At this Sun Web site you can choose to purchase the portal server software from the Sun Store, the Sun Download Center, Worldwide Sales offices, and more.

The Java Enterprise System combines software as a single entity, for a single price, per employee, per year. When you purchase the Java Enterprise System software, you receive the following:

- Network Identity Services
  - Directory Server
  - Identity Server
  - Directory Proxy Server
- Web and Application Services
  - Application Server Platform Edition
  - Application Server Standard Edition
  - Message Queue Enterprise Edition
  - Web Server
- Collaboration and Communication
  - Messaging Server
  - Calendar Server
  - Instant Messaging
- Portal Services
  - Portal Server
  - Portal Serer Secure Remote Access
- Availability Services
  - Sun Cluster

For details and pricing, go to
`http://wwws.sun.com/software/javaenterprisesystem/index.html`

Patching the Portal Server Software

While Patch Consolidations are cumulative, it's in your best interest to stay current by installing the latest patches. This keeps the delta to a minimum, making it easier to certify new releases for deployment into production environments.

To obtain portal server 3.x patches, open a customer support case at the following URL:

`http://cgi.iplanet.com/cgi-bin/c/ct-newcase.cgi`

Most portal server 6.x patches are available from the SunSolve℠ program Web site:

`http://sunsolve.sun.com/pub-cgi/show.pl?target=patchpage`

Because of the level of customization the portal server product enables, special attention should be paid during patch applications. Portal server 6.x patches contain release notes that include essential information to provide a surprise-free upgrade process. The table of contents will look similar to FIGURE 1-3.

FIGURE 1-3   Portal Server 6.1 Patch Consolidation 1 Release Notes

Two sections in particular are important to read before every 6.x patch consolidation:

- The Pre-installation Considerations section includes changes that will be noticeable after the patch has been applied. This section attempts to capture those functions that may be assumed to work a certain way or depend on a private interface that may change in the patch release. This is an important section for changes to the Rewriter because it may affect Web pages accessed using the Gateway or scraped using the URL scraper.

- The Template Modifications Required section lists all of the flat files that will be affected by the patch installation. These files should all be present in the default templates directory to ensure that the patching is performed correctly.

See the section of the release notes titled Tips for Customizing Templates for best practice approaches to customizing the portal server desktop templates. The Template Modifications Required section includes the affected nodes and summarizes exactly what is done to each file. FIGURE 1-4 shows what this section might look like.

Template and Flatfile Modifications Made by Portal 6.1 Patch Consolidation 1:

Name	Component	Change
`/etc/opt/SUNWps/desktop/default \ /Login/display_AuthLDAP.html` `/etc/opt/SUNWps/desktop/default \ /LoginProvider/display_AuthLDAP.html`	Server and Platform	Fixed typo in the FORM NAME attribute value. Changed from `login_form2` to `userid_form` so that JavaScript form verification will now work.
`/etc/opt/SUNWps/desktop \ /default/JSPLayoutContainer/layout1.jsp` `/etc/opt/SUNWps/desktop/ \ default/JSPLayoutContainer/layout2.jsp` `/etc/opt/SUNWps/desktop/default \ /JSPLayoutContainer/layout3.jsp`	Server and Platform	Added logic for JSPs to check whether channels are movable or not before displaying the channels on the layout page.

FIGURE 1-4 A Portion of the Template Modifications Required Section (Portal Server 6.1 PC1 Release Notes)

If you have modified any of the files listed in this section of the release notes, then your changes must be made manually by comparing the updated file in the default templates directory with the equivalent file in the customized template directory. There is an ongoing effort to improve the level of automation for portal patches to reduce the administrative overhead associated with their uptake.

Important Terms and Concepts

In this section, common terms and some basic concepts are defined in the context of how they are used throughout this book.

Portal Server Components

Best practices for deploying a portal server involve choosing which portal server features to use, then installing and configuring those features. The portal server components (FIGURE 1-5) include:

- Netlet
- NetFile
- Rewriter
- Gateway

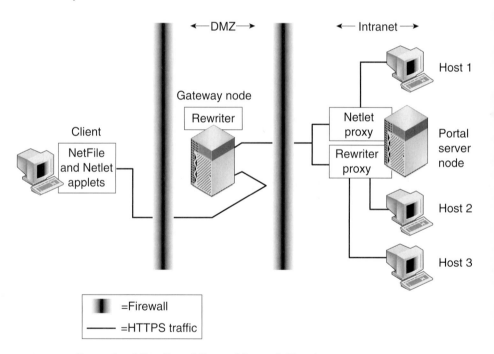

FIGURE 1-5   Example of Sun Portal Server Network Topology

Netlet

The Netlet enables users to run common TCP/IP services securely over public networks. You can run TCP/IP applications (such as Telnet, SMTP, and FTP), and any other fixed-port applications. The technology provided by the Netlet is similar to a virtual private network (VPN) with an important difference: VPNs encrypt all IP-level traffic, while the Netlet only encrypts data that must be secured, leaving the other communication unencypted.

See Chapter 2 "Netlet: Secure Remote Access Through On-Demand VPNs."

NetFile

NetFile enables remote users to securely transfer files bidirectionally to back-end systems. The NetFile provides the following secure features:

- Facility to add or remove shares or folders
- File upload and download
- Search for files and folders
- File compression using GZIP and ZIP
- Mail facility within the NetFile environment

See Chapter 3 "NetFile: Secure Remote Access for Exchanging Files With Internal File Systems."

Rewriter

The Rewriter component of the Sun portal server SRA software extends the notion of VPN-on-demand capability by allowing remote users to navigate and interact with internal Web pages as though they were accessing them from a local area network (LAN) connection.

When a user tries to access intranet Web pages through the Gateway, the Web pages are made available through the use of URL rewriting.

See Chapter 4 "Rewriter: Secure Remote Access to Internal Web-Based Applications."

Gateway

The Gateway, similar to a reverse proxy, provides the interface and a level of security between remote user sessions originating from the Internet and your corporate intranet. The Gateway presents content securely from internal Web servers and application servers through a single interface to a remote user.

The Gateway provides the portal server components (Netlet, NetFile, and Rewriter) with the following secure functions:

- Differentiates between Netlet traffic and HTTP traffic, and can off-load either or both to proxies to reduce internal firewall administration.

- Makes sure that users have a valid session and the appropriate access policy when fetching internal data.

- Manages HTTP message headers, rewriting when appropriate, and tagging responses with no-caching headers.

See Chapter 5 "Gateway: Gluing It All Together."

Additional Terms and Concepts

Nodes, Platforms, and Instances

A *node* is a physical box that is usually used for a specialized purpose. For example, it would be rare (and discouraged) for a Gateway and portal server to be installed as a single tier on the same box (two nodes on one box). Instead, a *Gateway node* is installed on one box, a *portal server node* is installed on a separate box, and each box is sized independently.

The Gateway component is either called a *Gateway node* or just simply *the Gateway*.

A portal installation can include one or more *portal platform node*s and one *portal server node*. *Portal server* generally refers to a portal server node, unless stated otherwise.

The term *instance* is used to indicate multiple processes running on the same physical box. This is different than multiple installations where the entire product is installed multiple times on the same physical box. Multiple installations should only be done on large machines that are separated using hardware domains (such as the Sun Fire™ 6800 server).

Rules and Rulesets

A *rule* is an individual entry that tells the Rewriter component what specific content requires URL rewriting.

A *ruleset* is a combination of rules for multiple content types that can be mapped to host names, addresses, and Gateway instances, so that multiple rulesets can be mutually exclusive. Both rules and rulesets are represented in XML and must follow guidelines set forth in the ruleset Document Type Definition (DTD).

Portal Server Desktop

The *portal server desktop* is the presentation layer for aggregated content displayed as channels. The portal server desktop is the primary portal end user interface.

Channels

Channels are the content containers on the portal server desktop.

Portlets

The term *portlet* can have several meanings. Used in a generalized way, it is interchangeable with the term channel. IBM, for instance, frequently uses the term portlet to indicate the content containers on the portal server desktop. Portlet is also the JSR168 specification for interchangeable application logic from one portal to another. This latter definition is how the term portlet is used in this book.

## CHAPTER 2

Netlet: Secure Remote Access Through On-Demand VPNs

This chapter discusses the Netlet, one of three primary technologies employed by the Sun's portal server SRA software product, to enable integration with, and provisioning of, internal applications to authenticated end users securely over the Internet.

This chapter contains the following sections:

Note – In this book, the term *portal server* refers to Sun's portal server software with the SRA software unless specified otherwise. *Portal server node* and *portal platform node* refer to the portal server core product.

What is the Netlet?

The Netlet is used to establish a secure tunnel for TCP/IP traffic over insecure networks such as the Internet. The technology provided by the Netlet is synonymous with virtual private network (VPN) on-demand technology. VPN-on-demand differs from traditional VPNs in that not all IP-level traffic on a VPN-on-demand system is tunneled through a VPN server. Instead, only data that must be handled through a secure tunnel is exchanged through the VPN server, and only when required. The rest of the communication is made between the browser and publicly assessable content servers.

There are advantages and disadvantages to both traditional VPN technology and VPN-on-demand (or Netlet) technology. Neither fully displaces the other because their aims are different. For example, a VPN can be used for an always-on business-to-business type of connection. Or a VPN can be used by remote access employees connecting with their own laptops or desktops from remote offices that are running VPN client software. On the other hand, VPN-on-demand can be used from an Internet kiosk, or from a remote workstation to pull up email. It can also be used for an internal application demonstration shown to a business partner from within the partner's network.

A VPN is only as secure as the client machine (and server) initiating the connection. If a machine is compromised before a VPN connection is established, the VPN can do little to ensure security. For instance, if a remote employee's system has contracted a virus, has a keylogger (physical or virtual) running, or other kinds of spyware or screen-scraping software, the connection might not be as secure as it appears. You must understand the limitations of any security software before deploying it, and understand the potential of opening your network to possible unwanted dissemination of valuable intellectual property or trade secrets.

The Internet is founded on a delicate balance between the convenience of free and open information and providing enough security so business itself is not undermined by the misuse, abuse, or vast distribution of confidential or otherwise protected information. With that in mind, VPN and VPN derivative software seek to mitigate the risk associated with accessing sensitive information over public wires and airways. With VPNs, data is encrypted, explicit user authentication is generally required, user sessions can be logged and audited, and the access to specific types of information from a remote location can be allowed or denied.

VPNs and Netlets provide convenience for end users as well as administrators.

- Traditional VPNs are convenient for end users because all internal network resources are accessed as those the users are physically present inside the corporate intranet.

- Netlets are convenient for end users because they can be used in a more flexible fashion, without requiring special VPN software to connect to the internal resource. For example, a company that outsources human resources (HR) solutions might use a Netlet to allow their employees to access their HR information remotely. In this case, the HR application runs on a machine hosted by the HR company, and access is provided using screen-scraping software such as a Citrix MetaFrame with the Independent Computing Architecture (ICA) client over a Netlet. The user experience is maintained on the company's application server, and security is provided by a Netlet, creating a secure tunnel for the Citrix ICA client to communicate back to the server. For more information about these kinds of deployments and how the Netlet can be leveraged to implement them, see "How Do I Deploy the Netlet?" on page 23.

Besides requiring a client footprint, another disadvantage of the traditional VPNs is that all traffic, except that which has been programatically excluded, passes through the VPN server. This is meant to increase the level of security that the VPN provides, but there are a variety of scenarios where this traffic requirement does not provide any greater security than a Netlet. In addition, the extra traffic creates an unnecessary burden on the VPN server. The more traffic that passes through the VPN server which could otherwise be serviced through a direct connection, the greater the burden on the VPN server.

In our HR example, only traffic between the Citrix applet and the Citrix server is tunneled. The Citrix applet is configured to communicate with the Citrix server using the localhost address, so the traffic is encrypted and decrypted by the Netlet applet listening on the configured port. If an end user accesses other pages (for example, their Yahoo stock quotes, or their own internal information), a traditional VPN would either fail outright or it would run very inefficiently. In some cases, if access to Internet resources is blocked or misconfigured, end users would not be able to access resources for which they had explicitly been granted permission.

VPN software is very difficult to employ in another company's complex proxy environment, and specialized arrangements are becoming rare as security personnel do everything they can do to reduce potential risk to network attacks and break-ins. Even companies with good working relationships are hesitant to share internal network and proxy information with one another. Thus, connections between them should be transparent, and should not require any client configuration or any change to the network infrastructure.

A Netlet connection can be used to tunnel traffic for any fixed-port TCP/IP application. It enables the native application client to communicate directly with the server application over an encrypted tunnel from a remote location. There are a few exceptions to the fixed-port rule, including the FTP protocol that operates over two channels, and Microsoft Outlook access to Exchange. These exceptions are described, along with other popular Netlet applications, in "How Do I Deploy the Netlet?" on page 23.

Why Should I Use the Netlet?

The primary purpose of the Netlet is to provide a transparent, secure connection to remote data without the need for client-side software other than a Java-enabled Web browser with a supported Java™ Virtual Machine (JVM[1]). No client reconfiguration or network infrastructure changes are required. The Netlet is a mature technology that has adapted to the needs of remote employees, customers, and partners alike. It has been used successfully in all of these applications, and continues to be used at Sun for secure remote access to internal applications and information.

Today's remote workforce and virtual teams require an extraordinarily flexible, yet dependable, security solution. The solution must be flexible enough to include support for differing infrastructures, a multitude of platforms and browsers, different bandwidths, and different geographical areas, while maintaining guaranteed up-time, and reasonable quality of service. It also has to work where there might be port restrictions, protocol restrictions, configuration restrictions, proxies, and where no client footprint is allowed. Secure remote access to applications using Sun's Netlet technology has extended to last-mile users ranging from users on sailboats over satellite links, to highly secure banking networks, airport lounges, convention kiosks, widely used modem pools, and consumer broadband connections. In all of these cases, Netlets are ideal for information-on-demand purposes. They enable time-critical, location-independent access to data using a secure, trusted technology.

A Netlet can be used to tunnel mail protocols like IMAP and SMTP to native email clients like Netscape Messenger and Outlook Express. A Netlet connection can be used as an alternative to NetFile (covered in Chapter 3) for secure file transfers using the raw FTP protocol and spec-compliant clients. For example, an insurance company might use this technology to enable doctor offices to upload sensitive patient data for consideration in offering a prospective customer a life insurance policy. In the past, this was done using fax technology, which is inherently insecure in transit, receipt, and even at the point of origin. It was also done through the mail, which is slower, affecting the turnaround time for extending or denying a policy, and more expensive in the long run.

---

1. The terms "Java Virtual Machine" and "JVM" mean a Virtual Machine for the Java™ platform.

Another popular use of a Netlet is to provide secure remote access to an employee desktop using Citrix, Tarantella, VNC, or a similar screen-scraping, or terminal-services technology. This configuration enables end users to have a remote point of presence to their own internal desktop, and locally installed native applications that might not be network aware.

How Does the Netlet Work?

Netlets are referred to as *static* and *dynamic*. They are configured using *Netlet rules*.

Static Netlets cannot be configured by the end user. If the Netlet provider (sometimes referred to as a Netlet channel) is visible on the desktop, static Netlets are launched as soon as the user logs into the portal server desktop.

Dynamic Netlets, however, can be created and edited by the end user and are launched only when the URL associated with the individual Netlet rule is selected. Dynamic Netlets are used for general-purpose protocols such as Telnet and FTP, when the end users might need to specify the host name of the machine where they want to establish a connection.

A Netlet session is established when a user launches the Netlet, the Netlet applet is downloaded, and the Netlet rules associated with the individual connection are loaded. The Netlet then listens on local ports where the rules have been configured and maps them to the ports on a destination host machine. As traffic comes across any of the ports where the Netlet applet is listening, the traffic is encrypted using the selected RC5 algorithm for that particular rule, cloaked as Secure Sockets Layer (SSL), and sent on its way to the portal Gateway machine using secure HTTP (HTTPS). The portal Gateway looks at the individual packets and determines whether or not they are Netlet traffic. If they are Netlet traffic, the Gateway decrypts them and sends them directly to the specified host if a Netlet proxy has not been configured. A Netlet proxy is used if there is a firewall between the Gateway node and the destination host that does not allow direct communication between the two over the specified host and the port indicated by the Netlet rule. A client application would interact with the destination server by using `localhost` instead of the actual server name and a local port number identified by the Netlet rule.

Once the Netlet applet is downloaded, it must determine which proxy to use to communicate with the Gateway (covered in Chapter 5). The proxy information can be retrieved in a variety of ways, due to the multitude of browser and proxy configurations that can be used. The Netlet applet first checks the browser proxy settings. If the settings specify whether to use a direct connection or a static proxy, the Netlet immediately communicates with whichever connection is specified. Otherwise, one of the following proxy configurations applies:

- If an automatic proxy configuration (PAC) file URL is specified, the Netlet applet attempts to retrieve the PAC file contents. If the browser allows the virtual machine (VM) to retrieve the PAC file, the Netlet sends the PAC file contents back to the portal Gateway over HTTPS. The Gateway then sends the PAC file contents to the portal node, which must have Rhino (the Mozilla™ open source JavaScript™ engine written in the Java programming language) installed on it. Rhino parses the PAC file and returns the proxy list to the Gateway and back to the client. The client then determines the first available proxy from the list returned and continues using it for the remainder of the session.

There are several important things going on here that deserve a closer look. First, Rhino is sitting on the portal platform because it would bloat the Netlet applet if it were downloaded with the rest of the applet. Second, Rhino use by the portal server might be deprecated when the Java™ Plug-in becomes ubiquitous, and the Netlet applet will be able to ask the plug-in what proxy to use to communicate with the Gateway at a specific IP address.

Finally, the PAC file must have an entry that allows either a direct connection or a proxy connection to retrieve the PAC file itself. This might seem strange, but the applet is not allowed by the browser to download the PAC file if the PAC file does not have such an entry. It is assumed that there must be direct access between the browser and the PAC file, but that is not always evident in the PAC file itself. For instance, some PAC files contain decision code (such as an else block) that returns a proxy that only handles Internet connections, instead of returning DIRECT in the event that no other specific matches were made earlier. This and other PAC-related information is discussed further in "Integrating Automatic Proxy Configuration (PAC) Files" on page 39.

- If an autoconfiguration URL (ins file extension) is encountered and no other proxy option is specified, the ins file must have a PROXY entry that the Netlet applet can extract and use. If the PROXY entry is a PAC URL, it follows the same process as stated above. If the PROXY entry is not a PAC URL, the entry is used for Netlet applet and Gateway communication thereafter. For information about autoconfiguration URLs, see "Using Custom Built Browsers" on page 62 and "Integrating Automatic Configuration (ins) Files" on page 55.

Note – The proxy behavior differs somewhat when the applet is running from within the Sun Java Plug-in software. Java Plug-in versions later than 1.5 allow for proxy transparency. Plug-in versions 1.3 and 1.4 require a portal server patch to use PAC files.

How Do I Deploy the Netlet?

To deploy the Netlet, you must understand the environment where it will be deployed and the environment from which it will be accessed. You must also be familiar with Netlet administrative options and how they affect functionality, security, and usability.

This section guides you through Netlet preferred practices, and describes advantages and disadvantages of making certain system-level decisions.

Configuring a Netlet Rule

The portal server SRA software comes out-of-box with several default Netlet rules already configured. IMAP, FTP, and Telnet are included as dynamic Netlet rules. The fact that these default rules are dynamic means that users can add their own rules from within the Netlet provider on their portal server desktop to specify the host to which they want to connect.

The out-of-box configuration may or may not be the ideal configuration for your intended use, so it is important to understand the Netlet options and how they affect the deployment of the Netlet. This section discusses the Netlet options and the configuration decisions you need to make:

- "Netlet Service Admin Window" on page 23
- "Selecting a Netlet Rule to Add, Delete, or Edit" on page 26
- "Assigning an Encryption Algorithm" on page 28
- "Associating a URL With a Netlet Rule" on page 29
- "Downloading an Applet from a Remote Host" on page 30
- "Selecting Extend Session" on page 30
- "Configuring the Network Ports" on page 31

Netlet Service Admin Window

The Netlet Service Admin window is shown in FIGURE 2-1 for portal server version 6.0, and FIGURE 2-2 for portal server versions 6.1 and 6.2. Netlets can be configured at the root, organization, role, and user levels.

The right panel is where the Netlet configuration process starts. The sections that follow describe the factors you need to consider while creating Netlet rules to suit your needs.

The steps for launching the Netlet Service Admin screen are slightly different for each version of the Sun portal server software. Consult the product documentation for the specific steps that you need to perform.

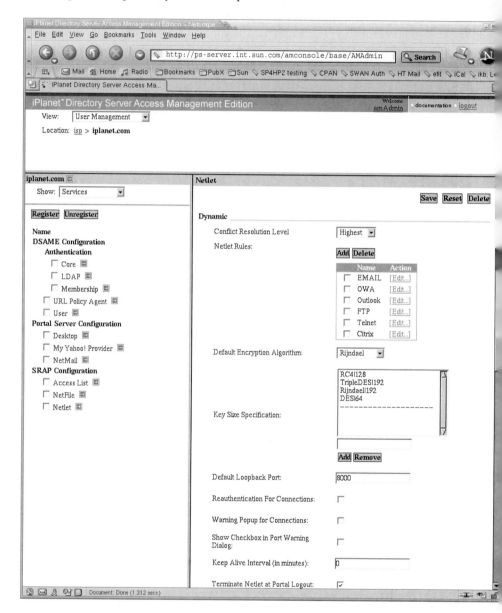

FIGURE 2-1   Netlet Service Admin Screen (Sun ONE Portal Server 6.0 Software)

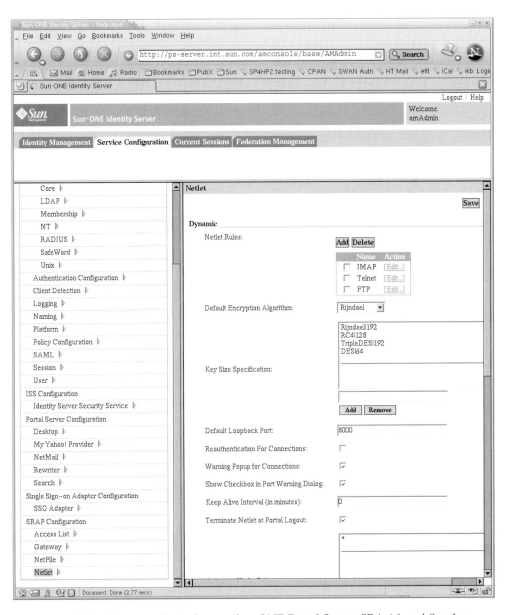

FIGURE 2-2   Netlet Service Admin Screen (Sun ONE Portal Server SRA 6.1 and Sun Java System Portal Server 6.2 Software)

Selecting a Netlet Rule to Add, Delete, or Edit

FIGURE 2-3 shows the existing Netlet rules (for example, IMAP, FTP, and Telnet), and the links you use to add, delete, or edit Netlet rules.

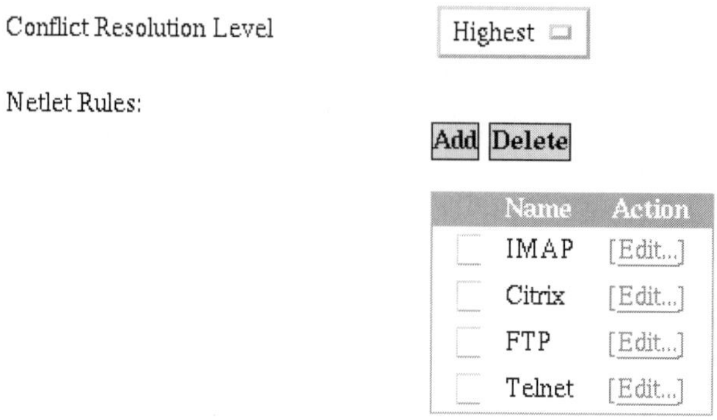

Conflict Resolution Level

Highest ▢

Netlet Rules:

Add **Delete**

Name	Action
IMAP	[Edit...]
Citrix	[Edit...]
FTP	[Edit...]
Telnet	[Edit...]

FIGURE 2-3 Admin Console Page (Sun ONE Portal Server 6.0 Software Example)

Selecting the Edit link for any of the Netlet rules brings up a page that contains the pertinent information for that specific rule (FIGURE 2-4).

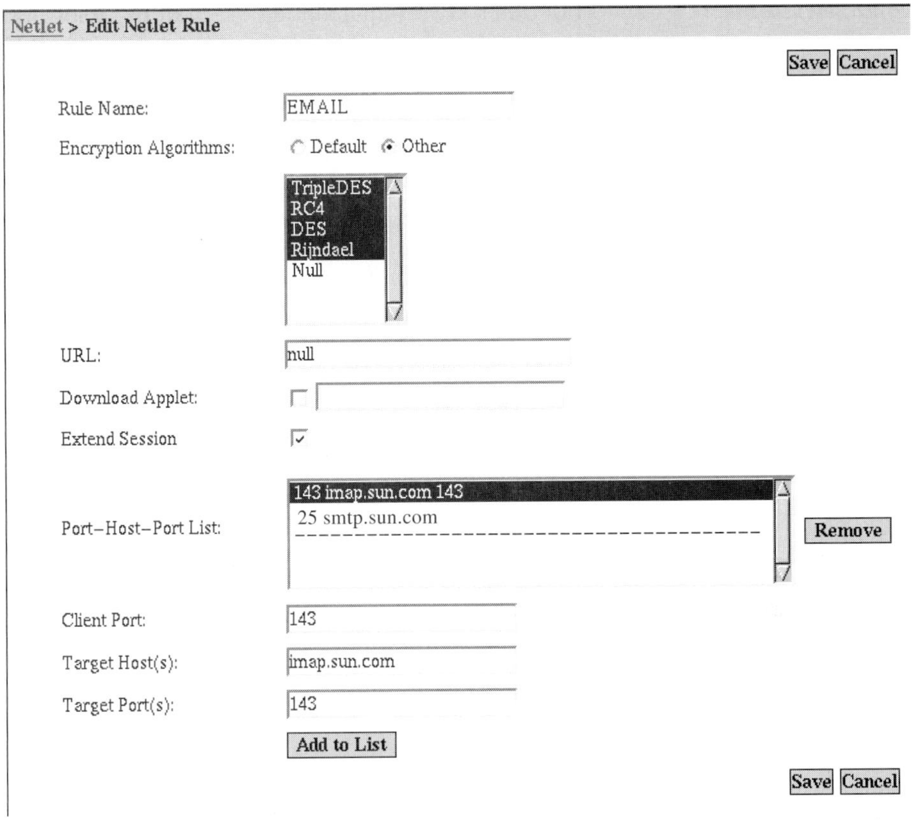

Save Cancel

Rule Name: EMAIL

Encryption Algorithms: ○ Default ● Other

> TripleDES
> RC4
> DES
> Rijndael
> Null

URL: null

Download Applet: ☐

Extend Session   ☑

Port–Host–Port List: 143 imap.sun.com 143
                        25 smtp.sun.com
                        --   Remove

Client Port: 143

Target Host(s):   imap.sun.com

Target Port(s):   143

Add to List

Save Cancel

FIGURE 2-4   Edit Netlet Rule Panel

Assigning a Netlet Rule Name

Specify the name for the rule you are creating in the Rule Name field (FIGURE 2-5). Best practices for rule naming conventions suggest selecting a name that reflects the service or protocol for which the Netlet is being used. Some applications might use a multitude of protocols, where it makes more sense to use the service name instead. This follows a similar practice of creating firewall filtering rules where the configuration is easier to maintain if the rule name states a clear purpose.

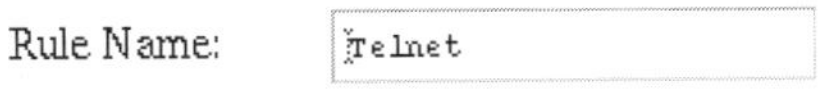

Rule Name: Telnet

FIGURE 2-5   Rule Name Entry

The rule name should also be unique among other Netlet rules that could be launched from the same Netlet provider. This makes rules easier to manage, but also helps avoid cross-pollination, a situation where traffic associated with one rule is unintentionally sent to a destination host associated with a different rule. For dynamic rules, the rule name is used as part of the link to launch that particular Netlet.

The Admin Console prevents you from making some of the most common mistakes when naming rules, but you should follow the guidelines described here in the event that Netlet rules are manipulated directly through directory modifications or using a command-line interface. The restriction on multiple Netlets sharing the same name does not prevent users from defining multiple dynamic Netlets with the same name, targeted at different hosts. The different host name makes the URL unique and the Gateway will be able to independently handle two sessions with the same Netlet rule, as long as the target host uses the same local port to communicate back to the client (with the exception of FTP).

Assigning an Encryption Algorithm

The next section of the Netlet configuration panel (FIGURE 2-6) deals with cryptographic algorithms.

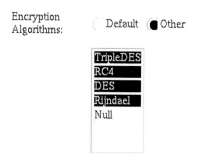

FIGURE 2-6 Algorithm Selection Field of the Netlet Configuration Panel

The ordering of these algorithms is important because they are listed from strongest to weakest, and eventually go to none (null). The algorithms that you select translate directly to what end users can select as the algorithms they want to use from the Netlet provider, with the strongest algorithm being the default.

Selecting Default uses a single encryption algorithm defined at the Netlet service level. To select multiple algorithms, use the Control key while simultaneously selecting individual entries. For information about the encryption options, see "Netlet Cryptography" on page 64.

Note – Do not select null, because this can result in chunks of client-bound Netlet traffic from being transmitted in the clear. Null is intended for use in test or staging environments to test application integration, or in load testing individual algorithms to be used in sizing considerations when the Netlet is deployed to a production environment.

Associating a URL With a Netlet Rule

Following the encryption options is a field for the URL to load when the Netlet is launched. As shown in FIGURE 2-7, you can specify protocol URLs.

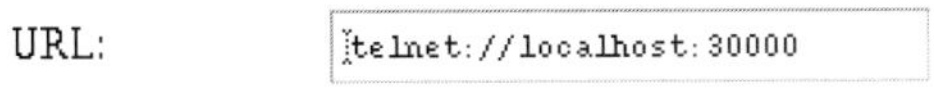

URL: `telnet://localhost:30000`

FIGURE 2-7   Specifying a URL to Launch for Dynamic Netlets

When you provide a URL in the URL field, the associated helper application will automatically launch when the Netlet launches, rather than the user having to manually open the application and configure it to communicate with the appropriate port. The port number should be the same as the client port where that particular Netlet rule is listening. Using the URL specified in FIGURE 2-7, the Telnet helper application would load once the dynamic Netlet link is selected.

Note – Do not add a URL that contains the Gateway's address with a protocol the Gateway doesn't understand. Doing so results in the following error:
`Exception java.lang.NullPointerException occurred while processing your request`

Static rules and dynamic rules with multiple listeners do not launch with a URL. In these cases you should enter null in the URL field. For dynamic FTP rules, you must also define the user name in the URL, or the connection is assumed to be anonymous. For example, `ftp://user@localhost:300021` passes the FTP user ID to the FTP server, and the user is prompted for the password. Otherwise the connection fails or the directory listing automatically defaults to the directory for public anonymous access. For information about Netlet FTP, see "Netlet Deployment Scenarios" on page 81.

Downloading an Applet from a Remote Host

The Download Applet field (FIGURE 2-8) is used in conjunction with the URL field when the page returned by the URL contains an embedded applet that needs to be fetched from a remote machine.

Download
Applet: I

FIGURE 2-8 Download Applet Field

Specifically, the Download Applet field is used to circumvent Java security that does not allow an applet to communicate with a host that it was not downloaded from. The applet must communicate with the Gateway through the local network port, so the Download Applet field, when enabled (checked), is specified using the following syntax:

clientport : *machinename* : *serverport*

The *clientport* is the local port on which the Netlet would be listening for traffic originating from the Applet. The *machinename* is the name of the server where the applet is to be downloaded from, and the *serverport* is the port used to download the applet (if the URL field is fully qualified, then this would be the same port specified in that URL).

Following the example for Citrix, the URL field would contain the URL pointing to the web page containing the citrix applet/object tag, and would be specified as `/third_party/citrix_start.html`. The Download Applet field would then be specified as `5000:ps-server.int.sun.com:80`. In this case, `5000` is the port that the `citrix_start.html` page indicates in the applet parameter to use for communication with the Citrix Server.

Selecting Extend Session

Use the Extend Session checkbox (FIGURE 2-9) to determine whether or not Netlet traffic should be considered when extending the portal server desktop timeout.

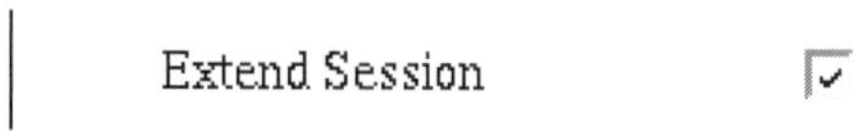

Extend Session   ☑

FIGURE 2-9 Extend Session Checkbox

If you do not check this box and the primary portal usage is the Netlet, the Netlet connection might be unexpectedly dropped when the user session idle timer is reached. Check this option if the portal is used primarily for secure remote access to Citrix or other screen-scraping products, or if the Netlet is used to access push servers, such as stock quote tickers. For more information about how this option affects timeouts and how to better determine what its state should be for your own purposes, see "Understanding and Handling Timeouts" on page 75.

Configuring the Network Ports

The next section of the Netlet configuration panel (FIGURE 2-10) is where you configure the client server ports and host names associated with the Netlet rule.

Port–Host–Port List:

```
30000 TARGET 23
------------------------------------------
```
[Remove]

Client Port: `30000`

Target Host(s): `TARGET`

Target Port(s): `23`

[Add to List]

FIGURE 2-10 Network Port Configuration

- In the Port-Host-Port list, you can define multiple listeners for a single-Netlet rule. This means that a service operating over multiple channels, like FTP, will not require multiple rules.

- In the Client Port field, provide the port number on which the Netlet applet listens. This value should ordinarily not be a reserved port on the OS or the default protocol and service ports. Specifying higher port numbers is good practice to avoid conflicts with services already running on lower port numbers. Exceptions to this rule that provide the Netlet with some additional capabilities are described in "Netlet Deployment Scenarios" on page 81.

- In the Target Host(s) field, define a Netlet as being static or dynamic. This is done by entering either TARGET or the actual host name. Entering TARGET in this field allows end users to define their own hosts in the Edit field of the Netlet provider, which results in a dynamic rule. Deciding whether or not to make the rule dynamic is primarily a policy decision.

- In the Target Port(s) field, define the port being used by the service on the back-end system (target system). If a Netlet is used for business partners or customers to upload sensitive data to a secure FTP server, the fully qualified host name of that FTP server would be added to the Target Host(s) field, the Client Port would be 30021, and the Target Port(s) field would be 21. The other channel is handled internally, which is why the Client Port must be 30021. This is explained further in "Scenario A: Running FTP Over a Netlet Connection" on page 81.

Once you've configured your Netlet rule, save your changes using the Save button.

Securing Access to the Netlet Service

To prevent end users from forging their own static rules, you should add a policy to the Netlet service level to allow specific rules, but deny all other rules. This idea is similar to a packet filtering firewall where the allow list is matched first. If the allowed rule is not there, everything else is denied. Out-of-box, all Netlet rules are allowed.

FIGURE 2-11 shows the Netlet service panel where you configure the options that control the security of a Netlet rule.

Continuing to use FTP as an example, if policy dictated that a user is a remote employee and should be able to FTP to any internal host where they have existing permissions, then the Target Host(s) field should specify TARGET, and all other port information should stay the same.

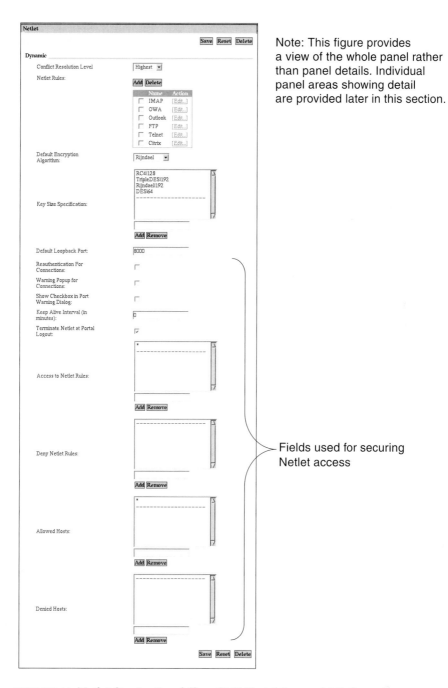

Note: This figure provides a view of the whole panel rather than panel details. Individual panel areas showing detail are provided later in this section.

Fields used for securing Netlet access

FIGURE 2-11 Netlet Service Panel (Sun ONE Portal Server 6.0 Software)

Don't be confused by the plurality of the field names. Only one entry can be specified per form field at a time. Also, as defined by the Netlet rule, there should be a one-to-one mapping between client ports and target host ports. Do not use one client port in conjunction with multiple server ports. For dynamic Netlets, users can define multiple rules that may use the same client port, but in that case, the host name should be unique to prevent the cross-pollination of Netlet sessions.

At the service level, there are several other Netlet configuration options to be aware of when deploying a Netlet. The first is a checkbox for the Warning Pop-up for Connections.

Warning Popup for Connections: ☑

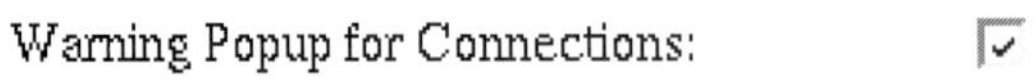

FIGURE 2-12 Warning Pop-up for Connections Checkbox

Enabling the warning pop-up provides an additional security precaution to ensure that an unauthorized user is not attempting to hijack, forge, or take over the Netlet connection. If the user who has permission to access the Netlet is getting port warnings without initiating any actions, there is a possibility that someone else is communicating with a port where the Netlet is listening. This is one reason client ports should be randomly chosen and should not be any of the default ports of well-known protocols. Port warnings, reauthentication, and a more secure Netlet access list all help reduce the likelihood of hijacked or forged Netlet connections.

The Netlet applet is not intended to be used on a time-shared machine where two users who both have the same Netlet configuration can be logged in. The second user would see the following error in the Java Console:

```
Socket DoConn tcpNoDelay exception: java.net.SocketException:
The specified address is not available from the local computer
```

After a short while, during repeated attempts to bind to the socket, the connection would eventually fail. This prevents a user from taking over the client port. If port warnings are enabled, and the warning is canceled rather than accepted, it prevents the second user from hijacking the first user's Netlet connection. Port conflicts on local multiuser systems are a primary reason the portal Netlet was not extended to Sun Ray™ systems until portal server version 6.2 version. Sun Ray clients all share a single network interface card (NIC) on the Sun Ray server for their network fabric. Netlet rules use static client ports, so they would not be iterated for different Sun Ray clients, and the client Ethernet address is not used to sort out individual Netlet sessions.

If FTP or Outlook (fat client) Netlets are extended to end users, port warnings should be turned off. These two services are special in that they make use of dynamic ports that the Netlet has been specially designed to handle. Unfortunately, this also means that every connection that is open on a different port results in a port warning even if the checkbox is selected not to show future warnings. The other problem specific to FTP is that the port warning can pop under the FTP client and give the perception that the file is downloading when in fact the Netlet is waiting for confirmation of the port warning. That fact is visible in the Java Console, but that is of little consequence to the average end user.

If Netscape™ Communicator software is used as the FTP client, the situation can worsen if a user, when uploading a file, receives a dialogue box that has only a Cancel button. A lock situation arises if the Netlet warning pop-up window is under the Netscape Communicator FTP window, because the browser window cannot be moved until the end user selects the cancel button, or until the user selects OK on the port warning pop-up window, which is not accessible.

Users can select the checkbox on the Netlet warning pop-up window to prevent future port warnings for specific port numbers from appearing. For example, if a user received a port warning for a Telnet connection on port 30000 and ended the Telnet connection, the next time the user established a Telnet connection to that same port, a port warning would not be shown. Generally speaking, port warnings are disabled in production environments because they are a usability hassle, but if there is concern about untrusted clients accessing sensitive data accessed over the Netlet, port warnings can be a nice security addition. However, the information about how to interact with the warnings must be conveyed properly to the end user.

Setting the Reauthentication for Connections Checkbox

The Reauthentication For Connections checkbox (FIGURE 2-13) is a handy mechanism to ensure that abandoned portal sessions that have not timed out cannot re-establish Netlet connectivity without a Netlet password.

The logistics of disseminating a Netlet password are a bit tricky because the Netlet password cannot be defined at user creation. The default Netlet password is *srap-Netlet* rather than the portal user password, and that information must be conveyed to end users.

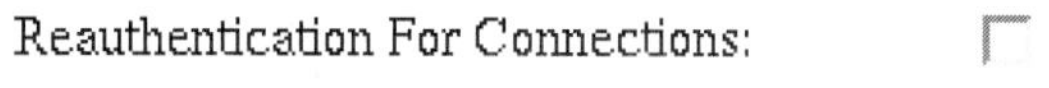

Reauthentication For Connections: ⌐

FIGURE 2-13 Reauthentication For Connections Checkbox

Reauthentication and warning for pop-ups are not mutually exclusive. The authentication pop-up overrides the warning. This option should definitely not be used if FTP Netlets are going to be deployed to the desktop, because the user will have to reauthenticate after every command since the port number will change.

Implementing the Netlet KeepAlive Interval Field

The Netlet KeepAlive Interval (FIGURE 2-14) is included mostly for historical reasons. Its namesake implies that the feature takes some kind of proactive measure to ensure that the connection between the Netlet applet and the application server remains intact, even during idle, and as dictated by other portal idle timers such as the desktop idle timer.

In portal server 6.0 software, however, the feature automatically kills the Netlet session once the interval time is reached while the Netlet is at idle. This is somewhat redundant because when the desktop idle timer is reached, the desktop idle timer supersedes the setting for the Netlet KeepAlive Interval, so the Netlet connection drops.

The portal server 6.1PC1 and 6.2 versions have been changed. These versions send dummy packets periodically to maintain network connections even when the Netlet is idle. Depending on how interim firewalls are configured, the connection might time out and be dropped if the Netlet idle exceeds the threshold configured by the firewall.

Keep Alive Interval (in minutes):   0

FIGURE 2-14 Keep Alive Interval Field

Enabling the Terminate Netlet at Portal Logout Option

The Terminate Netlet at Portal Logout option (FIGURE 2-15) is checked by default.

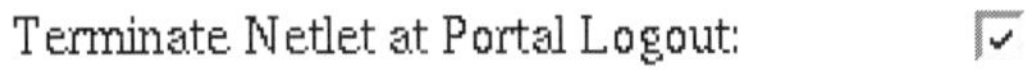

Terminate Netlet at Portal Logout: ☑

FIGURE 2-15 Terminate Netlet at Portal Logout Checkbox

By enabling this option, no new Netlet sessions can be initiated once the user has logged out of the portal server desktop. The name implies that the existing sessions terminate immediately upon portal logout, but it is worth noting that the existing sessions remain active until the session service Max Caching time threshold is reached. The default maximum caching time is three minutes, which means that existing Netlet sessions that are not individually closed by the end user remain active up to three minutes after the user has logged out of the portal. If the Max Idle Time is reached, however, all of the Netlet sessions are dropped. So, if the Max Idle Time is less than the Max Caching time, the idle time determines when the Netlet sessions are dropped if the sessions are idle. If the Netlet sessions remain active after portal logout, they remain open until the Max Caching time is reached.

Defining Netlet Rule Access Lists

Netlet rule access lists are used to define which rules an end user has the right to use.

Netlet access lists work by first attempting to match any entry in the allow list. If Netlet does not find such an entry, access to the Netlet rule is denied. If it does find an entry, the Netlet compares the entry to the deny list. If the entry is found in the deny list, the connection is denied. If there is no match in the deny list, then the connection is allowed. So, there can be explicit denials but not explicit allowances. For example:

- If `host.domain.com` was in the Allow Host list and `*.domain.com` was in the Deny Host list, the Netlet connection would be denied for a Netlet rule that contained the target value `host`.

- If the entries were configured such that `*.domain.com` was in the Allow Host list and `host.domain.com` was in the Deny Host list, the connection would still fail for a Netlet rule containing `host` as the target machine.

- If either `host.domain.com` or `*.domain.com` were in the Allow Host list, and if the Deny Host list was empty or contained neither of these entries, the Netlet connection would be approved for the rule.

When you install the SRA software, a wildcard is placed in the Access to Netlet Rules list. This means that users have access to any Netlet rule defined by the administrator. They also have access to any Netlet rule they might contrive by manipulating the Netlet applet parameters on their own. This manipulation of a Netlet rule is referred to as *forging Netlet rules*.

Forging Netlet rules is not straightforward, but it is possible by a motivated and knowledgeable user, which is why access lists are important. Netlet rules can also be forged by using the same name as an allowed rule. Removing the wildcard from the access list disallows all rules unless explicitly granted. This prevents the first type of Netlet forging by allowing access to only specific Netlet rules that have been added to the access list. To prevent the second kind of Netlet forging, the wildcard must also be removed from the Allowed Hosts list. This level of security is usually unnecessary for an employee portal, and is better suited for a business-to-business or customer-facing portal where users gaining access to or otherwise interfering with Intranet resources could pose a problem.

For instance, in the earlier example where an HR company deployed a Netlet to partner companies so their employees could access sensitive HR-related information, a single Netlet rule would be defined in the access list for the HR application, and the wildcard would be removed. A single host would also be defined in the allowed list in place of the wildcard (assuming that the HR application uses only one host).

To summarize, if the Netlet is being used as a remote-employee entry point, modifying the rule and host access lists might not be necessary. This is especially true if dynamic Netlets are being deployed where the administrator might not know the host name of the machine an end user intends to connect to, and therefore can't add it to the Allow Hosts list. Removing the wildcard in the access list so that remote employees can only use Netlets that they've been granted access to does not pose problems and is often a reasonable thing to do. If a remote employee forges a Netlet using an allowed name, there is usually some level of authentication on the application side, which should prevent the employee from gaining access beyond that which would be available from within the company Intranet. A log audit might also turn up this kind of activity.

For other types of portals where users accessing the Netlet are not trusted, modify both access lists to reflect only those resources that the end user absolutely must have access to. In addition, you can create roles in an Identity Server and different Netlet profiles if users in the same organization have different Netlet connectivity requirements. The rule of thumb should be that users who are trusted the least should be given the least amount of access. Think of access lists as a valet key for the Netlet.

Integrating Applications

Application integration requires careful understanding of which protocols and network ports an application uses and how it makes use of the ports. As previously stated, Netlets only work for fixed-port TCP/IP applications. There is no exception to the protocol requirements, and only two exceptions to the fixed port requirements: FTP protocol and Microsoft Exchange access through the Netlet using the Outlook fat client. In these cases, the Netlet keeps track of what port to use to continue communicating with the back-end server.

When integrating applications, you also need to know which client should be used to communicate with the application. The client might need to be configured to communicate with the port where the Netlet is listening. For example, if IMAP is tunneled through a Netlet to a non-default client port, the mail application used to access the IMAP server would have to configure the server name as localhost and the port equal to the Netlet client port for that rule. Dynamic Netlets and Netlet URLs can be used in some cases so end users don't have to manually configure client applications. For example, a Telnet Netlet rule can have a Netlet URL associated with it that causes the browser to launch the helper application associated with the Telnet protocol. Also in the URL are the correct host name to use (localhost) and the correct port where the Netlet is listening for that particular rule.

Considering Network Topology

Understanding how different network topologies affect the Netlet enables you to deploy it in an optimized fashion. Part of the challenge in using a Netlet is how to work with, and in some cases work around, an existing security infrastructure while remaining secure. Because the Netlet operates in a network environment, it has to be flexible enough to work in end-user environments, highly restrictive environments, and with the wide array of infrastructure products and policies that are already in place to control the flow of information that passes in and out of the internal network. The following sections describe the kinds of environments, products, and policies that affect the successful deployment of the Netlet. These sections also provide preferred practices for managing areas that are under your control, and describe the minimal requirements for successfully using the Netlet.

Integrating Automatic Proxy Configuration (PAC) Files

Automatic proxy configuration (PAC) files are a widely popular means of simplifying the management of complex proxy environments used in corporate, enterprise, and other highly secure, large-scale networks. An automatic proxy configuration file is written in JavaScript and defines a single function called FindProxyForURL, which determines which proxy server, if any, the browser should use for each URL. Because the Netlet only needs a communication path back to the portal Gateway, this decision needs to be made only once in the case of a Netlet connection. The simplest PAC file returns only DIRECT (meaning no proxy should be used).

The easiest way to test whether a Netlet is properly configured to use PAC files is to create a simple PAC file and test it on one of the default dynamic Netlet rules, such as Telnet.

CODE EXAMPLE 2-1   Example of a Simple PAC File

```
// sample proxy pac file
function FindProxyForURL(url, host)
{
  // strings to return -- obviously substitute actual proxy server
address
  var proxy_yes = "PROXY myproxy.subdomain.domain.com:8080";
  var proxy_no = "DIRECT";

  // ...etc.
  // Proxy everything else
return proxy_no;
}
```

The preceding example is a little more complex than it needs to be. This was done on purpose to show that a PAC file is JavaScript and, therefore, JavaScript syntax rules apply. There is a fair amount of flexibility in evaluating which proxy to use.

A PAC file evaluates which proxy to use based on the URL, host, or both parameters passed to the `FindProxyForURL` function. A PAC file can be deployed on the client machine and created at the time the browser is installed. Custom-built browsers created using the Internet Explorer Administrator Kit (IEAK) or Netscape Mission Control Desktop can have the proxy URL address locked down (hard-coded) so that a script installed locally is used to determine proxy addresses. In this case, the URL might be a `file:///` URL, or it might point directly at the local path, such as `c:\browsers\Netscape\mypac.pac`. Pointing to a local path is one of the less popular methods for deploying PAC files, because of the maintenance required to update each individual client with new proxy information or to create a new browser build and force end users to reinstall it. End users who are fairly technical can also write their own PAC files and store them locally on their machines. A Netlet connection might fail if the end user has misconfigured the PAC file, or the PAC file does not contain necessary entries to connect with the appropriate proxy.

Another method for deploying PAC files is to store them on a Web server. This is the most widely used PAC deployment method. Deploying a PAC file on a Web server is easy and straightforward, and standard source code control policies can be put in place for its strictly controlled modification. Deploying a PAC file on a Web server is advantageous when using the Netlet. This is because Web servers tend to adhere to certain HTTP protocol requirements necessary for the Netlet to fetch and interpret the PAC file contents.

▼ To Install a Simple PAC File on a Sun ONE Web Server

1. **To install the example PAC file shown in** CODE EXAMPLE 2-1 **on a Sun ONE Web Server, simply copy the file to the doc root and save it as** `simple.pac`.

2. **As the Web server administrator, add the following entry to the server instance's** `config/mime.types` **file:**

```
type=application/x-ns-proxy-autoconfig exts=pac
```

If the PAC file is being stored on the Web server that was installed with the Identity Server software, you can add the PAC file to *install_dir*/SUNWam/public_html/sample.pac.

Note – You might have to change the existing entry for `type=audio/x-pac` if you want to use .pac as the file extension. It is recommended that you use `.pac` as the file extension for automatic proxy files and `.ins` for autoconfiguration files so the Netlet has two methods for determining the file type. File extensions are also important in cases where a PAC file is stored locally and there is no MIME type to use to determine what type of file it is. This ambiguity arises because Internet Explorer (IE) can have either an `ins` file or a PAC file specified in the automatic configuration field of the browser settings.

PAC files can also be dynamically created by an application. There are a couple of reasons you might choose to deploy PAC files in this way. The first reason, and probably the reason with the most historical significance, is that the user agents have a file size limit on PAC files. To avoid downloading the PAC file for the entire corporate network topology, a dynamically created PAC file can be custom tailored to the client IP address, GEO, URL query string, or other factors. This reduces the final file size and improves the PAC parse time, to some degree. PAC applications also allow network administrators to work in one particular area without affecting other areas because the application can be logically separated and easier to maintain than a huge static file.

PAC applications are usually scripted in CGI using Perl. Because the file extension is `.pl`, `.cgi`, or something similar, it is important that the script return the appropriate content type. A simple PAC file deployed as an application might appear as shown in CODE EXAMPLE 2-2.

CODE EXAMPLE 2-2   Example Autoproxy Application

```perl
#!/usr/bin/perl
########################################################
##      proxy.pl
##              Perl application which returns PAC file
##              contents
########################################################
print "Content-Type: application/x-ns-proxy-autoconfig\n\n";

# Print the opening PAC JS function
print <<ENDOFPAC;
function FindProxyForURL(url, host)
{
  var newHost = host.toLowerCase();
ENDOFPAC

# Bring in external proxy definitions from a file
open(FILE, "./domain-matches.txt");
while(<FILE>) {
  chomp;
  print "$_\n";
}
close(FILE);

# Host matches
print <<ENDOFPAC2
/////////////////////
  if (shExpMatch(newHost, "ps-gateway.domain.com")) {
    return "PROXY external.mydomain.com:8080";
  }
  if (shExpMatch(newHost, \"localhost\")) {
    return "DIRECT";
  }
  else {
    return "DIRECT";
  }
}
ENDOFPAC2
```

This PAC application reads in a file that might be managed by another group that
controls the proxy environment for different corporate domains and subdomains. In
this case, a special entry was made specifically for the portal Gateway fictitiously
named here as ps-gateway.domain.com. This entry specifies to use the proxy
running on external.mydomain.com at port 8080. The else block returning
DIRECT gives the Netlet applet the appropriate permissions to retrieve the PAC file
results generated from the PAC application URL. Notice the required print

`Content-Type` string towards the beginning of the script. This string is necessary so that the Netlet knows that the result of executing this script will be a valid PAC file that it can parse.

Finally, PAC files can be delivered as a service. A PAC service is used in the absence of a Web server. It can serve a static PAC file or a PAC application. A PAC service is unique because it can be defined to respond to the default HTTP port 80. It can have no path in the PAC URI, and it can have no Content-Length header. A PAC service might be defined in the Solaris™ Operating System (Solaris OS) as shown in the following procedure.

▼ To Define a PAC Service in the Solaris OS

A direct HTTP request to a configured port returns the execution results of the Perl program.

1. **As `root`, add the following line to the** `/etc/inet/services` **file:**

```
pac     80/tcp # Automatic Proxy Configuration
```

2. **Add the following line to the** `/etc/inet/inetd.conf` **file:**

```
pac stream  tcp     nowait  root     /export/proxy.pl
```

3. **Restart the** `inetsvc` **service.**

4. **Add the following line (HTTP status response) above the** `print "Content-Type: . . ."` **line in the autoproxy application file** (CODE EXAMPLE 2-2) **.**

```
print "HTTP/1.1 200 OK\n";
```

You only add this line for this particular method of deployment.

Because no Content-Length header is explicitly defined in the PAC service model, larger PAC files might be truncated because the Java method `in.available()` can return the incorrect length. This bug is fixed in the Sun ONE Portal Server 3.0 software, and there is a patch fix for the portal server 6.0 and 6.1 versions. The portal server 6.0 and 6.1 PAC truncation can be identified in the Java Console where the PAC file content length is printed as `-1` but the stream size is a positive nonzero integer. An additional identifier is the null entry specifying what proxy to use. The null entry alone does not necessarily indicate the PAC file truncation problem, and frequently arises when the Rhino has not been installed at all, or it was installed into a JDK™ release not in use by the portal server. The following Java Console output example shows what might indicate PAC file truncation:

```
Netscape Communications Corporation -- Java 1.1.5
Type '?' for options.
Netlet running on Netscape
Netlet config:
https://gateway.sun.com/http://portal.int.sun.com/portal/NetletC
onfig?func=loadResources
gateway protocol : https
gateway host : portal.sun.com
gateway port : 443
PAC file content length -> -1 , stream size -> 4031
https://gateway.sun.com/http://portal.int.sun.com/portal/NetletC
onfig?func=parsePacFile&PacFileUrl=
http://proxy.int.sun.com&ServerURL=
https://gateway.sun.com/http://portal.int.sun.com/portal/NetletC
onfig&ClientIPAddr=10.10.10.220.
null
Netlet no-proxy hosts:localhost
Netlet using proxy (Netscape): host:  port:0
Netlet config: https://ps-gateway.sun.com/http://ps-
server.int.sun.com/portal/NetletConfig?func=setLoaded
```

Advanced PAC File Configuration

There are two steadfast requirements for the Netlet connection to correctly function within automatic proxy environments:

- The PAC file must contain an entry with an appropriate proxy to use to communicate with the portal Gateway. This can be done using a host match, substring match, or a domain lookup.

- The PAC file must contain an entry to retrieve the PAC file itself. The entry should be direct, or have a proxy that has access to the PAC file.

  This might seem strange, but because the Netlet applet runs in the browser JVM, the browser has to give it permission to retrieve the PAC file. The browser determines this based on the PAC file contents. This chicken-and-egg scenario should become moot once the Java Plug-in software has become ubiquitous and the Netlet applet can make direct calls to the plug-in for which proxy to use. Until then, backward compatibility must be maintained, which means that the browser enforces its own security model dictated by the PAC about what URIs that applet can and can't access. This requirement surfaces most often in two instances. The first instance is when a PAC file doesn't contain a final else block with a DIRECT return statement. The second instance is when a PAC file returns a default proxy that can't communicate with the Gateway component.

PAC Deployment Security Concerns

There are two primary security concerns associated with using autoproxy files with the Netlet.

The first concern is that the client PAC file is transmitted to the portal server to be evaluated there rather than being parsed by the applet itself. This is an issue for companies who have deployed the portal server in a business-to-business fashion and their clients might not be aware that the Netlet must be granted specialized operating permissions by the end user. These permissions include the ability of the Netlet to read the browser preferences so that it can extract the proxy settings, in addition to connection privileges, so the Java applet can make network connections back to the server (the Gateway) where it was downloaded.

The applet also needs file access permissions if the PAC file is stored locally. Because downloading a fully featured JavaScript engine with the Netlet applet is not realistic, especially when you consider that many remote users do not connect using a broadband connection, the solution is to send the PAC file through a secure tunnel back to the portal server. The portal server passes the PAC contents with the help of Rhino and sends the results back to the Netlet client. If there is a possibility that end users will connect through their own intranet proxies using PAC files, it is highly recommended that you deploy the Netlet with a Netlet proxy so that the PAC file contents are never in the clear in the DMZ. Some companies might consider their PAC data to be of a sensitive nature, while others understand that information can be freely available on the Web applications where their users connect.

To reduce the likelihood of PAC file contents being intercepted in transit, use the Netlet proxy so that the data is transferred end-to-end in a secure manner. The PAC file contents are parsed only to retrieve the correct proxy to use to communicate with the Netlet and are themselves not permanently stored or cached on the portal node.

The other security issue is the possibility of the Rhino JavaScript engine executing rogue server-side JavaScript code. The risk here is minimal because only the predefined JavaScript functions necessary for automatic proxy configuration have been implemented. Any other JavaScript functions would have to implement their function definitions using the predefined JavaScript functions and limited additional JavaScript logic available within the body of the PAC file itself. Because of the narrow operating domain, there is very little chance that executing this code would result in anything more serious than causing it to throw a null pointer exception.

Note also that unless the PAC URL is changed just prior to launching the Netlet itself (as in the case of a dynamic Netlet rule), the browser also needs to get the result of the same PAC file to determine the network path necessary to reach the portal Gateway component. If the PAC file is syntactically incorrect at that time, it is caught and dismissed by the browser before a connection to the portal Gateway is made.

PAC Method Implementations

The following predefined JavaScript functions are implemented by the portal server for the Netlet to make use of PAC files:

- Host name-based conditions:

```
boolean dnsDomainIs(host, domain)
boolean isInNet(host, pattern, mask)
boolean isPlainHostName(host)
boolean isResolvable(host)
boolean localHostOrDomainIs(host, hostdom)
```

- Related utility functions:

```
int dnsDomainLevels(host)
string dnsResolve(host)
String myIpAddress()
```

- URL and host-name-based condition:

```
boolean shExpMatch(str, shexp)
```

- Time-based conditions:

```
boolean dateRange(day1, month1, year1, day2, month2, year2, gmt)
boolean timeRange(hour1, min1, sec1, hour2, min2, sec2, gmt)
boolean weekdayRange(wd1, wd2, gmt)
```

Use of time-based conditions in PAC files is rare. If a time-based condition is implemented such that a different proxy should be used to reach the portal Gateway sometime during the Netlet session, end users might have to terminate their Netlet sessions, close the Netlet pop-up window (and possibly the browser as well), and restart it to make use of the new proxy. In addition, the Netlet supports the nesting of functions, a functionality that is heavily used in complex proxied environments. It is a good idea to make the external Gateway address resolvable by the portal server platform so that when Rhino evaluates a PAC file any calls to the utility function dnsResolve() will resolve to the correct IP address. Otherwise, if `dnsResolve()` returned the private interface IP address, the PAC file might evaluate the incorrect proxy to use if there are internal IP address mapping overlaps between the two companies.

CODE EXAMPLE 2-3   Example of `dnsResolve()` Utility Function Use

```
function FindProxyForURL(url, host) {
  hostIP= dnsResolve(host);
  if (isInNet(hostIP, "10.0.0.0", "255.255.254.0") ||
      isInNet(hostIP, "10.10.220.0", "255.255.252.0"))
  {
    return "PROXY yxorp.domain:8080";
  }
  ...
}
```

Determining Causes of Failure in PAC File Deployments

Another important facet of PAC file use with the Netlet is being able to determine causes of failures. Because most PAC usage failures feature the same result condition, it is useful to know why certain failures might occur.

Possible Cause A – Cannot Fetch PAC File Contents

One PAC usage failure, mentioned earlier in this chapter, has to do with the PAC file contents not containing a DIRECT return statement or proxy to use to fetch the PAC file contents. For instance, some banking environments allow very few direct connections and might have an else block for all other content that has not matched anything prior and returns a proxy that cannot access the PAC file.

CODE EXAMPLE 2-4   Example PAC That Will Not Work With Netlet

```
function FindProxyForURL(url, host) {
  hostIP= dnsResolve(host);
  if (isInNet(hostIP, "10.10.220.0", "255.255.254.0"))
  {
    return "PROXY yxorp.domain:8080";
  }
  else {
    // Return external proxy for everything else
    return "PROXY ext_net.yxorp.domain:8080";
  }
}
```

For example, if the PAC file is hosted from a Web server with an IP address of 10.10.221.10, the IP address would have to be directly reachable from the browser itself for autoproxy to function at all. But in this case, the Netlet applet would not be able to download the PAC file because the browser security model would force the applet to download the file using the ext_net proxy which, in this example, would not be able to communicate directly with 10.10.221.10. Looking at the Java Console output for the failed connection, an end user might see the following:

```
Netlet running on Netscape
Netlet config: https://ps-gateway.sun.com/
http://ps-server.int.sun.com/portal/NetletConfig?func=
loadResources
gateway protocol : https
gateway host : ps-gateway.sun.com
gateway port : 443
java.lang.NullPointerException
at BrowserProxyInfo.g(Compiled Code)
at BrowserProxyInfo.<init>(Compiled Code)
.
.
.

https://ps-gateway.sun.com/http://sips-
server.int.sun.com/portal/NetletConfig?func=
parsePacFile&PacFileUrl=http://10.10.221.10/proxy.pac&ServerURL=
https://ps-gateway.sun.com/http://ps-
server.int.sun.com/portal/NetletConfig&ClientIPAddr=127.0.0.1
null
.
.
.
```

Having failed to grab the PAC file contents, the Netlet applet might attempt to locate another proxy to do the job, but a successful connection is not guaranteed.

Possible Cause B – Rhino Parser Missing

Another easy oversight resulting in a null pointer exception is to not have the Rhino JavaScript parser installed. Unfortunately, because Rhino is assumed to be available at runtime, no clearly identifiable errors occur such as "You forgot to install Rhino. I hope you don't expect your Netlet users to be able to use automatic proxy configuration files." Instead, you might just ensure that the required Java™ Archive (jar) file is in place. You can do this from the portal node as shown in the following example.

```
# file /usr/java*/jre/lib/ext/js.jar
/usr/java_1.3.1_04/jre/lib/ext/js.jar:   java program
```

Make sure that the `js.jar` is stored in the JDK runtime directory used by the portal server. This can be verified by taking a look at the `jvm12.conf` file of the Web server being used by the portal as follows:

```
# grep "/usr/java"
install_dir/SUNWam/servers/https*com/config/jvm12.conf | grep -v
"SUNWam"
#jvm.option=-
Xbootclasspath:/usr/java_1.3.1_04/lib/tools.jar:/usr/java_1.3.
1_04/jre/lib/rt.jar
```

Must match the Java version as determined in the previous code box.

This is a situation where you'll want to kick yourself for not reading the product documentation, or for simply forgetting to install Rhino when the portal moves to production and all of a sudden no remote users are able to access the Netlet.

Note – Rhino is available on the third-party software CD that ships with the portal software. Additional information about Rhino can be found at `mozilla.org`. Aditional information about installing Rhino with the portal server is available at: `http:// docs.sun.com/source/816-6731-10/ app_optional.html#wp12411`.

Possible Cause C

Another frequent cause for a null pointer exception is PAC file truncation. This is the situation already mentioned where a Content-Length header is not returned by the application serving the PAC contents, and the Netlet applet fails to read the PAC file in its entirety.

Other Possible Causes

Further diagnosis of PAC-related failures can be done by requesting the PAC file contents from the end user and the client IP address from where they are connecting. With this information, you can use a Java application to evaluate the PAC file contents. The following procedure describes how to do this.

▼ To Compile and Run the PAC Test Program

1. **Set your** `CLASSPATH` **variable to the same value set in the Web server** `jvm12.conf` **file as follows.**

```
# CLASSPATH=`/usr/bin/cat /opt/SUNWam/servers/https-ps-
server.int.sun.com/config/jvm12.conf | /usr/bin/grep
"jvm.classpath" | cut -d '=' -f2`:$CLASSPATH
# export CLASSPATH
# echo $CLASSPATH
/opt/SUNWam/servers/plugins/servlets/examples/legacy/beans.10/SD
KBeans10.jar:/opt/SUNWam/lib:/opt/SUNWam/locale:/opt/SUNWam/lib/
jss311.jar:/opt/SUNWam/lib/am_sdk.jar:/usr/java_1.3.1_04/lib/too
ls.jar:/opt/SUNWam/lib/am_services.jar:/opt/SUNWam/lib/am_sso_pr
ovider.jar:/opt/SUNWam/lib/swec.jar:/opt/SUNWam/lib/acmecrypt.ja
r:/opt/SUNWam/lib/iaik_ssl.jar:/opt/SUNWam/lib/jaas.jar:/opt/SUN
Wam/lib/crimson.jar:/opt/SUNWam/lib/jaxp.jar:/opt/SUNWam/lib/mai
l.jar:/opt/SUNWam/lib/activation.jar:/opt/SUNWam/lib/servlet.jar
```

Note – Your `CLASSPATH` might differ depending on the path for your Identity Server install directory.

---

2. **Create a** `PACtest.java` **file similar to the following example to test the PAC file evaluation.**

This file is available for download. See "Obtaining Downloadable Files for This Book" on page xxi.

CODE EXAMPLE 2-5   `PACtest.java` Example

```
import java.util.*;
import java.io.*;
import java.net.*;

public class PACTest {
  public static void main(String[] args) {
    try {
      if (args.length != 4) {
        System.out.println("PACTest:Incorrect number of arguments
("+args.length+")");

        System.out.println("Usage:\tjava PACTest <localPACFile>
<URL> <remoteHost> <clientIP>");

  System.out.println("EX:\tjava PACTest /h/export/simple.pac \\");
```

```
      System.out.println("\thttps://ps-
gateway.domain.com:443/http://ps-
server.domain.com:80/NetletConfig \\");
      System.out.println("\tps-gateway.domain.com \\");
      System.out.println("\t10.10.220.10");
    }
    else {
      FileInputStream fIn=new FileInputStream(args[0]);
      DataInputStream in = new DataInputStream(fIn);
      String url = args[1];
      String host = args[2];
      String clientIP = args[3];

      byte data[]=new byte[in.available()];
      in.readFully(data);
      String pacFileBody = new String(data);

      Runtime rt = Runtime.getRuntime();

      String command="/usr/java_1.3.1_04/bin/java
com.sun.portal.netlet.servlet.EvalPAC "+URLEncoder.encode(pacFile
Body)+" "+url+" "+host+" "+clientIP;

      String env[] = new String[1];
      env[0]=new String("CLASSPATH=
/usr/java_1.3.1_04/jre/lib/ext/js.jar:/opt/SUNWps/lib/ips_netlet.
jar:.");

      //System.out.println(command + env );
      Process proc = rt.exec(command,env);
      DataInputStream Conin = new DataInputStream(
proc.getInputStream());
      String result= Conin.readLine();
      System.out.println(result);
    }
  }
  catch(Exception ex) {
    ex.printStackTrace();
  }
 }
}
```

3. Check the following administrative settings:

   a. Make sure that your `CLASSPATH` environment variable is set to the correct Java directory.

   Example:

   ```
   # setenv CLASSPATH /usr/java_1.3.1_04
   ```

   b. Make sure that the Java path specified for the `String command=` string in your `PACtest.java` file is set to the proper Java directory.

   Example:

   ```
   String command="/usr/java_1.3.1_04/bin/java
   com.sun.portal.netlet.servlet.EvalPAC "+URLEncoder.encode(pacFile
   Body)+" "+url+" "+host+" "+clientIP;
   ```

   Do not specify a link (such as `/usr/bin/java`) to the `String command=` string because the link might not point to the correct version of Java software needed for your PAC file deployment.

4. Test the program by using the `simple.pac` file described earlier with a bogus URL and IP address.

   ```
   # java PACTest ./sample.pac https://ps-
   gateway.domain.com:443/http://ps-
   server.domain.com:80/NetletConfig ps-gateway.domain.com
   10.10.220.10
   PROXY myproxy.subdomain.domain.com:8080
   ```

This is a helpful approach for diagnosing connectivity problems related to automatic proxy configuration files. If null is returned by the test program, it might be due to a syntax problem in the PAC file itself. Other outside network factors would obviously not be in play. The purpose of the test program is to make sure that, given the client IP address and portal Gateway IP address, the PAC file can be evaluated successfully, and that it returns the appropriate proxy for the client to use to successfully connect with the Gateway and download the Netlet applet.

PAC Deployment Tips

While you might not have control over the proxy environments of your end users, the following tips can help ensure successful connectivity:

- Ensure that the PAC file contains a DIRECT entry or proxy to be used to fetch the PAC file itself.

- Use a Content-Length header, set by a server delivering proxy contents, to help eliminate the possibility of PAC file truncation.

- Keep overall PAC file sizes down. Older browsers like Internet Explorer 4 and 5.0 have file size limitations on PAC files.

- Keep your environment as simple as possible. The more complex the autoproxy environment, the higher the possibility for the wrong proxy to be returned.

- Make sure that the Gateway address resolves to the public interface from the portal node, otherwise dnsResolve() and dnsDomainIs() references to the host IP (portal Gateway in this case) might fail or be inaccurate.

- Make sure end users are connecting with a supported browser and JVM combination.

Limitations On PAC File Deployment

There are two bugs in the Sun ONE Portal Server 6.0 and 6.1 software that directly impact the successful evaluation of most PAC files. Patches are available for these bugs. In the portal server 6.2 release, these bugs are fixed.

The first bug is the PAC file truncation for large PAC files and PAC files served from applications that do not set a Content-Length HTTP header.

The second bug is that the incorrect client IP address is used during PAC file evaluation. This directly affects any PAC files making references to myIpAddress() in determining which proxy to use as shown in CODE EXAMPLE 2-6.

CODE EXAMPLE 2-6   Sample PAC File Making Use of `myIpAddress()` Function

```
function FindProxyForURL(url, host)
{
  myaddr=myIpAddress();
  hostIP=dnsResolve(host);
  //
    if ( isInNet("127.0.0.0", myaddr, "255.255.255.0") )
      {
        return "DIRECT";
      }
    else
      {
        return "PROXY myproxy.domain.com:8080";
      }
  //
}
```

Note – The `hostIP=dnsResolve(host)` is not used in this example, but is shown in case the `isInNet` comparison were to look at the host address instead of the client IP address. This is why it is necessary to have the external gateway address resolvable by the internal network. Otherwise, the wrong proxy, or no proxy might be selected instead.

Although the `localhost` address is explicitly passed as a parameter to the Netlet servlet, the value stored for the `iPlanetUserId` cookie is used during PAC file evaluation. Sun ONE Portal Server 6.0 software might return a Network Address Translation (NAT) IP address or the network gateway (`defaultrouter`) address. This can be checked by adding a second proxy to return (so that it isn't used), which prints the client IP address.

CODE EXAMPLE 2-7   Client IP Address Debug PAC File

```
function FindProxyForURL(url, host)
{
  myaddr=myIpAddress();
//
if ( isInNet(myaddr,"127.0.0.0","255.255.255.0") )
      {
        return "PROXY myproxy.domain.com:8080";
      }
    else
      return "DIRECT; PROXY " + myaddr;
//
}
```

Using the same test program with this PAC file returns the following message:

```
DIRECT; PROXY 10.10.220.10
```

When accessed remotely, the incorrect client IP address that would be visible in the Java Console output might be returned.

Integrating Automatic Configuration (ins) Files

Automatic configuration files are used to configure browser settings dynamically once the browser is launched. Autoconfiguration files are an offshoot from Netscape mission control desktop configuration (cfg) files, combined with autoproxy configuration files. The syntax of ins files is that of section names followed by key-value pairs for each section. Autoconfiguration files are used for branding purposes and to lock down specific features and functions for corporate users. A custom browser can be built using the Internet Explorer Administrator Kit (IEAK) that locks down the autoconfiguration URL location. This way, the autoconfiguration file can be modified as business needs change without having to spin another browser and deploy it across the entire company. Additional information is provided in "Using Custom Built Browsers" on page 62. For more details about the Internet Explorer Administrator Kit (IEAK), visit Micosoft's Web site.

Because the proxy settings can be specified in the autoconfiguration file, the Netlet applet needs to retrieve and parse out that information if the browser is configured to make use of autoconfiguration files. Microsoft autoconfiguration files are also referred to as ins files because of their file extension. ins files can be created manually, or by using the IEAK Profile Manager. A simple ins file is shown below.

CODE EXAMPLE 2-8   Example ins (Autoconfiguration) File

```
;;;;;;;;;;;;;;;;;;;;;;;;;;;;;;;;;;;;;;;;;;;;;;;;;;;;
;;    example.ins
;;    Autoconfiguration file which refers to
;;    a Perl application that returns the PAC
;;    file contents
;;;;;;;;;;;;;;;;;;;;;;;;;;;;;;;;;;;;;;;;;;;;;;;;;;;;
[URL]
AutoConfig=1
AutoDetect=0
AutoConfigJSURL=http://yourURL/genpac.pl
AutoConfigURL=http://yourURL/corp.ins
[Proxy]
HTTP_Proxy_Server=
FTP_Proxy_Server=
Gopher_Proxy_Server=
Secure_Proxy_Server=
Socks_Proxy_Server=
Use_Same_Proxy=1
Proxy_Enable=0
Proxy_Override=<local>
```

Note – Once an ins file is enabled, it continues to be used unless it is explicitly replaced by another ins file, such as clean.ins, which would be configured to have empty values for the AutoConfigJSURL and AutoConfigURL entries.

CODE EXAMPLE 2-9   Example `clean.ins` File

```
[Branding]

[URL]

[ActiveSetupSites]

[HideCustom]
{61274460-bf8c-11d1-994c-00c04f98bbc9}=1
{B57EA2D1-1C31-11d2-B9C1-00A0C9B7C9C1}=1
{CC2A9BA0-3BDD-11D0-821E-444553540000}=1
{3bf42070-b3b1-11d1-b5c5-0000f8051515}=1
{45ea75a0-a269-11d1-b5bf-0000f8051515}=1
{4f216970-c90c-11d1-b5c7-0000f8051515}=1
{36f8ec70-c29a-11d1-b5c7-0000f8051515}=1
{BEF6E001-A874-101A-8BBA-00AA00300CAB}=1
{C9E9A340-D1F1-11D0-821E-444553540600}=1
{9381D8F2-0288-11D0-9501-00AA00B911A5}=1
{630b1da0-b465-11d1-9948-00c04f98bbc9}=1
{44BBA842-CC51-11CF-AAFA-00AA00B6015C}=1
{44BBA842-CC51-11CF-AAFA-00AA00B6015B}=1
{7790769C-0471-11d2-AF11-00C04FA35D02}=1
{44BBA840-CC51-11CF-AAFA-00AA00B6015C}=1
{22d6f312-b0f6-11d0-94ab-0080c74c7e95}=1
{9a2e4ab0-9a7e-11d2-9da1-00c04f98bbc9}=1
{283807B5-2C60-11D0-A31D-00AA00B92C03}=1
{10072CEC-8CC1-11D1-986E-00A0C955B42F}=1
```

For the Netlet to successfully run on IE clients with autoconfiguration enabled, the
ins file must have either a Proxy section with a value for `Secure_Proxy_Server`
if the portal Gateway is running in HTTPS mode (which it should be in most cases),
or a value for `HTTP_Proxy_Server` otherwise. If an autoproxy configuration file is
used instead, the ins file must contain a URL section with an entry for
`AutoConfigJSURL`. This URL should point to something that the Netlet applet can
download that is syntactically valid JavaScript. There is some circular logic built into
ins files that enables an ins file to point to an additional ins file. The Netlet
follows the ins redirection until it finds an `AutoConfigJSURL` entry or there is no
`AutoConfigURL` entry in the redirected ins file. Redirected ins files should be
avoided, if possible.

IE uses the same form field for ins files as PAC files (FIGURE 2-16). The Netlet
decides which one is specified by looking at the file extension in addition to the
MIME type.

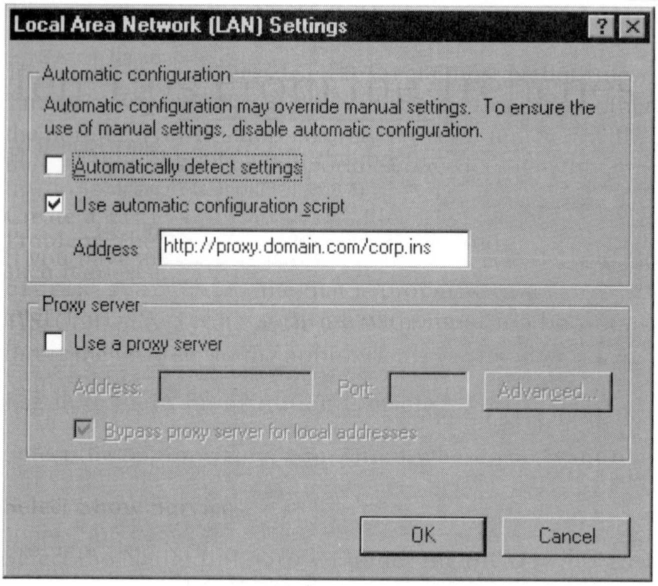

FIGURE 2-16 IE Configured to Use an `ins` File

The Java Console output, when a Netlet connection is being established, doesn't look any different regardless of whether an autoconfiguration file or an autoproxy file has been specified. When testing with an `ins` file, it's a good idea to change the window title under the Branding section so that you know which `ins` file is active.

CODE EXAMPLE 2-10   Example of a Branding Section in an `ins` File

```
[Branding]
Language Locale=en
Language ID=1033
Window_Title_CN=Put message here!!!
Window_Title=Microsoft Internet Explorer -->  Put message here!!!
FavoritesOnTop=0
Platform=2
CabsURLPath=http://proxy.domain.com/example3_config.cab
InsVersion=2001.05.15.01
Type=0
DeleteAdms=1
ImportIns=c:\autoconfig\example3.ins
Wizard_Version=5.50.4309.1200
Custom_Key=DEMOWIZ
CompanyName=Sun Microsystems Inc
Win32DownloadSite=0
UseDefAddon=1
NoIELite=1
```

In addition to creating custom `ins` files to troubleshoot Netlet connections, follow these general rules:

- **Case matters**. The JavaScript function `FindProxyForURL`, predefined JavaScript functions, and the `ins` entry `AutoConfigJSURL` must all match the case shown.

- **Arbitrary JavaScript cannot be added to the PAC file content**. Aside from comments and other JavaScript functions implemented in the PAC file body, any other arbitrary or rogue JavaScript prevents the proxy evaluation from being returned to the client.

- **Syntax matters**. For instance, return statements cannot have dangling plus signs. The following is an example of unacceptable syntax:
  ```
  return "PROXY proxy.domain.com:8080;" +
  ```

- **URLs must include protocol identifiers**. For example, the Netscape `prefs.js` file might contain an entry such as:
  ```
  user_pref("network.proxy.autoconfig_url", "pac.com:8080/pac");
  ```
  In this case, `pac.com` is not a valid URL, but `http://pac.com:8080/pac` is a valid URL.

CODE EXAMPLE 2-11 Netscape Autoconfiguration File

```
/////////////////////////////////////////////
// sample.jsc
//   example Netscape autoconfig file
/////////////////////////////////////////////

with (PrefConfig) {
lockPref("network.proxy.autoconfig_url",
"http://yourURL/test.pac");
lockPref("network.proxy.type", 3);
}
```

This autoconfiguration file prepopulates the PAC file URL in the browser and locks that setting so that the user is unable to modify it. The value for `network.proxy.autoconfig_url` must contain the protocol identifier, and be a fully qualified URL for the Netlet applet to be able to fetch the PAC file.

Browser and JVM Support

The 6.x version of the portal server software expands the list of supported browsers and JVMs that can be used to access the NetApps and the portal server desktop. Portal server mobile access expands this list to include mobile device browsers. For the most part, browser functionality for the portal Rewriter remains in line with what would be required to view the content itself.

The Sun ONE Portal Server Secure Remote Access NetApps comprised of Netlet and NetFile, in addition to the portal server Netmail application, have a narrower supported scope. To determine supported browsers for your environment, refer to the product documentation for the specific portal version you are using.

The list of supported browsers is selected at the time the portal server software is initially released. Because browsers are released so quickly and features are deprecated or changed equally fast, it would not be useful to spend much time talking about the individual browser releases. Instead, I will speak more generally about why some browsers not on this list may or may not work with the NetApps.

To begin with, the browser security model has to be identified so that the Java applet can be granted the appropriate permissions to execute and work properly. This is done by the applet checking for the existence of a Netscape security library and also by checking user agent values. Sometimes the security library might have been manually copied to Internet Explorer's CLASSPATH, causing the Netlet to incorrectly ascertain the browser type and eventually causing Netlet connection failure. Despite that fact, this approach is generally a dependable method for determining browser versions. In the case of Internet Explorer, however, when the browser looks for the Netscape security library, it results in nuisance logging in the Web server error log.

CODE EXAMPLE 2-12 Example Web Server Entry for IE Request

```
[25/Jan/2004:23:01:44] warning (14475): for host 10.10.220.10
trying to GET /netlet/netscape/security/PrivilegeManager.class,
send-file reports: can't find
/opt/SUNWips/public_html/netlet/netscape/security/PrivilegeManager
.class (File not found)
```

This might look frightening, but adding the class file to that directory makes the Netlet assume that all connections are originating from a Netscape browser. So resist the temptation, and write a script using the grep command to remove these entries to make the log more readable. This can be done immediately after log rotation to the inactive log.

CODE EXAMPLE 2-13 Example Command to Remove Nuisance Log Entries

```
# grep -v "PrivilegeManager.class" errors > errors.032904_filtrd
```

The proxy settings specific to the portal browser must also be determined, which are different from browser to browser. As mentioned already, IE uses a single ambiguous form field for autoconfiguration files, and autoproxy files alike.

The rendering engines in Mozilla and Netscape 7 are essentially identical, so most features and functionality work. A JVM earlier than 1.4 might have to be used for reliable results, and "Allow Website icons" might have to be turned off in Netscape 7 for end users to log in to the portal server 6.0 Gateway. More details about this configuration requirement are discussed in Chapter 4 "Rewriter: Secure Remote Access to Internal Web-Based Applications" and Chapter 5 "Gateway: Gluing It All Together."

For Netlet connections that do not require network proxies, Mozilla 1.2.1, Netscape 6x, and Netscape 7 should work well with a JVM 1.3.1. The Netscape Communicator 4x software functions okay. However, due to slow rendering of nested tables, Communicator software is not the optimal browser to use with the portal server 6.x desktop, especially if the portal server desktop contains URL-scraped channels that have additional nested tables. At ten deep, Netscape Communicator software freezes up, and in most cases produces a segmentation fault within two refreshes of the page. Granted, ten nested tables is borderline insanity, especially if you're trying to figure out where a table tag might be missing. Netscape 6 is generally not as well revered in the Web community as Netscape 7, and most enterprises still using an IE alternative have switched to Mozilla because of the absence of AOL branding and features.

In the Microsoft browser camp, IE 5.0 and 5.0SP1 can limp along, but 5.5SPx tends to be the most reliable entry-level version of IE. IE 6.0 can be used with the 1.3.1_02 Java Plug-in software and most later versions of the Microsoft VM when they were still shipping with the client.

Each browser version has its own advantages and disadvantages. Some are purely related to taste, but adoptions of certain Web technologies in personalized portal content, tag syntaxes, security considerations, and other preferences might dictate a required user agent and release level. Other browsers are likely to have mixed results, but none of them are currently supported for use with the NetApps. When in doubt, check the product documentation for the most recent SRA-supported browsers and VMs.

Using Custom Built Browsers

Corporate IT departments often make custom browser versions available to desktop users to reduce security risks, add branding and configuration, and lock down preferences to reduce internal support-related calls. In addition to the browser and VM support requirements already stated, there are some things to keep in mind if customized browsers are going to be used to access Netlet functionality. Most browser features and functionality that can be changed by end users can be locked down by creating customized browsers. Mission Control Desktop (MCD) is the software administration package used to create customized Netscape Communicator browsers for corporate use. No comparable software package exists for more recent versions of Netscape, and because Internet Explorer now owns a significant browser market share, the Microsoft MCD equivalent, Internet Explorer Administrator Kit (IEAK), is discussed instead.

Follow these guidelines to ensure that Netlets work in customized browser environments:

■ Java software must be enabled and supported JVM software must be installed. See "Browser and JVM Support" on page 60 for more information about specific version information.

■ Non-persistent cookies must be enabled. The portal server and Identity Server technology both use cookies for session management.

■ JavaScript programming language must be enabled. The Netlet provider and Netlet pop-up window both operate using JavaScript, as do a significant portion of other functionality on the portal server desktop like the Bookmark provider and URL rewriting technology.

■ The Do not Save Encrypted Pages to Disk option should be selected if sensitive data will be downloaded through HTTP by redirecting through the Gateway. This is not related to the Netlet functionality, but the option is an important security consideration because of the way Internet Explorer handles encrypted content. Whether or not this option is enabled, IE caches or briefly caches SSL content that needs to be handed off to helper applications. For instance, if a Microsoft Word document is downloaded from an SSL-enabled Web server, the document is first decrypted and cached before the data is sent to the Microsoft Word application. This contrasts with the behavior of the Netscape browser that streams the content to the helper application as soon as it is decrypted. This is important to note because content other than the portal server desktop may be cached when accessed through the Gateway. In most cases this is considered a security risk, so HTTP no-cache headers are used to prevent the problem from occurring. IE treats a no-cache header differently than it treats its own "Do not Save Encrypted Pages to Disk," and by doing so, setting a no-cache header might prevent end users from accessing data with MIME types not handled internally by IE. In fact, they will not even be able to choose Save As because IE must cache the content before a user can actually save the content. This is discussed in more detail in Chapter 4

"Rewriter: Secure Remote Access to Internal Web-Based Applications" and in Chapter 5 "Gateway: Gluing It All Together." Check the Microsoft Knowledge Base for affected Internet Explorer browser versions.

Infrastructure: Firewalls and Proxies

The uniqueness and flexibility of the Netlet VPN-on-demand technology makes it ideal to plug into existing infrastructure to grant secure remote access to authenticated users. Because the Netlet is most frequently deployed to run over port 443, additional ports generally do not have to be opened on client-side or server-side firewalls. There have been no reported cases of correctly configured packet filtering firewalls interfering with Netlet traffic. Sometimes firewall timeouts can force a premature Netlet session disconnect. This topic is discussed further in "Understanding and Handling Timeouts" on page 75.

That said, there is a small group of network traffic infrastructure products that might interfere with Netlet connectivity. These firewalls and proxies perform packet-level inspection on the individual data packets and make sure that they adhere to protocol standards that they claim to support. The Netlet operates on the basis that it cloaks the encrypted traffic as though it were SSL, so SSL verification might fail depending on the level of inspection done. Packet inspection is usually a feature that can be turned on or off. The only products known to affect Netlet traffic when the feature is enabled are the Gauntlet firewall and the Squid Web proxy. Up to now, SSL has not been fully supported because the encryption strength is not as strong as the proprietary implementation offered natively by the Netlet. Because SSL has become a standard for secure transactions over the Internet, it is accepted as a reasonable level of security for most e-commerce activity, and because many companies offer SSL hardware accelerators to speed up handshakes and bulk data transfer, SSL has been added to the list of supported Netlet algorithms in portal server version 6.2. See "New Netlet Technology in the Java Enterprise System" on page 125.

Static VPNs

Netlet technology is not expected to compete directly with traditional static VPNs. In many cases, where a static VPN is present, the Netlet can complement it, and can in most cases work perfectly well over the VPN itself. VPNs are widely used in wireless 802.11 networks and for remote employees using their own or corporate-owned hardware to access the network. So long as the VPN does not exclude connections originating from localhost to the VPN network, the Netlet ought to function normally. As you might expect, this is somewhat redundant. One example of using both a VPN and a Netlet would be a business-to-business portal with an access control list (ACL) in place that only allows connections from partnering corporate networks rather than from the Internet. This is not a widely used form of security, due to the ease by which an end user is able to spoof their own IP address, but it can be used as another security layer. In this usage scenario, the end users working remotely would log on to their own network through the VPN, then go to the remote portal and launch the Netlet session from there.

In most cases, however, the Netlet is used instead of a VPN. The reason for this is due to the Netlet's lack of a client footprint, and the Netlet's ability to function between secure networks over public wires without having to lock down all IP traffic, or require manual key (certificate) exchange prior to establishing a connection.

Netlet Cryptography

The portal server 6 versions expose the cryptographic algorithm it uses and adds some additional choices. Despite the fact that the Netlet provider edit page enables end users to select what algorithms they would like to use, the choice is usually made by the portal administrator or third-party security consultant. There might be applications such as government agencies and banks that require triple DES, but for most applications RC4 is considered adequate. RC4 might be considered in cases where Solaris™ Secure Shell (SSH) software runs over a Netlet connection and the traffic is already encrypted to begin with, which makes the crypto-per-rule a handy feature. To avoid any confusion, and to prevent end users from being able to select Null, the default encryption algorithm should be set to whatever you find suitable, and it should be fixed for all of the Netlet rules. Setting the crypto to Null might be useful for performance benchmarking against the other algorithms, but not all the communication is in the clear, so the difference between the two might not be as large as you would expect. If all of the rules are selectable, the strongest one is chosen by default unless an end user specifically changes it. Exposing this to the end user is a bit like allowing an employee to choose whether or not they want to use a badge to enter the office building, or if they prefer to use the secret handshake with the receptionist.

Using the Netlet Proxy

The Netlet proxy is used when the Gateway is deployed to a DMZ to avoid the need to open additional holes in the secondary firewall for each Netlet rule. It's easy to turn the proxy on and off by using the Admin Console and selecting which port it should use from the Gateway properties configuration. Defining services per machine fits well with Sun's strategy of blade architectures, but the system should be sized well enough to handle bulk encryption and decryption. SSL accelerators can be used for bulk encryption and decryption in portal server 6.2 when SSL ciphers are configured in the Gateway. SSL accelerators have a limited impact on earlier versions, because only the SSL handshake is positively affected.

Netlet Pop-Up: Friend or Foe?

The purpose of this section is less to answer this baited question than it is to discuss the purpose of the pop-up window, reasonable customizations you can make on it, and some handy tricks for managing it.

The Netlet pop-up exists because the client portion of the Netlet is a Java applet. If the applet were run from within the Netlet provider, Netlet sessions would be lost when channels were edited, another tab was navigated to, channels were removed or added to the desktop, and a whole host of other desktop actions. The three biggest complaints about this approach are:

- Why can't I choose whether the applet loads on the desktop or the pop-up?
- Pop-up blockers prevent the Netlet from running.
- Pop-ups are annoying and take up valuable desktop real estate.

It doesn't make sense to run the applet on the portal server desktop given that a portal is dynamic in nature. In addition, there is logic in the pop-up window that gives rudimentary status about the Netlet using customizable messages. Pop-up blockers might be a problem for static Netlet rules where pop-ups are created without user intervention. Dynamic Netlets require the user to select a link on the portal server desktop before the Netlet pop-up launches, and should work through most pop-up blockers. The exception to this behavior is where URLs are launched in helper applications. If pop-up blocking is enabled, the helper application might need to be opened manually and directed to the local port where the Netlet has been configured to listen. If that fails, end users might have to add the fully qualified host of the Gateway server to the blocker's allow list to successfully use the Netlet. However, most agree that pop-ups are often annoying, requiring additional user intervention to deal with them.

When a user logs in to the portal server with the Netlet provider visible on their desktop, the Netlet pop-up window loads automatically if there are any static rules defined for them. This determination is made by looking at the Port-Host-Port list to see if there are any hosts not matching TARGET. If a static rule is found, the following code in the Netlet provider launches the pop-up window:

```
netletWinOpen("https://ps-gateway.sun.com/http://ps-
server.int.sun.com/portal/NetletConfig?func=makepage", true );
```

This differs slightly from dynamic Netlet rule links, which instead use the following code:

```
netletConfigOpen('https://ps-gateway.suncom/http://ps-
server.int.sun.com/portal/NetletConfig?func=makepage',
'https://ps-gateway.sun.com/http://ps-
server.int.sun.com/portal/NetletConfig?func=Telnet&machine=
www.sun.com')
```

This is useful to know if you would like to launch a Netlet from somewhere on the desktop other than the Netlet provider. Because JavaScript is a top-down programming language, be sure that the Netlet functions are defined prior to any places they might be called from. The query string parameter `func` is the Netlet rule name and `machine` is the destination host. Because these URLs can be contrived, it's important to make use of the allow and deny lists defined at the Netlet service level to aid in limiting access to specific hosts as business requirements might demand.

Customizing the Pop-Up

The pop-up (FIGURE 2-17) is composed of a single frameset. The top frame provides Netlet status, while the bottom frame loads the Netlet applet. You can modify the customizable portion of the Netlet status window by changing the properties in the `.properties` file at
install_dir/SUNWam/locale/srapNetletServlet.properties

Before

After

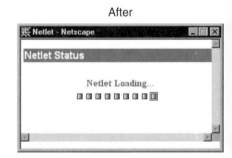

FIGURE 2-17 Netlet Pop-Up Windows, Before and After Customization

The HTML source for the frame shows you what you can modify:

```
<html>
<BODY TEXT="#000000" BGCOLOR="#FFFFFF">
<p><h2>Netlet runs from this browser window.</h2><p><b><font
color=red>Note:</font>  Do not close this window while using
netlet connections.  You may close this window when you no longer
want to use netlet connections.</b></body>
</html>
```

Most of the values in this example are self explanatory. Those you might care about the most are nc1–nc5, which specify the Netlet states. Be sure to keep all of the property values on a single line, or you risk truncating the text. The following example shows a customized Netlet pop-up window with an nc3 value.

```
nc3=<TABLE WIDTH="100%"><TR BGCOLOR="#594FBF"><TD><FONT SIZE="+0"
FACE="Sans-Serif" COLOR="#FFFFFF"><B>Netlet
Status</B></FONT></TD></TR><TR><TD><p><BR><b><font color=
red><CENTER>Netlet Loading...<BR><IMG SRC=
"/portal/desktop/images/loading.gif" BORDER="0"></font> 
</TD></TR></TABLE>
```

The loading image has been added to the desktop service as an example. In portal server 6.0, it is not generally recommended that you make changes to the web-apps or web-src directories. In certain instances, such as modifying the appearance of channel buttons, the images must be stored in the desktop images directory. In this case, the images should be changed in the following directory:
install_dir/SUNWps/web-src/desktop/images/

Note – For the portal server 6.2 software only:
To push the changes to the portal instances, as root, run the redeploy command from the *install_dir*/SUNWps/bin/deploy redeploy directory.

Note – The redeploy option of the deploy command is a private interface and can change at any time. Do not use the deploy command if you are using l versions 6.0 or 6.1 of the portal server software. See the "Risks and Workarounds for the deploy Command" on page 411" in Appendix B.

Be sure to restart the portal server after making changes to the Netlet properties files.

```
# /etc/init.d/amserver startall
```

You can modify the Netlet window properties by making changes to the Netlet `display.template` file, and you can add JavaScript event handlers to spawn additional actions when the Netlet launches. Because this template file is used for functional reasons, changing it might result in the customizations being overwritten or corrupted when upgrading. For this reason, copy the template file to a customized template directory prior to making changes to it, in addition to backing it up to a non-portal server directory or to off-disk media. This might seem like overkill, but it is necessary because you are changing a file that is not typically considered to be modifiable. In portal server 6.0, the Netlet templates are stored in the default container directory. With the demo desktop installed, this would be at `/etc/opt/SUNWps/desktop/default/MyFrontPageTabPanelContainer/Netlet` If this is not the container you have currently chosen, copy the `Netlet` directory contents to the appropriate location. For example, as `root`, type the following command:

```
# cp -R
/etc/opt/SUNWps/desktop/default/MyFrontPageTabPanelContanier/Netlet
/etc/opt/SUNWps/desktop/custom/JSPTableContainerProvider/Netlet
```

Before making any modifications to the `display.template` file, it is important to be aware of some of the limitations in doing so. First and foremost, the frameset should remain intact, and, at a minimum, the pop-up window name must continue to be `nWin` because that is the handle used by the Netlet servlet to update the window status. If the window status cannot be updated, the Netlet connection fails. The `netletWinOpen` function is called when all of the TARGET hosts are fixed (static) and no URL is specified to launch once the Netlet has fully loaded. The `netletConfigOpen` function is used to launch the Netlet rules with specific hosts. If the Netlet is loading for the first time using `netletConfigOpen`, an interim window opens with a Continue button. If the URL associated with the Netlet rule is null, the window simply closes when the Continue button is selected. Otherwise, the URL is loaded in the interim window by calling `netletActionOpen`.

While the Netlet pop-up window is a useful notification service about the status of the Netlet, and while it is important to separate the Netlet from the portal server desktop to avoid losing Netlet sessions when users interact with the portal server desktop, some applications of the Netlet might require it to be a bit more discrete. See "Scenario C: Integrating Citrix ICA With a Netlet" on page 88 for examples of instances when the Netlet should be more discrete than it is by default. There are a couple of ways to lessen the impact of the Netlet pop-up on client desktop real estate and to minimize user intervention required by the Netlet pop-up window. Unfortunately, most of them require you to modify the Netlet template and are browser specific. For example, the Netscape client does not allow Netlet pop-up windows to be smaller than 100x100 pixels without the JavaScript being signed. Be sure that you are familiar with these types of browser-specific limitations and requirements before making changes to the template.

The default Netlet window size is 320x170, as shown in the following example:

```
nWin = window.open( url, "Netlet","width=320,height=
170,scrollbars");
```

To change the size and remove the scrollbars, modify the window.open parameters in the NetletWinOpen function as shown in the following code box:

```
nWin = window.open( url, "Netlet","width=100,height=
100,noscrollbars");
if (navigator.appName.indexOf("Microsoft") < 0) {
  nWin.screenX=screen.width;
  nWin.screenY=screen.height;
}
```

This is far from a perfect solution, but the space required by the Netlet pop-up window is at least minimized. In portal sever version 6.0, the FRAME attributes are hardcoded, so there is no way to turn off the scrollbars to make better usage of the Netlet pop-up window. To avoid users having to explicitly close the Netlet pop-up, a script can be added to the portal server desktop logout link as follows:

```
<a href="dt?action=logout" onClick="if (nWin)
{nWin.close();}">LOGOUT</a>
```

Without explicitly closing the Netlet window, Netlet sessions that remain open might be active for an extended period of time. See "Understanding and Handling Timeouts" on page 75 for more information about this.

There are a few other advanced techniques for hiding the unsightly Netlet pop-up window. For browsers that support it, the IFRAME tag can be used to embed the Netlet pop-up in the portal server desktop itself. An IFRAME statement that embeds the Netlet pop-up window might appear as follows:

```
<IFRAME SRC="/portal/NetletConfig?func=makepage" HEIGHT="0"
WIDTH="0" ID="embedWin" STYLE="visibility:hidden"></IFRAME>
```

The /portal string is the default DEPLOY_URI chosen at install time. To make the Netlet visible, you can change the size back to the default 320x170 and change the CSS STYLE attribute to visibility:show. The IFRAME attributes can be modified a bit to look similar to other portal channels except for the scrollbar that results from hardcoded window frame size attributes.

Similar embedding functionality might be possible in Netscape to use inline layers. However, because of the vast flexibility in the different desktop containers, it is probably better to hide the Netscape pop-up if you don't want your end users to worry about the Netlet status. You can do this using the Netscape JavaScript security model by requesting UniversalBrowserWrite privileges and then moving the pop-up window off of the screen. With code base principles enabled, this can be done as follows in the Netlet template file:

```
<SCRIPT LANGUAGE="JavaScript1.2" CODEBASE=
"http://contentserver.com" ID="nWinMod">
  netscape.security.PrivilegeManager.enablePrivilege("UniversalBr
owserWrite");
  nWin.moveTo(screen.width+100, screen.height+100);
  netscape.security.PrivilegeManager.revertPrivilege("UniversalBr
owserWrite");
</SCRIPT>
```

To enable CODEBASE principles, add the following line in the Netscape preferences file: user_pref("signed.applets.codebase_principal_support", true);

Without the JavaScript being signed, or if the root certificate authority (signer) isn't trusted, users must accept a warning similar to FIGURE 2-18 for the window-handling script to be executed.

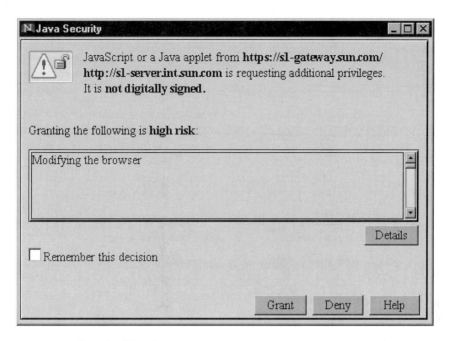

FIGURE 2-18 Security Warning

In a production environment, the script should be signed using the Netscape signtool program so that end users have some additional assurance that the code requesting the additional privileges is from a trusted source. To use signtool, you must have a current valid signer certificate in your communicator `cert` database. Modify the preceding example as follows:

```
<SCRIPT LANGUAGE="JavaScript1.2" ARCHIVE="http://ps-
server.int.sun.com/js/nWin.jar" SRC="http://ps-
server.int.sun.com/js/modWin.js" ID="1">
</SCRIPT>
```

The source of `modWin.js` should look something like the following example.

```
nWin = window.open( "/portal/NetletConfig?func=makepage",
"Netlet", "width=320,height=170,noscrollbars,alwayslowered");
nWin.moveTo(screen.width+100, screen.height+100);
```

After you download signtool, sign the script by running the following command.

```
# signtool -d"$HOME/.netscape" -k"signer-cert-name"
-Z"$PS_HOME/htdocs/js/modWin.jar" $PS_HOME/htdocs/js
```

$PS_HOME is the path to your shared portal documents or to a secondary content directory, signer-cert-name is the nickname of your signer certificate, and js is a directory containing a modWin.js script, which opens the window and then moves it off of the screen.

▼ To Sign the JavaScript Code With an iButton

For information about Java iButtons visit http://www.ibutton.com/ibuttons/java.html.

1. **Make sure that the iButton is readable by typing the following command.**

```
$ ./readpkcs
```

The following message is displayed.

```
        ---------------------------------------------------------
        |        Dallas Semiconductor, PKCS Testing Tool        |
        |             for the Java Powered iButton               |
        |          Version 1.00 - Release date 11/29/2000        |
        |     - Serial/Parallel ports supported on Linux/Win32.  |
        |     - Only serial ports supported on Solaris           |
        ---------------------------------------------------------

Compiled: Nov 29 2000 14:47:43
Java iButton 1-Wire Address: 96 6c 2e 00 00 90 00 c5
Java Powered iButton - Firmware Revision 2.2.0007
DS1957 -52
Selected RSATools applet
applet version: 05.07
1 certificate(s) are loaded

Press 'Q' to quit, <Enter> to continue: q
```

2. **Use the** `signtool` **command in conjunction with the cert nickname stored on the iButton to create the signed JavaScript.**

```
$ signtool -d"$HOME/.netscape" -k"iButton:Portal Server's Sun
Microsystems Inc ID" -Z"./modWin.jar" $HOME/test_cases/js
```

The following message is displayed.

```
using certificate directory: /home/uid/.netscape
Generating /home/uid/test_cases/js/META-INF/manifest.mf file..
--> modWin.js
adding /home/uid/test_cases/js/modWin.js to
./modWin.jar...(deflated 48%)
--> modWin.jar
Generating zigbert.sf file..
Enter Password or Pin for "iButton":
Enter Password or Pin for "Communicator Certificate DB":
adding /home/uid/test_cases/js/META-INF/manifest.mf to
./modWin.jar...(deflated 30%)
adding /home/uid/test_cases/js/META-INF/zigbert.sf to
./modWin.jar...(deflated 36%)
adding /home/uid/test_cases/js/META-INF/zigbert.rsa to
./modWin.jar...(deflated 33%)
tree "/home/uid/test_cases/js" signed successfully
```

To get a code signing certificate, visit the Verisign Web site at:
`http://www.verisign.com/products/signing/index.html`

Be sure to select Netscape Object Signing Digital ID* as the product of choice.

When the `signtool` process completes, the generated `modWin.jar` file contains the certificate and the script. If the CA used to create the signer certificate is trusted by the end user's browser, which it should for Verisign, the user will not have to explicitly accept the certificate for the Netlet pop-up window to move. For more information about signing JavaScript and Mozilla-specific signed script requirements, visit the Mozilla Web site at:
`http://www.mozilla.org/projects/security/components/signed-scripts.html`.

To wrap everything up in a single, handy package, you can create a JSP channel on the desktop that contains the following Netlet launch code.

```
<%
String ua = request.getHeader("User-Agent");
if (ua.indexOf("MSIE") != -1) {
%>
    <IFRAME SRC="/portal/NetletConfig?func=makepage" HEIGHT="0"
WIDTH="0" ID="embedWin" STYLE="visibility:hidden"></IFRAME>
<%
  }
  else {
%>
    <SCRIPT LANGUAGE="JavaScript1.2">
    nWin = window.open( "/portal/NetletConfig?func=makepage",
"Netlet", "width=320,height=170,noscrollbars, alwayslowered");
    </SCRIPT>
<%
    if(ua.indexOf("Mozilla") != -1) {
%>
    <SCRIPT LANGUAGE="JavaScript1.2" CODEBASE="<%=
application.getRealPath(contentPage) %>" ID="nWinMod">

netscape.security.PrivilegeManager.enablePrivilege("UniversalBro
wserWrite");
    nWin.moveTo(screen.width+100, screen.height+100);
    </SCRIPT>
<%
  }
  }
%>
```

The Pop-Up Blocker Phenomenon

Like any filtering technology, pop-up blockers have a negative side effect in that they might block access to functionality or information that users are genuinely interested in. Most end users attempting to turn cookies off or micro-manage their usage and storage quickly find they spend more time scrutinizing their cookie contents than simply relying on the cookies to not store personal or sensitive data in clear text or use a simple encoding. Like cookie managers, pop-up blockers require a great deal of hand-holding to get them to block the incessant minicamera ads while letting good stuff, like the Netlet, through.

Pop-up blockers vary in their administration requirements and invasiveness. If you are deploying a secure remote access corporate portal to employees, you might want to consider recommending a specific pop-up blocker to use and recommend how to configure it to allow the Netlet to function through it. If client control is out of the question and the portal server is being used solely as a secure remote access solution to back-end applications through the Netlet, you might consider embedding the Netlet pop-up window, which works for any browser supporting the IFRAME HTML tag.

Here are some general guidelines about pop-up blockers and how they might need to be configured for the Netlet to operate normally.

- Pop-up blocker software that contains ACIs should have the Domain Name Service (DNS) domain of the portal Gateway stored so that any pages fetched through the Gateway will be trusted because the Gateway will be matched as the point of origination.

- With pop-up blockers that require a simultaneous keystroke, the key must be held down as long as it takes the Netlet window to open, load, and launch the interim window (in the case of dynamic rules). In some cases, this additional key is the Control key. The key may have to be pressed again if the Continue button on the interim window is selected.

- Passive pop-up blockers work for dynamic rules with a null URL. Passive blockers generally allow explicit JavaScript onHandlers like onClick to open new windows, while others like onLoad or onUnload are blocked.

- Active pop-up blockers rigorously prevent any `window.open JavaScript` calls from functioning and affect not only the Netlet from, but much of the portal server desktop (such as detached channels). Active functioning pop-up blockers or passive pop-up blockers configured to be "aggressive" are not recommended.

Pop-up and pop-under advertising will likely become irrelevant by the massive use of blockers now, and the use of both will diminish in the future when pop-up blocker functionality becomes a feature of the user agent. Until then, be aware that, by default, the Netlet will not run correctly if a pop-up blocker does not allow the Netlet pop-up to open and initialize the Netlet applet.

Understanding and Handling Timeouts

Successfully configuring the built-in portal timeouts and application-specific timeouts helps ensure a smooth interruption-free end-user experience. Similar to closing the Netlet pop-up window, or any actions that cause the Netlet applet to restart, a timeout can result in the loss of all open Netlet sessions. This section describes timeouts, and how they should be sensibly configured for your particular business needs.

Portal Server Desktop Timeouts

Calling these timeouts *portal server desktop timeouts* is a bit misleading in the portal server 6 versions because the user sessions and their corresponding timeouts are actually managed by the Identity Server. I'm referring to the user-session timeouts as the portal server desktop idle timeout because the session idle timer is updated through end-user interaction with the portal server desktop. By default, the session service is registered and administrated at the service management level. There are three values that can be configured in the service:

- **Max session time** – This is the maximum amount of time, in minutes, that an active user can remain logged in to the portal server without having to reauthenticate. If users only log in periodically for a matter of minutes, or if they frequently time out from being idle, this value should be set low. If the portal is used by off-site employees for remote access to compute resources, then this value should be set high. The value should not be excessively high because user sessions that have been invalidated but not destroyed might remain in memory until they are selectively removed by a thread that attempts to cleanup invalid sessions. Because session handling at this level is a function of the underlying Identity Server, session cleanup and expiration can change in newer versions of the Identity Server that might be included in portal upgrades.

- **Max idle time** – Specifies the total time, in minutes, of portal server desktop inactivity before the user session is invalidated. This is usually considered an important security decision so that unattended portal sessions do not remain active and accessible to other passersby. The value should be set high enough not to be a nuisance to end users, but low enough to reduce exposure to security risk.

- **Max caching time** – As the name implies, this is the total time, in minutes, that an invalidated session remains in memory, but in truth, it is the interval used in determining how often user sessions are refreshed. So an invalid session is refreshed and remains invalid up to the max session time limit. The sole reason for this is to catch the user's next action (if there is one that occurs prior to the max session time being exceeded) and inform them that their session has timed out. At this time, the user session is destroyed and another immediately created when the Login link is selected. The max caching time value should be set low for a dynamic desktop where users may be constantly customizing their visible content, layout, tab settings, and so on. For a mostly static, informational portal that has hardcoded preferences made at the organization or role levels, the value can be higher because it isn't expected that channel lists and other user data will be modified throughout the duration of the user session.

The session service can be registered at the organization level, but this is not recommended for portal server 6.0. In addition, there are some oddities with how the first action is handled after the desktop idle timer is reached. These actions range from a browser error being returned if accessing the portal through the Gateway due to an infinite redirection, to a serious desktop error. To reduce the memory footprint of thousands of invalid user sessions, or potential problems when users try to perform a desktop function such as minimizing a channel unaware that their session has timed out, you can create an idle timer in the top-level container JSP that explicitly calls `logout`. This destroys the session and proactively informs users when their sessions timed out. The timer can be extended to inform the users prior to a timeout as well. Unfortunately, the implementation of such a script-based solution is a bit tricky. In the event that a future version of Identity Server exposes a way to synchronize the remaining idle time, this will be a more useful option.

Netlet and Application Timeouts

The portal server desktop idle time is not the only game in town. Any application accessed through the Netlet can have its own associated timeouts, as well as infrastructure like firewalls, load balancers, and operating environments. These do not keep individual sockets open for an indeterminate amount of time (for good reasons).

In versions of the portal server software prior to 3.0 SP5, the Netlet timeout and the portal server desktop timeout were considered two different entities and were updated separately. This created problems where an idle timeout would occur on either the desktop or the Netlet when the user was actively using the other. Because the user session is now maintained by the Identity Server in the portal server 6 software, the primary idle timeout is the session max idle time value. This means that both Netlet activity and portal server desktop activity update the same timer. Therefore, there is no way to have an active Netlet session without having an active portal session. This might seem less of an SRA-only solution as a result, but you will see many examples of how to launch the Netlet from something other than the Netlet provider on the portal server desktop throughout this chapter. If the portal server desktop is not used, the end user will be completely unaware that their Netlet session is also used as a portal session.

Stayin' Alive

Keeping connections open for active for users, while remaining vigilant about destroying idle sessions and associated connections, depends entirely on your business requirements and security restrictions. Keep in mind that there are application timeouts and KeepAlives, infrastructure timeouts, Netlet timeouts and KeepAlives, and portal (Identity) timeouts to mix and match to achieve the desired result. To determine whether a Netlet session should remain active, the following path is roughly followed:

1. **The max session value is checked.**

    If exceeded, the user session is destroyed, the login page is redirected, and all open Netlet sessions are terminated. Otherwise, the next step is performed.

2. **The idle timer is checked.**

   The user's last activity time is checked. If the difference between the current time and the last activity time exceeds the max idle time value, the user session is invalidated, and the open Netlet sessions are terminated. Otherwise, the next step is performed.

3. **The KeepAlive interval is checked.**

   If exceeded, all open Netlet sessions are terminated in portal server 6.0. In later versions of the portal server software, KeepAlive packets are sent to the Gateway to keep the connections active across infrastructure products such as the firewall.

Note – In Sun ONE Portal Server 6.0 software the Netlet KeepAlive does not do anything except explicitly kill the Netlet session once the value is reached. It does not proactively maintain the Netlet session during that period of time, and should only be used to prevent unwanted session extensions due to application KeepAlive packets.

In portal server 6.2, the Netlet KeepAlive interval is no longer the total time that an idle Netlet session should be kept active, but rather, the specific period of time where KeepAlive packets are sent to keep the connections open. An application KeepAlive interval, such as that provided in Citrix, specifies the interval that packets should be sent, is similar to how this option now behaves.

The portal server 6.1 software adds a configurable platform entry to ignore client-bound traffic. This prevents the idle session from being reset automatically as a result of application KeepAlive packets being sent to the application client. An easy way to see how this works is to create a Telnet rule, and reduce the max idle time to something very low like two minutes. Start the Telnet session and run a KeepAlive script that appears similar to the following:

```
#!/bin/sh
while(true)
do {
  touch /tmp/ping
  if (test -f "/tmp/ping") then {
    /bin/rm /tmp/ping
    echo "Alive .."
    echo
  }
  else {
    date
  } fi
  sleep 60
} done
```

Because the sleep time (60 seconds) of the script that sends the terminal echo back to the Telnet client is less than the max idle time (120 seconds), the idle timeout is extended as long as the client program is running or the maximum session time has not been reached. The client-bound traffic is ordinarily not differentiated from user-initiated, application-bound traffic. Citrix can be deployed with a similar KeepAlive mechanism that does the same thing. Because the 6.0 version of the portal server software cannot currently ignore client-bound traffic, the only way to handle this problem is by setting the ceiling of the max session time lower. Changing the Netlet KeepAlive value will not help in this instance because the session is not considered idle. Some problem scenarios follow that illustrate this.

TABLE 2-1   Problem Scenario 1

Remote stock broker with a trading system accessed through the portal server desktop	
Problem	Netlet/portal session terminates unexpectedly as a result of the idle timeout value being reached.
Solution	Increase both the maximum session time and the maximum idle time. The maximum session time could be set to the approximate amount of time the broker spends logged in to the portal during normal working hours. The maximum idle time could be approximated to be slightly greater than the average time between stock trades.
Considerations	Time between stock trades might be sporadic, making it difficult to determine an average for the idle that will prevent session termination between stock trades. Intermediary infrastructure might drop the connection. In the portal server version 6.1 software, KeepAlive can be fully utilized, which sends bogus messages to keep the connection open between the client and the Gateway. A patch is available for portal server version 6.0 software to do the same.

TABLE 2-2   Problem Scenario 2

Employee portal that offers employees secure remote access to their PC desktops using Citrix accessed from a kiosk

Problem	A remote user has open access to their desktop machine behind a corporate firewall, and presumably access to any machines and resources in that environment.
	The Netlet session extends automatically until the max session time is reached, even when the kiosk is left unattended, resulting in a potential security risk.
Background	Citrix has a configurable option for sending KeepAlive packets to Citrix clients to prevent connection loss due to network timeouts. If the KeepAlive interval is less than max idle time, the session remains active even if there is no user-initiated action (which might indicate the desktop has been left unattended).
Solution	The solution is to disable "Extend Portal Session for Client-bound Netlet Traffic," and reduce the maximum idle time. This ensures that if the desktop is left unattended, the session will not remain active for long. Because the portal server 6 software does not have this same capability, only the max idle time can be reduced. Alternately, the Citrix KeepAlive interval can be configured so it is greater than the idle timeout (after reducing the idle timeout as previously suggested).

Netlet Deployment Scenarios

There are all kinds of applications that can be deployed and used through a Netlet connection. The important thing to consider is that the applications must be TCP/IP compliant, and in most cases must also use fixed ports for communication. The only exceptions to the latter requirement are FTP and Microsoft Outlook. The following sections describe a few of the most widely used and most powerful deployment scenarios.

Scenario A: Running FTP Over a Netlet Connection

FTP over a Netlet connection is a very useful method for creating secure file transfer using spec-compliant native FTP client applications. FTP over the Netlet can also be used to implement `ftp://` URLs that the portal Gateway does not understand.

FTP over a Netlet connection is well suited for organizations that want a single FTP server with controlled end-user accounts making secure remote FTP transfers from an end-user system to a single repository. For example, a health care provider might provide Netlet access to a doctor's office for the purpose of uploading sensitive patient files for insurance consideration. FTP over a Netlet connection is also ideal for remote employees who need to securely transfer files to and from back-end FTP servers.

Providing end-user access to multiple FTP servers is a bit more challenging because dynamic FTP rules do not allow an end user to specify a user ID to be used in the FTP URL when connecting to the FTP server. The user ID has to be prepopulated in the rule itself to avoid automatically connecting as an anonymous user, or the URL must be left blank (null), requiring the user to type in the FTP URL manually. A third approach is handcrafting a URL that can be launched from the portal server desktop. Some examples are presented in the following paragraphs that clearly explain this limitation and how to circumvent it.

FTP comes in two flavors: active and passive. The one you use is dictated by your inner firewall restrictions. This limitation can be bypassed using the Netlet proxy, or by making sure that the FTP mode is correct on the client FTP program. The Netlet reserves client port 30021 for FTP traffic. This is required for the Gateway to keep track of the dynamic port allocation from PASV FTP (passive FTP) commands.

> **Note –** FTP Netlet rules should only use a port-host-port mapping of `30021 ftp-server 21` to prevent FTP clients from attempting to make direct connections to the FTP server during PASV FTP command responses.

The Netlet does not provide any additional security beyond what is implemented in the FTP server itself, and in the Netlet rule and host access control lists provided to all Netlet rules. Some FTP servers and clients offer the capability to limit user's FTP sessions to their home directories (`chroot`). The configuration of the FTP server is dictated by your business needs. The Netlet serves as a secure access mechanism to your FTP server file systems. NetFile must be used to transfer files securely to Windows Server Message Block (SMB) file systems, but FTP over a Netlet should work for any WU[2] FTP-compliant client and server pairs.

▼ To Set Up an FTP Netlet Rule

An FTP rule is provided out-of-box when the portal SRA software is installed. If you have removed the SRA software, or are curious about ways to tweak the rule for your own needs, read on. This first procedure describes how to set up an FTP rule at the organization level.

1. **Log in to the Administration Console.**

2. **Select the appropriate organization where you want to add FTP access.**

3. **Select Show Services.**

4. **Select the Netlet link under the SRAP Configuration section of the left pane.**

5. **If there is already a rule called FTP, select the Edit link to make changes, otherwise, select Add.**

6. **Enter the configuration information for the FTP Netlet rule, following these guidelines:**

   a. **Select a name such as FTP, and an appropriate encryption algorithm.**

   b. **Enter 30021 for the client port.**

   The only required element in an FTP Netlet rule is that the client port must be 30021.

   c. **Select a URL to use when the Netlet is launched.**

   - For Anonymous access, use: `ftp://localhost:30021`. This URL assumes that the user ID is anonymous. In most cases, the user is only prompted for a password (the user's email address by default).

---

2. Washington University

- For a non-browser FTP client or a browser that might not have an FTP helper application defined, enter: `null` (or blank). Once the Netlet is launched, the end user must manually open their FTP client and select `localhost` and `port 30021` to connect to the remote FTP server through the Netlet.

- For a dynamic Netlet defined at the user level, not at the organization level, use: `ftp://username@localhost:300021`.

If you hard code the user name, the Netlet does not automatically perform an anonymous FTP login. This is a required administrative action or the user must have delegated administration privileges to change the URL of the Netlet rule because the Netlet provider only extends dynamic hosts, not dynamic user names, or dynamic FTP URLs. This is the same URL a user would have to type manually in a user agent that supports FTP URLs to manually connect through a Netlet connection.

d. **If download applet is selected, deselect it.**

No client component besides the Netlet applet itself is required for FTP access over a Netlet connection.

e. **Check Extend session if the end user's primary activity will be file transfers rather than portal server desktop interaction.**

f. **Create or modify the Port-Host-Port list.**

The out-of-box FTP rule is dynamic, which means that end users are able to determine which FTP servers they would like to connect to. To change this to a static rule and define a single FTP archive for the entire organization, remove the port-host-port mapping and add a new mapping with the hard-coded, fully qualified FTP server host name. If access should not be allowed to a subset of FTP servers, you can keep the FTP server dynamic and limit the FTP server access in the Allowed and Denied hosts lists defined at the Netlet service level.

Note – When adding or modifying the Netlet service to include an FTP rule, for usability reasons you should deselect port warnings, reauthentication for connections, and warning `pop-up` for connections. Because the FTP protocol allows for the use of dynamic ports, each PASV FTP request might result in a barrage of pop-ups. Some user agents lose focus on the pop-ups, giving the end user the appearance that an FTP transfer is ongoing when in fact it is waiting on user intervention for some sort of confirmation.

Managing the FTP Netlet Rule from the Portal Server Desktop

If the Netlet rule is static, be sure that the Netlet provider is available and visible on the user's desktop. If the Netlet rule is dynamic, a TARGET must be defined in the Netlet provider under the FTP rule name.

Using the Communicator FTP Client

To use FTP over a Netlet connection, you must have already defined a Netlet rule as described in "To Set Up an FTP Netlet Rule" on page 82. After a user logs in to the desktop and the Netlet applet is started, the user simply opens an additional browser window (Alt+n), and enters the URL as `ftp://username@localhost:30021`. This is only necessary if the Netlet rule URL is equal to null. Otherwise, the URL loads automatically after the user selects the link in the Netlet channel. Communicator software then prompts for a password and the user has a valid and secure FTP session.

Note – Because the user is now using FTP instead of HTTPS, the browser might indicate that they are no longer using an encrypted session. However, the communication between the Netlet and the Gateway component is encrypted, so the connection is actually an encrypted session as seen over the public wire.

Sample FTP Commands in Communicator

- To upload – Select File ➤ Upload to upload a file to the directory you are currently viewing.
- To download – Use the left mouse button to download to the same browser window, or use the right mouse button and select Save As.
- To change the current working directory (CWD) – Add or delete any portion of the path information that appears after the Netlet port number in the URL field and press Enter.

Note – Communicator software uses PASV FTP commands for things such as transfers and file listings.

Using the Internet Explorer FTP Client

IE users can also access an FTP server using the same FTP URL syntax. Unlike Communicator software, however, IE uses an interface with a similar look and feel to the Microsoft Explorer file manager so files can be moved around with drag and drop. Additionally, IE forces a home directory restriction (`chroot` to the users home directory). Because navigation is done by modifying the browser's URL field, there is no way to change to a directory higher than the user's root directory. This is a nifty security enhancement for FTP users who do not need access to the root file system, but can be a nuisance for users that have administrative privileges but cannot access the files they need to upload or download.

Sample FTP Commands in Internet Explorer

- To upload – First create a file folder in your UNIX® platform home directory (for example, you might call it `uploads`). Drag files from anywhere on your desktop to the `uploads` folder and securely transfer them. This intermediate directory creation is not necessary if you are using Windows 2000.
- To download – Double-click on any of the files. Windows 2000 allows you to drag files directly to your desktop.
- To change the CWD – You can add or change any path information beyond the Netlet port number in the URL field, but you can never go higher than your home directory because it is hardcoded when you login.

Note – For IE 5.0SP2 + the additional browsing pack is the minimal IE version required to use the IE FTP client with the Netlet. Otherwise, a connection to `localhost` at a specific port number might not be possible.

Using Other FTP Clients

The FTP Netlet rule is also compatible with many FTP command-line programs and other graphical FTP programs such as CuteFTP.

Caution – If any of these other clients implement PASV commands, the Port warnings for Netlet connections should be turned off. One reason for this, other than the annoyance factor of receiving warnings, is there could be a contention between the authentication window and the Netlet warning window that prevents the user from being able to log in to the FTP server.

Tips for Administrating the Solaris Core `ftpd`

The Solaris OS provides a full-featured, robust FTP server that is installed when you install the `SUNWftpr` package. Here are some hints to make use of this feature set.

- If you or your users are using any uncommon shells, it is a good idea to list all of the shells (including their paths) that FTP users might use in the `/etc/shells` file. You might have to create this file, because it does not exist by default.
- To prevent users with login accounts to other UNIX platform resources from using FTP, force them to use a shell not in `/etc/shells`, or add the user to the `/etc/ftpusers` file, which denies them access.
- To add a customized banner that can be seen by command-line FTP clients, add a directive for BANNER in the `/etc/default/ftpd` file. For example:
  `BANNER="`echo "This is a restricted access server."`

Scenario B: Tunneling Mail Protocols Through the Netlet

Tunneling mail protocols is a very useful capability that enables remote users to use their preferred email client to access corporate mail. End users only need to configure an account on their mail client to point to `localhost` as the server name and the port where the Netlet rule is configured to listen. IMAP, SMTP, and POP3 all work over a Netlet connection. POP3 is less widely used because downloading message headers and bodies to the client is considered less secure, and less dependable than keeping them on the mail server. Sometimes this might be necessary for certain nomadic users, in which case POP3 might be allowed for them but denied for others.

▼ To Configure Netlet Rules Required for Tunneling Mail Protocols

1. **Log in to the Administration console.**

2. **Select the appropriate Organization name.**

3. **Select Show: Services.**

4. **Expand the Netlet properties by selecting the arrow next to Netlet under the SRAP Configuration section in the left pane.**

5. **Add Netlet rules for IMAP, SMTP, and POP3, or a single service group.**

Note – POP3 is not recommended as a secure solution because sensitive mail (message headers as well as bodies) can be downloaded and saved on the client machine. You might consider only supporting IMAP and SMTP.

---

a. **Select a unique name for the rule, such as the protocol name.**

IMAP might be there by default. SMTP and POP3 can be added as well. If defining a Netlet service group, use a more generic name such as mail.

b. **Choose an appropriate encryption algorithm.**

Usually the service default is satisfactory. Government and banking institutions might consider using an algorithm with a longer key length. See "Assigning an Encryption Algorithm" on page 28 for more details on what to use.

c. **Select null for the URL.**

Because the native mail client is used instead of an HTML-based email client, there is no associated URL to launch.

d. **Deselect download applet.**

Because email communication does not require a Java applet, one does not have to be independently downloaded.

e. **Put a checkmark next to extend session.**

This should be selected if users will be interacting with their native email program for an extended amount of time with little or no interaction with the portal server desktop. See "Understanding and Handling Timeouts" on page 75 for more information about this feature and its intended usage.

f. **Add the port-host-port mappings.**

If you are defining a Netlet service group, add all of the mappings to the one Netlet rule. Otherwise, add one mapping per rule. The default mappings for the protocols are:

10143   mail-server   143 # IMAP

10025   mail-server   25 # SMTP

10110   mail-server   110 #POP3

Note – Use TARGET instead of the actual mail server name to allow end users to specify their own email server.

---

g. **Select Save.**

6. **Restart the Gateway so that it can reread its updated profile.**

Scenario C: Integrating Citrix ICA With a Netlet

Citrix is one of the more widely used applications that is accessed through the portal Netlet. The Netlet technology is used as the security framework, while Citrix deals with the details of licensing, terminal services, screen scraping, and load balancing of x86-based applications. Citrix has an entire suite of applications, but the integration discussed in this section is for the ICA client, a Java applet that provides browser-based access to a Citrix session. For Citrix NFuse integration with the Sun's portal server software, contact your Sun Sales representative or Sun Professional Services.

As of the portal server 6.x versions, Citrix ICA and Netlet integration is not provided out-of-box, but getting it to work is straightforward enough. You must create a file called `citrix_start.html` (CODE EXAMPLE 2-14). This file describes which Java applet archive to load and which startup parameters to use.

Note – The Sun ONE Portal Server 3.0 software ships with a `citrix_start.html` file, located at
install_dir/SUNWips/public_html/third_party/citrix_start.html.
If you use this file for version 6.x of the portal server software, you might need to make minor modifications, as discussed in this section.

CODE EXAMPLE 2-14   Sample `citrix_start.html` File (Sun ONE Portal Server 3.0 Software)

```
<HTML>
<BODY>
<SCRIPT LANGUAGE="JavaScript1.2">
if (navigator.platform.indexOf("PPC") != -1 &&
navigator.appName.indexOf("Microsoft") != -1) {
   document.writeln("<APPLET CODE=\"com.citrix.JICA.class\"
ARCHIVE=\"JICAEngJ.jar\" width=800 heigh=600>");
}
else {
   document.writeln("<APPLET CODE=\"com.citrix.JICA.class\"
ARCHIVE=\"JICAEngN.jar\" width=800 height=600>");
}
   document.writeln("<PARAM NAME=\"cabbase\" value=\"JICAEngM.cab\
">");
   document.writeln("<PARAM NAME=\"address\" value=\"localhost\
">");
document.writeln("<PARAM NAME=\"ICAPortNumber\" value=1494>");
   document.writeln("</APPLET>");
</SCRIPT>
</BODY>
</HTML>
```

By specifying an HTML file for the Netlet to load rather than the Netlet downloading the applet byte code itself, the parameters, and even the archives, are determined dynamically at runtime, offering a high level of flexibility. The preceding `citrix_start.html` file might need to be changed slightly to work with the Sun ONE Portal Server 6.0 SRA software due to a limitation in how the Rewriter handles dynamically created HTML containing APPLETs and OBJECTs. Used as it is, the Rewriter might force the creation of a CODEBASE attribute out of context so that applet CODE and parameters are evaluated relative to the CODEBASE. For example, the preceding page might be rewritten as follows.

```
    .
    .
    .
  document.writeln("<APPLET codebase="https://ps-
gateway.sun.com/http://ps-server.int.sun.com:8080/third_party/"
CODE=\"com.citrix.JICA.class\"  ARCHIVE=\"JICAEngJ.jar\" width=
800 heigh=600>");
    .
    .
    .
```

The problem might be subtle, but if your eyes are attuned to one of the all-too-frequent JavaScript errors, you'll notice that the double quotes for the CODEBASE value are not escaped. This is because the Rewriter is interpreting the APPLET tag in the context of HTML, not as part of a dynamically created HTML block. For more discussion on rewriting DHTML, applets, or general rewriting information, see Chapter 4 "Rewriter: Secure Remote Access to Internal Web-Based Applications"

This limitation is easily worked around by explicitly setting a CODEBASE attribute (with escaped quotes) in your `citrix_start.html` file. The CODEBASE should not contain the portal Gateway address, because the address is rewritten correctly when it is present. To enable a portal end user to access Citrix over the Netlet, create a Citrix rule, and grant access to that rule for users who have permission to use it. Refer to the SRA product documentation for information about the basics of creating a Netlet rule if you are unfamiliar with the steps involved.

▼ To Configure a Netlet Rule for Use With Citrix ICA

This is the same process used to create most Netlet rules. What sets Citrix, Tarantella, and VNC over the Netlet apart from most other Netlet applications is that the portal server desktop is rarely if ever interacted with, and a single application is the primary reason for the portal server deployment.

1. **Create a** `citrix_start.html` **file.**

   If you have an existing Sun ONE Portal Server 3.x version, you can use the `citrix_start.html` file that is provided. You can also use this file for the Sun ONE Portal Server 6.x software with minor modifications, or you can create one from scratch.

2. **Log in to the Administration Console.**

3. **Select the appropriate organization where you want to add the Citrix rule.**

4. **Select Show Services.**

5. **Select the Netlet link (arrow) under the SRAP Configuration section in the left pane.**

6. **In the Netlet Rules box in the right panel, select Edit next to the Citrix rule.**

   If you do not have an existing Citrix rule to Edit, select Add instead, and enter the rule name (such as Citrix).

7. **Enter the configuration information for the Citrix rule, following these guidelines:**

   a. **Select a name such as Citrix, and an appropriate encryption algorithm.**

      See "Assigning an Encryption Algorithm" on page 28 for details.

   b. **Select a URL to use when the Citrix Netlet is launched.**

      The URL must be the fully qualified URL to the `citrix_start.html` file.

   c. **If Download applet is selected, deselect it.**

      In addition to deselecting the Download applet, make sure that there aren't any rules specified.

   d. **Check Extend session.**

      Enabling Extend session is especially important when users will be primarily interacting with Citrix over the Netlet rather than with the portal server desktop. If extend session is deselected, the Citrix session might be unexpectedly lost when the portal server desktop idle timeout is reached. For more information about Netlets and timeouts, see "Understanding and Handling Timeouts" on page 75.

e. **Use the following syntax to specify the ports in the Port-Host-Port list:**

client-port citrix-server citrix-port

Because port 1494 is the default port specified as the ICA port number in the `citrix_start.html` file, the correct entry for the Port-Host-Port field is usually similar to the following:

```
1494 citrix.int.sun.com 1494
```

Port 1494 does not have to be open on the outer firewall. If a Netlet proxy is used, port 1494 does not have to be opened on the internal firewall either, assuming that the Gateway has been deployed to a traditional DMZ where there is a secondary firewall. See "Using the Netlet Proxy" on page 64 for more information.

As with all Netlet rules, the actual application server name can be swapped out with TARGET to make the Netlet dynamic, thereby launching the Netlet automatically with a user-initiated or scripted action. Whether you configure the Citrix Netlet as a dynamic or static rule is dependent on how you want the portal SRA software used. If the primary use of the SRA software is to provide users secure access to their PC desktops, the Netlet rule should be static so that it is launched as soon as they log in to the portal. If additional flexibility is required or preprocessing is necessary before the Citrix session is launched, the rule can be made dynamic so that a link from the Netlet provider must be selected for the Citrix session to launch, or the Citrix session can be launched as soon as the necessary preprocessing is complete.

f. **Enter 1494 for the client port.**

g. **Enter your target host in the Target Host field.**

h. **Enter 1494 in the Target Ports field.**

8. **Select Save.**

Deployment Considerations for Citrix

Most people trying to deploy Citrix over the Netlet have two major complaints:

- Opening the Citrix session through a dynamic Netlet link results in a cluttered desktop with too many open windows. If port warnings and reauthentication are enabled, that scenario worsens.

- The Netlet pop-up window is virtually uncustomizable.

I'm surprised by the number of people I've encountered integrating Citrix who completely ignore the portal server desktop altogether. In this section I suggest a solution that puts the two big complaints to rest while taking advantage of the portal server 6 desktop.

The Netlet pop-up window is used to inform end users of a change to the Netlet status, and to isolate the Netlet applet so that it is unaffected by portal server desktop refreshes. Hiding the Netlet by moving it back to the portal server desktop would prevent either of these intended features from working. However, this may be acceptable if you have a single channel desktop containing Citrix.

In the portal server 6 software, the launch code is not exposed, but the pop-up messages can still be customized in the Netlet Servlet properties file. Because most people who want to use Citrix through the Netlet want it to be transparent, you might want to know how to bypass the pop-up feature without interrupting or modifying the way the pop-up is used.

▼ To Make Pop-Ups Disappear

The following steps provide an outline of the tasks you can perform to make the pop-ups disappear. There are a variety of ways to make the Netlet pop-up less intrusive, including adding a focus to the portal server desktop, creating signed JavaScript to minimize the pop-up on load, and embedding it. The following tasks use an IFRAME and some cascading style sheet (CSS) code.

1. **Create a static Citrix rule for the organization.**

   The Citrix Netlet rule must be static because there is no way for an end user to specify a Citrix server once the Netlet provider has been removed from the portal server desktop. Follow the steps outlined earlier for Citrix Netlet rule configuration in "To Configure a Netlet Rule for Use With Citrix ICA" on page 90, or refer to the SRA product documentation for information about Netlet rule configuration. Be sure to select Extend Session because most of the portal activity will be going through the Citrix applet, and therefore the Netlet, rather than with the portal server desktop.

2. **Create a customized template directory and assign it to the organization.**

   Customized template directories are very important for a variety of reasons. A custom template directory helps you keep track of what you have customized and what you haven't. It also makes upgrading less hazardous to customizations assuming that your customized template directory is not a mirror image of the default template directory. You should copy into your customized template directory only what you intend to customize or have already customized, and nothing more. The template directory needs to be assigned to the organization so that the template lookup mechanism in the portal starts with your customized template directory instead of the default template directory. Put your template directory at the same hierarchy level as the default template directory to avoid confusing the portal installer in the event of upgrade, and to maintain the same relative link level. That said, the customized template directory should be either a directory or symbolic link in the `/etc/opt/SUNWps/desktop/` directory. The new customized template directory can be assigned to the organization from the desktop view of services management by changing the value of the desktop type. The value should be the directory name (not the fully qualified path) of the customized template directory.

3. **Copy the existing SampleJSP code to the customized template directory.**

The SampleJSP code is provided with the portal server desktop demo software that can be installed with the portal server product at install time. The `SampleJSP` directory contains the code necessary to create a portal channel written in JSP.

As stated in the previous step, only the templates that are actually customized should reside in the customized template directory. Run the following command to copy the `SampleJSP` code to your custom template directory.

```
# cp -R /etc/opt/SUNWps/desktop/default/SampleJSP \
/etc/opt/SUNWps/desktop/citrix/SampleJSP
```

In this example, *citrix* is the name of the customized template directory. Using a common naming scheme for desktop template directories makes it easier to keep track of larger, more complex deployments such as those for secure remote access applications service providers (ASPs).

4. **Modify the sample JSP code to include the dynamic portion of the** `citrix_start.html` **file and change the** `applet` **parameter to** `localhost`.

For simplicity's sake, I am using the existing SampleJSP code for this example. The method of embedding the Netlet pop-up only works in user agents that support the iFRAME tag (a similar technique might work for other user agents that only support layers). Here is an example of the modified `samplecontent.jsp` code. This code listing is available for downloading. See "Obtaining Downloadable Files for This Book" on page xxi.

CODE EXAMPLE 2-15 Modified `samplecontent.jsp` File

```
<%@ page import="java.util.Enumeration" %>
<%@ page import="java.io.*" %>

<%@ taglib uri="/tld/jx.tld" prefix="jx" %>
<%@ taglib uri="/tld/desktop.tld" prefix="dt" %>
<%@ taglib uri="/tld/desktopProviderContext.tld" prefix="dtpc" %>
<dt:obtainChannel channel="$JSPProvider">
  <dtpc:providerContext>
  <dtpc:getStringProperty key="contentPage" id="contentPage"/>
  <jx:declare id="contentPage" type="java.lang.String"/>
  <dtpc:getStringProperty key="fontFace1" id="fontFace"/>
  <jx:declare id="fontFace" type="java.lang.String"/>

<HTML>
<BODY>
<FONT FACE="<%=fontFace%>">
<%
   String ua = request.getHeader("User-Agent");
   // codebase should be the fully qualified URL where your ICA jars
```

```
  // are stored
  String codebase = "http://ips-
server.iplanet.com:8080/third_party/";
  String code,archive = "";
  if (ua == null) {
    code = "com.citrix.JICA.class";
    archive = "JICAEngN.jar";
}
  else if (ua.indexOf("MSIE") != -1) {
    code = "com.citrix.JICA.class";
    archive = "JICAEngJ.jar";
  }
  else if (ua.indexOf("MOZILLA") != -1) {
    code = "com.citrix.JICA.class";
    archive = "JICAEngN.jar";
  }
  else {
    code = "com.citrix.JICA.class";
    archive = "JICAEngN.jar";
  }

%>
<IFRAME SRC="/portal/NetletConfig?func=makepage" HEIGHT="0"
WIDTH="0" ID="embedWin" STYLE="visibility:hidden">
</IFRAME>

<APPLET CODEBASE="<%= codebase %>" CODE="<%= code %>" ARCHIVE="<%=
archive %>" width=600 height=800>
  <PARAM NAME="cabbase" value="JICAEngM.cab">
  <PARAM NAME="address" value="localhost">
  <PARAM NAME="ICAPortNumber" value=1494>
</APPLET>
</FONT>
</BODY>
</HTML>
  </dtpc:providerContext>
</dt:obtainChannel>
<!-- Channel width is p.getWidth() -->
```

Note – Refer to "Netlet Pop-Up: Friend or Foe?" on page 65 for information about modifying the JSP code to be friendly to Netscape in addition to Internet Explorer.

5. **Remove other channels from the Available And Visible list (including the Netlet provider).**

At the very least, the Netlet provider must be removed from the portal server desktop to prevent the Netlet pop-up window from launching automatically as soon as the end user logs in. This is the expected behavior when static Netlet rules have been defined. Given the overall size of the Citrix applet, the channel width should be changed from thick to full_top, or full_bottom, depending on how you want the desktop layout to look.

Note – Changing tabs, maximizing or minimizing the Citrix channel, loading bookmarks on the portal server desktop, and other similar actions, stop and restart running Java applets. The result is that all Netlet sessions are lost, including the Citrix session, and these sessions must be restarted.

---

6. **Change the SampleJSP attributes.**

To limit the number of ways Citrix sessions can be lost, it is a good idea to modify the Citrix channel so that users cannot maximize, minimize, detach, or edit the SampleJSP (citrix) channel. You can also modify the default attributes such as the channel title to reflect the actual channel purpose and contents. Using the Sun ONE Portal Server SRA 6.0 software, perform these changes as follows:

Note – These steps might vary slightly in future releases. Refer to the Sun ONE Portal Server 6.x product documentation for information about how to set the channel states like isEditable and other channel properties.

---

a. **Remove the tabbed desktop.**

The out-of-box tabbed desktop does not maintain channel states or keep applets running when switching from tab to tab. To prevent session loss due to end users selecting a different tab, it is better to add the providers they might use below the Citrix channel in the desktop layout. To do this, change the default channel name in the desktop service configuration screen of the administration console from JSPTabContainer to JSPTableContainer.

b. **Customize the look and feel of the JSPTableContainer desktop.**

You can add brand and company identity to the portal server desktop. The modifications should be made in the customized template directory. As `root`, type the following:

```
# cp -R /etc/opt/SUNWps/desktop/default/JSPTableContainerProvider \
/etc/opt/SUNWps/desktop/custom_template_dir/JSPTableContainerProvider
```

In this example, *custom_template_dir* represents your own directory name. In FIGURE 2-20, I changed `header.jsp`, and `menubar.jsp`.

c. **Modify SampleJSP channel properties**

Edit the Display Profile entry for the SampleJSP provider. Change both properties to reflect the channel name. The title string value in the Locale element is the one that is actually used when the desktop is rendered. Also, change the value of isEditable to false. Finally, add a helpURL string property with a null (empty) value to remove the help button from the channel, or specify a URL that contains help relevant to the Citrix channel. To do this, select `Download XML` from the desktop service configuration screen.

Note – Make sure you don't have any unintended line breaks. Also, be sure to edit the Display Profile using an editor that does not add DOS end-of-line characters to the file. Editors such as Windows Notepad append each line with an end-of-line character. If you do use such an editor, run the UNIX command called `/usr/bin/dos2unix(1)`, which removes the DOS end-of-line characters.

The XML block should look something like CODE EXAMPLE 2-16:

CODE EXAMPLE 2-16   Channel Entry in the Display Profile

```
<Channel name="SampleJSP" provider="JSPProvider" advanced="false"
merge="fuse" lock="false">
        <Properties advanced="false" merge="fuse" lock="false" name=
"_properties" propagate="true">
                <String name="title" value="Citrix" advanced="false"
merge="replace" lock="false" propagate="true"/>
                <String name="description" value="This is the sample
for the Jsp Provider" advanced="false" merge="replace" lock=
"false" propagate="true"/>

        <Locale language="en" country="US" advanced="false" merge=
"fuse" lock="false" propagate="true">
                <String name="title" value="Citrix" advanced="false"
merge="replace" lock="false" propagate="true"/>
```

```
            <String name="description" value="This is the sample
for the Jsp Provider" advanced="false" merge="replace" lock=
"false" propagate="true"/>
        </Locale>
        <String name="helpURL" value="" advanced="true" merge=
"replace" lock="false" propagate="true"/>
    <Boolean name="isEditable" value="false" advanced="true"
merge="replace" lock="false" propagate="true"/>
        <String name="width" value="full_top" advanced="false"
merge="replace" lock="false" propagate="true"/>



        </Properties>

    </Channel>
```

d. **Once the changes have been made, re-import the XML, and log in to the Gateway to make sure that the changes have taken affect.**

e. **Remove any remaining channel action buttons.**

   Removing the additional provider actions further reduces the likelihood of an unexpected Netlet session termination. From the desktop services view in the Administration Console, select Channel and Container Management. Select the Edit link next to JSPTableContainer. Add a boolean property to the three channel state collections (channelsIsRemovable, channelsIsMinimizable, channelsIsDetachable) with a property name of SampleJSP or whatever you might have changed the channel name to (not to be confused with the channel title).

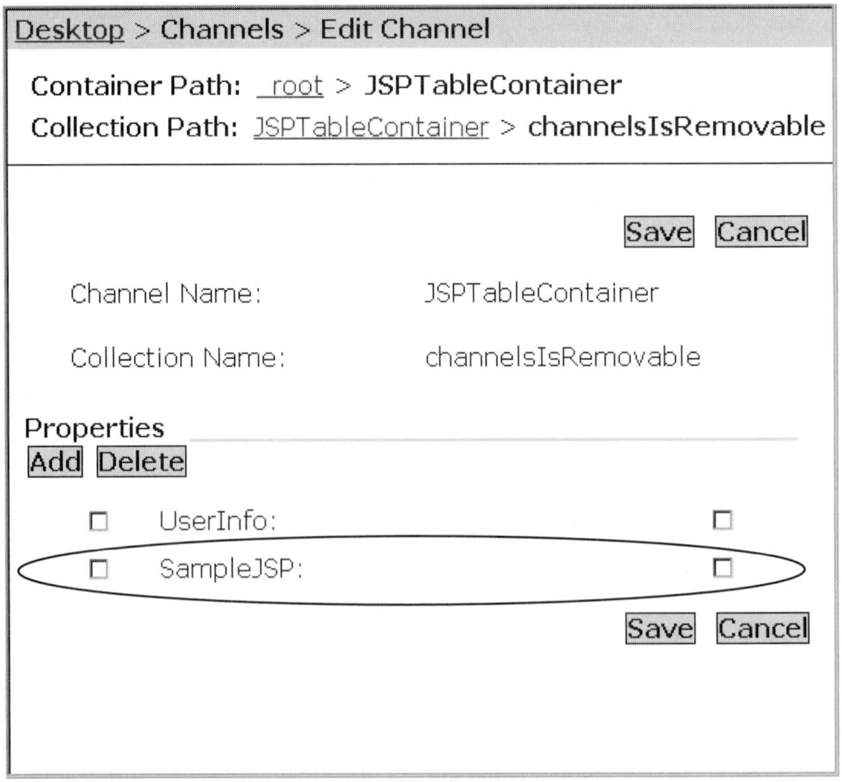

FIGURE 2-19 Example Property Addition to `channelIsRemovable` Collection (Sun ONE Portal Server SRA 6.0 Software)

Note – If the Bookmark provider is going to be added to the desktop in addition to the Citrix channel, the windowPref property should be set to all_new or a named window to avoid the bookmarks loading in the same window for which Citrix is running.

FIGURE 2-20 Example of What Citrix Might Look Like Running Through the Netlet on the Portal Server Desktop

Scenario D: Integrating Exchange With the Netlet

For a good long while, before Outlook Web Access (OWA) came along, followed by Exchange 2000 and all of its ancestry, the Netlet was the only way to integrate Microsoft Exchange with the portal server. In many cases, this was a key differentiator because it meant that the Exchange server did not have to be moved to the DMZ, and specialized extranet appliances and applications did not have to be used for remote users to access their Exchange data. As Microsoft continued to grow and mature the Exchange product, the requirements and caveats for its method of integration with the portal have changed along the way. OWA has become the de facto standard for accessing Microsoft Exchange. There is a substantial amount of information about the Exchange integration through the Rewriter in Appendix A, "Application Integrations for the Rewriter."

Even though OWA is positioned to eventually obsolete the Microsoft fat clients like Outlook, there are still ways to leverage the Netlet technology to access Exchange data depending on your requirements. There are a variety of approaches, each with their own caveats, in addition to the Rewriter integration, and all of them should be read and understood fully before deciding which is the most appropriate.

Integrating Portal in Legacy Windows Environments

Legacy environments refer to environments with clients that access Microsoft Exchange using the Outlook fat client, and from a pre-Windows 2000 operating environment. So the integration's scope is limited to Windows 95, 98, 98SE, ME, and NT. This is how the original portal and Exchange integration is done. It involves the Netlet listening on the `localhost` port 135, which is the hardcoded port the Outlook client uses to communicate with the Microsoft Exchange server.

Note – In Windows 2000, and Windows XP, port 135 is reserved by the operating system, which does not make this integration viable for more recent Microsoft platform releases.

The integration can be done at the server level using a single Netlet rule. End users would be able to access their Exchange data by adding `localhost` as an Exchange server. In this implementation, the Netlet would have to be launched prior to Outlook being opened for the Exchange connection to be successful. Newer versions of Outlook might allow users to add multiple Exchange servers so that the configuration would not have to be changed every time the user's location changed. Basically, the connection would succeed for whichever Exchange Server was available at the time.

▼ To Deploy SRA Using Legacy Environment Integration

1. **Configure a Netlet rule to listen to Exchange traffic on client port 135.**

   By listening on port 135, the Netlet applet can route traffic through a secure encrypted tunnel over the public wire directly to the portal Gateway where it is then proxied to the Exchange Server. Use static Netlet rule if there is only one Exchange Server or if users are not able to choose which Exchange Server they want to use. Likewise, use a dynamic rule when there is more than one Exchange server and when end users are allowed to choose which Exchange server they would like to use. If you are not using version 6.0 of the portal server, refer to the accompanying SRA product documentation about how to create the appropriate Netlet rule. Using the portal server administration console, the Netlet rule can be added as described here.

   a. **Log in to the Administration Console.**

      Log in to the Identity Server as `amadmin` or an administrator with the appropriate authority to create organization level changes to the Netlet configuration.

      For example, `http://s1identity.domain.com/amconsole`

   b. **Select the appropriate organization.**

      From the root DN (default is `isp`) under the User Management view, select the organization name for users who will be using the Exchange Netlet rule.

   c. **Select Show Services.**

      This option is available from the drop-down form menu.

   d. **Register the Netlet service, if not registered already.**

      Select register from the left panel and then select Netlet and Register.

   e. **Expand the Netlet properties by selecting the arrow next to Netlet under the SRAP Configuration section in the left pane.**

   f. **Select Add.**

      Under the Add Netlet section of the right panel, select Add.

   g. **Fill in Netlet Rule Properties.**

      - Give the Netlet rule an acceptable encryption level.
      - If the end user is going to be interacting with Exchange more than the portal server desktop, be sure to select Extend Session.
      - Delete the default URL and deselect Download Applet.
      - Add an entry to the Port-Host-Port list that looks like `135 ex-server 135` where `ex-server` is the fully qualified name of the Exchange server.
      - Remove the default port-host-port entry and select Save at the bottom of the right panel.

2. **Set the Exchange Server address in Outlook as the local loopback address** (`localhost` **or** `127.0.0.1`)

   For Outlook to make use of the Netlet, the Exchange address must be set to `localhost` so that the Netlet can ferry the information to the Exchange server rather than the Outlook client attempting to directly communicate with the Exchange server.

   a. **From the Control Panel, select the Mail icon.**

   b. **From the E-Mail accounts window select View or change existing e-mail accounts.**

   c. **Select Next.**

   d. **Select the Exchange server instance name.**

   e. **Select Change.**

   f. **Enter** `localhost` **in the Server address field titled Microsoft Exchange Server.**

   g. **Enter the user name of the mailbox in the User Name Field.**

   h. **Select More Settings.**

   i. **Change the name of the Connection to Exchange, Remote, or something else easily discernible.**

   j. **Confirm the warning that you cannot log on to the Exchange server (if the Netlet is not running).**

   Be sure in the future to launch the Netlet before the Outlook to avoid similar warnings.

   k. **Select Next and Finish.**

3. **Verify Exchange connectivity through the Netlet.**

   Test that the connection not only works, but that it is communicating using the Netlet before moving the integration in to production. As with rewriting URLs, sometimes it can appear that connectivity is working perfectly well on the corporate intranet, but this can be misleading if direct connections to applications are being made that are not possible outside of the corporate firewall to remote users.

   a. **Log in to the portal Gateway as an end user.**

   b. **If the Netlet rule is dynamic, launch the rule using the appropriate link from the Netlet provider.**

   c. **Open the Windows Control Panel.**

   d. **Select the Mail Icon and Email Accounts.**

   e. **Select View or Change Existing Accounts.**

f. **Type in the user name and password.**

g. **Open the Java Console and make sure that the output looks like it contains entries indicating connections are being made to the Exchange server from port 135.**

CODE EXAMPLE 2-17 Java Console Output

```
Microsoft (R) VM for Java, 5.0 Release 5.0.0.3802
=================================================
?  help
c  clear
f  run finalizers
g  garbage collect
m  memory usage
q  quit
t  thread list
=================================================
Netlet running on IE
Netlet config: https://ps-gateway.sun.com/http://ps-
server.int.sun.com/portal/NetletConfig?func=loadResources
gateway protocol : https
gateway host : ps-gateway.sun.com
gateway port : 443
Netlet not using proxy (IE)
Netlet rule 0: local:1494   destination:citrix.int.sun.com:1494
Netlet rule 1: local:8000   destination:ps-server.int.sun.com:80
Netlet rule 2: local:30021  destination:TARGET:21
Netlet rule 3: local:10025  destination:TARGET:25
Netlet rule 4: local:10143  destination:TARGET:143
Netlet rule 5: local:135    destination:ex-server.int.sun.com:135
Netlet rule 6: local:30000  destination:TARGET:23
Netlet config: https://ps-gateway.sun.com/http://ps-
portal.int.sun.com/portal/NetletConfig?func=setLoaded
Netlet got connection on port: 1494 from port:1123 to gateway:ps-
gateway.sun.com on port:443
Passing Cipher to Proxy from RWGroupCrypt .....

com.sun.portal.netlet.crypt.ciph.CipherGroup
Netlet got connection on port: 135 from port:1125 to gateway:ps-
gateway.sun.com on port:443
Passing Cipher to Proxy from RWGroupCrypt .....

com.sun.portal.netlet.crypt.ciph.CipherGroup
Netlet Exchange
rpc packet size is 60
rpc packet size is 152
Netlet Exchange Dynamic Port: 1075
```

CODE EXAMPLE 2-17 Java Console Output *(Continued)*

```
Netlet got connection on port: 1075 from port:1127 to gateway:ps-
gateway.sun.com on port:443
Passing Cipher to Proxy from RWGroupCrypt .....

com.sun.portal.netlet.crypt.ciph.CipherGroup
Netlet got connection on port: 135 from port:1134 to gateway:ps-
gateway.sun.com on port:443
Passing Cipher to Proxy from RWGroupCrypt .....

com.sun.portal.netlet.crypt.ciph.CipherGroup
Netlet Exchange
rpc packet size is 60
rpc packet size is 152
Netlet Exchange Dynamic Port: 1026
Netlet got connection on port: 1026 from port:1136 to gateway:ps-
gateway.sun.com on port:443
Passing Cipher to Proxy from RWGroupCrypt .....

com.sun.portal.netlet.crypt.ciph.CipherGroup
Netlet got connection on port: 1026 from port:1138 to gateway:ps-
gateway.sun.com on port:443
Passing Cipher to Proxy from RWGroupCrypt .....

com.sun.portal.netlet.crypt.ciph.CipherGroup
Netlet got connection on port: 1026 from port:1140 to gateway:ps-
gateway.sun.com on port:443
Passing Cipher to Proxy from RWGroupCrypt .....

com.sun.portal.netlet.crypt.ciph.CipherGroup
```

Note – If you do not see dynamic Exchange connections being made, you might not have set the Exchange server address to `localhost`. If you get a pop-up window with an error indicating the Netlet could not bind to port 135, then it is either being used by a local service, or you are using a version of Windows that had reserved this port.

Tunneling Exchange Mail to Outlook Express Clients

Many companies use Exchange solely as a messaging solution. By creating Netlet tunnels for messaging protocols like IMAP, SMTP, and POP3, any standards-compliant client, such as Netscape Messenger, can be used to send and receive email securely once configured to use the local loopback address as the email server without having to move Exchange in to the DMZ where it is more vulnerable. This, of course, only works if the port is not already bound by another service. Nondefault client ports can be used to avoid this situation as well. Because it is unlikely that the mobile workforce is running messaging servers from their clients, this is generally not a problem. With both a remote account and a local account created, when Outlook Express is launched, either one or the other will be able to successfully synchronize with the Exchange Server and a warning will be displayed regarding the other.

To reduce the amount of traffic, Messaging Express also allows specific synchronization options such as synchronizing only new messages. This is a good solution for companies that have more proficient end users who are able to make configuration changes to their email client and who do not require access to anything other than their internal email and news.

If you plan to use Exchange calendaring and other services, you should use a split DNS (see "To Configure the Netlet Rule Required for Exchange Split DNS Integration at the Organization Level" on page 111) or a Rewriter integration (see Appendix A, "Microsoft Exchange Integrations"). Tunneling mail protocols using a Netlet connection is a frequently used, reliable way to make internal email available to remote users accessing it using their native mail client over a secure connection.

▼ To Configure Netlet Rules Required for Exchange Messaging in Portal Server 6.x at the Organization Level

1. **Log in to the Administration console.**

2. **Select the appropriate Organization name.**

3. **Select Show: Services.**

4. **Expand the Netlet properties by selecting the arrow next to Netlet under the SRAP Configuration section in the left pane.**

5. **Add Netlet rules for IMAP, SMTP, and POP3, or a single service group.**

Note – POP3 is not recommended as a secure solution because sensitive mail (message headers, as well as bodies) can be downloaded and saved on the client machine. You might consider only supporting IMAP and SMTP.

---

a. **Select a unique name for the rule, such as the protocol name.**

IMAP may be there by default. SMTP and POP3 can be added as well. If defining a Netlet service group, use a more generic name such as "mail."

b. **Choose an appropriate encryption algorithm.**

Usually the service default is satisfactory. Government and banking institutions might consider using an algorithm with a longer key length. See "Assigning an Encryption Algorithm" on page 28 for more details on what to use.

c. **Select null for the URL.**

Because the native mail client is used instead of an HTML-based email client, there is no associated URL to launch.

d. **Deselect download applet.**

Because email communication does not require a Java applet, one does not have to be independently downloaded.

e. **Put a checkmark next to extend session.**

This should be selected if users will be interacting with their native email program for an extended amount of time with little or no interaction with the portal server desktop. See"Understanding and Handling Timeouts" on page 75 for more information about this feature and its intended usage.

f. **Add the port-host-port mappings.**

If you are defining a Netlet service group, add all of the mappings to the one Netlet rule. Otherwise, add one mapping per rule. The default mappings for the protocols are as follows:

10143   exchange-server   143 # IMAP

10025   exchange-server   25 # SMTP

10110   exchange-server   110 #POP3

g. **Select Save.**

6. **Restart the Gateway so that it can reread its updated profile.**

▼ To Configure Accounts on the Client Machine

1. **Launch Outlook Express.**

2. **Select Tools ➤ Accounts.**

3. **Select Add ➤ Mail.**

4. **Enter your internal work address.**

5. **Select Next.**

6. Enter your work email address next to the E-mail address field.

7. Select IMAP from the drop-down menu bar.

8. Enter `localhost` in both the incoming and Outgoing mail fields.

9. Select Next.

10. Enter the Username and password.

11. Select Remember password if the client machine is not a shared resource and if your own security requirements permit it.

12. Select Next.

13. Verify connectivity by logging in to the portal Gateway.

14. Launch Messaging Express and select `localhost` (or whatever you have chosen as the account name).

Note – If a nondefault port is being used for the protocol (like 10143 instead of 143), the port number must be changed in the Advanced tab of the Account properties.

---

15. Select OK to download the folder list and select which folders to view.

16. Select account name again.

17. Select a few of the folders to make sure the contents are present (FIGURE 2-21).

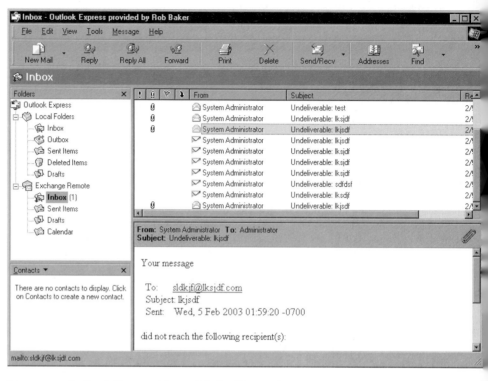

FIGURE 2-21 Outlook Express Over a Netlet Connection

Note – If a test message fails due to the inability to relay, you might have to modify the SMTP relay restrictions. If the test machine is isolated from the outside network completely, the restrictions can be removed completely. Otherwise, a great deal of care should be taken to ensure that the appropriate filtering is done to avoid creating a wide-open relay.

---

18. **View the Java Console to verify that connections are being made to the Netlet. The output might appear as shown in** CODE EXAMPLE 2-18.

CODE EXAMPLE 2-18   Java Console Output

```
Microsoft (R) VM for Java, 5.0 Release 5.0.0.3802
==============================================
?   help
c   clear
f   run finalizers
g   garbage collect
m   memory usage
q   quit
```

```
t  thread list
================================================
Netlet running on IE
Netlet config: https://sps-gateway.sun.com/http://ps-
server.int.sun.com/portal/NetletConfig?func=loadResources
gateway protocol : https
gateway host : ps-gateway.sun.com
gateway port : 443
Netlet not using proxy (IE)
Netlet rule 0: local:1494  destination:citrix.int.sun.com:1494
Netlet rule 1: local:8000  destination:ps-server.int.sun.com:80
Netlet rule 2: local:30021  destination:TARGET:21
Netlet rule 3: local:25  destination:ex-server.int.sun.com:25
Netlet rule 4: local:143  destination:ex-server.int.sun.com:143
Netlet rule 5: local:135  destination:ex-server.int.sun.com:135
Netlet rule 6: local:30000  destination:TARGET:23
Netlet config: https://ps-gateway.sun.com/http://ps-
server.int.sun.com/portal/NetletConfig?func=setLoaded
Netlet got connection on port: 1494 from port:1537 to gateway:ps-
gateway.sun.com on port:443
Passing Cipher to Proxy from RWGroupCrypt .....
com.sun.portal.netlet.crypt.ciph.CipherGroup
Netlet got connection on port: 143 from port:1539 to gateway:ps-
gateway.sun.com on port:443
Passing Cipher to Proxy from RWGroupCrypt .....

com.sun.portal.netlet.crypt.ciph.CipherGroup
Netlet got connection on port: 25 from port:1541 to gateway:ps-
gateway.sun.com on port:443
Passing Cipher to Proxy from RWGroupCrypt .....

com.sun.portal.netlet.crypt.ciph.CipherGroup
Netlet got connection on port: 143 from port:1543 to gateway:ps-
gateway.sun.com on port:443
Passing Cipher to Proxy from RWGroupCrypt .....

com.sun.portal.netlet.crypt.ciph.CipherGroup
```

▼ To Allow Email Relaying in the Test Environment

1. **Launch the Exchange System Manager.**

2. **Expand Servers.**

3. **Expand the server instance.**

4. **Expand Protocols.**

5. **Expand SMTP.**

6. **Right-click over Default SMTP Virtual Server and select Properties.**

7. **Select Access tab from the properties window.**

8. **Select the Relay button.**

9. **Checkmark All Except the List Below.**

10. **Choose OK.**

Integrating Outlook Web Access Over a Netlet Using Split DNS

Outlook Web Access (OWA), which ships with Exchange 2000 SP2, SP3, and possibly newer versions of Exchange to come, uses new underlying technologies that make OWA integration using the Rewriter somewhat more difficult. These specific challenges are discussed in further detail in Appendix A, "Application Integrations for the Rewriter"

Depending on your business needs and network topology, some of these configuration challenges can be overcome by tunneling the communication between the browser (specifically, Internet Explorer) and the Exchange server using a Netlet connection. The basic requirements of this integration approach are to use a single Netlet rule that listens on the client's local port 80 (or whatever the Exchange server is listening on). To be sure that Exchange traffic is routed through the `localhost` address, a dummy (split) external DNS entry must be configured so that the Exchange server address is externally resolvable to `localhost` or 127.0.0.1. The advantage to this approach is that no changes are required to the Exchange server controls scripts and component files, and no Rewriter rules are necessary. The drawback is that internal email with internal embedded URLs might not be accessible. This is the same problem as creating extensive mappings on reverse proxies. Most companies do not want to create split DNS for all of their internal subnets, nor do they want to create reverse proxy mappings for them. In this case, integrating OWA through the Rewriter might be a better solution.

The final step in this integration is to create a link on the portal server desktop that is not rewritten, so the browser's own DNS resolution is used instead of the Gateway resolving the Exchange server address. The reason for this is that many internal URLs in OWA are created dynamically using the contents of the browser's URL field. ActiveX requests are then generated using these dynamically created URLs that would otherwise result in direct requests to the Exchange server rather than through the Netlet tunnel.

▼ To Configure the Netlet Rule Required for Exchange Split DNS Integration at the Organization Level

1. **Log in to the Administration console.**

2. **Select the appropriate organization name.**

3. **Select Show: Services.**

4. **Expand the Netlet properties by selecting the arrow next to Netlet under the SRAP Configuration section in the left pane.**

5. **Add Netlet rules for HTTP default port 80 or whatever port the Exchange server is listening on.**

Note – If client port 80 is already in use, Exchange Netlet connectivity fails because the Netlet applet is not able to bind to the port. Also, because 80 is the default HTTP port, all of the client's HTTP traffic is tunneled through Netlet creating a bottleneck at the Gateway not unlike bottlenecks encountered by traditional VPN servers. Using nonprivilaged ports (higher than 1024) helps to not preclude UNIX and UNIX-like platforms.

---

   a. **Select a unique name for the rule, such as OWA.**

   b. **Choose an appropriate encryption algorithm.**

   Usually the service default is satisfactory. Government and banking institutions might consider using an algorithm with a longer key length. See "Assigning an Encryption Algorithm" on page 28 for more details on what to use.

   c. **Select null for the URL.**

   Because the native mail client is used instead of an HTML-based email client, there is no associated URL to launch.

   d. **Deselect download applet.**

   Because email communication does not require a Java applet, one does not have to be independently downloaded.

e. **Put a checkmark next to extend session.**

This should be selected if users will be interacting with their email for an extended amount of time with little or no interaction with the portal server desktop. See "Understanding and Handling Timeouts" on page 75 for more information about this feature and its intended usage.

f. **Add the following mapping to the Port-Host-Port field.**

The mapping should look like this:

```
80   exchange-server   80
```

In this example, *exchange-server* represents the fully qualified address of the externally resolvable Exchange address.

g. **Select Save.**

6. **Restart the Gateway so that it can reread its updated profile.**

▼ To Create a DNS Entry That Publicly Resolves the Exchange Server Address to the Loopback Address

The DNS resolution must be made from a public DNS server.

Most companies have internal subdomains that are subsets of their external second-level domains. In this case, an entry needs to be added to the start of authority (SOA) of the second-level domain to resolve the fully qualified Exchange server address to `localhost`.

1. **Add a DNS entry.**

This example uses BIND 8 as follows (using `int` as a fictitious subdomain of `int.sun.com`):

a. **Add a zone entry for to the BIND configuration file (`/etc/named.conf`).**

```
////////////////////////////////////////////
//   Zone info for int.sun.com domain
zone "int.sun.com" in {
        type master;
        file "named.sun_int_hosts";
        //   Restrict zone transfers to localhost
        allow-transfer { 127.0.0.1; };
};
```

b. Create a Start of Authority in the `hosts` **file.**

```
@       IN      SOA     int.sun.com.
postmaster.int.sun.com.
  (
                        101         ; serial number
                        3600        ; refresh
                        600         ; retry
                        2073600     ; expire
                        3600      ) ; minimum TTL

        IN      NS      ns-sun.int.sun.com.

; hostname of Exchange server
exchange-server         IN      A       127.0.0.1
```

c. Push DNS maps.

```
# pkill -HUP named
```

d. Perform a test lookup.

```
# nslookup exchange-server
Server:   ns-sun.int.sun.com
Address:  10.0.0.1

Name:     exchange-server.int.sun.com
Address:  127.0.0.1
```

Note – For internal testing purposes, the mapping can be done by adding an entry in the client's hosts file. An example for Windows 98 might involve adding the line in the `c:\windows\hosts` file. . .

127.0.0.1 *exchange-server*

. . . where *exchange-server* is the fully qualified address of the publicly resolvable Exchange Server.

▼ To Create a Link to Launch OWA That Will Not be Rewritten on the Portal Server Desktop

The link should not be rewritten because you want the browser to perform the DNS lookup of the Exchange server. This way it uses `127.0.0.1` in its communication (and thus tunnels through the Netlet), but the browser URL field continues to have only Exchange-specific information in it. If the browser URL field is modified in any way, there might be miscommunication between the client and server. Some of the ActiveX requests are generated using the value of `docutment.location.hostname`, which would return the Gateway instead of the exchange server, if the URL in the browser URL field has been rewritten.

1. **Copy the default** `Bookmark` **file to your customized template directory.**

   Example:

   ```
   # cp /etc/opt/SUNWps/desktop/default/Bookmark
   /etc/opt/SUNWps/desktop/custom/Bookmark
   ```

2. **Edit the** `display.template` **file created in the customized template directory and add the following lines of code just prior to the bookmarks tag:**

   Note – A bookmark template is available for download called `display.template.OWA`. See "Obtaining Downloadable Files for This Book" on page xxi. To use the downloadable file, rename it to `display.template` and copy it in to the `Bookmark` directory of your customized template directory.

   ```
   <TR><TD>
   <FONT FACE="Sans-serif" SIZE="-1">
   <A HREF="javascript: " onClick="javascript: exWin =
   top.window.open('http://ex-server/exchange'); exWin.focus();
   return false;">Launch Microsoft Outlook Web Access</A>
   </font></TD></TR>
   [tag:bookmarks]
   ```

   Note – The `top.window.open` function is used instead of the more generalized `window.open` function to enable you to modify the Rewriter rules so that its parameter value does not get rewritten.

If multiple Exchange servers are going to be used, and you do not want the Netlet pop-up for the static rules to launch as soon as the users log in, you can move the Netlet provider logic into the customized bookmark provider and create some additional script to launch the Netlet, then the OWA interface. The OWA interface cannot be launched by the Netlet because the URL will be rewritten. That is why the URL field was left blank when you configured the Netlet rule.

Each bookmark link might look like this:

```
<A HREF="javascript: " onClick="launchOWA('OWA',
'ex-server');">Launch Outlook Web Access
</A>
```

OWA is the name of the Netlet rule (*OWA*, *OWA1*, and so on) and *ex-server* instances are the individual fully qualified Exchange server names (*ex-server1*, and so on). The code to launch Netlet might look like this:

```
//function to launch nelet
function launchOWA (ruleName, exServer){
  netletConfigOpen('/portal/NetletConfig?func=makepage',
'/portal/NetletConfig?func=' + ruleName + '&machine=' + exServer);
  exWin=top.window.open('http://' + exServer + '/exchange');
  exWin.focus();
  return false;
}
```

In this example, */portal* represents the value of DEPLOY_URI you specified at installation time.

Note – Hard coding the Netlet functionality in a different provider than the Netlet provider is risky because the underlying Netlet functionality might change in future releases.

---

3. **Change the value of exchange-server to the fully qualified value of your Exchange host.**

▼ To Change the Rewriter Rules so `top.window.open` is Not Rewritten

By default, all `window.open` JavaScript function calls are rewritten. Because this behavior is too generalized for this procedure, you must make sure that the first `window.open` function parameter continues to be rewritten, but that the `top.window.open` function parameter is not.

1. **Log in to the Administration console.**

2. **Select View Service Management.**

3. **Select Gateway.**

4. **Under the Domain-based rulesets section, check the ruleset associated with the DNS domain in which the Exchange server is installed.**

   By default, the `generic_ruleset` is applied to all DNS domains. The `default_gateway_ruleset` is applied to the default portal domain. Any ruleset that contains the rule `*open` must be removed or commented out from the Rewriter XML associated with the ruleset that is applied to the portal server desktop, because that is where the link to launch OWA is residing. In this case, both the `default_gateway_ruleset` and the `generic_ruleset` must be modified.

5. **Select Rewriter from the left panel of the Administration console.**

6. **Modify the XML by downloading it, or editing it inline as follows:**

```
<!--window.open-->
<!-- <Function type="EXPRESSION" name="*open" paramPatterns="y"/>
-->
```

Note – Do not edit the XML if it has been downloaded with a text editor that inserts end-of-line characters at the end of each line. The UNIX platform editors `vi` and `emacs` and Microsoft Windows Wordpad usually work well for large rulesets.

---

7. **Restart the Gateway to read in the new profile.**

Note – To create a single logout, use the `exWin` handle from the Logout link defined in the `menubar.jsp` template file in the top-level container. For example, to change the logout link for a non-tabbed desktop, modify the file at:
`/etc/opt/SUNWps/desktop/custom/JSPTableContainerProvider/menubar.jsp`
or `/etc/opt/SUNWps/desktop/custom/JSPTableContainerProvider/header.jsp`
if it has been modified to contain the `menubar.jsp` commands. A single sign-off link might appear as follows:
`<a href="dt?action=logout" onClick="if (exWin)`
`{exWin.close();}">LOGOUT</a>`

▼ To Test a Successful Integration Using a Split DNS Entry With a Netlet Rule

1. **Using a test DNS server, or by modifying the client `hosts` file, make sure that the `ex-server` address resolves to `localhost`.**

2. **Log in to the portal Gateway and select the Launch Outlook Express link from the Bookmark provider.**

3. Verify the Netlet connection.

Once the Netlet is loaded, and after the OWA interface presents the Basic Auth login, check the portal Java Console (example below) to make sure the communication is going over the Netlet connection.

```
.
.
.
Netlet got connection on port: 80 from port:1183 to gateway:si-
gateway.sun.com on port:443
Passing Cipher to Proxy from RWGroupCrypt .....

com.sun.portal.netlet.crypt.ciph.CipherGroup
Netlet got connection on port: 80 from port:1185 to gateway:ps-
gateway.sun.com on port:443
Passing Cipher to Proxy from RWGroupCrypt .....

com.sun.portal.netlet.crypt.ciph.CipherGroup
Netlet got connection on port: 80 from port:1187 to gateway:ps-
gateway.sun.com on port:443
Passing Cipher to Proxy from RWGroupCrypt .....
.
.
.
.
```

Scenario E: Using a Secure Shell Through a Netlet

The Solaris Secure Shell (SSH) software is frequently used as an alternative to `Telnet` for remote terminal access. Having an SSH session tunnel through a Netlet connection is somewhat redundant, but it does offer some unique capabilities such as remote X tunneling (assuming an X server is running on the client) and Secure File Transfer Protocol (SFTP). By using the Netlet for the SSH session, the external firewall does not have to have ports open for SSH. Only authenticated users coming in through the Gateway will be able to access internal machines using an SSH client. The portability of this solution depends on how your secure shell daemon (`sshd`) server is set up. If it requires client public keys to already be stored locally before end users initially connect, then the portability is limited because you can only connect using the client with the SSH software installed containing a specific public/private key pair. If SSH is configured to store the client's public key upon authentication to establish the trust relationship, then any SSH client can be used once the Netlet has been launched. Even if the SSH credentials are stored locally upon successful authentication, a connection cannot be re-established from that machine without a valid Netlet session.

▼ To Configure a Netlet Rule Required for SSH

1. **Log in to the Administration console.**

2. **Select the appropriate Organization name.**

3. **Select Show: Services.**

4. **Expand the Netlet properties by selecting the arrow next to Netlet under the SRAP Configuration section in the left pane.**

5. **Add a Netlet rule for the SSH default port 22 or whatever port the SSH server has been configured to listen on.**

Note – If the Gateway is sitting in the DMZ, either the Netlet proxy will have to be configured to pass through the inner firewall, or the SSH port will need to be opened on the inner firewall so that the SSH traffic will be allowed through to the SSH server. No additional firewall rules must be opened on the outer firewall.

---

   a. **Select a unique name for the rule, such as SSH2.**

   b. **Choose an appropriate encryption algorithm.**

   Usually the service default is satisfactory. Government and banking institutions might consider using an algorithm with a larger key length. See "Assigning an Encryption Algorithm" on page 28 for more details on what to use. Because the data is encrypted twice, a longer key length might be unnecessary in this particular instance.

   c. **Select null for the URL.**

   Because most user agents do not have a SSH helper application defined and you are not using a locally installed client to access the SSH server, there is no need to have a URL here.

   d. **Deselect download applet.**

   No client applet besides the Netlet applet itself is required to be downloaded for SSH to work over a Netlet connection.

   e. **Put a checkmark next to extend session.**

   This should be selected if users will be interacting with their SSH terminal session for an extended amount of time with little or no interaction with the portal server desktop. See "Understanding and Handling Timeouts" on page 75 for more information about this feature and its intended usage.

f. Add the port-host-port mappings.

The mapping should look like the following:

```
30022   ssh-server   22
```

ssh-server is the fully qualified address of the SSH server. Unlike FTP Netlet rules, the client port does not have to be fixed to 30022.

g. Select Save.

h. Restart the Gateway so that it can reread its updated profile.

▼ To Establish an SSH Session Over a Netlet Connection

Once the Netlet has launched when an end user logs in and they have configured a TARGET host if the SSH rule was made dynamic, all they need to do to establish an SSH session is launch their SSH client and connect to `localhost` on the client port specified in the Netlet rule (30022 as shown above). If connecting for the first time, and password authentication is used, the public key for the SSH server can be stored on the client. If you are not on your own machine, you should probably answer no, even though the password is not stored locally. Also, if end users will be connecting to different hosts, there is no reason to associate a specific public certificate with `localhost`.

FIGURE 2-22 shows an example of an SSH session being initiated to run over a Netlet connection.

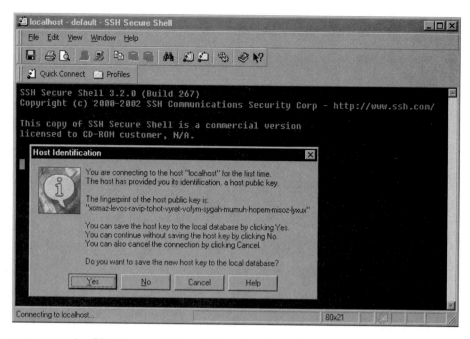

FIGURE 2-22 An SSH Session Being Initiated to Run Over a Netlet Connection

Once the authentication completes successfully, the Java Console output looks something like this:

```
Netlet got connection on port: 30022 from port:1097 to gateway:ps-
gateway.sun.com on port:443
Passing Cipher to Proxy from RWGroupCrypt .....
com.sun.portal.netlet.crypt.ciph.CipherGroup
```

You now have a secure tunnel with remote X on-demand capability. To take advantage of remote X, an X server must also be running on the client machine. This functionality is not provided in the Netlet itself. X servers like ReflectionX and Exceed work well for Win32 systems. Linux and UNIX platforms have native X servers running on them, so no additional software is required.

FIGURE 2-23 shows an example of a remote X command running through an SSH session encapsulated by a Netlet session.

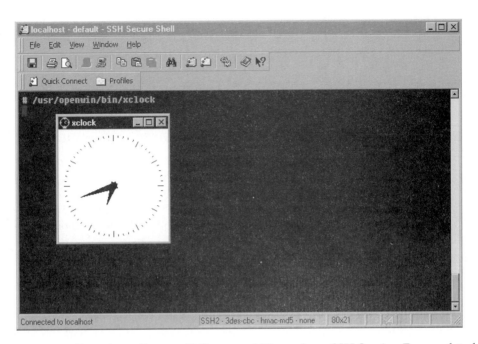

FIGURE 2-23 Running a Remote X Command Through an SSH Session Encapsulated by a Netlet Session

Ten Tips From the Trenches

This section presents ten of the most frequent Netlet-related problems, and offers tips for solving each problem.

Problem: The Gateway does not understand `FTP:///` URLs, and therefore rejects such requests.

Tip: Configure a Netlet rule for FTP to a specific host. FTP URLs can be used, which direct the browser to the appropriate port number where the Netlet is listening. For example, `ftp://`*uid*`@localhost:30021`. For more information about how to accomplish this, see "Scenario A: Running FTP Over a Netlet Connection" on page 81.

Problem: The Netlet session ends intermittently and unexpectedly.

Tip: This can happen for a variety of reasons. First, there may be some intermediary infrastructure like a firewall or a proxy closing the network connection. If this turns out to be the case, the Netlet KeepAlive interval should be set to a nonzero value. In portal server 6.x, this value is specified in seconds. Portal server 6.0 requires a patch for this feature to work properly. Another possibility is that the user session idle timer is being reached. Although Netlet activity will update the idle time, if there is no activity, both the Netlet and portal sessions will become inactive and require the user to log back in and re-initiate the Netlet session.

Problem: When an automatic proxy configuration file is used, the Java Console reports that the resolved proxy to use is null.

Tip: This situation can occur in portal server 6.0 when very large PAC files are sent, resulting in a chunked transfer encoding being used, and the PAC file being truncated. The more likely scenario is simply that Rhino has not been installed on the portal server or the `js.jar` that ships with Rhino is in the wrong location.

Problem: The Netlet pop-up window remains open, even after a portal logout.

Tip: To take care of this problem in the Sun ONE Portal Server 6.0 and 6.1 software, a JavaScript event handler can be added to the logout link on the portal server desktop that checks if the window exists, and if it does, closes it. In Sun ONE Portal Server 6.1PC1 software, the Netlet window was added to the detached windows list so that it is automatically cleaned up upon portal logout. To do this in earlier versions, modify the Netlet `display.template` file:
`/etc/opt/SUNWps/desktop/`*desktop_name*`/MyFrontPageTabPanelContainer/` `Netlet/display.template`.

The `netletWinOpen` and `netletActionOpen` functions both contain `window.open` method invocations. Immediately following the `nWin` variable assignment, add the following line:

```
detachedWindows[detachedWindows.length] = nWin;
```

Problem: Users are not able to specify their own UID when Netlet FTP is set up using dynamic Netlet rules. Internal FTP machines assume the user is anonymous.

Tip: There is no way for an end user to modify the administratively preset URL, and a missing UID implies that the FTP connection is for an anonymous user. The FTP client built into Internet Explorer will prompt for both the user name and password, ignoring the UID specified in the URL. One solution is to change the URL to something like `ftp://bogus@localhost:30021`. This prevents the browser from automatically authenticating as an anonymous user. If this is not an option, the only straightforward way to include the UID is to set the URL in the user's profile. If the portal UID and FTP UID are the same, this should not be too difficult. If they differ, then FTP URLs should not be able to be used with the FTP Netlet rules.

Problem: Netlet thinks that the browser vendor is Netscape instead of IE, and thus cannot connect.

Tip: Sun ONE Portal Server 6.0 and 6.1 versions attempt to determine the browser type by looking for the Netscape security libraries in the client `classpath`. If these libraries have been added, then the Netlet connectivity may fail for IE. Additionally, no IE clients will be able to connect if the libraries have been added on the server side as a result of warnings similar to the following in the Web server error logs:

```
[12/Feb/2004:18:24:54] warning (21723): for host 10.10.10.220
trying to GET /portal/netlet/netscape/security.class, send-file
reports: can't find /opt/SUNWps/web-apps/https-
portal.int.sun.com/portal/netlet/netscape/security.class (File
not found)
```

This warning should be ignored, and is actually indicative of the browser type determination working as expected.

Problem: The Netlet creates too many pop-up windows.

Tip: This can be an issue for end users that have enabled pop-up blockers, or it may be considered a usability issue. The primary Netlet pop-up is used so that the Netlet applet runs in a separate window from the portal server desktop. This way desktop refreshes to not affect the Netlet sessions by causing the applet to stop, restart, or reinitialize. There are some suggestions in "Netlet Pop-Up: Friend or Foe?" on page 65 describing how to embed the Netlet popup window, make it invisible, or place it inconspicuously off the screen. The Netlet status functionality is lost in these cases, and it is not an ideal solution in most cases.

Problem: Mac OSX browsers are not able to use the Netlet.

Tip: The MAC platform is not supported for use with NetApps, however, OSX.2 with the latest JVM and Sun ONE Portal Server 6.1 PC1 software is one combination known to work. OS9 will not work with any portal server release.

OSX browsers have been tested and should work as expected in Sun ONE Portal Server 6.1PC1 software. This is the only portal server 6.x release that currently works with this platform. Mac OS9 will not work with any of the Java-based portal NetApps.

Problem: Netlet connections are failing. The Java Console output indicates I/O exceptions similar to the following:

```
Netlet showing port warning dialog:30000
ProxyMsg: IOE writing proxy info: java.io.IOException: The virtual
circuit was aborted due to timeout or other failure
```

Tip: The most likely cause of this failure is that a firewall or proxy has been configured in one of two ways:

- To disallow SSL traffic altogether
- To perform packet-level inspection to make sure that the traffic indeed is SSL

Sun ONE Portal Server 6.0 and 6.1 versions cannot be configured to use SSL encryption, so packet-level inspection must be turned off. Portal server 6.2 should be configured to use SSL ciphers so that the traffic will pass scrupulous inspection.

Problem: Netlets cannot be used in conjunction with Sun Ray servers.

Tip: Due to the fact that Sun Ray server software runs on a single machine, the lack of dynamic port allocations in the Netlet applet prevents more than one Sun Ray client from being able to make use of the Netlet at a time. Sun Ray system support has been added in Sun Java Enterprise System Portal Server 6.2 software. Refer to the product documentation for additional details.

New Netlet Technology in the Java Enterprise System

The Netlet now offers a half dozen selectable cryptographic algorithms. Now that SSL is available, you can use the Netlet with packet sniffers in proxying firewalls. This includes functionality with proxies that perform protocol compliance on the traffic that comes across its interfaces. Onboard hardware accelerators can churn through bulk-loaded SSL encryption/decryption, improving overall throughput, and off-board hardware accelerators can perform all of the cryptography on behalf of the Gateway.

Another advantage offered by the latest Netlet technology is in serving applications to thin clients such as Sun Ray network appliances. Doing so moves the administration from a per-machine basis to the servers in the data center, while extending the same desktop-level functionality or a role-based portal. Sun Ray systems operate off of a single network fabric with all of the appliances sharing a single machine. Because the Netlet uses `localhost`, administrating per-user Netlet rules to avoid hijacked Netlet sessions or attempts at listening on already-bound ports is very difficult. A dynamic port allocation similar to how the FTP protocol operates can be used for hundreds of Sun Ray users requiring access to the same Netlet rules and machine resources.

## CHAPTER 3

NetFile: Secure Remote Access for Exchanging Files With Internal File Systems

This chapter discusses NetFile, one of the three primary technologies provided by the portal server, secure remote access software. NetFile enables integration and provisioning of internal applications to authenticated end users securely over the Internet. NetFile securely exposes internal file systems to remote users so that files can be viewed, uploaded, and downloaded.

This chapter contains the following sections:

- "What is NetFile?" on page 128
- "Why Do I Need NetFile?" on page 128
- "How Does NetFile Work?" on page 130
- "How Do I Deploy NetFile?" on page 132
- "Deployment Scenarios" on page 145
- "Logging" on page 163
- "Ten Tips From the Trenches" on page 164
- "New NetFile Technology in the Java Enterprise System" on page 166

Note – In this book, the term *portal server* refers to Sun's portal server software with the SRA software unless specified otherwise. *Portal server node* and *portal node* refer to the portal server core product.

What is NetFile?

NetFile is a component of the portal server Secure Remove Access software that enables remote users to securely transfer files bidirectionally to back-end systems. These types of systems include WU-FTP compliant FTP servers, Network File System (NFS) mount points, Server Message Block (SMB) file systems, and Novell (Netware) FTP servers. From a single graphical interface, users can add and save systems and mount points (shares), transfer files, email files, search for files, and perform a basic set of file manipulations including file compression and renaming. Administrators can also prepopulate hosts and shares.

Why Do I Need NetFile?

Here are ten good reasons to take advantage of the NetFile component.

- Reason 1 – NetFile provides an alternative to using FTP over a Netlet connection. This is useful when end users do not have the necessary skills to configure their own FTP client software appropriately to connect through the Netlet. It also extends the number and types of hosts available to transfer files to and from. For more detail, see "NetFile Versus Netlet FTP" on page 130.

- Reason 2 – NetFile supports prepopulating of hosts.
  The ability to prepopulate hosts is very useful in deployment scenarios where the portal server is used for secure file uploads of sensitive data such as medical records from multiple client locations. In portal server, this feature is referred to as *common hosts* rather than *prepopulated hosts*, as in the portal server 3. For more information about the usefulness of this feature and information about using it, see "Prepopulating Hosts and Shares" on page 144.

- Reason 3 – NetFile provides access to SMB and Netware file systems.
  Besides increasing the flexibility of file transfers to include heterogeneous network environments, enabling file transfers to these additional file systems reduces the need to invest in and implement an extranet solution. Extranets are frequently used to extend the native network out to trusted areas of the Internet. The reasoning for this is that proprietary authentication mechanisms, or proprietary client-server communication, often prevent the insertion of Internet Web proxies between clients and back-end systems. Additionally, most companies want as few holes in the firewall open to the outside world as possible. Using NetFile with the portal Gateway means no additional holes have to be opened in the external-facing firewall.

- Reason 4 – You can avoid having to open up a Secure Shell (SSH) or Telnet connection to find files. The search feature in the NetFile interface makes it easier to find files without having to enable SSH or Telnet connections to initiate a file search from the command line. The administrator has control over search scope to avoid root-level searches that might unnecessarily bog down compute resources.

- Reason 5 – NetFile does not limit client access to the file system. Internet Explorer has a feature for FTP where the only files that can be accessed by the end user are those files residing in whatever directory the FTP server initializes the user to. Users can never step above that directory in the file system to transfer files to another location (sometimes referred to as *chrooted*). The FTP server should be configured to operate with limited access, if that is the intended behavior, rather than the browser or some other FTP client enforcing it.

- Reason 6 – You are looking for a platform-independent file-transferring solution. Because the NetFile client runs as a Java applet, it is able to transfer files to and from any system running a compatible Java Virtual Machine (JVM), including the Sun Java plug-in. There are no hassles with additional client software licensing, because the Sun Java plug-in is freely distributed.

- Reason 7 – You require file transfer capabilities in a heterogeneous network environment. Remote users typically don't store their own files on an FTP server. Thus, they need a means by which to upload and download files on a variety of systems and system types. In addition to FTP servers, NetFile also works well with SMB, NFS, and Netware file systems.

- Reason 8 – You require access to multiple systems from a single interface. NetFile is designed to have multiple hosts and shares set up so that transfers can be done between any of these mount points without having to initiate individual sessions in multiple client windows.

- Reason 9 – You do not want to have to log in individually to each host prior to transferring files. Single sign-on (SSO) can be accomplished by saving the NetFile session upon exit once shares are mounted. Assuming that the password itself has not changed since the last time a user accessed the host, the user is automatically logged in the next time NetFile is launched.

- Reason 10 – You need to email files stored remotely.
  Using NetFile, files stored locally or remotely can be sent as attachments. Multiple selected files are sent in one email, rather than one per email as was the case with portal server 3.

How Does NetFile Work?

NetFile runs as a Java applet that is launched from the portal server desktop. NetFile serves as a buffer between commands and command responses to and from native file systems. Like the Netlet, NetFile traffic is encrypted across the public wire between the Netlet applet and the portal Gateway, and between the Gateway and portal node if so configured.

Hosts and shares can be added, deleted, and configured by both portal administrators (for prepopulated and common hosts) and end users. Access permissions and ability to read and write to shares and files contained in the shares is determined by the security implementation on the native file systems.

NetFile Versus Netlet FTP

Historically, Netlet FTP came about as a solution to limitations imposed by the difficult-to-use, non-internationalized NetFile user interface (UI). Netlet FTP is advantageous over NetFile in several deployment scenarios. The first such scenario is for remote employees who needed to access a known internal FTP server, and who possess an appropriate skill set to configure the FTP client software to connect through the Netlet. Another common deployment scenario applies when a substantially large number of users need to download files from an anonymous FTP server. In this case, an FTP file URL can be used that automatically loads a familiar file manager window for downloading files. The third deployment scenario applies when the average file size being uploaded or downloaded is greater than 10 Mbytes. Netlet FTP uses native FTP protocol, so it is ideal for transferring large files.

Because the NetFile UI that ships in portal server 6 is more suitable in localized environments, internationalization is no longer a primary reason to choose Netlet FTP over NetFile. NetFile has obvious advantageous over Netlet FTP in other deployment scenarios. NetFile can transfer files between a variety of file system types, connect without requiring additional authentication once a share has been added, and transfer from multiple systems and mount points using a single window. NetFile can also perform some file manipulations that cannot be done using an FTP client application.

Two UIs, One Purpose

To make portal server 6 backward-compatible with browsers containing earlier JVMs, two UIs are currently maintained. The first is referred to as the NetFile Java 1 UI, and it is visually similar to that which is shipped in later versions of portal server 3. The second UI is referred to as the NetFile Java 2 interface. It offers an iconified menu bar and supports the Java 2 Virtual Machine (VM) shipping in the current Sun Java plug-ins.

FIGURE 3-1 shows the legacy Java 1 interface. This interface should be used by older browsers that include a Java 1 VM and do not have the Sun Java plug-in installed and enabled.

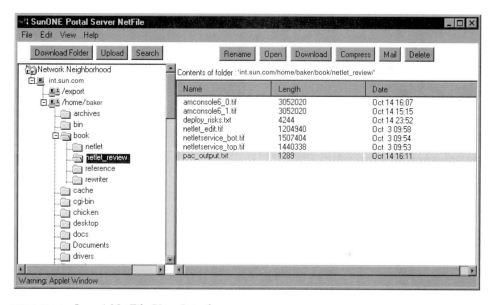

FIGURE 3-1   Java 1 NetFile User Interface

FIGURE 3-2 shows NetFile with a face lift. The Java 2 UI also has a few more options on the toolbar, and more consistent host and share tree expansion.

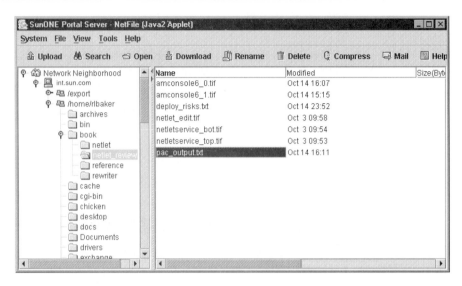

FIGURE 3-2   Java 2 NetFile User Interface

How Do I Deploy NetFile?

Deploying NetFile requires administrative tasks on the portal side to ensure that users have access to the NetFile service. Administrative tasks must be performed on the back-end systems to ensure that the portal server node can communicate with the necessary file systems. Additionally, there may be some end-user tasks that include specifying hosts and shares, and performing basic file transfers and file manipulations.

Configuring NetFile

Before using NetFile for the first time, the NetFile service must be registered, the service templates created, and default NetFile runtime options selected. Additional tasks might be required, depending on the host types that need to be supported. Two of the more tricky configurations to support NFS and SMB are described in "Deployment Scenarios" on page 145.

System Administrator Tasks

This section describes administrative portal tasks that must be accomplished for the successful deployment of the NetFile component of portal server SRA. "Initial Configuration" on page 133 discusses post-portal installation requirements to get NetFile up and running, while "Tuning the NetFile Service" on page 136 speaks a bit more about choosing appropriate default organization attribute values for the NetFile service.

Initial Configuration

NetFile can be used once you assign the NetFile service to the user in the Identity Server (FIGURE 3-3) and the Application channel (App channel) is configured with string values for NetFile Java 1 (FIGURE 3-1) or NetFile Java 2 (FIGURE 3-2). In portal server 6.1, if the portal was installed using the SRAP installer, both of these steps should have been done by default and all of the necessary SRA services should have also been automatically registered with the Identity Server. Some additional administrative steps must be taken after installing portal server 6.0 to ensure that users will have access to the SRA services. Refer to the product documentation for specifics. By adding the properties set in the App channel, NetFile can be launched from the App channel on the portal server desktop (FIGURE 3-5).

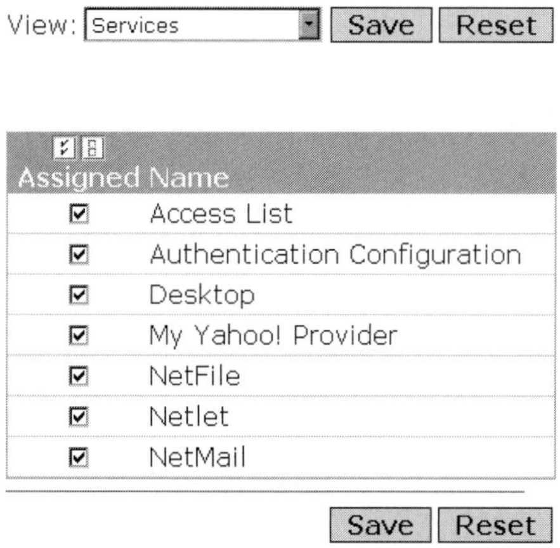

View: [Services ▾] [Save] [Reset]

☑☐	
Assigned Name	
☑	Access List
☑	Authentication Configuration
☑	Desktop
☑	My Yahoo! Provider
☑	NetFile
☑	Netlet
☑	NetMail

[Save] [Reset]

FIGURE 3-3   User Service Configuration Panel

FIGURE 3-3 shows the user Service Configuration panel in the Identity Server 6.0 console. The checkboxes represent user-assigned services. Be sure that NetFile is selected. If it is not, select it, and choose Save. This ensures that the specified user is able to use the Netlet functionality. Typically, this and other SRA-specific services are selected at user creation time.

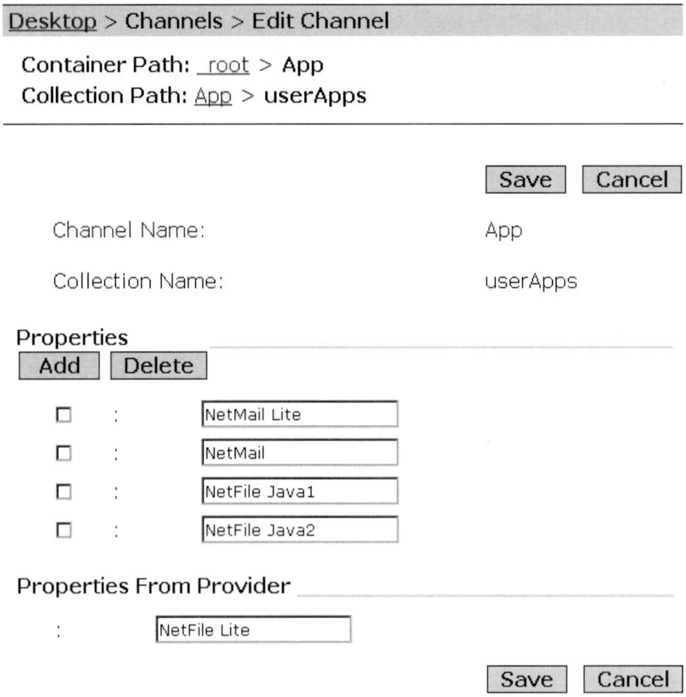

Container Path: _root_ > App
Collection Path: _App_ > userApps

| Save | Cancel |

Channel Name: App

Collection Name: userApps

Properties

| Add | Delete |

☐ : | NetMail Lite |
☐ : | NetMail |
☐ : | NetFile Java1 |
☐ : | NetFile Java2 |

Properties From Provider

: | NetFile Lite |

| Save | Cancel |

FIGURE 3-4   Channel Edit Panel

FIGURE 3-4 shows that the App channel has two properties configured for the NetFile links displayed on the portal server desktop. While these properties appear here as boolean values, as evidenced by the checkboxes, they are actually string values in the display profile's XML. Bold text in CODE EXAMPLE 3-1 shows what the App channel looks like in the display profile XML.

CODE EXAMPLE 3-1 XML Representing App Channel in the Portal Desktop Display Profile

```
<Channel name="App" provider="AppProvider" advanced="false"
merge="fuse" lock="false">
        <Properties advanced="false" merge="fuse" lock="false"
name="_properties" propagate="true">
        <String name="refreshTime" value="600" advanced="true"
merge="replace" lock="false" propagate="true"/>
        <Collection name="targets" advanced="false" merge=
"fuse" lock="false" propagate="true">
            <String value="NetMail Lite|NetMailServlet?nsid=
newHTMLSession" advanced="false" merge="replace" lock="false"
propagate="true"/>
            <String value="NetMail|NetMailServlet?nsid=
newAppletSession" advanced="false" merge="replace" lock="false"
propagate="true"/>
            <String value="NetFile Java1|NetFileApplet?Refer=
java1" advanced="false" merge="replace" lock="false" propagate=
"true"/>
            <String value="NetFile Java2|NetFileApplet?Refer=
java2" advanced="false" merge="replace" lock="false" propagate=
"true"/>
        </Collection>
        <Collection name="userApps" advanced="false" merge=
"fuse" lock="false" propagate="true">
        <String value="NetMail Lite" advanced="false" merge=
"replace" lock="false" propagate="true"/>
            <String value="NetMail" advanced="false" merge=
"replace" lock="false" propagate="true"/>
            <String value="NetFile Java1" advanced="false"
merge="replace" lock="false" propagate="true"/>
            <String value="NetFile Java2" advanced="false"
merge="replace" lock="false" propagate="true"/>
        </Collection>
        <String name="title" value="My Applications" advanced=
"false" merge="replace" lock="false" propagate="true"/>
        </Properties>
    </Channel>
```

If the channel is edited using channel and container management in the Admin Console, it is not as obvious that targets and user applications are actually collections. The string values in both collections must match for the link to be displayed in the channel content.

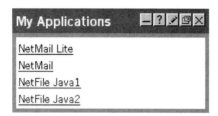

FIGURE 3-5   App Channel Containing NetFile Launching Links

FIGURE 3-5 shows what the links look like on the default portal server desktop inside of the App channel. The properties are not locked, so end users can remove them if they wish. To lock them, simply edit the display profile, and set lock to true on the bolded items in shown in CODE EXAMPLE 3-1. Locking the entire collection has the same effect, but in addition to not being able to remove the NetFile links, end users cannot add any of their own.

Tuning the NetFile Service

Unless there is a specific reason to modify the NetFile attributes at the user level or role level, it is better from an administrative perspective to modify them at the organization or service level and propagate the changes using the Identity Server's template conflict resolution feature. At the organization level, the conflict resolution should be set at its highest level. If a service template exists for NetFile at the role level, set its conflict resolution to the lowest level, or delete the template. At the user level, you may have to select one of the drop-down menus and choose Inherit, then Save, in order for the service attribute values to be reflected accurately in the Admin Console. Be sure to return to the service view of the organization when modifying NetFile attribute values to propagate the attributes changes to all NetFile users in that organization.

Note – For information about modifying the static NetFile attributes, refer to the product documentation. For information regarding the SMB client location, see "Working With SMB Shares" on page 147.

The following changes are performed at the organization level in the Admin Console.

One dynamic attribute that can be changed is the NetFile interface window dimensions (FIGURE 3-6). By default, a size of 700x400 is selected, and this setting works reasonably well across a wide variety of platforms and screen resolutions. You can reduce the size if you expect the file listings to be relatively small, with a minimal number of subdirectories that need to be expanded. The starting location for the window can also be modified by changing the x/y coordinates for the upper left corner of the NetFile UI. Be sure to use integer values in these fields and not JavaScript.

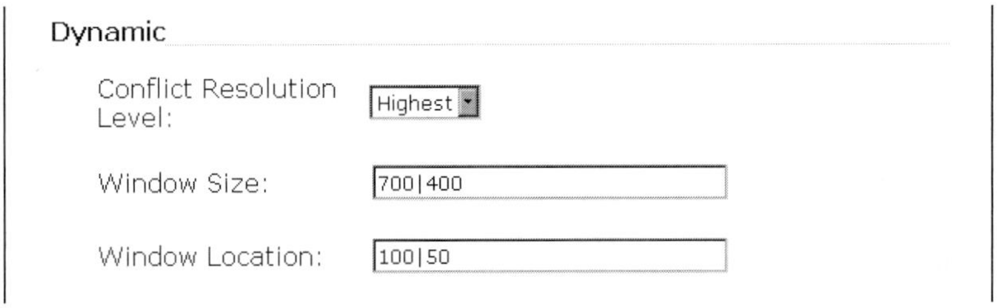

FIGURE 3-6   Window Size and Window Location Fields

The four checkboxes for the host types (FIGURE 3-7) should remain unchecked unless the host type is going to be explicitly allowed. This prevents auto-detection from choosing a host type that may not be appropriately configured on the portal node, or one that is not being supported in the portal deployment.

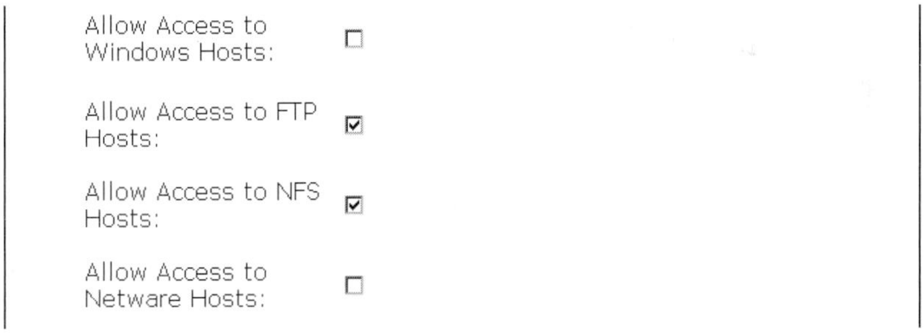

FIGURE 3-7   Host Type Checkboxes

The Common Hosts field (FIGURE 3-8) should remain empty unless otherwise required by the specific deployment scenario. See "Prepopulating Hosts and Shares" on page 144 and the deployment scenario titled "Deploying NetFile for Use in Business-to-Business Environments" on page 154.

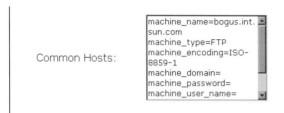

Common Hosts:

```
machine_name=bogus.int.
sun.com
machine_type=FTP
machine_encoding=ISO-
8859-1
machine_domain=
machine_password=
machine_user_name=
```

FIGURE 3-8   Common Hosts Field

The Allowed Hosts and Denied Hosts fields (FIGURE 3-9) are each used to define an access list of allowable hosts for end users to use through the NetFile interface. By default, all hosts are allowed. Depending on the security requirements of your NetFile deployment, specific hosts can be either denied or allowed. For trusted users such as internal employees, the default may suffice, while other deployment scenarios may dictate greater control over what hosts can be accessed using NetFile. Removing the default asterisk (*) from the allow list results in all hosts being disallowed. Adding a single host to the allow field allows that host and denies all others. Avoid the mistake of adding an asterisk (*) to the deny field because all hosts, including those listed in the allow field, will be denied access. Be sure to only add hosts in the allow field that can be accessed by the portal server node itself. Otherwise, users will get connection failures when trying to add or access the host of their choice.

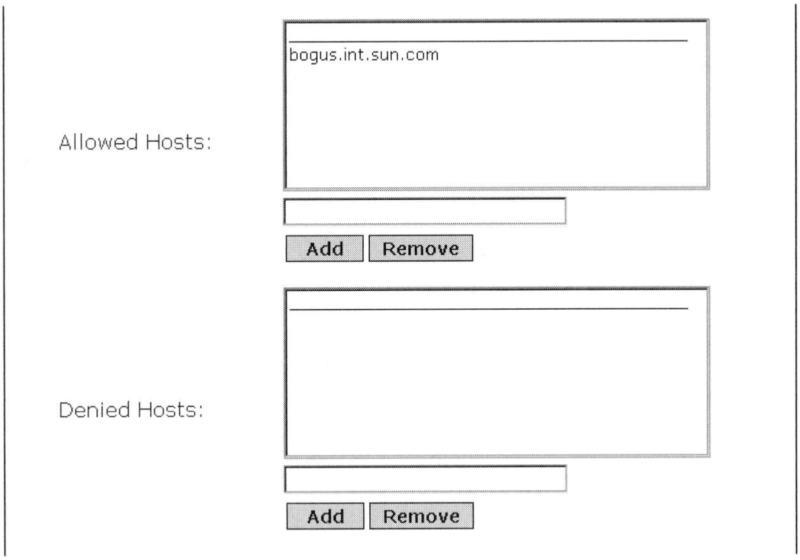

FIGURE 3-9 Allowed Hosts and Denied Hosts Fields

The file modification checkboxes (FIGURE 3-10) that include file deletion, renaming, changing the (UID), and changing of windows domains should be configured according to the security policy put into place for the portal deployment. If NetFile will be used by remote access service (RAS) employees, then file deletion and renaming capabilities are important. Changing the UID is useful when FTP servers might have different kinds of login accounts, and in cases where end users want to have differing host types visible and usable in a single NetFile interface. Changing the windows domain may be necessary where there is a complex windows networking environment on the back end that remote users already understand and need access to.

FIGURE 3-10 File Modification Checkboxes

The File Upload Limit (FIGURE 3-11) is a very important administrative setting and it must be sized according to approximated usage. There are two aspects of the file size limit. The first is that NetFile should not be used to transfer large files in the range of 50 Mbytes or greater. Netlet FTP is a much better solution for these kinds of workhorse transfers because Netlet FTP uses the FTP protocol and no interim temporary directory is used. The second aspect of sizing this limit has to do with the expected number of concurrent users, average file size, and the disk partition size where the organization's Temporary Directory Location (a static NetFile service attribute) resides. For example, with a hundred concurrent users averaging 100-Kbyte file transfers, a theoretical maximum might be 5 Mbytes or even less. The dedicated partition size can be about three times the concurrent user count times the average file size, or about 30 Mbytes, in this simple example. If disk space is not an issue, this number can be increased to three times the maximum file size times the average concurrency (or the highest load, if necessary) to guarantee adequate file space needed by NetFile to perform file transfers. The Temporary Directory Location should not be on the root (/) partition.

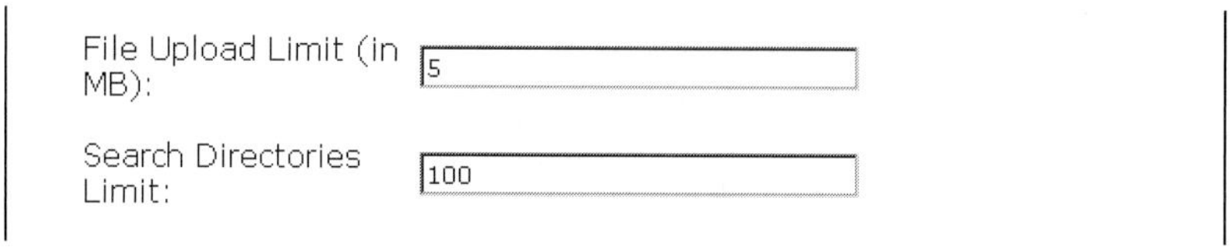

File Upload Limit (in MB): `5`

Search Directories Limit: `100`

FIGURE 3-11 File Upload Limit and Search Directories Limit Fields

The Default DNS Domain and Windows Domain/Workgroup settings (FIGURE 3-12) can be specified at the organization level so that end users do not have to include this information when adding hosts and shares to the NetFile user interface unless they differ from the default.

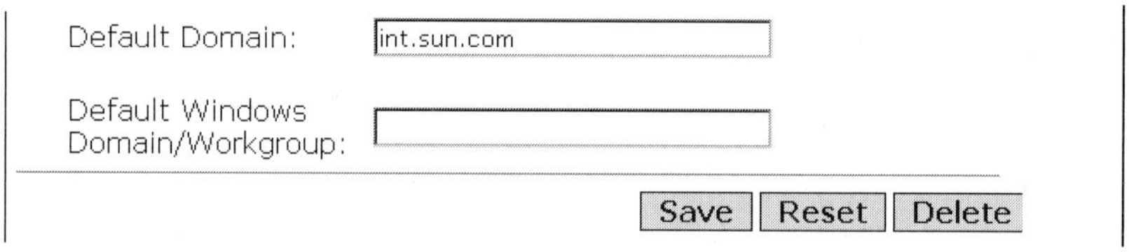

Default Domain: `int.sun.com`

Default Windows Domain/Workgroup:

[Save] [Reset] [Delete]

FIGURE 3-12 Default Domain and Default Windows Domain/Workgroup Fields

End-User Tasks

Once the NetFile service is configured for use, configuring hosts and shares as an individual is straightforward. Begin by launching the appropriate interface (Java 1 or 2) from the App channel after logging in to the portal server desktop. If you have a Sun Java plug-in installed, enable it for the browser you are using, then launch the Java 2 interface from the App channel on the portal server desktop.

Note – When using Microsoft Windows, the Java plug-in can be enabled by going to the Control Panel and selecting the installed Java plug-in. More recent versions of the plug-in enable you to specify a particular browser for which the plug-in works (FIGURE 3-13). When the plug-in control panel loads, be sure that Enable Java plug-in is checked, and that the browser you plan to use is also selected.

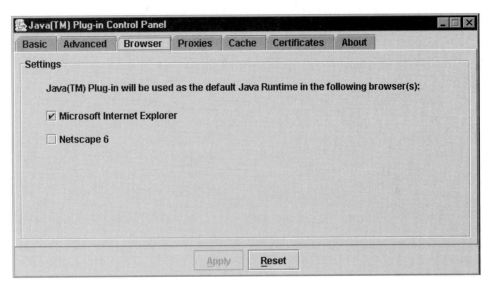

FIGURE 3-13 Example Java Plug-in Control Panel

The Java plug-in should be backward compatible with the Java 1 NetFile UI, but it is better not to go back and forth between the two NetFile UIs or get used to an older version that might be deprecated in the near future once the Java 2 VM becomes more ubiquitous. If a newer NetFile UI is chosen than what the browser JVM supports, a NetFile pop-up window indicates that the browser is not supported with the NetFile Java 2 applet.

Once the NetFile interface loads, the left panel contains a house icon labeled Network Neighborhood. If the administrator has assigned any prepopulated hosts and shares, the key next to Network Neighborhood is expanded and the hosts and shares are also displayed in the same pane. The product documentation explains in detail how to add and configure hosts and shares.

Although the NetFile Java 2 interface is much cleaner than its predecessor, it does lack right mouse-driven action menus, drag and drop, and the MIME type file icons that appear in many content shelves of Active X applications and in third-party FTP software. None of these shortcomings greatly impair the usability of NetFile itself, but they make it seem a bit unfamiliar when compared to most popular file management applications.

One thing to keep in mind when adding shares for the first time is that the entire interface runs faster the more specific the share names are. For example, in a network environment, you would not want to add a share such as /home that might contain a large number of mounted user home directories. Instead, adding a more specific share such as /home/uid/downloads is a better practice. Avoid anything with a huge folder tree that would be displayed on the left pane.

This same approach should be used when establishing a search base for file searches. It's worth the reduced wait to be a bit more specific in search scope. There are no search indexes maintained for the shares, so the files are located by applying a brute force algorithm limited only by the administratively governed search directories limit (maximum folder count) that can be set through the Identity Server Admin Console.

End users might be confused by the message they receive in the event that the maximum folder count value is exceeded:

Search is Complete. There are no results to display.

The only way to tell whether this message was received because the file was not present, or because the maximum folder count was exceeded, is to look at the srapNetFile debug log. By following the same thread ID through the log, you can see that it eventually reaches the limit set by the administrator. The limit is 100 by default, so a snippet from the log might look like the following:

```
    .
    .
    .
03/04/2004 02:25:31:273 AM PST: Thread[Thread-490,5,main]
Directory number being searched = 101
03/04/2004 02:25:31:277 AM PST: Thread[Thread-490,5,main]
Search over
```

This is another reason why the search base should be set to something reasonably specific. Starting at the root of a file system, for instance, might take a very long time, and is almost guaranteed to hit the directory limit, even if the maximum folder count has been moderately increased.

Selecting Appropriate Host Types

Auto-detect is a handy feature when the actual method for transfer is not an issue. Otherwise, the host type should be explicitly set from the drop-down menu when adding new hosts.

The FTP type and Netware type require no additional intervention by either the end user or the administrator.

Note – There are some restrictions on specific versions of the Novell product that work as a result of the syntactical irregularities in the command responses from one version of Netware to another. Netware 4 and 5 have been tested with the portal server 6.x software, but you should refer to the portal product documentation to be sure that the version of Netware you are using is compatible.

The FTP host type works with most WU-FTP compliant FTP servers. There is some difference between the command responses on individual FTP servers, but Microsoft FTP and Solaris FTP have both been tested and are certified for use with all currently shipping versions of portal server SRA software. To use NFS or SMB hosts, refer to "Working With NFS Shares" on page 145 and "Working With SMB Shares" on page 147.

Server-Side File Manipulations

A rudimentary set of server-side file manipulations can be performed using NetFile. While fairly basic, these manipulations, including rename, delete, and compress, are quite handy because these functions would otherwise need to be done from a terminal or on the local machine itself. The ability to email files stored on remote systems means that the files never have to be downloaded to an intermediate machine from which to be emailed. This is particularly useful if the intermediate machine is an Internet kiosk or some other similarly untrusted machine where sensitive information could be accidentally exposed when the user leaves the system.

Opening and Downloading Files

One or more selected files can be downloaded or opened by selecting the associated action button from the menu bar. To select noncontiguous files, use the Ctrl key simultaneously with the mouse selection. Downloading files brings up a Save As dialog box and enables you to place the file wherever you like on the local file system. Selecting to open a file or double-clicking on the file enables the Web browser to open the file using the appropriate helper application, if applicable, for the MIME type of the remote file. To use the bundled Web server MIME types, be sure that the NetFile service attribute value corresponding to the MIME-types Configuration File Location in the NetFile service configuration is pointing to the appropriate location. To use another MIME-types file, change the directory location to point to the nondefault file location on the portal node. This file is used to determine the appropriate Content-Type HTTP header to return to the Web browser so it can determine the most likely candidate needed to display the file.

Note – NetFile does not perform any virus screening on uploaded or downloaded files. For file systems that are particularly susceptible to viruses, it is the responsibility of the administrator or end user to make sure the files are clean.

Prepopulating Hosts and Shares

Prepopulating hosts and shares is a useful way for administrators to define a set of machines and directories that end users can automatically access. These prepopulated hosts and shares are configured in portal server 6 by modifying the Common Hosts attribute value of the NetFile service. A single host can be specified using the `machine_name` keyword, followed by any number of additional supporting key values. The keys and values that can be included in the Common Hosts field are explained in detail in the *Sun ONE Portal SRA Administrator Guide*. Not all of the fields must be included per prepopulated host.

There may be a security policy in place that prevents the prepopulating of passwords. This limits the ability to prepopulate NFS shares unless end users know the root password of the machine they are attempting to access. The password list is not exposed to end users, but depending on how the Identity Server has been configured, delegated administrators may have permission to view the Common Hosts list. The following is an example of what a Common Host list value might look like:

```
machine_name=ftp.int.sun.com
machine_type=FTP
machine_user_name=anonymous
share_name=/downloads
share_password=email@sun.com
machine_name=win-host.int.sun.com
machine_type=WIN
machine_user_name=Administrator
share_name=address
share_password=mypassword
```

This example prepopulates two shares of different types, on two separate hosts. The `share_password` value can be removed to force the end user to enter the appropriate password.

When a user belonging to this organization logs in to NetFile, both of these hosts are automatically added to the Network Neighborhood, and the hosts are expanded to include the shares. It is a good idea to put the most frequently used share first because the first share is automatically selected once NetFile completes loading, as shown in FIGURE 3-14.

FIGURE 3-14 Left Panel Displaying Prepopulated Hosts

Deployment Scenarios

There are a variety of scenarios in which the NetFile component can be useful in a secure portal deployment. This section includes some of the trickier deployment scenarios, in addition to a walkthrough of one example explaining how to deploy NetFile in a business-to-business environment.

Working With NFS Shares

Before configuring NetFile to work with NFS shares, you must first enable and configure UNIX authentication. In Sun ONE Portal Server 6.1 software, this is done through the Identity Server Administration Console following the steps below.

▼ To Enable and Configure UNIX Authentication

1. **Log in to the Administration Console.**

2. **Select View: Services in the left pane of the Identity Management tab.**

   This assumes that an organization has already been selected.

3. **Register the service, if necessary.**

   If UNIX displays in the right pane, it means that UNIX authentication service is not registered. To register it, select the checkbox to the left of the UNIX, and select Register.

4. **Create the service template.**

   Once the service is registered, it is displayed in the left pane. Select the expansion arrow, and choose Create in the right panel to create the template.

5. **Select Save.**

6. **Log out of the Administration console.**

7. **Restart the Identity Server.**

   As `root`, or as the user that the Identity Server is configured to run as, type:

   ```
   # /etc/init.d/amserver startall
   ```

8. **Verify that the** `doUnix` **process is running.**

   ```
   # ps -ef | grep doUnix
       root  5348    1  0 18:31:35 ?        0:00 /opt/SUNWam/bin/doUnix
   -c 58946
   ```

9. **Configure UNIX Authentication.**

   Connect to the UNIX helper from the command line as `root`, and configure the options.

   ```
   # telnet localhost 58946
   Trying 127.0.0.1...
   Connected to localhost.
   Escape character is '^]'.
   Enter Unix Helper Listen Port [57946]:
   Enter Unix Helper Session Timeout [3]:
   Enter Unix Helper Max Sessions [5]:
   get_config_info: doUnix configured successfully
   Connection closed by foreign host.
   ```

10. **Create a common host share for NFS, or allow users to create their own shares.**

   Note – Because of limitations in WebNFS, the share must be mounted as `root`.

   The `root` password must be known to connect to an NFS mount, so it is most likely that an NFS server would be prepopulated, and would only have read-access mounts to prevent end users from uploading files as `root`. Also, it is a good idea not to create an NFS mount from the root directory of the NFS server, but rather to specify something less harmful such as `/export`. Users would have shared level access control, so NFS mounts should only be used for read-only purposes (downloads), unless NetFile is being used by remote access employees who wish to add NFS mounts to their own personal machines, or administrators who require an additional level of access.

Working With SMB Shares

Server Message Block (SMB) is commonly used with many Windows OS versions for user-level access to remote file systems. Samba is an open source program that opens the proprietary SMB protocol for UNIX and UNIX-like clients such as Linux. By using Samba's `smbclient` program, NetFile can interact with Windows file systems, while at the same time provide the common look and feel NetFile extends to other file system types. The next section details how to set up and deploy WIN share types with NetFile following best practice guidelines.

Note – The use of the `smbclient` in portal server 6.2 for NetFile interoperability with Windows file systems has been replaced with support for using Java Common Internet File System (jCIFS). jCIFS is the underlying protocol used by networked Windows file systems. jCIFS proves to be advantages to NetFile in several ways. First, it eliminates the need to fork off individual `smbclient` processes for each request. This eliminates the need for temporary files for NetFile subcommands including open, download, compress, mail, and upload. Also, jCIFS extends native Java calls at the protocol level, eliminating the need to parse responses from the `smbclient` command executions.

Configuring the Portal to Allow the Addition of WIN Share Types in Portal Server 6.0 and 6.1

Samba is used by the portal server for accessing SMB shares on Windows file systems. You must install Samba on the portal server node prior to adding WIN share types. After running `pssetup` from the portal third-party product distribution, Samba is installed in the default location of `/usr/sfw/bin`.

▼ To Install the Samba Client on the Portal Server Node

1. **Run** `pssetup` **from the third-party product distribution.**

```
# ./pssetup
****************************************************************
****
@PRODUCTNAME@ (@PRODUCTVERSION@)
****************************************************************
****

Log at /var/sadm/install/logs/pssetup.install.6710/setup.log

This product will run without a license. However, you must either
purchase a
Binary Code License from, or accept the terms of a Binary Software
Evaluation
license with, Sun Microsystems, to legally use this product.
Do you accept? yes/[no] yes
```

2. **After accepting the license, select the option to install the Samba client.**

```
Install options:
1) Install Samba Client
2) Exit
Choice? [2] 1

Patch 108827-15 is required.
One or more required patches may be missing from your system.
Please refer
to the Release Notes for more information regarding patches.
Abort setup? [y]/n n

Samba Client installation summary
---------------------------------
Base Directory: /usr/sfw/bin

Installing Samba Client...

Installation took .06 minute.

All available components have been installed.
Setup complete.
```

Note – The Portal Installer does not check if a patch has been made obsolete by a later patch with a different patch base. If you have installed an additional patch which lists 108827-15 or later in the patch obsolescence list, you do not need to worry that the specific patch mentioned is missing from your system as noted in the preceding screen output. Up-to-date patch information is available from the SunSolve Web site.

Once Samba is installed, the Identity Server must be configured to make use of it. The first change needs to be done at either the organization or service level for NetFile.

▼ **To Specify the SMB Client Location at the Organization Level in Portal Server 6.1**

1. **Log in to the Identity Server Admin Console.**

2. **Select View: Services.**

3. **Select the link next to NetFile.**

4. **If a service template has not been created for NetFile, select Create.**

5. **Add** /usr/sfw/bin **to the SMB Client Location field.**

6. **Select Save.**

7. **Log out of the Admin Console.**

8. **Restart the Identity Server.**

9. **Specify the** smbclient **location.**

At this point, if you attempt to add a WIN share, users will likely see an error indicating that the smbclient cannot be found. While accurate, the message is a bit misleading, since you have already modified the SMB Client Location to point to the appropriate place. If debug logging is enabled, you may also see something like this

```
Add System win-client.int.sun.com
Domain name is
Request to add system of type WIN
Char Set to be used is ISO-8859-1
11/12/2003 05:08:33:697 PM PST: Thread[Thread-388,5,main]
All hosts are allowed
11/12/2003 05:08:33:699 PM PST: Thread[Thread-388,5,main]
smbclient not found at /smbclient
```

This problem must be resolved before SMB/WIN shares can be added to the NetFile Interface. The first approach works around the problem by creating a a symbolic link from the file system root to the smbclient binary, and to the smb.conf file if one exists. This enables WIN hosts to be added and accessed, but it does not do anything to reduce the exceptions thrown, and growth of the debug logs, as a result of not being able to read the default organization attributes.

You can do this using one of the following procedures:

- (Workaround) "To Perform a Workaround so WIN Shares Can Be Added" on page 151

- (Fix) "To Assign a Single User to the NetFile Role" on page 151

- (Another fix) "To Assign Multiple Users Simultaneously to the NetFile Role" on page 151

▼ To Perform a Workaround so WIN Shares Can Be Added

This approach should only be used as a temporary workaround. The appropriate change should be made at the user level, by assigning users granted NetFile execution permissions to the NetFile role. For individual users, this can be done in portal server 6.1 as described in the next two sections.

● **Create a symbolic link from the root of the file system.**

```
# cd /
# ln -s /usr/sfw/bin/smbclient smbclient
# ln -s /etc/sfw/smb.conf smb.conf
```

▼ To Assign a Single User to the NetFile Role

1. **Log in to the Identity Server Admin Console.**

2. **Select View: Users.**

3. **Select the link next to the user you wish to add to the role.**

4. **In the right panel, select View: Roles.**

5. **From the list of roles that appears, put a checkmark in the box next to NetFile User Role.**

6. **Select Save.**

▼ To Assign Multiple Users Simultaneously to the NetFile Role

1. **Log in to the Identity Server Admin Console.**

2. **Select View: Roles.**

3. **Select the link next to the NetFile User Role.**

4. **In the right pane, select View: Users.**

5. **Select Add.**

6. **Enter an asterisk (*) in the UserID field and select Filter.**

7. **Put a checkmark next to all of the users that have already been allowed to execute the NetFile service.**

8. **Select Submit.**

Specifying an `smb.conf` File

An `smb.conf` file is not required to add WIN-type shares to NetFile. It is frequently used by administrators who are already using Samba. For a portal server to pass the `smb.conf` file to `smbclient` when it is called, the `smb.conf` file must be stored in the same directory as the `smbclient` binary. This must also be the same location that was specified in the SMB Client location field.

When creating a `smb.conf` file (or when using a version of the `smbclient` not shipped with the portal product), be careful to only use flags or options that are not compatible with the version of `smbclient` included on the portal server third-party product distribution. Additionally, the NetFile host access list provided in portal server 6.0 and 6.1 versions takes precedence over the logical equivalents that might be specified in the `smb.conf` file. It is important to note that in portal server 6.0 and 6.1, the access lists are enforced in the opposite manner of Samba. So moving an entry with a value of *ALL* from the hosts deny field of the *global* section of the `smb.conf` file to the equivalent value in NetFile (*) results in no hosts being allowed. The difference between the two policy enforcements is that Samba continues to allow any servers in the hosts allow field, while portal denies even those hosts. The behavior is similar in portal, if there isn't an * in the deny list. In that case, the host is denied unless explicitly allowed.

Note – In portal server 6.0 and 6.1, the host access entries in the `smb.conf` file are ignored in favor of the access lists specified in the NetFile.

If you have a requirement to run `smbd` on the same machine as the portal server, two different `smb.conf` files should be used so that the full feature set of the global section of the file is available to the SMB server without negatively affecting NetFile. Be aware that NetFile clients would be unable to connect to a Samba server running on the portal node because of security restrictions imposed by NetFile. To verify that `smbclient` is working before adding a WIN-type share, try accessing it from the command line. This works even before you have created an `smb.conf` file.

Consider the following example, given a Windows NT domain of WORKGROUP, a machine named win-client that has an IP address of 10.10.10.220, and the connection made using the Administration login.

```
# /usr/sfw/bin/smbclient //win-client/address -I 10.10.10.220 -W
workgroup -U Administrator%password
load_client_codepage: filename
/usr/sfw/lib/codepages/codepage.850 does not exist.
load_unicode_map: filename /usr/sfw/lib/codepages/unicode_map.850
does not exist.
added interface ip=10.1.1.1 bcast=10.10.10.255 nmask=
255.255.255.0
Domain=[WORKGROUP] OS=[Windows NT 4.0] Server=[NT LAN Manager 4.0]
smb: \>
```

Once you see the smb prompt you can navigate and transfer files using FTP-like command syntax. Using the smbmount command (an additional command available with the full Samba suite), a Windows file system can be permanently mounted to a Samba server (not running on the portal server node) and then exported as an FTP directory to work around some of the NetFile WIN-type share complexity.

Note – The unicode map warning goes away if you download the entire Samba suite and run make_unicodemap. This might be done by default on other precompiled Samba distributions.

The smb.conf file used by smbclient does not need a great deal of information in it. One thing frequently added to the smb.conf file for smbclient is the IP address of the WINS server hosting shares that end users will be accessing, so that end users do not have to fully qualify their host names when adding WIN-type shares. For example, if the following smb.conf file is used:

```
[global]
wins server = 10.10.10.220
```

10.10.10.220 happens to be the IP address of win-client in the previous example, so the host can be added to the NetFile interface without including the fully qualified domain name, as seen in FIGURE 3-15. Similarly, smbclient can be used from the command line without requiring the -I flag because it reads the smb.conf file entry.

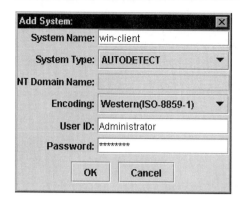

FIGURE 3-15 Adding a Host Without a Fully Qualified DNS Address

Depending on how the shares are configured on the Windows hosts, directories might or might not be readable, writable, and browsable by remote users. When connecting through NetFile using Samba, an explicit share need not be defined because all of the available shares on that particular host are listed automatically once the host has been added to the NetFile interface.

Deploying NetFile for Use in Business-to-Business Environments

While there are many possibilities as to how NetFile can be deployed, this deployment example covers aspects of one particular deployment, a business-to-business portal between an insurance company and medical professionals. This is a fictitious example, but it details many aspects of ensuring that patient data remains secure while staying flexible enough so that doctors from anywhere are able to quickly figure out how to use the system.

This deployment requires that remote access doctors be able to securely upload patient data to the insurance company for proof of treatment to secure payment for services provided. While all kinds of bells and whistles can be thrown in to make this deployment more realistic and user friendly, this example keeps things simple.

The first consideration is the authentication method. In this example, there is already an NIS server, and the remote server is already configured for UNIX authentication. The remote server can be configured to use the same LDAP user entries as portal server for authentication so that the doctors don't have to remember two user names and passwords. But there is no easy way to propagate this information in the common host data, and we do not want to store the users' passwords in the clear along with the rest of the data. Assuming that each doctor has a UNIX user name and password, the portal can be configured to use UNIX authentication.

This deployment begins by creating an organization that includes all of the doctors. SRA does not support self registration out-of-box, so the doctors must receive their user names and an initial password through email or some other mechanism. The doctors can change their password the first time they log in by creating an additional authentication method that checks if it is the first time they are logging in.

When creating the new organization, do not make it active until it has been completely configured. Once the organization is created (from the View: Organizations panel), select the organization name (not the link next to it). Some basic services now need to be added to the organization.

The following steps assume that portal server version 6.1 software is installed. Refer to the specific product documentation for exact steps for the version you are using.

▼ To Add Required Services

1. **Select View: Services in the left panel of the administration window.**

2. **Select Register and place a checkmark next to the following services in the right pane:**

   - Core (located under Authentication)
   - UNIX (located under Authentication)
   - Policy Configuration (located under Authentication)
   - Desktop (located under Portal Server Configuration)
   - Access List (located under SRAP Configuration)
   - NetFile (also located under SRAP Configuration)

   FIGURE 3-16 shows what the services look like.

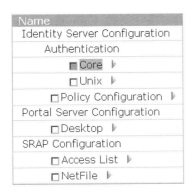

FIGURE 3-16 Registered Services for the New Organization

3. **Select Register from the right pane.**

4. **Create a service template at the organization level for each of the services:**

a. Select the link to the right of the service name.

b. Select Create in the right pane.

c. Select Save each time a service template is created.

Note – When the policy configuration service template is created, be sure to fill in the LDAP bind password.

---

5. Follow the guidelines for enabling and configuring UNIX authentication in the NFS deployment scenario section.

▼ To Make UNIX Authentication Available to Users in the New Organization

There are a few additional administrative tasks that need to be performed. These changes are made to the core authentication service for the organization.

1. From the left side of the organization panel, select View: Services.

2. Select the link to the right of Core under the Authentication heading.

3. From the right pane, deselect LDAP from the Authentication list, and select UNIX instead.

4. Change the User Profile to indicate Dynamically Created or Required.

Required is a bit more secure because it means that the portal administrator must create the users, rather than assuming every user with a UNIX account can log in to the portal server. If you select Dynamically Created, then as soon as a user successfully authenticates, a user profile is created.

5. Select the Edit link next to Organization Authentication Configuration.

6. In the new window, select the checkbox next to LDAP, then select Delete.

7. Select Add.

8. Choose the module name as UNIX, and Flag as REQUIRED.

9. Select OK.

This redirects to the appropriate authentication page from the Gateway using the organization in the URL. For example, the login URL might look like `https://gateway.sun.com/Insurance`, where `Insurance` is the name of the new organization.

10. **Change the Default Success Login URL to something containing the Portal DEPLOY_URI value.**

By default, this looks something like (where `/portal` is the `DEPLOY_URI`):

`%protocol://%host:%port/portal/dt`

11. **Select Save.**

▼ To Create a New Top-Level Referral Policy

The policies defined at the top level of the directory must be configured to be inherited by the new organization. This is done by creating a new top-level referral policy. For more information about creating policies and referrals, refer to the Identity Server product documentation. Briefly, the necessary policies can be added as follows:

1. **From the top-level directory view, select View: Policies.**

2. **Select New.**

3. **Choose Referral as the Policy Type, and pick an appropriate name like** `patientRecordReferral`.

4. **Select Save.**

5. **Enter a useful description and select Save.**

6. **Select View: Rules from the left pane.**

7. **Select Access list from the list and choose Next.**

8. **Choose a rule name that follows some kind of intelligent naming convention (such as** `patientAccessList`**)**

The final rules look something like what you see in FIGURE 3-17.

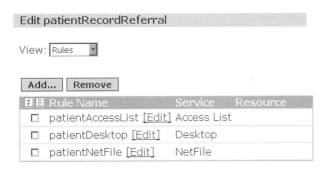

FIGURE 3-17 Rules Added to the New Referral Policy

9. **Select Save.**

10. **Continue to add rules for the Desktop and NetFile services in the same way.**

    Be sure to select Save for each rule created.

11. **Select Save again.**

12. **Select View: Referrals.**

13. **Select Add.**

14. **Select a name for the Referral and be sure that the organization name is selected in the Value field.**

15. **Select Save, and Save again.**

▼ To Modify the Portal Server Desktop

With the referral policy in place, new users created in the Organization have the necessary policies to perform portal and SRA-specific tasks. Because a very simple portal server desktop is needed with nothing more than a branded page with a NetFile launching link, the Desktop service can be modified as described in this procedure.

1. **Select the link next to Desktop under the Portal Server Configuration heading in the left panel of the Admin Console.**

2. **Change the default channel name field from JSPTabContainer to JSPTableContainer.**

    This simplifies the configuration of the portal server desktop substantially by removing tabs from the interface.

3. **Change the desktop type from** *default* **to something like** *patient_records.*

4. **Select Save.**

5. **Select Channel and Container Management.**

6. **Select the JSPTableContainer link (not the Edit link).**

7. **Remove all unused Channels from the Available and visible list, leaving App and possibly UserInfo channels.**

8. **Select Save under Channel Management.**

9. **Select the __root container path from the top of the right pane.**

▼ To Create a New Desktop Type

The rest of the desktop service can be configured later, but first the desktop type `patient_records` must be created on the portal node. To create the `patient_records` desktop, perform these steps.

1. **Log in to the portal node as** `root` **or the user which the portal is running as.**

2. **Create the new desktop directory by typing:**

```
# cd /etc/opt/SUNWps/desktop
# mkdir patient_records
```

3. **Copy the necessary customizeable files to the new desktop directory.**

```
# cp -R ./default/JSPTableContainerProvider ./patient_records/
```

4. **Back up the files so that change control is easier.**

```
# cd patient_records/JSPTableContainerProvider
# mkdir bak
# for files in `ls | grep -v bak`
> do
> cp $files bak/$files.bak
> done
```

5. **Modify the** `header.jsp` **file in some way so that when it is tested, it will be obvious that the new desktop type is being used correctly.**

   To simplify things, I simply added a `TITLE` element after the opening `HEAD` tag so it would be immediately obvious that the customized JSP was being used. More customization can be done later.

▼ To Create a Test User

Now that the new desktop type is configured, a desktop test user can be created to make sure that the authentication and desktop are working correctly. If you have selected to dynamically create user profiles, it isn't necessary to create a test user in the portal because each user is automatically able to log in with their UNIX credentials. Each user must be added to the NetFile role, however.

1. **Select View: Users after selecting the appropriate organization name from the list.**

2. **Place checkmarks next to Access List, Desktop, and NetFile to assign the new user the appropriate services.**

3. Create a user ID like `inittest` and be sure that the user status is set to active.

4. Make sure the `inittest` user has an associated UNIX login on both the portal node and the FTP host.

   This should be the same user with the same UID rather than two local users with the same login name.

5. Log in to the new organization through the Gateway by specifying the organization in the URL path.

   For example, use the URL `http://gateway.sun.com/Insurance` where `Insurance` is the new organization name.

6. Verify that the portal server desktop shows up and includes the customization made to the `header.jsp` file.

   The portal server desktop should look like FIGURE 3-18:

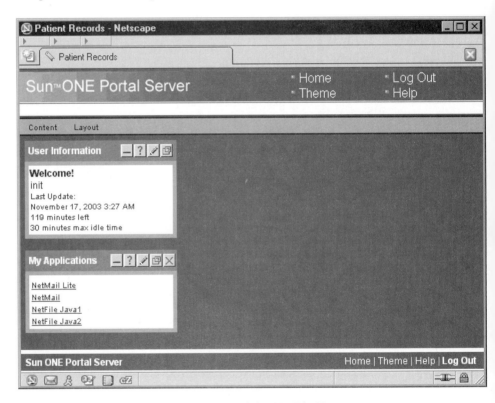

FIGURE 3-18 New Portal Server Desktop (6.1) for NetFile Users

▼ To Configure the NetFile Service

Notice that in FIGURE 3-18, both the browser tab and the window title indicate that the correct JSP is being used because it shows "Patient Records." With all of the groundwork laid out, the next thing to do is configure the NetFile service to suit the needs of the deployment scenario. From the organization view do the following:

1. **Select the link to the right of the NetFile Service.**

2. **In the right pane, change the temporary directory location to something other than** /tmp **(like** /export/tmp**). Change the ownership of** /export/tmp **to the portal user and be sure that it has file mode permissions set to 700.**

3. **Deselect all host types except for FTP.**

4. **Edit the common hosts field and add something similar to the following:**

```
machine_type=FTP
machine_encoding=ISO-8859-1
machine_domain=
machine_password=
machine_user_name=
share_name=/export/patient_records
share_password=
```

5. **Remove the asterisk (*) from allowed hosts.**

6. **Adjust the file upload limit as necessary to accommodate expected patient record file sizes.**

7. **Select Save.**

8. **Verify that the new common share is displayed automatically, as shown in** FIGURE 3-19.

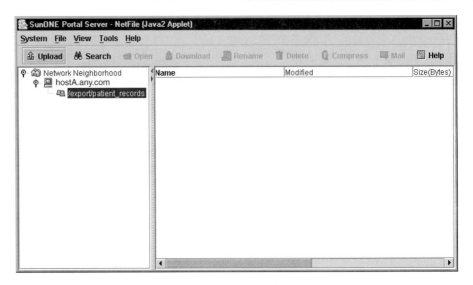

FIGURE 3-19 Prepopulated Host and Share

The end user must configure the host info and the share info with their own FTP user name and password. The authentication error to the FTP host can be ignored, and the limitation may be fixed in a later release of portal server 6.x.

▼ To Create a NetFile User Role for the Organization

The last thing that needs to be configured on the portal side is to create a NetFile user role and assign users in the organization that will be accessing NetFile.

1. **From the organization view in the left panel, select View: Roles.**

2. **Select New.**

3. **In the right panel, use the name NetFile User Role, and the Type as Service.**

4. **Select Create.**

5. **Select the link to the right of the NetFile User Role.**

6. **Select View: Users.**

7. **Add the users who will be accessing the NetFile service.**

Additional Deployment Considerations

From the portal server perspective, the basic configuration for this deployment scenario is complete. There are some additional steps that can be taken to further secure the environment. The first is to run SSL between the Gateway and the Server.

This prevents the snooping of traffic on the Gateway network interface in the DMZ. Also, because an internal server is exposed to the outside world, it is a good idea to limit (chroot) the FTP server user directories so that end users cannot move above the predetermined directory location. Doing this also prevents end users from overriding the prepopulated share by attempting to create one of their own on the same machine.

Logging

Both access and debug logging is provided by the NetFile component. The access log is provided at /var/opt/SUNWam/logs/srapNetFile.access, and the debug log, once enabled, is at /var/opt/SUNWam/debug/srapNetFile. To enable debug logging, change the value of com.iplanet.services.debug.level from error to message in the *install_dir*/SUNWam/lib/AMConfig.properties file, and restart the portal node using the amserver startall command.

Ten Tips From the Trenches

This section presents ten of the most frequent NetFile problems and offers tips for solving each one.

Problem: Searches return Not Found when users are positive that the file being searched for exists.

Tip: Start searches from the highest directory possible. Netfile uses a brute force approach to finding files in the directory hierarchy, so the search should be initiated from the most specific directory possible. The other reason for this is that the administrator may have put a limit on the number of subdirectories and files that can be searched. Instead of indicating the search limit was exceeded, a message saying the file was not found may be returned instead.

Problem: The portal server node cannot be added to the Netfile hosts list.

Tip: This limitation is mainly for security purposes because the NetFile process operates using different user permissions on these nodes than on the target host. Thus, the portal nodes are used only as jump points to target hosts and cannot themselves be targets. If remote access to the portal node is absolutely necessary, consider using FTP over a Netlet connection or Secure FTP (SFTP) instead.

Problem: When the Netfile link is selected from the portal desktop, a huge pop-up window appears.

Tip: Unlike the Netlet Application that has logic to keep the window size in check, NetFile opens using the default window size of the browser. First try changing the NetFile window size attributes through the Identity Server console. If that fails, remove NetFile from the Application channel through the Admin Console, and then add a link above the apps tag in the application provider template file called /etc/opt/SUNWps/desktop/*desktop_name*/App/display.template. The added link looks similar to the following:

```
<TABLE CELLPADDING=1 CELLSPACING=0 WIDTH="100%"><TR><TD><FONT
FACE="Sans-serif" SIZE="+0"><TR><TD BGCOLOR="#FFFFFF"><FONT FACE=
"Sans-serif" SIZE="-1"><A HREF="javascript:" onClick="javascript:
window.open('/portal/NetFileApplet?Refer=java2', 'NetFile_Java2',
'width=320, height=170')";>NetFile
Java2</A><BR></FONT></TD></TR></TABLE>
[tag:apps]
```

Problem: NetFile search hangs or takes an extremely long time.

Tip: Recommended to users that they use NetFile search as a last resort. As mentioned earlier in this tips section, its brute force search method makes Netlet less than ideal for searching through huge amounts of files and directories. Consider using the UNIX `find` command with a Telnet Netlet rule for more savvy users, or a predefined search index for shared file systems.

Problem: The root partition of the portal server is getting close to full or has become full and caused the system to panic.

Tip: Size the temporary directory that Netfile uses on the portal nodes appropriately. This temporary location should not be mounted on the root partition, and it should be sized according to expected download sizes and concurrency. Some sizing suggestions are made in the preceding sections.

Problem: Users are not able to access shares created using the NetFile Java 1 UI when using the NetFile Java 2 UI.

Tip: Don't go back and forth between NetFile user interfaces. The Java 1 interface in NetFile should be used for legacy purposes only. If there is not a specific need for it, then it is recommended that it be removed from the list of applications in the applications channel. This will prevent any problems caused by interchanging the two interfaces.

Problem: End users can override admin-created hosts and shares.

Tip: The product was originally designed to allow this activity to occur. Certain situations may mandate that users not be able to modify prepopulated hosts and shares. Currently, the best way to do this is to modify the NetFile service attributes. First, modify the allow list to only include those machines listed in the prepopulated shares. Next, only select the machine types that are listed in the prepopulated shares. Finally, uncheck the Allow changing userID field. A future version of portal server may allow more flexibility with respect to the administration of prepopulated hosts and shares.

Problem: NFS clients cannot be added as NFS share types.

Tip: Do not try to add an NFS host type that is not configured as an NFS server. WebNFS is used to communicate directly with the NFS server to access its file system. An NFS client cannot be added as a NFS host type in NetFile. Instead, FTP should be used, and the NFS mount point can be added as a share instead of a host type.

Problem: WIN type shares cannot be added using a custom `smb.conf` file.

Tip: Avoid adding SMB server settings to the `smb.conf` file for portal server 6.0 and 6.1. Some `smb.conf` settings prevent WIN shares from being able to be added. In fact, there are very few `smb.conf` entries that are useful for the `smbclient` command, so you might consider just the bare minimum needed for the command to run properly. Additionally, most of the information supplied to the `smbclient` command is extracted from the directory store, so it need not be saved in two different places.

Problem: When the a NetFile session is restarted, unsaved session data is displayed.

Tip: When starting a new Netfile session, restarting the browser will prevent a cached applet from being used. If changes were made to the host and share data, but not saved prior to exiting or session timeout, these changes may appear to have been saved when Netfile is restarted. The reason for this is that the browser might choose to restart an applet rather than download it again, making it appear as though the changes were automatically written to the user profile.

New NetFile Technology in the Java Enterprise System

After undergoing a full rewrite in portal server 6.0, NetFile has made major strides. NetFile now includes minor usability enhancements, and additional administrative features that enable greater control over prepopulated hosts and shares. Additional character sets have also been added to support an even greater number of file system types and locales.

## CHAPTER 4

Rewriter: Secure Remote Access to Internal Web-Based Applications

This chapter discusses the Rewriter, one of the three primary technologies offered by the Sun's portal server SRA software—to enable integration with, and provisioning of, internal applications to authenticated end users securely over the Internet.

This chapter contains the following sections:

Note – In this book, the term *portal server* refers to Sun's portal server software with the SRA software unless specified otherwise. *Portal server node* and *portal platform node* refer to the portal server core product.

What is the Rewriter?

The Rewriter component of the portal server secure remote access software extends the notion of VPN-on-demand capability by allowing remote users to navigate and interact with internal Web pages as though they were accessing them from a local LAN connection.

Depending on the complexity of the Web content passing through the Gateway, rewriting can happen automatically, or through the creation of rules that tell the Gateway what content to rewrite. Rewriting involves the translation of URLs embedded in Web content and HTTP headers to control the destination of future browser requests. This is necessary for remote access users who only have one entry point to the Intranet— through the Gateway. The idea is similar to a VPN where all network traffic must come across the VPN server. However, unlike a VPN solution, URLs that are externally resolvable by the browser or content originating from external domains is not rewritten. In these cases, a direct connection can be established, thus reducing the Gateway as a bottleneck since internal proxies are no longer required to service unnecessary requests.

With the advent of broadband connectivity, more and more remote access users share the same connection for work and play. A VPN is not an ideal solution when thousands of users are not only checking their internal mail but also connecting to their online banking and bill paying, Yahoo stock quotes, and daily horoscope through the VPN server. With the portal Rewriter, only requests for the corporate email or other internal content go through the Gateway; the rest of the connections are established directly between the client's browser and the Internet servers. Since there is no direct TCP connection between the client and the corporate Intranet, the rewriter can even help prevent the spread of computer viruses and worms that may originate from an infected remote machine running Windows.

A more visible differentiating factor between the Rewriter and a traditional VPN is the lack of a client-side footprint. VPNs usually have some fat client software that must be preloaded onto a client machine before a VPN connection can be established. The lack of a footprint is advantageous for nomadic users connecting over a variety of networks and from devices such as Internet kiosks found at airport terminals. The Rewriter has even less client requirements than the Netlet because it is not dependent on the Java VM. Most JavaScript version 1.2-enabled browsers work without a problem. Some differences between how browsers handle content are discussed in the sections that follow.

Why Do I Need the Rewriter?

URL rewriting enables requests for internal URLs by authenticated remote users to be serviced by the Portal Gateway. The Gateway handles the requests on the browser's behalf, similar to a reverse proxy. By modifying the URLs as content passes back through the Gateway, URL rewriting indirectly tells the browser what proxy to use to fetch internal content by prepending the Gateway's address to the fully qualified original URLs before sending the data back to the end user. This approach can, among other things, be applied in a variety of deployment scenarios including corporate extranets, B2B relationships, and remote employee network access.

Here are ten additional reasons URL rewriting is successfully used by existing portal SRA deployments:

- Reason 1 – Field personnel and nomadic users might be unable to connect using a VPN. Most portals are designed as aggregate jump points to the most widely used applications and information, so users might require access from an array of devices such as SSL-enabled phones, PDAs, Internet Kiosks, wireless LANs, and satellite connections. VPN software might not be available for all of the devices, or security policies might already be in place that prevent a VPN from functioning correctly. In other cases, users may require access from public or client devices. For instance, consider the scenario where a remote systems engineer wants to demonstrate a software product to a business partner using the partner's systems, on which the software engineer's company VPN software is not installed. Instead, the engineer can log in to his company's portal and launch the demo from a link on his personal desktop or by specifying the internal URL in the Bookmark provider form field.

- Reason 2 – Creating reverse proxy mappings for all Intranet content is not feasible. Many companies have tried to implement secure remote access to all of their internal applications and content using a single secure reverse proxy. Sometimes this turns out to be an ideal solution for a single application like a Peoplesoft application where there isn't enough understanding about how the application works to warrant figuring out how to rewrite the content correctly. Some third-party applications, such as Peoplesoft may require domain expertise to make sure that all of the functionality is working properly due to the high level of complexity involved. Some advanced third-party application integrations through the Rewriter are discussed in Appendix A. However, trying to handle all of the possible URLs a remote user might want to retrieve quickly becomes overwhelming and a significant administrative burden. Additionally, a split DNS solution is usually required, the client browser must be configured to use a specific proxy for access to the application, or an automatic proxy configuration file must be used. Portal 6.2 provides a feature for obfuscating internal URLs so much of the same security gained from implementing a split DNS configuration to hide internal network information can also benefit secure portal deployments. For business-to-business applications where there might be a complex existing proxy infrastructure, or where the proxy settings are locked down on all of the browsers corporate wide, this is not feasible. Proxies might also reside on nonprivileged network ports that are not allowed direct access through strictly configured firewalls. Many applications and content are instantly accessible through the portal Gateway out-of-box. By following best practices outlined in this chapter, you will be able deploy the Rewriter component, thereby shifting a significant portion of the administrative burden to the software, where it should be.

- Reason 3 – You want to deploy your Web-based applications to the extranet or Internet. Web applications that do not contain complex dynamic content work easily through the Rewriter with little or no administrative effort. More complex applications like Outlook Web Access, Lotus iNotes, and SAP require additional administrative attention, integration solutions, or professional services help to work well through the Gateway. One of the purposes of this book is to provide information that makes deploying both existing Web applications and more complex applications through the portal a feasible solution.

- Reason 4 – You do not want any of your content servers or application servers to be deployed to the DMZ. This is probably one of the most underutilized features of the portal Rewriter. The secure portal recommended network topology architecture is designed for the Gateway to handle denial of service (DOS) attacks while your internal applications remain unaffected and secure. This is a key feature, and is often why the Rewriter is used by some customers only for secure remote access to their existing homegrown portal or other internal Web-based applications.

- Reason 5 – You do not want to extend your native network using specialized appliance devices which do not offer any identity management or granular access control. There are a handful of companies offering extranets in a box. These products are often compared side by side with the portal server secure remote access software, though their purpose is usually quite different. Often, extranet devices do not offer any additional access control, security, or identity management, that is afforded through the use of Sun's portal server.

- Reason 6 – You want to minimize the number of ports opened in your external firewall to allow remote access to applications. Most organizations maintain strict control over ports that can be opened in the external firewall to reduce the likelihood of successful port scanning and outside network attacks. SRA deployments typically have the Gateway running on port 443, so that Netlet traffic and other HTTPS traffic share the same port. Usually no additional ports are created in the firewall because SSL traffic is already allowed by the firewall filtering rules. If a DMZ is in place, the number of ports opened on the internal firewall for HTTPS requests redirected through the Gateway can be reduced by using portal proxies.

- Reason 7 – You want a method for remote users to connect to internal resources that is not browser dependent and does not require any client-side configuration changes. The Rewriter implements Web standards suggested by the World Wide Web Consortium (W3C) as industry standards. Using the Rewriter means that the user (or the IT department) can choose to use whatever browser works best for their purposes.

- Reason 8 – You want to deploy a business-to-business portal where only a specific subset of internal servers, services, and content can be accessed by business partners. Many companies do not want to open their entire internal network to outside partnering companies and typically create an isolated environment only accessible through authorized proxies or some other means of isolation. The Gateway component offers an access list feature where individual URLs, hosts, and domains can be allowed or denied so only selected content can be exposed and accessed by partners. This feature, in conjunction with the URL Rewriter, makes a subset of content available to authenticated business-to-business users from remote locations.

- Reason 9 – You do not want any data that is retrieved from the internal network to be cached on the client machine. This is a frequent request from companies wishing to allow access to their portal from a public resource such as an Internet kiosk, airport data terminal, or library computer. The Gateway can be configured to add appropriate "no-caching" HTTP (1.0/1.1) headers to responses containing the rewritten message bodies. This increases the load on the Gateway due to repeat requests, but it ensures that sensitive information is not inadvertently left on a shared, public system.

- Reason 10 – You do not want to require a client footprint to access internal information. Using the Rewriter requires no more than a standards-compliant Web browser that supports at least CSS1, JavaScript 1.2, and HTML 4. Any other browser requirements are determined only by your own internal content, not by the portal server product. For instance, if you are performing client-side XML transforms in some of your content, the browser would need to have an XML parser. The portal server Rewriter supports the rewriting of XML content, and the core portal server product ships with a simple Web services provider that performs some entry level SOAP handling.

How Does the Rewriter Work?

Whether content is rewritten at all is determined by the content type specified in the HTTP header of the server or the application servicing the client's initial request. The Gateway instance profile maintains a mapping of content types under the MIME mapping section that controls whether the Gateway will rewrite content of a given type.

Note – Portal server 6.0 requires the 6.0PC1 or later 6.0 patch consolidation patch in order to rewrite CSS syntax.

There is currently no mechanism in the Gateway to extend this list to arbitrary content types because specific parsing engines on the Gateway correspond to the default entries in the MIME mapping section. The out-of-box MIME mappings include text/html, text/htm, text/x-component, text/wml, text/vnd.wap.wml, application/x-javascript;text/javascript, text/vnd.wap.wmlscript, text/xml, and text/css. Additional entries cannot be added; only the existing ones can be removed, if desired.

Once the content type has been ascertained, the Gateway looks to see if the FQDN where the content originates is in the Proxies for Domains and SubDomains section of the profile for the Gateway instance handling the request on behalf of the client. If the entry is missing, the content is passed on as-is. If the entry is listed, the Gateway decides which ruleset to use to translate the content, as determined by the Domain-Based Rulesets section.

The Sun ONE Portal Server 6.0 software allows the left side of the Domain-Based Rulesets to specify a fully qualified host name, a domain including a subdomain, a domain, or a wildcard for general applicability. The most specific rule that applies to the content's origin is selected, regardless of the order in which the rules appear in the list. Once the Gateway knows what ruleset to use and what Rewriter engine to use, it proceeds top down through the content looking for URLs that the ruleset indicates require rewriting. This is determined by the individual rules in the ruleset itself. The ruleset itself is comprised of XML text defining the semantics of what a URL is and how to find it for the purpose of URL rewriting. Once a URL that matches a rule is encountered, the method used to rewrite it is determined by the URL type specified. For example, if a rule type is *EXPRESSION*, the URL will be rewritten at runtime by calling client-side JavaScript inserted into the document when it is initially rewritten.

EXPRESSION is the most generalized rule type, and it is best used in rulesets that generally apply to a multitude of content and applications. When the Gateway matches the expression, it determines if the URL is a raw URL— described later, but for now, a raw URL is a string that the Gateway can identify as one that represents a

URL. If, for example, the expression is matched in a JavaScript variable assignment, and the right-hand side (RHS) of the assignment is a string representing a fully qualified URL, that is considered a raw URL. In contrast, if the RHS is a string object variable, the expression is not considered a raw URL.

In the case of a raw URL, the Gateway first makes the URL fully qualified, if it is not already, and then prepends the Gateway's address to the result. If the expression is not a raw URL, the entire expression is wrapped in a function call (if the Content type is JavaScript), so that the URL can be rewritten dynamically at execution time. For instance, in the case where the RHS of an assignment is a variable, this variable is given a value at runtime when the browser's JavaScript engine interprets the content, and its value is rewritten upon assignment to the new value. By contrast, if the rule type is URL, the value is rewritten if it is a raw URL and ignored otherwise.

Note – Best practices for creating the right rules for the right content are described in "Application Integration" on page 223.

Once the URL is fully qualified, the Proxies for Domains and Subdomains list and the Rewrite all URLs checkbox are used to determine if the URL needs to be rewritten, as shown in the following example.

Rewriter Example

The default ruleset contains a rule for the portal Bookmark provider that looks like this:

```
<Variable type="EXPRESSION">surf_form_URL</Variable>
```

Assume that int.sun.com is listed in the Proxies for Domains and Subdomains, and that the HTML page shown in CODE EXAMPLE 4-1 contains the JavaScript variable surf_form_URL.

CODE EXAMPLE 4-1   HTML Page Containing Various JavaScript Assignments

```
<HTML>
<HEAD>
<SCRIPT>
<!--

//tmpURL should not be rewritten because there is no rule for it

var tmpURL = "http://server.int.sun.com";

//surf_form_URL should not be rewritten because the netscape.com
//domain is not included in the domain and subdomains list
```

```
var surf_form_URL = "http://www.netscape.com";

//surf_form_URL will now be rewritten because the domain
//int.sun.com is included in the domain and subdomains list

surf_form_URL = "http://server.int.sun.com";

//tmpURL will still not be rewritten because there is no rule for
it

tmpURL = surf_form_URL;

//surf_form_URL will be rewritten because the URL type is
Expression.

surf_form_URL = tmpURL;

//The first parameter will not be rewritten because the alert
function
//has not been added to the ruleset.  But, surf_form_URL will
//already have been rewritten in the previous statement.

alert(surf_form_URL);
// -->
</SCRIPT>
</HEAD>
<BODY BGCOLOR="#FFFFFF">
</BODY>
</HTML>
```

This example shows the inherent power of the Rewriter, and at the same time the potential for complexity when rewriting certain applications. Fear not though, because the purpose of this chapter is to show you how to get the Gateway to do the hard part for you! When the content is rewritten, a view of the source page reveals what you see in CODE EXAMPLE 4-2.

CODE EXAMPLE 4-2   Results After Rewriting

```
<HTML>
<HEAD>

<SCRIPT>
<!--
// All of the function definitions to rewrite content at runtime
//psSRAPRewriter_convert_expression... etc.
</SCRIPT>
.
```

```
    .
    .
    .
<SCRIPT>
-->

//tmpURL should not be rewritten because there is not rule for it

var tmpURL = "http://server.int.sun.com";

//surf_form_URL should not be rewritten because the domain is not
//included in the domain and subdomains list

var surf_form_URL ="http://www.netscape.com";

//surf_form_URL will now be rewritten because the domain is
//included in the domain and subdomains list

surf_form_URL =
"https://gateway.sun.com/http://server.int.sun.com";

//tmpURL will not be rewritten because there is no rule for it

tmpURL = surf_form_URL;

//surf_form_URL will be rewritten because the URL type is
Expression.

surf_form_URL =psSRAPRewriter_convert_expression( tmpURL);

//The first parameter will not be rewritten because the alert
function
//has not been added to the ruleset.  But, surf_form_URL will
//already have been rewritten in the previous statement.

alert(surf_form_URL);
// -->
</SCRIPT>
</HEAD>
<BODY BGCOLOR="#FFFFFF">
</BODY>
</HTML>
```

> **Note –** In CODE EXAMPLE 4-2, some output was omitted for clarity. Also, the first SCRIPT element was added by the Rewriter to define the function body of `psSRAPRewriter_convert_expression`.

What you see is that the first assignment of `tmpURL` is not rewritten, even though it contains a URL with a domain that should have been rewritten. This is expected because there isn't a rule for `tmpURL` in the JSRules section of the ruleset. The first assignment for `surf_form_URL` is also not rewritten, even though a rule exists for the variable name, because `netscape.com` is not added to the Proxies for Domains and Subdomains list, or Rewrite all URLs is not enabled (the Rewrite all URLs checkbox is not checked in the Gateway service panel of the Admin Console).

> **Note –** `www.netscape.com` should be resolvable by the client, so any actual request generated using this value would be made directly to the Netscape Web server instead of unnecessarily bogging down internal proxies to service requests for publicly available content. If Rewrite all URLs is enabled, that would be the same conceptually as adding a * (wildcard) to the Proxies for Domains and Subdomains list, and the Gateway would have to be configured so that it could download external content.

The second assignment for `surf_form_URL` was rewritten. This is because it not only existed in the ruleset, but the URL contained a domain that was in the Proxies for Domains and Subdomains list, even though Rewrite all URLs is not enabled. The second `tmpURL` assignment is still not rewritten because there is no rule specified for the variable in the ruleset. The third assignment for `surf_form_URL` was rewritten at runtime because the RHS of the assignment is a variable instead of a raw URL.

One thing to be aware of is that the FQDN of the URL cannot be compared to the Proxies for Domains and Subdomains list at runtime, so the URL is automatically rewritten with a redirect string included between the Gateway address and the original URL.

For example:

```
tmpURL = http://www.netscape.com
surf_form_URL = tmpURL;
alert(surf_form_URL);
```

The result is that `surf_form_URL` is rewritten to `https://gateway.sun.com/redirect/http://www.netscape.com`.

The redirect tells the Gateway to refer to the Proxies for Domains and Subdomains list to see if the request should be handled by the Gateway or if it should be redirected so that the browser can make a direct connection. In the absence of the domain entry, a 302 redirect response is sent back to the browser, which initiates a follow-up request directly to `www.netscape.com`.

Is a Raw URL Some Kind of Sushi?

Understanding what a raw URL is helps in determining what type of rules to create or modify and where they should reside in the ruleset.

Raw URLs are any strings that can be clearly identified as URLs. Raw URLs have relevance when rewriting HTML attributes, FORM INPUT tags, and APPLET and OBJECT parameters, but it is most useful to differentiate a raw URL in JavaScript content where a variable assignment occurs. As such, the following is a good rule of thumb for determining raw URLs in JavaScript content. A raw URL in JavaScript content must follow these conventions:

1. It must be a string literal enclosed by matching single or double quotes.

2. It usually, but not always, contains prepended path information.
   - Prepended path information can be relative or absolute.
   - The prepended path information must all be in the first string literal after the variable assignment.
   - If no prepended path information is provided, the FQDN + path to the parent document is used as the BASE equivalent. This value is often derived from the HTTP referrer header if one exists.

3. It is not built on separate lines by using a concatenation operator.

The underlined portion of the following examples represents the portion of the URL that the Gateway uses to rewrite the URL for URL rule types. For Expression types, raw URLs are less of an issue, because the entire RHS of the assignment is passed into the Rewriter function at runtime and any string concatenations are done prior to calling the Rewriter function. The only exception to this is dynamically created HTML generated from string concatenations. See "Rewriting JavaScript and JScript Content" on page 239 for details.

Examples of JavaScript variable assignments that *are* raw URLs include the following:

- Fully qualified URL with no path or object:

```
var myURL = "http://www.sun.com/" + prodPath + "solaris";
```

- Relative prepended path with path remainder and object:

```
img = "../../images/myimg.gif";
```

- Relative prepended path with no path remainder or object:

```
newImg = "../../" + "images/newimg.gif";
```

- No prepended path with partial path remainder and no object:

```
URL = 'images/' + imgNum + '.gif';
```

The following are examples of JavaScript variable assignments that *are not* raw URLs:

- Prepended path that is split:

```
var offImg = "../" + "../" + "images/off.gif";
```

- up2dir is a variable:

```
var mouseOverImg = up2dir + "images/mouseover.gif";
```

- Multiple assignments using the += operator:

```
surfToNewPage += '?param1=val&' + param2Name + '=val2';
```

JavaScript variable assignments that are known to contain raw URLs can have URL types specified in their associated rules. Otherwise, the type should be either Expression or DHTML depending on the context.

Why Do Relative URLs Have to be Made Absolute?

There are several reasons that the URLs must be made absolute by the portal server. Absolute URLs in this case include not just a path beginning from the server document root, but the server address, and protocol identifier as well. The first reason the portal server makes URLs absolute applies mostly to URL scraped content that is displayed on the portal server desktop. Relative URLs are typically resolved by the browser, using the location field to complete the address. Because the portal server desktop aggregates content fetched from a variety of locations, the browser location field is not useful in completing any of the individual relative URLs. To prevent incorrect URL resolution that might break image display and page functionality, the URLs are made absolute. This is done in HTML by first checking if a BASE tag is present in the document. If it is, the BASE tag is commented out and the relative URLs in the remainder of the page are resolved using the rewritten value of the BASE HREF attribute value. Some URLs can be rewritten indirectly using a CODEBASE attribute value. Imported content is rewritten using an HTTP referrer header if one exists. In the absence of a referrer header, the URI used to make the request is used to make the individual URLs absolute. Usually the only tricky relative URLs to catch are those that occur in JavaScript; especially where a block of HTML code might be dynamically generated.

The second reason URLs have to be made absolute is so that when they are rewritten, the Gateway knows what server and path to use to fetch the content. For instance, if a URL relative to the server root is rewritten without a protocol and server address, the Gateway tries to service the request itself, or presumes that it was intended to be a login request. The latter can result in a portal session loss and the user being redirected to the default authlessanonymous page if it has been configured as a non-authentication URL.

The final reason URLs are made absolute is so that the Gateway policy for access control to internal content can be enforced. Access to internal content can be allowed or denied based on the URL used to fetch it. This is advantageous in deployments such as business-to-business portals where only a small subset of internal servers and applications should be exposed and accessible to users logging in to the portal, even if they attempt to surf to other content directly, or by using the Bookmark provider.

Rewriter Versus the Netlet

The Netlet is typically used to provide secure remote access to specialized, fixed-port TCP/IP applications that talk to their own client application (downloaded to, or residing on, the end-user machine). The Netlet does this by establishing a secure tunnel between the client and server, using a preconfigured local port that communicates directly with the Gateway. Telnet, Citrix, SSH, and IMAP are just a few of the programs and protocols that can take advantage of Netlet functionality.

The Netlet is not typically used for Web surfing because of the difficulty in configuring it to work in that manner. You would have to use a proxy that specifies the localhost address, along with a specific port, for all content accessed from an internal domain. Or you would have to use a split DNS to publicly resolve the DNS name to the localhost with a default port (if port mapping is not in use). An internal Web proxy that knows how to handle the incoming Netlet HTTP requests might also have to be configured. Those requests might be for content outside of the corporate Intranet and have to be handed off to another proxy. While this extends the portal server to include more VPN-like functionality, it is difficult to implement, puts undue strain on the Gateway, and requires client customizations that may not be feasible. Take, for example, a business-to-business portal that provides a parts-ordering interface. The company providing the interface would not be able to dictate Web browser configuration requirements to the parts-ordering company. The Netlet would be used in this case, if the parts-ordering interface was a TCP/IP application that had a separate client application to interact with it, rather than a HTML-based interface.

In contrast to the Netlet, the Rewriter enables remote access through the use of most SPEC-compliant Web browsers because there is no JVM requirement as is needed for the Netlet. The Rewriter uses functionality similar to a full-featured reverse Web proxy, with the added benefit of rewriting the URLs so that no browser configuration is required to make sure requests for Intranet content are routed back to the Gateway. This prevents the browser from trying to make direct requests to content that is not available outside of the corporate firewall.

Rewriter Versus the Browser

In most cases, the Rewriter mimics how the browser would resolve relative URLs as though the page were being accessed directly instead of being redirected through the portal Gateway. Relative URLs are frequently used so that the content is more portable by not hardcoding the server address in the content itself. When content from multiple sources is displayed on the same page (with the exception of frames), the relative URLs must be made absolute before the content is presented to the browser. This is so the browser does not attempt to resolve the URLs incorrectly using the location field which is out of context. For instance, a location field when accessing the portal server desktop might look like the following:

```
https://gw.sun.com/http://ps.int.sun.com/portal/dt
```

Assuming that the default top-level container presents the channels as table cells, you would not want a situation where a URL-scraped channel contains an IMG tag that looks like the following to be resolved using the location field:

```
<IMG SRC="../images/pic.gif">
```

The incorrect image might be fetched, or no image would be fetched at all. The image tag would incorrectly be interpreted by the browser as:

```
<IMG SRC=
"https://gw.sun.com/http://ps.int.sun.com/portal/images/pic.gif">
```

If the content was fetched using the following URL, the resolved image address would be completely wrong:

```
http://ch.int.sun.com/ch/stocks_ch.html
```

Even if the content was served up from a Web server instance on a portal node, the path would likely be incorrect. Relative URLs that are not rewritten to absolute URLs are avoided for the following reasons:

- You want to be sure that requests to get internal content always come back to the Gateway component.
- Absolute URLs are used to determine if the URLs need to be rewritten based on their domain or subdomain value.
- Absolute URLs are compared to the user's access list to see whether or not the user has permission to retrieve the specified content.
- Absolute URLs avoid situations where the browser might resolve a relative path to the incorrect fully qualified path.

How Do I Deploy the Rewriter?

The Rewriter component is used by both the portal server and the Gateway. The portal server uses the Rewriter to translate content from pages fetched by the URL scraper. This usually consists of nothing more than fully qualifying the URLs. The `default_ruleset` is used by the URLScraper provider out-of-box. The ruleset for URL-scraped channels can be modified using the Identity Server Admin Console by going to the Channel and Container Management panel for the organization and changing the inherited urlScraperRulesetID property for the channel.

The exact method to deploy the Rewriter component used by the Gateway might differ depending on the portal server 6.x version that you are using, due to changes in the underlying Identity Server software. Refer to the product documentation to install and register the SRA-specific services. Once that is done, a Gateway profile called `default` is created that uses the default ruleset called `default_gateway_ruleset`.

For specific instructions on how to integrate several complex third-party applications through the Rewriter, see Appendix A.

Out-of-Box Rulesets

There are three primary rulesets provided by the portal server software out-of-box.

- `default_ruleset` is used by the URLScraper and it provides a set of rules that would be most applicable to scraped content. Most HTML content is handled by the ruleset, and some attempts are made at catching widely used JavaScript such as built-in methods like `window.open`.

- `default_gateway_ruleset` provides Rewriter rules for SRA applications and portlets. In addition to most of the basic HTML rules, this ruleset contains quite a few rules to make sure that the SRA applet parameters are rewritten correctly.

- `generic_ruleset` is a catch-all ruleset that attempts to automatically rewrite known JavaScript methods that manipulate or reference URLs. Unfortunately, some of the wildcarded rule entries tend to be overzealous, and can create as many problems as their simplicity solves.

All three rulesets are generated by following the DTD defined in the `RuleSet.dtd` file. The DTD can be extracted from *install_dir*/`SUNWps/lib/rewriter.jar`, as shown in the following example:

```
# mkdir /tmp/dtd
# cd /tmp/dtd
# jar xvf install_dir/SUNWps/lib/rewriter.jar resources/RuleSet.dtd
resources/StrictRuleSet.dtd
     extracted: resources/RuleSet.dtd
     extracted: resources/StrictRuleSet.dtd
```

The DTD is also available in Chapter 5 of the *Sun ONE Portal Server 6.0 Secure Remote Access Administration Guide*.

Creating a new ruleset from the Admin Console is the easiest way to start with a skeleton ruleset from which to work without inadvertently breaking the default rulesets. The only thing you must do before saving the new ruleset is to change its ID attribute value from the following default. . .

```
<RuleSet id="ruleset_template">
```

. . . to something else, taking care to keep the value of the ID in lowercase as the DTD requires.

The out-of-box rulesets have three key sections:

- HTMLRules – handles HTML tag attribute values, JavaScript event handlers, form data, and applet/object parameters

- JSRules – handles user-defined JavaScript variables, system variables, function parameters, event handlers, and DHTML

- XMLRules – handles text data, attribute values, and PCDATA

The out-of-box rulesets give a pretty good idea how to specify the rules themselves, but additional information on how to create rules for specific content and scenarios is provided in later sections of this book. CODE EXAMPLE 4-3 through CODE EXAMPLE 4-9 show the default_ruleset file provided in portal server 6.0 piece by piece, with important information about individual rules.

CODE EXAMPLE 4-3   default_ruleset (part 1)

```
<?xml version="1.0" encoding="UTF-8"?>
<!DOCTYPE RuleSet SYSTEM
"jar://rewriter.jar/resources/RuleSet.dtd">
<RuleSet id="default_ruleset">
<!-- Rules for Rewriting HTML Source -->
<HTMLRules>
<!-- Rules for Rewriting Form Input/Option Values List -->
<!-- Rules for Rewriting Applet/Object Parameter Values List -->
<!-- Rules for Rewriting HTML Attributes -->
    <Attribute name="action" />
    <Attribute name="background" />
    <Attribute name="codebase" />
    <Attribute name="code" />
    <Attribute name="href" />
    <Attribute name="src" />
    <Attribute name="value" />
    <Attribute name="imagePath" />
    <Attribute name="lowsrc" />
    <Attribute name="archive" valuePatterns=
"***;**,**,**,**,**,**,**,**,**,**,**,**"/>
    <Attribute name="style" />
    <Attribute name="content" tag="meta" />
```

Note – If the CODE attribute is present in this section, it should be removed because it might prevent embedded objects from loading correctly. The code location is fetched relative to the codebase attribute that is already rewritten.

These rules handle the rewriting of HTML tag attribute values. HREF, SRC, and BACKGROUND are recognizable. STYLE is a bit tricky because it contains CSS contents that might have a URL reference to a background image.

For instance, the following content results in the background image being correctly displayed in FIGURE 4-1 as a result of the CSS URL method parameter being rewritten.

CODE EXAMPLE 4-4 Example of Style Rule Application by `default_ruleset`

```
<HTML>
<BODY STYLE="background-
image:URL(https://gw.sun.com/http://ps.int.sun.com/img/tkns2k.jp
g);background-repeat:repeat;width:770px">
</BODY>
</HTML>
```

FIGURE 4-1 Example of Default Ruleset Application by the Rewriter

CODE EXAMPLE 4-5 `default_ruleset` (part 2)

```
<!-- Rules for Rewriting HTML Attributes containing Java Script -->
    <JSToken>onAbort</JSToken>
    <JSToken>onBlur</JSToken>
    <JSToken>onChange</JSToken>
    <JSToken>onClick</JSToken>
    <JSToken>onDblClick</JSToken>
    <JSToken>onError</JSToken>
```

```
        <JSToken>onFocus</JSToken>
        <JSToken>onKeyDown</JSToken>
        <JSToken>onKeyPress</JSToken>
        <JSToken>onKeyUp</JSToken>
        <JSToken>onLoad</JSToken>
        <JSToken>onMouseDown</JSToken>
        <JSToken>onMouseMove</JSToken>
        <JSToken>onMouseOut</JSToken>
        <JSToken>onMouseOver</JSToken>
        <JSToken>onMouseUp</JSToken>
        <JSToken>onReset</JSToken>
        <JSToken>onSelect</JSToken>
        <JSToken>onSubmit</JSToken>
        <JSToken>onUnload</JSToken>
    </HTMLRules>
```

Unless you have a specific reason why you do not want the Rewriter to assume that specific JavaScript event handlers should not be rewritten, the JSTokens can all be abbreviated as they are in the generic_ruleset using a single wildcarded rule that looks like this:

```
<JSToken>on*</JSToken>
```

One of the most popular event handlers is onClick. It can be used for page navigation or form submission. For example, the portal server desktop uses a JavaScript event handler to open the help window for individual channels:

```
<A HREF="/portal/docs/en_US/desktop/userinfo.htm" TARGET="wthelp"
onClick="javascript: var helpWin=
window.open('/portal/docs/en_US/desktop/userinfo.htm', 'wthelp',
'width=600,height=500,hotkeys=no,status=no,resizable=
yes,scrollbars=yes,toolbar=yes'); helpWin.focus();return false;">
```

In this case, if onClick did not match a rule, or the wildcarded rule previously suggested wasn't added, the first parameter to window.open is not considered for rewriting because the onClick attribute value (the RHS) is ignored.

FIGURE 4-2 shows the resulting window after the onClick event fires due to a user selecting the help button from the User Info channel. If the URL had not been rewritten at all, the resulting window would not display properly.

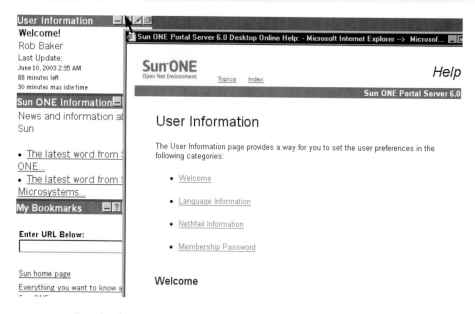

FIGURE 4-2 Result of Rewriting a JavaScript Event Handler

Continuing to examine the `default_ruleset`, the following code box shows the JSRules section.

CODE EXAMPLE 4-6 `default_ruleset` (part 3)

```
<!-- Rules for Rewriting JavaScript Source -->
<JSRules>

<!-- Rules for Rewriting JavaScript variables in URLs -->
    <Variable type="URL"> imgsrc </Variable>
    <Variable type="URL"> location.href </Variable>
    <Variable type="URL"> _fr.location </Variable>
    <Variable type="URL"> mf.location </Variable>
    <Variable type="URL"> parent.location </Variable>
    <Variable type="URL"> self.location </Variable>
    <Variable type="EXPRESSION"> location </Variable>
    <Variable type="SYSTEM"> window.location.pathname </Variable>
```

JavaScript Variables can be used to manipulate URLs, create URLs from a series of string concatenations, or have specific significance to the Document Object Model (DOM) where a built-in JavaScript variable value change could result in the browser location being updated. Images can also be prefetched and loaded into JavaScript arrays, where the array indexes might need to be rewritten for the images to be fetched using the appropriate URLs.

For example, consider a page that contains images that change once they are selected, as shown in CODE EXAMPLE 4-7.

CODE EXAMPLE 4-7   Example of Rewriting JavaScript Image Object Assignment

```
<HTML>
<HEAD>
<SCRIPT>
<!--
   function depress(imgNum){
      if (imgNum == 1) {
         document.images["IMG"+imgNum].src =
"../../img/Back_lit.gif";
         liftUp(2);
      }
      else if (imgNum == 2) {
         document.images["IMG"+imgNum].src =
"../../img/Forward_lit.gif";
         liftUp(1);
      }
   }

function liftUp(imgNum) {
      if (imgNum == 1) {
         document.images["IMG"+imgNum].src = "../../img/Back.gif";
      }
      else if (imgNum == 2) {
         document.images["IMG"+imgNum].src = "../../img/Forward.gif";
      }
   }
//-->
</SCRIPT>
</HEAD>
<BODY BGCOLOR="#FFFFFF" TEXT="#000000">
<A HREF="#" onClick="depress(1);"><IMG SRC="../../img/Back.gif"
NAME="IMG1" BORDER="0"></A>
<A HREF="#" onClick="depress(2);"><IMG SRC=
"../../img/Forward.gif" NAME="IMG2" BORDER="0"></A>
</BODY>
</HTML>
```

In this case, the following rule would have to be added to the JSRules section:

```
<Variable type="URL"> document.images*.src </Variable>
```

Note – The '#' URL is mishandled in portal server 6.0. This character is used to create named anchors in hypertext documents to enable navigation within the document itself. The document will not be reloaded as long as the HREF value that precedes the hash mark is the same as the browser location field. In the case of portal server 6.0, the hash mark was being dropped during the rewriting of these URLs which resulted in an additional page request when attempting to navigate within the page. A patch is available for this problem for portal 6.0 and it has been addressed in other portal 6 releases.

FIGURE 4-3 shows the results of successfully rewriting the JavaScript Image Object. If the image URLs were not rewritten, broken image icons would be displayed in place of the button images. This behavior will be explained later in further detail later when discussing the rewriting of the portal desktop.

FIGURE 4-3   Images Correctly Displayed After Rewriting

If the image array index is not rewritten correctly, the result is a bounding box or broken image icon when either of the buttons is selected.

The next section of the `default_ruleset` (CODE EXAMPLE 4-8) describes the rules necessary to rewrite JavaScript functions and function parameters.

CODE EXAMPLE 4-8   `default_ruleset` (part 4)

```
<!-- Rules for Rewriting JavaScript Function Parameters -->
    <Function type="URL" name="openURL" paramPatterns="y"/>
    <Function type="URL" name="openAppURL" paramPatterns="y"/>
    <Function type="URL" name="openNewWindow" paramPatterns="y"/>
    <Function type="URL" name="parent.openNewWindow"
paramPatterns="y"/>
    <Function type="URL" name="window.open" paramPatterns="y"/>
    <Function type="DHTML" name="document.write" paramPatterns=
"y"/>
    <Function type="DHTML" name="document.writeln" paramPatterns=
"y"/>

</JSRules>
```

For multiwindow applications, `window.open` function calls are frequently used. The first parameter to this function is a URL that might need to be rewritten at the point of the function call. Consider the following example where a link on a page opens a detached channel:

```
<HTML>
<HEAD></HEAD>
<BODY>
<A HREF="javascript:var popupstock=
window.open('http://ch.int.sun.com/channels/stocks_channel.html'
,'Stocks','width=300,height=250,directories=no,location=
no,menubar=no,scrollbars=yes,status=no,toolbar=no,resizable=
yes')">Open Channel</A>
</BODY>
</HTML>
```

If the first parameter of the `window.open` function call is not rewritten, the browser attempts to directly connect to the content server that, more than likely, is not accessible from outside the corporate firewall. The paramPatterns attribute value in the rule definition indicates which parameters to rewrite by marking them with a y. So a paramPatterns value of `y,,y` rewrites the first and third function parameters.

FIGURE 4-4 shows the result of a user-initiated window pop-up.

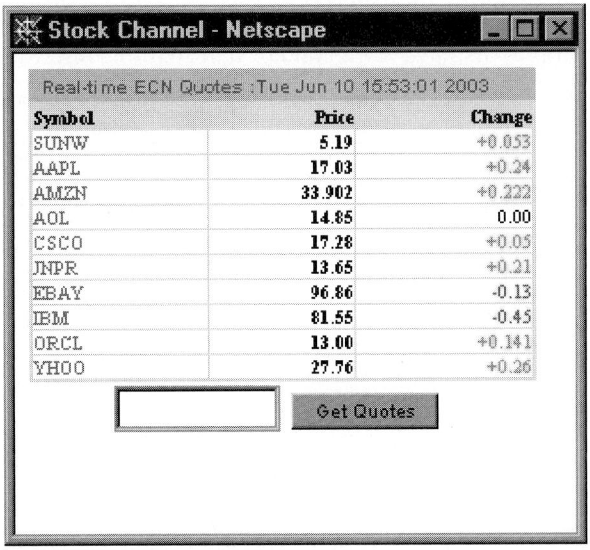
Stock Channel - Netscape
Real-time ECN Quotes :Tue Jun 10 15:53:01 2003
Symbol
Price
Change
SUNW 5.19 +0.053
AAPL 17.03 +0.24
AMZN 33.902 +0.222
AOL 14.85 0.00
CSCO 17.28 +0.05
JNPR 13.65 +0.21
EBAY 96.86 -0.13
IBM 81.55 -0.45
ORCL 13.00 +0.141
YHOO 27.76 +0.26
Get Quotes

FIGURE 4-4 Example of a Pop-up Window Created from a JavaScript `window.open` call

CODE EXAMPLE 4-9 is used to rewrite XML attributes and text data.

CODE EXAMPLE 4-9   default_ruleset (part 5)

```
<!-- Rules for Rewriting XML Source -->
<XMLRules>

<!-- Rules for Rewriting Attributes -->
    <Attribute name="xmlns"/>
    <Attribute name="href" tag="a"/>

<!-- Rules for Rewriting TagText -->
    <TagText tag="baseroot" />
    <TagText tag="img" />
</XMLRules>
</RuleSet>
```

Many modern browsers now include XML parsers, so there may be instances where XML content contains URLs that require translation. ActiveX, for example, is sometimes used to create XML/HTTP requests directly to a server. The XML response can be used to create a block of HTML that is inserted directly in to the DOM. In this case, the PCDATA in the XML response must be rewritten prior to the transform to ensure that a request is not made prematurely by the browser for the incorrect URL. For more information regarding this and similar XML rewriting issues, see "Rewriting XML" on page 271.

The following example displays XML content that requires rewriting.

CODE EXAMPLE 4-10   library.xml File

```
<?xml version="1.0" encoding="UTF-8"?>
<?xml-stylesheet type="text/xsl" href="library.xsl"?>
<!-- This comment is in the prolog -->
<library>
<book ISBN="0131483382">
<title>Making the Net Work: Deploying a Secure Portal on Sun
Systems</title>
<author>Rob Baker</author>
</book>
</book>
</library>
```

The following example is the XSL code imported by the previous example.

CODE EXAMPLE 4-11 `library.xsl` File

```
<?xml version="1.0" encoding="UTF-8"?>
<xsl:stylesheet version="1.0" xmlns:xsl=
"http://www.w3.org/1999/XSL/Transform">
<xsl:template match="/">
<html>
<body>
<TABLE BGCOLOR="#EEEEEE" BORDER="0" CELLPADDING="2" CELLSPACING=
"0">
<TR BGCOLOR="#DDDDDD"><TD>TITLE</TD><TD>AUTHOR</TD></TR>
<xsl:for-each select="library/book">
  <TR><TD><xsl:value-of select="title"/></TD>
      <TD><xsl:value-of select="author"/></TD></TR>
</xsl:for-each>
</TABLE>
</body>
</html>
</xsl:template>
</xsl:stylesheet>
```

The resulting display through rewritten XML, is shown in FIGURE 4-5.

TITLE	AUTHOR
Making the Net Work: Deploying a Secure Portal on Sun Systems	Rob Baker

FIGURE 4-5 Example of Rewriting an XML Attribute Value

Configuring the Rewriter

While the out-of-box ruleset might be adequate for simple proof-of-concept deployments, chances are you need to create new rulesets. You can modify the default rulesets and create new Gateway instances to handle a production-level secure remote access portal that is used to access a multitude of applications and content from different sources. This section discusses how to root out tricky URLs, and how to configure the Gateway to rewrite them. Some new terminology, such as rule trumping, is introduced.

Methodology for Rule Extraction

Rule extraction from Web applications accessed through the Gateway can be difficult, particularly if the applications were not created inhouse, and because debugging tools are not provided as a part of the portal server. Depending on how the application is written, integrating the it with the Gateway usually falls into one of three categories:

- "Integration Out-Of-Box (Category 1)" on page 192
- "Integration Through Profile Configuration (Category 2)" on page 197
- "Integration With Special Attention Required (Category 3)" on page 203

Integration Out-Of-Box (Category 1)

This category usually applies to Web applications that are delivered to the browser in pure HTML or HTML, and some other content that is imported but does not contain any URLs. For example, CSS content that only defines font styles can be imported. Content falling into this category is usually straightforward to integrate, requiring little to no administrative intervention for it to be accessed by remote users through the Gateway. This content tends to be static in nature, contains absolute URLs, adheres to generally accepted published specifications, and is well formed. Well formed here means that the entire content is syntactically correct and that basic formatting practices are in place. The content does not have complex forms, Java applets, or imported scripts that require special attention. The IMG SRC, A HREF, FORM ACTION, APPLET CODEBASE, and JAVASCRIPT SRC tag attributes are just a few that are handled by the Gateway out-of-box.

CODE EXAMPLE 4-12 shows part of a page that contains two tag attributes that need to be considered for rewriting.

CODE EXAMPLE 4-12   Category 1 Content (Example 1)

```
<HTML>
<HEAD><TITLE>Category 1 Content</TITLE>
<BODY BGCOLOR="#FFFFFF">
<A HREF="http://www.sun.com"><IMG SRC=
"http://www.sun.com/im/sun_logo.gif" BORDER="0">
</BODY>
</HTML>
```

The first attribute of concern is HREF. It is identified by the rule:

```
<Attribute name="href" />
```

This rule must appear in the ruleset that is applied to the contents FQDN origin. Additionally, for the HREF attribute value to be rewritten, the domain `sun.com` must appear in the Proxies for Domains and Subdomains section of the Gateway instance's profile used to fetch the content.

The second attribute of concern is SRC. It is identified by a similar rule:

```
<Attribute name="src" />
```

In the 6.0 version of the portal server, the SRC attribute of the image tag is rewritten whether the rule exists or not, or if the URL's domain is in the Proxies for Domains and Subdomains list. This is done mainly to avoid the usability problem of mixed content, meaning some of the content is encrypted while other content is not. In this case, either the images will be displayed as broken icons on the web page, or end users will have to select OK to popup windows warning of the mixed content if the browser is able to access the images directly. The browser encryption key icons will also be broken indicating the page less secure. The only problem with this option not being configurable is that the Gateway must be able to fetch the remote image, which may be a bit more difficult if a Web proxy is being used or another security policy prevents the Gateway from making a connection to the content when the browser could in fact connect to it directly.

If the Gateway is unable to fetch images, you might see broken image icons throughout the content displayed on the portal server desktop, as shown in FIGURE 4-6.

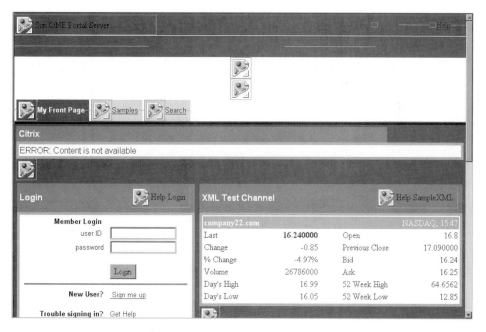

FIGURE 4-6   Broken Image Icons Resulting From an Improperly Configured Ruleset

In addition to the Gateway simply not being able to establish a connection to the server, this situation may hint at some Rewriter rules that might be required for the content to be displayed correctly. Consider the following example:

CODE EXAMPLE 4-13   Category 1 Content (Example 2)

```
<HTML>
<HEAD>
<SCRIPT LANGUAGE="JavaScript">
lnk = "http://ch.int.sun.com";
document.write('<A HREF="'+lnk+'/test_cases/foo.html">\n');
document.write('<img border="0" src=
"'+lnk+'/test_cases/cgi/images/test.jpg" alt="ALT"><BR>\n');
document.write('<img border="0" src=
"/test_cases/cgi/images/test.jpg" alt="ALT">');
document.write('</A>');

</SCRIPT>
</HEAD>
<BODY>
</BODY>
</HTML>
```

The following rule ensures that the document.write parameter is rewritten as HTML:

```
<Function type="DHTML" name="document.write" paramPatterns="y" />
```

The difference between the two IMG tags is that the first image is created using a JavaScript variable, and therefore is not a raw URL. The second IMG SRC is relative to the server root and is rewritten correctly. Accessing this page through the Gateway results in something similar to the following:

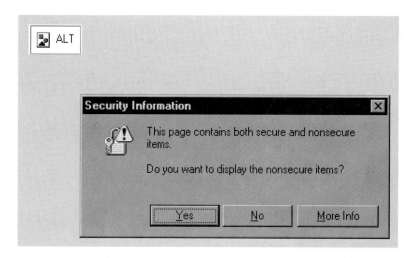

FIGURE 4-7   Broken Image Icon Due to Incorrectly Rewritten URL or IMG Tag

The reason for the broken image icon is that the `lnk` variable value was not rewritten, so the browser attempted to fetch `http://ch.int.sun.com/test_cases/cgi/images/test.jpg`. In this particular case, even if the user selects Yes, the image is not displayed properly because the browser is not able to connect directly to `ch.int.sun.com`. The solution is to add the following rule to the JSRules section of the appropriate ruleset:

```
<Variable type="URL">lnk</Variable>
```

Now the security alert is not displayed, and both images show up as expected, as shown in FIGURE 4-8.

FIGURE 4-8 Image Results When the Rules are Correct

Integration Through Profile Configuration (Category 2)

This category applies to Web applications, including those in Category 1, but which are increasingly complex. Category 2 content contains URLs in the following:

- FORM data
- Applet parameters
- JavaScript event handlers
- Assignment to built-in JavaScript variables
- Mixed content types including CSS, JavaScript code, and XML
- Dynamically created content

Some Category 2 content is handled with out-of-box rules, while other Category 2 content requires special consideration. CODE EXAMPLE 4-14 shows an example of Category 2 content, with the URLs in bold.

CODE EXAMPLE 4-14   Category 2 Content (Example 1)

```
<HTML>
<HEAD>
<TITLE>Category 2 Content</TITLE>
<STYLE>
<!--
.menuskin{
  position:absolute;
  width:165px;
  background-color:#594FBF;
  border:2px solid #FBE249;
  font:normal 12px Verdana;
  line-height:18px;
  z-index:100;
  visibility:hidden;
}
.menuskin a{
  text-decoration:none;
  color:black;
  padding-left:10px;
  padding-right:10px;
}
.menuitems li{list-style-type : square;list-style-
image:url("http://www.sun.com/css/ic_bullet_white.gif");margin:0
px 0px 0px -20px;padding:0px}
#mouseoverstyle{
  background-color:#FBE249;
}
#mouseoverstyle a{
  color:white;
}
-->
```

CODE EXAMPLE 4-14   Category 2 Content (Example 1) *(Continued)*

```
</STYLE>
<SCRIPT LANGUAGE="JavaScript" src="cat2.js">
</SCRIPT>
</HEAD>
<BODY BGCOLOR="#FFFFFF">
<DIV ID="popmenu" CLASS="menuskin" onMouseover=
"clearhidemenu();highlightmenu(event,'on')" onMouseou
t="highlightmenu(event,'off');dynamichide(event)">
</DIV>
<A HREF="/link1.html" onMouseover="showmenu(event,lnk[0])"
onMouseout="delayhidemenu()">Sun Links</A
><BR>
<A HREF="/link2.html" onMouseover="showmenu(event,lnk[1])"
onMouseout="delayhidemenu()">Java Links</A>
</BODY>
</HTML>
```

The corresponding Category 2 imported JavaScript source is shown in CODE EXAMPLE 4-15.

CODE EXAMPLE 4-15   Category 2 (Example 2)

```
//Pop-it menu- By Dynamic Drive
//For full source code and more DHTML scripts, visit
http://www.dynamicdrive.com
//This credit MUST stay intact for use

var lnk=new Array()
//SPECIFY MENU SETS AND THEIR LINKS. FOLLOW SYNTAX LAID OUT

lnk[0]='<UL><div class="menuitems"><LI class="menuitems"><a href=
"http://www.sun.com/blueprints">Sun
 Blueprints</a></div>'
lnk[0]+='<div class="menuitems"><LI class="menuitems"><a href=
"http://www.sun.com/software">Sun Soft
ware</a></div>'
lnk[0]+='<div class="menuitems"><LI class="menuitems"><a href=
"http://wwws.sun.com/software/products
/portal_srvr/home_portal.html">SunONE Portal
Server</a></div></UL>'

lnk[1]='<div class="menuitems"><a href="http://java.sun.com">Java
Homepage</a></div>'
lnk[1]+='<div class="menuitems"><a href=
"http://java.net">Java.net</a></div>'
```

```
lnk[1]+='<div class="menuitems"><a href=
"http://javafreeware.com">Java Freeware</a></div>'

////No need to edit beyond here

var ie4=document.all&&navigator.userAgent.indexOf("Opera")==-1
var ns6=document.getElementById&&!document.all
var ns4=document.layers

function testurl(e, tst1)
{
e=tst1;
return e;
}
function showmenu(e,which){

if (!document.all&&!document.getElementById&&!document.layers)
return

clearhidemenu()

menuobj=ie4? document.all.popmenu : ns6?
document.getElementById("popmenu") : ns4? document.popmenu
: ""
menuobj.thestyle=(ie4||ns6)? menuobj.style : menuobj

if (ie4||ns6)
menuobj.innerHTML=which
else{
menuobj.document.write('<layer name=gui bgColor=#E6E6E6 width=165
onmouseover="clearhidemenu()" onmo
useout="hidemenu()">'+which+'</layer>')
menuobj.document.close()
}

menuobj.contentwidth=(ie4||ns6)? menuobj.offsetWidth :
menuobj.document.gui.document.width
menuobj.contentheight=(ie4||ns6)? menuobj.offsetHeight :
menuobj.document.gui.document.height
eventX=ie4? event.clientX : ns6? e.clientX : e.x
eventY=ie4? event.clientY : ns6? e.clientY : e.y

//Find out how close the mouse is to the corner of the window
var rightedge=ie4? document.body.clientWidth-eventX :
window.innerWidth-eventX
var bottomedge=ie4? document.body.clientHeight-eventY :
window.innerHeight-eventY
```

```
//if the horizontal distance isn't enough to accommodate the width
of the context menu
if (rightedge<menuobj.contentwidth)
//move the horizontal position of the menu to the left by it's
width
menuobj.thestyle.left=ie4? document.body.scrollLeft+eventX-
menuobj.contentwidth : ns6? window.pageXO
ffset+eventX-menuobj.contentwidth : eventX-menuobj.contentwidth
else
//position the horizontal position of the menu where the mouse was
clicked
menuobj.thestyle.left=ie4? document.body.scrollLeft+eventX : ns6?
window.pageXOffset+eventX : eventX

//same concept with the vertical position
if (bottomedge<menuobj.contentheight)
menuobj.thestyle.top=ie4? document.body.scrollTop+eventY-
menuobj.contentheight : ns6? window.pageYOf
fset+eventY-menuobj.contentheight : eventY-menuobj.contentheight
else
menuobj.thestyle.top=ie4? document.body.scrollTop+event.clientY :
ns6? window.pageYOffset+eventY : e
ventY
menuobj.thestyle.visibility="visible"
return false
}

function contains_ns6(a, b) {
//Determines if 1 element in contained in another- by Brainjar.com
while (b.parentNode)
if ((b = b.parentNode) == a)
return true;
return false;
}

function hidemenu(){
if (window.menuobj)
menuobj.thestyle.visibility=(ie4||ns6)? "hidden" : "hide"
}

function dynamichide(e){
if (ie4&&!menuobj.contains(e.toElement))
hidemenu()
else if (ns6&&e.currentTarget!= e.relatedTarget&&
!contains_ns6(e.currentTarget, e.relatedTarget))
hidemenu()
```

```
}

function delayhidemenu(){
if (ie4||ns6||ns4)
delayhide=setTimeout("hidemenu()",500)
}

function clearhidemenu(){
if (window.delayhide)
clearTimeout(delayhide)
}

function highlightmenu(e,state){
if (document.all)
source_el=event.srcElement
else if (document.getElementById)
source_el=e.target
if (source_el.className=="menuitems"){
source_el.id=(state=="on")? "mouseoverstyle" : ""
}
else{
while(source_el.id!="popmenu"){
source_el=document.getElementById? source_el.parentNode :
source_el.parentElement
if (source_el.className=="menuitems"){
source_el.id=(state=="on")? "mouseoverstyle" : ""
}
}
}
}

if (ie4||ns6)
document.onclick=hidemenu
```

This is an extensive example, but it represents real-world content. The page loads with two links, Sun Links and Java Links. When a mouseover event occurs, showmenu is called with the mouse event and an array index reference. The array index represents an array that was created by concatenating strings of HTML text together. If the browser is Internet Explorer, the resulting text is inserted directly in to the DOM with the menu offset using the coordinates from the mouse location, and made visible. The corresponding CSS highlights links inside of the menu box. If the browser is Netscape, a layer is created and made visible instead. Without any modifications to the ruleset, the resulting page looks like what you see in FIGURE 4-9.

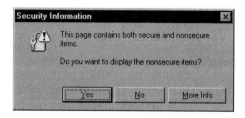

FIGURE 4-9 Warning Displayed for Incorrectly Rewritten Images

The warning is displayed because the CSS specifying the style for the bullets contains an image that was not rewritten:

```
.menuitems li{list-style-type : square;list-style-
image:url("http://www.sun.com/css/ic_bullet_white.gif");margin:0
px 0px 0px -20px;padding:0px}
```

In this case, you don't need a rule because the CSS content is rewritten by default. The problem is that either sun.com needs to be added to the Proxies for Domains and Subdomains section of the Gateway profile, or Rewrite all Urls must be enabled.

After you make these changes, the warning window goes away, but the links are still not rewritten. When the links inside of the menu are highlighted, the status bar on the browser shows they have not been rewritten. Consider the 0th array index initialization:

```
lnk[0]='<UL><div class="menuitems"><LI class="menuitems"><a href=
"http://www.sun.com/blueprints">SunBlueprints</a></div>'
lnk[0]+='<div class="menuitems"><LI class="menuitems"><a href=
"http://www.sun.com/software">Sun Software</a></div>'
lnk[0]+='<div class="menuitems"><LI class="menuitems"><a href=
"http://wwws.sun.com/software/products/portal_srvr/home_portal.h
tml">SunONE Portal Server</a></div></UL>'
```

By default, there is no rule for the `lnk` variable, so a rule must be added to make sure that the links are rewritten. The RHS of the assignment is not a raw URL, and there are multiple string concatenations along several lines of text, so the following rule must be added to the JSRules section of the appropriate ruleset:

```
<Variable type="DHTML">lnk*</Variable>
```

`lnk*` is used to avoid regular expression matching problems with the brackets `[]`. It is also used to generally apply to all of the `lnk` assignments. Specifying the type as DHTML ensures that the RHS of each of the assignments and concatenations is rewritten as HTML content.

For the previous example of JavaScript content to be rewritten, the SRC attribute value where the JavaScript is imported must first be rewritten. This is done by default because the SRC attribute value already has a corresponding rule. Similarly, the HREF attribute values for the links on the initial page are rewritten because there are already rules created for them.

Once the profile modifications are made and the Gateway component is restarted to reread its configuration, the page looks like what you see in FIGURE 4-10.

FIGURE 4-10 URLs Correctly Rewritten and Page Correctly Displayed

Integration With Special Attention Required (Category 3)

Category 3 content includes the following:

- Dynamically created URLs on the client side
- Complex scripts that have URLs in function parameters
- URLs built using several steps or in multiple locations in the code using string concatenation
- URLs contained in fractured JavaScript
- URLs hidden in nested function calls
- Integrations with unknown third-party applications
- URLs contained in code that has passed through an obfuscator

Category 2 content makes up the bulk of what most people would expect to see pass through the Gateway. However, for applications that are being created specifically for use with the Gateway, there are a multitude of content-based workarounds that you can use if it is difficult, or not possible, to create a rule that matches a specific URL.

Best programming practices later in this chapter provide information about possible workarounds for different corner cases or content types. The only concerns for the content are the URLs that are referenced. URLs that are not correctly rewritten can manifest themselves in a variety of ways. The applications might have problems when certain buttons are selected, or when forms are submitted, or when other actions occur, such as a mouseover. The browser might return an error message saying that a particular server is either down or inaccessible when a link has been selected. Users might be mysteriously redirected back to the portal server login page, even though they did not log out or have their session terminated. Images might show up broken, applets might not download completely or run correctly, and navigation bars might not work correctly. Any of these symptoms can be signs that the Rewriter requires additional configuration to work with the application.

For testing purposes, you should ensure that the browser cannot make a direct connection to any content server. All request should go through the Gateway. Otherwise, when the portal server is moved into production, a number of issues could arise because the browser is no longer able to talk directly to internal content. One way to determine if this is a problem is to use the `snoop` or `tcpdump` commands to watch the connection between the client and the content server. There should be no direct communication between the two when accessing the content server through the Gateway component. If there is, then it is likely that a URL has been overlooked and has not been rewritten.

Category 3 content presents a more difficult challenge in getting third-party applications to work through the Gateway.

One example of Category 3 content is the integration of Lotus iNotes where the JavaScript code is obfuscated and HTML elements are created and inserted into the DOM dynamically, as shown in the following example:

```
<script> function np(index) {if
(theWelcomeFrameset.frames[index].mL().readyState != "complete")
{setTimeout('np(' + index + ')', 3000);
return;)theWelcomeFrameset.frames[index].lz(true);}function
nq(index){theWelcomeFrameset.frames[index].lj(false);document.bo
dy.onclick= function(){theWelcomeFrameset.lj(true);{;var s=
"setTimeout('np(" + index + ")' + 3000 + ")"; haiku.LB.add(s);}if
(h_ClientBrowser.isIEF()){nq(ht); var mg=
theForm.document.createElement("IFRAME"); with(mg){id=ld(); src=
LayoutOption[ht]; style.disply="none";}
document.write(mg.outerHTML;}else{var s="<layer>nyi - " +
LayoutOption[ht] + "<\/layer>";document.write(s);}</script>
```

This example is on the extreme edge of challenges you might encounter when integrating existing Web applications through the Rewriter. In short, this code block creates an IFRAME containing a Web page using the URL that an end user has saved in their page Layout preferences. Because the URL is already fully qualified, only the src variable needs to be rewritten. Don't confuse SRC here with the HTML SRC attribute value, because SRC in this particular case is a JavaScript/JScript variable. To rewrite it so that the user-defined embedded Web URLs show up on their iNotes page, the following rule must be added to the appropriate ruleset:

```
<Variable type="EXPRESSION"> src </Variable>
```

FIGURE 4-11 shows a Lotus iNotes Layout edit page where panel three represents the URL used to create the IFRAME in the preceding code.

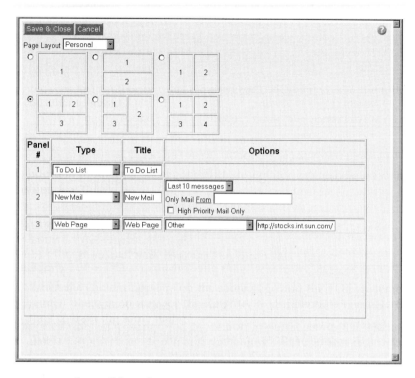

FIGURE 4-11 Lotus iNotes Layout

In addition to the DHTML used above, the code is also obfuscated, making it very difficult to determine what actually represents a URL, or what the URL might look like at the time of execution. Code obfuscation is a technique of removing code formatting, and translating variable names to more unreadable counterparts, in an attempt to stop or slow the proliferation of Intellectual Property to other people or companies.

Note – See "Lotus iNotes Integration" on page 391 for more information about integrating Lotus iNotes with the portal server. You can also obtain Rewriter integrations and portlet integrations from Sun BluePrints Online (http://www.sun.com/solutions/blueprints/online.html) or through Sun Sales for some of the most widely integrated third-party applications.

Adding and Modifying Rewriter Rules and Rulesets

You must understand how to create and modify rules and rulesets to configure and maintain a portal server, SRA deployment. The following sections discuss two ways that rulesets can be created and modified:

- "Using the Administration Console to Manage Rules and Rulesets" on page 207
- "Using the Command-Line Interface to Manage Rules and Rulesets" on page 208

Using the Administration Console to Manage Rules and Rulesets

The following steps are based on version 6.0. Steps may differ slightly depending on which version of the portal server software you are using.

▼ To Create a Ruleset

1. **Log in to the Admin Console.**

2. **Select View Service Management.**

3. **From the left panel under Portal Server Configuration, select the link next to Rewriter.**

4. **Select the New button at the top of the right panel.**

5. **In the text box below the Ruleset XML title, modify the RuleSet id attribute to some reasonable name, taking care to keep the name in lowercase.**

   Example: `<RuleSet id="paycheck_app">`

6. **Select Save above or below the text box.**

▼ To Add or Modify a Rule

1. **Login to the Admin Console.**

2. **Select View Service Management.**

3. **From the left panel under Portal Server Configuration, select the link next to Rewriter.**

4. **Select Edit next to the name of the ruleset to which you want to add a rule:**

   Example: `default_gateway_ruleset`

5. **Add the rule to the appropriate section:**

   Example, under JSRules, add: `<Variable type ="URL"> myURL </Variable>`

6. **Select Save above or below the text box.**

▼ To Associate a Rule With a Gateway Instance

1. **Log in to the Admin Console.**

2. **Select View Service Management.**

3. **From the left panel under SRAP Configuration, select the Link next to Gateway.**

4. **Select the edit link corresponding to the Gateway profile you would like to associate the new Ruleset with.**

5. **Next to the section titled Domain-based Rulesets, add the fully qualified host name or domain name corresponding to the Web application, a pipe separator, and the ruleset name.**

   Example: `echeck.int.sun.com|paycheck_app`

Using the Command-Line Interface to Manage Rules and Rulesets

▼ To Create a New Ruleset

1. **Create a new XML file by making a copy of one of the default rulesets.**

   Example:

   ```
   # cp install_dir/SUNWps/export/DefaultGatewayRuleSet.xml
   install_dir/SUNWps/export/MyNewRuleSet.xml
   ```

2. **Change the RuleSet id attribute, following a naming convention for how the ruleset is to be used.**

   Example: `my_new_ruleset`.

3. **Store the new ruleset.**

   Example:

   ```
   # install_dir/SUNWps/bin/rwadmin store --runasdn "uid=amAdmin,ou=
   People,o=sun.com,o=isp" --password "test"
   /opt/SUNWps/export/MyNewRuleSet.xml
   ```

> **Note –** Your DN value required for the `runasdn` command will differ from the example, but you can find your DN value in the *install_dir*/SUNWam/lib/AMConfig.`properties` file on your Identity Server.

4. **Verify that the new ruleset is stored.**

   The following example shows `my_new_ruleset` in the list.

   ```
   # install_dir/SUNWps/bin/rwadmin list --runasdn "uid=amAdmin,ou=
   People,o=sun.com,o=isp" --password "test"
   blank_ruleset
   default_gateway_ruleset
   default_ruleset
   desktop_ruleset
   generic_ruleset
   inotes_ruleset
   my_new_ruleset
   owa_sp3_ruleset
   ```

▼ To Add or Modify a New Rule

1. **If modifications have been made through the Admin Console since the RuleSet was created, you must retrieve the new contents and dump them to an XML file if you want to edit the ruleset using an XML editor. The reason for this is that the local XML file representing the ruleset may be out of sync with the same ruleset stored in the directory.**

   Example:

   ```
   # install_dir/SUNWps/bin/rwadmin get --runasdn "uid=amAdmin,ou=
   People,o=sun.com,o=isp" --password "test" --rulesetid
   "my_new_ruleset" > /opt/SUNWps/export/MyNewRuleSet.xml
   ```

2. **Make the necessary changes to the XML file.**

   a. **Remove the stored ruleset.**

      Example:

   ```
   # install_dir/SUNWps/bin/rwadmin remove --runasdn "uid=amAdmin,ou=
   People,o=sun.com,o=isp" --password "test" --rulesetid
   "my_new_ruleset"

   SUCCESS!
   ```

b. Verify that the ruleset was removed.

```
# install_dir/SUNWps/bin/rwadmin list --runasdn "uid=amAdmin,ou=
People,o=sun.com,o=isp" --password "test" | grep my_new_ruleset |
wc -l

0
```

c. Store the modified ruleset.

```
# install_dir/SUNWps/bin/rwadmin store --runasdn "uid=amAdmin,ou=
People,o=sun.com,o=isp" --password "test"
/opt/SUNWps/export/MyNewRuleSet.xml
SUCCESS!
```

d. Verify the ruleset was stored.

```
# install_dir/SUNWps/bin/rwadmin list --runasdn "uid=amAdmin,ou=
People,o=sun.com,o=isp" --password "test" | grep my_new_ruleset |
wc -l
1
```

Improvements in the Rewriter Since Portal Server 3.x

There are a variety of improvements in the portal server version 6.x software from the 3.x version. This section describes some of these improvements.

Reduced Rule Trumping

Rule trumping refers to the inaccurate determination of a variable value to be rewritten. In most cases, rule trumping occurs when one particular application requires a URL to be rewritten, while another application with the same variable name does not. For example:

Source from example page 1:

```
<HTML>
<HEAD>
<SCRIPT>
var theLocation = "http://www.sun.com/";
</SCRIPT>
<BODY BGCOLOR="#FFFFFF" TEXT="#000000">
</BODY>
</HTML>
```

Source from example page 2:

```
<HTML>
<HEAD>
<SCRIPT>
var theLocation = "Sun's Homepage";
</SCRIPT>
<BODY BGCOLOR="#FFFFFF" TEXT="#000000">
</BODY>
</HTML>
```

In the portal server 3.x software, if the variable theLocation was added to the Gateway profile, both instances would be rewritten. By contrast, if it was left out, the first instance that needed to be rewritten would be ignored. Portal server 6.x solves this problem by mapping rulesets to the point of origin of the Web content. This way, only the application that uses the variable in the context of a URL will have its value rewritten.

No More Gateway Profile Section Ambiguity

In portal server 3.x software, you have to make a judgment call as to which Gateway profile section to add JavaScript Variables or JavaScript Function Parameters. In earlier versions of portal server 3.x, this decision was made more difficult by the unpredictable way that the runtime Rewriter functions are inserted. For example, if JavaScript onHandlers contained function calls or variables that needed to be rewritten, the Rewriter function definition was inserted just after the variable reference, but inside the HTML tag itself. While this limitation was resolved in later versions of portal server 3.x, portal server 6.x reduces confusing aspects of administering the Rewriter by using type identifiers instead of separate sections for the same content.

For example, the first parameter of the `window.open` JavaScript method is a URL. This can either be a raw URL or a variable that had previously been assigned a URL. In portal server 3, a rule entry for the method can either be added to the Rewrite JavaScript Function Parameters section of the Gateway profile, or into the Rewrite JavaScript Function Parameters Function section. The value cannot exist in both places. If it does, only the first match is considered. If you use the former section, only raw URLs passed to the `window.open` method are rewritten and all others are ignored. If you place the entry in the latter profile section, all occurrences are rewritten using the runtime Rewriter functions, even if they do not require it. This causes problems not only within JavaScript specified in onHandlers, but also in dynamic HTML blocks containing references to `window.open`.

Portal server 6.x reduces this ambiguity by defining a single `type` attribute for each rule. By specifying an `EXPRESSION` type, a `window.open` parameter value that is a raw URL is directly rewritten. Otherwise, the parameter value is handled by the runtime Rewriter function. The new rule syntax looks something like the following:

```
<Function type="EXPRESSION" name="window.open" paramPatterns=
"y"/>
```

The rule is placed in a ruleset file represented entirely in XML between the JSRules tags so that the Gateway references the rule when inspecting JavaScript content. The tag identifier function indicates that the rule is for a JavaScript function. The `type` can be specified as `EXPRESSION`, `URL`, `DHTML`, or `DJS`. Function rules also have a pattern matching utility to specify which parameters to rewrite and which to ignore. In the case above, only the first parameter is rewritten, which is the expected behavior.

Ruleset Mapping Per Host/Domain

By mapping a ruleset to an individual host name, that ruleset is used for all content originating from that specific host. The ruleset is used as a guide to finding URLs that might require rewriting. However, the ultimate determination is made by the Proxies for Domains and Subdomains list that compares the fully qualified address's DNS value to determine whether or not the URL needs to be rewritten. Being able to specify rules that only matter to one particular application, or group of applications hosted on the same machine, reduces the likelihood that a change in the ruleset will break other applications being accessed through the Gateway. This also helps in the testing and verification process because there are no interaction problems with other applications and their rule requirements. Mapping at the domain and subdomain level is done so that a generalized ruleset can be used for all other content that does not require any special attention. Application-specific rulesets can be the glue needed to get internal content or third-party products to work through the Gateway. If the application ruleset is mapped to an individual host name, then its rollout does not affect any other applications already available through the Gateway. Portal server version 6.2 offers even further granularity by being able to map individual URLs with their own rulesets. Also, portal server 6.2 allows the rulesets to be extended so that generalized rules need not be duplicated in every ruleset.

Logging Enhancements

Using the log files in portal server 3.x to identify Rewriter misconfiguration is difficult. To begin with, the log only shows the rewritten version of the final page that was passed back to the browser. Viewing the browser source for this information is easier than trying to locate it in a log file that contains all kinds of other information. Also, the 3.0 logs do not contain imported content sources that are often the smoking gun for Rewriter problems. To get the contents of these files, you must handcraft a separate page with links that point to the JavaScript sources. By downloading the link targets, you can see the JavaScript source, but once again, it was already rewritten, unless there was direct access to the content server so that the link did not have to be downloaded through the Gateway. Oftentimes, to debug more difficult rewriting problems, you had to resort to changing the Gateway to HTTP mode, which cannot be done in a production environment. Then use the snoop command to view the traffic over the network interface to determine what the original source looked like.

Portal server 6.x offers several logging enhancements. Although you might want to write a script to parse the data, the logging enhancements make the work of integrating applications much easier. For example, a separate file records all of the pages before and after translation. Included with each entry in the file is the URI used to fetch the page, and the ruleset used for rewriting. When multiple Gateway instances are installed, a separate log file is kept for each instance. It is not advisable to keep verbose logging enabled for extended periods of time because certain content and HTTP headers may contain passwords or other sensitive data. Thus, this level of verbosity should be reserved for debugging purposes only. For more information about this and other logging enhancements, see "Rewriter Logging" on page 292.

Cleaner Ruleset Language

Rules are now specified as XML tags, rather than XML text data. The individual Gateway profile sections from portal server 3 for different content types have been consolidated into the HTMLRules, JSRules, and XMLRules sections.

Type attributes are used to determine what engine to use to parse the data, and how to go about rewriting it. For example, the type URL is used to rewrite raw URLs, while a type of EXPRESSION is used to rewrite variables or expressions that might contain string concatenations and the like. The following example shows the difference between the usage of the two types:

```
<HTML>
<HEAD>
<BODY BGCOLOR="#FFFFFF" TEXT="#000000">
staticURL = "http://www.sun.com";
catURL = protoCol + "://www.sun.com";
</BODY>
</HTML>
```

The RHS of the staticURL variable assignment contains a raw URL, so the following rule is added to the JSRules section of the appropriate ruleset:

```
<Variable Type="URL">staticURL</Variable>
```

The RHS of the catURL variable assignment, however, contains a JavaScript string concatenation, so the rule is modified to look like this:

```
<Variable type="EXPRESSION">catURL</Variable>
```

For more information about the new language, see "Migrating Portal Server 3.x Rewriter Rules" on page 216.

Content Handling Enhancements

The handling of content in a correct, predictable, browserlike fashion is of utmost importance to portal SRA administrators and end users. Portal server 6.x provides substantial improvements in the integration of existing Web application content. Some of the content handling enhancements in portal server 6.x include the following:

- Empty strings are no longer rewritten. Documents containing empty values like '' and "" are not rewritten. This prevents accidental file listings or unauthorized access in cases like empty frame sources where the contents are dynamically generated using JavaScript.

- Object constructors are not rewritten. This enables the use of rules to rewrite array data where the first entry is an object constructor, and the second is an assignment to the src property.

- Null initializations are not rewritten. Null initializations are now handled correctly by both the Gateway and the runtime Rewriter functions.

- Runtime Rewriter function definitions are not inserted in HTML element tags. Rules containing expression types can now be used to rewrite onHandler values and DHTML text bodies.

- Rewriting of imported JavaScript is now cross-browser compatible. Using its own referrer logic, the Rewriter can now determine how to correctly rewrite imported JavaScript, even if the browser does not send an HTTP referrer header as a part of the request.

Multiple Gateway Profiles

The addition of multiple Gateway profiles in portal server 6.x has increased its horizontal scalability and manageability by allowing each instance to operate independently with its own configuration. Gateway profiles now include multiple rulesets that can be mapped to individual hosts or domains. They can be applied to all content passing through the Gateway as well.

For example, a dedicated Gateway instance can now be set up and sized individually for remote users wishing to access their internal email being served up by Exchange. After following the integration recipe for Outlook Web Access (see Appendix A), a single Gateway instance can be used for the sole purpose of Web-based, secure, remote employee email access. The same can be done for other HTML-based email clients, such as Messaging Express, which ships with the Sun™ ONE Messaging Server software. At the same time, another Gateway instance can be created for general use or for access to less mission-critical applications.

Migrating Portal Server 3.x Rewriter Rules

Migrating existing Rewriter rules for an upgraded or new 6.0 installation is often easier than creating them again from scratch. Rule migration reduces the initial learning curve for syntax and administrative changes required in portal server 6.0, making it less of an impact on the early evaluation and proof-of-concept exercises required to upgrade your portal.

Portal Server 3 Gateway Profile Section Mappings

The migration tools (see "Automated Ruleset Creation Using Portal Server 6 Migration Tools" on page 219) convert your Gateway profile to a 6.0 Rewriter ruleset automatically. Otherwise, refer to TABLE 4-1 to manually configure the portal server version 6.0 equivalent Rewriter ruleset.

TABLE 4-1   Portal Server 3 to Portal Server 6 Rewriter Rule Mappings

Attribute Name Portal Server 3	Portal Server 3 Attribute Description	Example of Portal Server 6 Syntax Equivalent

iwtGateway-Tags	Rewrite HTML Attributes	`<HTMLRules>`
		`. . .`
		`<Attribute Name="foo"/>`
		`</HTMLRules>`

iwtGateway-JavaScriptTags	Rewrite HTML Attributes Containing JavaScript	`<JSRules>`
		`. . .`
		`<JStoken>on*</JSToken>`
		`</JSRules>`

iwtGateway-JavaScriptRewrite	Rewrite JavaScript Function Parameters	`<JSRules>`
		`. . .`
		`<Function type="URL" name=`
		`"openAppURL"`
		`paramPatterns="y"/>`
		`</JSRules>`

iwtGateway-JavaScriptVariables	Rewrite JavaScript Variables In URLs	`<JSRules>`
		`. . .`
		`<Variable type="URL">`
		`myURL`
		`</Variable>`
		`</JSRules>`

Attribute Name Portal Server 3	Portal Server 3 Attribute Description	Example of Portal Server 6 Syntax Equivalent

iwtGateway-JavaScriptVariableConvert	Rewrite JavaScript Variables Function	`<JSRules>`
		
		`...`
		
		`<Variable type=`
		`"EXPRESSION"> myURL`
		`</Variable>`
		`</JSRules>`

iwtGateway-JavaScriptSystemVariableConvert	Rewrite JavaScript System Variables Function	`<JSRules>`
		
		`...`
		
		`<Variable type="SYSTEM">`
		`*.location.pathname`
		`</Variable>`
		`</JSRules>`

iwtGateway-JavaScriptFunctionParameterConvert	Rewrite JavaScript Function Parameters Function	`<JSRules>`
		
		`...`
		
		`<Function type=`
		`"EXPRESSION" name=`
		`"window.open"`
		`paramPatterns="y"/>`
		`</JSRules>`

iwtGateway-JavaScriptHTML	Rewrite JavaScript Function Parameters in HTML	`<JSRules>`
		
		`...`
		
		`<Function type="DHTML"`
		`name="document.write"`
		`paramPatterns="y"/>`
		`</JSRules>`

iwtGateway-JavaScriptFunctionParameterJavaScript	Rewrite JavaScript Function Parameters In JavaScript	`<JSRules>`
		
		`...`
		
		`<Function type="DJS" name=`
		`"window.setTimeout"`
		`paramPatterns="y"/>`
		`</JSRules>`

iwtGateway-JavaScriptHTMLVariables	Rewrite JavaScript Variables in HTML	`<JSRules>`
		
		`...`
		
		`<Variable type="DHTML">`
		`myURL`
		`</Variable>`
		`</JSRules>`

Attribute Name Portal Server 3	Portal Server 3 Attribute Description	Example of Portal Server 6 Syntax Equivalent

iwtGateway-JavaScriptVaraibleJavaScript	Rewrite JavaScript Variables in JavaScript	`<JSRules>`
		
		`...`
		
		`<Variable type=`
		`"DJS">myURL</Variable>`
		
		`</JSRules>`

iwtGateway-AppletParamValues	Rewrite Applet/Object Parameter Values List	`<HTMLRules>`
		
		`...`
		
		`<Applet source="*/applets"`
		`code="map.class" param=`
		`"mapLocURL" />`
		
		`</HTMLRules>`

iwtGateway-FormInputValues	Rewrite Form Input Tags List	`<HTMLRules>`
		
		`...`
		
		`<Form source="*/signon"`
		`name="*" field=`
		`"homePageURL" />`
		
		`</HTMLRules>`

iwtGateway-XMLTextRewrite	Rewrite Text Data of XML Document	`<XMLRules>`
		
		`...`
		
		`<TagText tag="baseroot" />`
		`</XMLRules>`

iwtGateway-XMLAttributeRewrite	Rewrite Attribute Value of XML Document	`<XMLRules>`
		
		`...`
		
		`<Attribte name="href" tag=`
		`"a"/>`
		`</XMLRules>`

iwtGateway-JavaScriptFracturedHTML	Rewrite JavaScript Function Parameters in Fractured HTML	Discontinued in portal server 6.0. Can be handled using other Rewriter methods.

Note – HTMLRules and JSRules tags are only shown to determine what section the rule needs to be added to and does not indicate that the tags should wrap each individual rule. The "..." represents other rules that might or might not already be present in that specific section.

Automated Ruleset Creation Using Portal Server 6 Migration Tools

Portal server 6.0 ships with a migration suite that contains an export tool for converting Rewriter-specific data from the Gateway profile into rules. Refer to the *Sun ONE Portal Server 6.0 Migration Guide* for specifics on installing this software and other migration considerations. If you have a clean install and just want to migrate your ruleset from 3.0 to 6.x, you can install the Sun ONE Portal Server 3.0 Migration Suite on your Sun ONE Portal Server 3.0 software and run the export utility.

▼ To Migrate 3.x Rewriter Rules to 6.x Rulesets

The following steps are performed on the portal server 3.x system.

Note – You should migrate from 3.x to 6.x by installing 6.x on a separate system. This enables easier rollback in case problems that are encountered following the migration process.

---

1. **Install the Migration Suite on the 3.x system using the** `pssetup` **command.**

The Migration Suite and the `pssetup` command are available from the portal server 6.x product distribution.

```
# ./pssetup
*****************************************************************
Portal Server (6.0)
*****************************************************************
Log at /var/sadm/install/logs/pssetup.5107/setup.log
...
Sun ONE(tm) Portal Server 6.0 License/Rev 1.1
                30July02/WF
Do you accept? yes/[no] yes
Install options:
1) Install Portal Server
2) Install Directory Server only
3) Install Migration Tools
4) Exit
Choice? [4] 3
Migration Tools installations summary
-------------------------------------
Base Directory: /opt
Use these settings? [y]/n y
Installing Migration Tools...
Installation took .05 minute
Install options:
1) Install Portal server
2) Install Directory Server only
3) Exit
Choice? [3] 3
Setup complete
```

2. **Export the data using the** `exportps` **command.**

The `exportps` command dumps the necessary portal data required for migration to a temporary files.

3. **Run the** `convertps` **command, taking the following into account.**

```
# install_dir/SUNWps/migration/bin/exportps /tmp/ps3data
Found iPS version 3.0sp5
Begin Export process at Tue Jul 15 02:37:56 PDT 2003
Error file: /tmp/ps3data/logs/error.5429
Report file: /tmp/ps3data/logs/report.5429
Metrics file: /tmp/ps3data/logs/export_metrics.5429

Export Menu:
1) LDAP Database
2) Desktop
3) Certificate Databases
4) All of the above
5) Exit
Select one of the listed options to export: 1
Enter the LDAP admin passphrase
Dumping the ldap database
organizationalPersion
user
role
domain
application
Dumping xml
. . . . . . . . . . . . . . . . . . . .
Successful completion of export process at Tue Jul 15 02:43:39 PDT
2003
```

The `convertps` command only runs on systems that have the Sun ONE Portal
Server 6.x software installed, so you must do one of the following:

- Install the Sun ONE Portal Server 6.0 Migration Tools on the portal server version
  6.0 machine, copy the entire export directory contents (`/tmp/ps3data` in this
  example) to the portal server 6.x system, and run `convertps` from the portal
  server 6.x machine.

- Edit the *install_dir*/SUNWps/migration/modules/rules/45ruleconvert
  script that is installed on the 3.x machine. Comment out the `print` and `GETTEXT`
  statements and add the following lines above the `if` option for the menu at the
  beginning of the file:

```
#!/bin/ksh -a
exportDir=/tmp/ps3data
importDir=/tmp/ps6data
libDir=../../lib
JAVA_HOME=/usr/java1.2
if [ "$1" == "--menu" ];then
  .
  .
  .
```

Note – These files modifications should only be attempted if you are migrating portal server 3 Rewriter rules to a clean install of portal server 6.x. Making these changes and then performing a full migration is not recommended or supported.

---

4. **Run the** `45ruleconvert` **script as follows:**

```
# cd install_dir/SUNWps/migration/modules/rules
# ./45ruleconvert
```

The resulting `rules.xml` file is located in the `/tmp/ps6data/rewriter/rules` directory.

5. **Copy the** `rules.xml` **file to your 6.x machine.**

Copy this file to your portal server 6.x machine into the same directory where the XML is stored for the other rulesets (such as *install_dir*/SUNWps/export/).

6. **Import the ruleset using the guidelines described in "Adding and Modifying Rewriter Rules and Rulesets" on page 207.**

Comparing `rules.xml` and `iwtGateway.xml` helps you visualize how the rule definitions have been simplified in portal server 6.0, and makes the 3.0 Gateway profile section mapping more clear.

Application Integration

Application integration can require little to no administrative effort, or it can require an artful combination of log and source analysis to discern what needs to be rewritten for the application to work correctly when accessed through the Gateway. The following sections describe the special considerations and best practices to follow when configuring the Rewriter for application integration, or when developing content that will eventually be accessed through the Gateway.

Rewriting HTML Content and Attributes

Most of the needed HTML tag attributes are already provided in the out-of-box rulesets, but there may be instances where additional rules have to be added to handle new attributes supported in later revisions of the HTML specification, or for browser vendor-specific tag attributes.

For HTML content and attributes to be rewritten, the MIME type for the content must be text/HTML, and the attribute is usually a raw URL. If the attribute value instead contains JavaScript content, A JSToken rule must be added to the HTMLRules section of the appropriate ruleset. The following is an example:

```
<BODY onResize="this.location.href='hompage.html';">
<A TARGET="content" HREF="iim.jnlp" NAME="CHAT"
onMouseOver=document.images[0].src="images/chat2.gif"
onMouseOut=document.images[0].src="images/chat.gif";>
<IMG ALIGN="MIDDLE"
SRC="images/chat.gif" BORDER="0" ALT=" Chat"></A>
</BODY>
```

In the previous example, there are three tags: BODY, A, and IMG. The tag attributes are onResize, TARGET, HREF, NAME, onMouseOver, onMouseOut, ALIGN, SRC, and ALT. Only onResize, HREF, onMouseOver, onMouseOut, and SRC need to be considered for containing potential URLs. Of those, the HREF and SRC attributes are taken care of out-of-box by the following rules:

```
<HTMLRules>
.

.

.
<Attribute name="href"/>
<Attribute name="src"/>
.

.

.
</HTMLRules>
```

Similarly, onMouseOver and onMouseOut are taken care of by:

```
<JSRules>
.

.

.
<JSToken>onMouseOver</JSToken>
<JSToken>onMouseOut</JSToken>
.

.

.
</JSRules>
```

Three things remain for this example to work. The first is to add a rule for the onResize event handler if it is not present. Do this by adding an additional JSToken rule: `<JSToken>onResize</JSToken>`.

Second, to parse the attribute values for the onMouseOver and onMouseOut event handlers, a wildcarded rule needs to be added to the JSRules section. This might look like this: `<Variable type="URL">` *document.images*`*.src </Variable>`. A more generalized rule such as `<Variable type="URL"> *.src </Variable>` also works, but it is advisable to err on the conservative side so as to not mistakenly rewrite string literals that are not actually URLs.

HTML BASE Tag

It is important to understand the role that the BASE tag plays in how documents are rewritten, and what to expect in content that contains a BASE tag. The BASE tag is used by the browser for address completion of relative links. Instead of rewriting the BASE HREF attribute value and leaving the relative URLs alone, the Rewriter comments out the BASE tag entirely and rewrites the relative URLs throughout the document by using the translated value of the BASE tag for address completion. The only exception to this rule is when a BASE TAG contains a TARGET attribute, in which case the first BASE tag is still commented out entirely, but a new BASE tag is added that contains the same TARGET attribute and attribute value. The BASE and TARGET remain exposed to prevent the incorrect loading of a selected link to the current document.

The BASE tag and HREF attribute are commented out so that multiple scraped channels that each contain BASE tags will not affect each other or any other portal server desktop content containing its own relative URLs. Because the portal server desktop is essentially an HTML table after it is rendered, there is no way to have the relative URLs resolved correctly with multiple BASE tags. Similarly, scraped pages that contain CSS content can adversely affect the entire portal server desktop if the CSS content contains generalized style definitions for basic HTML elements such as the BODY and TABLE elements. For example, consider the following CSS contained in a URL scraped page that modifies the look of the scrollbars in Internet Explorer:

```
<HTML>
<STYLE>
  <!--
    BODY {
    scrollbar-face-color: #9999CC;
    scrollbar-highlight-color: CCCCFF;
    scrollbar-3dlight-color: #CCCCFF;
    scrollbar-darkshadow-color: #DDDDDD;
    scrollbar-shadow-color: #EEEEEE;
    scrollbar-arrow-color: #CCCCFF;
    scrollbar-track-color: #333366
    }
  -->
</STYLE>
<BODY>
Scraped page that changes the portal desktop scrollbars
</BODY>
</HTML>
```

The result is similar to that in FIGURE 4-12.

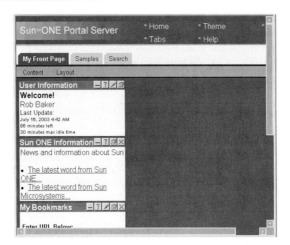

FIGURE 4-12 Modified Scrollbars in Internet Explorer

FIGURE 4-12 shows that scrollbars for the portal server desktop inherited style characteristics from remote content. This would be a nice effect had it been intended, or it can seriously clash with your meticulously planned desktop branding if you are not careful.

One other limitation to be aware of is when content contains a BASE tag and an APPLET or OBJECT tag that does not contain a CODEBASE attribute. In this particular case, when the BASE tag is commented out, the browser will no longer be able to find the APPLET or OBJECT code or any parameter data specified with relative URLs because there will not be any prepended path information supplied. Always be sure that a CODEBASE attribute is used for these and similar tags when a BASE tag is also used within the same document. Follow the same guideline for dynamically created APPLET tags because the CODEBASE attribute might be added out of context with the JavaScript `document.write` call, resulting in code that might look like the following:

```
Before rewriting:

document.writeln("APPLET CODE=\"com.citrix.JICA.class\" ARCHIVE=\
"JICAEngJ.jar\" width=800 height=600>");

After rewriting:

document.writeln("APPLET
codebase="https://gw.sun.com/http://ica-server.int.sun.com"
CODE=\"com.citrix.JICA.class\" ARCHIVE=\"JICAEngJ.jar\" width=800
height=600>");
```

Note – The unescaped quotes in the codebase attribute value results in an error such as `Expected ")"`. To prevent this from occurring, always make sure that object tags have a corresponding CODEBASE attribute.

Even though the BASE HREF attribute value can be a fully qualified URL that includes a resource name, you should end the HREF value with a directory name and a trailing slash. The following example uses a valid BASE tag, but doesn't have a trailing slash.

```
<BASE HREF="http://www.iplanet.com/docs/index.html">
```

The following example is sure to resolve relative URLs throughout the remainder of the document.

```
<BASE HREF="http://www.iplanet.com/docs/">
```

Additionally, BASE HREF attribute values with only host and port information and no path information, as in the following example, are not recommended because the relative URLs contained in the page may be rewritten incorrectly due to the lack of a path value in the BASE URL.

```
<BASE HREF="http://www.iplanet.com.80">
```

Best Practices—HTML Programming for Use Through the Gateway

Here are rough guidelines for content developers to follow when creating content that will be accessed through the Gateway.

- Always use CODEBASE attributes for tags that support them, as in the following example:

```
<APPLET CODEBASE="http://www.iplanet.com/java/"
CODE="helloWorld.class">
```

- End BASE HREF attribute URLs with a directory name or a directory name and a following slash, as in the following example:

```
<BASE HREF="http://www.iplanet.com/docs/">
```

Different browsers handle poorly written BASE tags differently, so it is good to make sure they each have host, port, and path information, and a trailing slash indicating that path is to be used to resolve relative URLs throughout the remainder of the document.

- Avoid fractured HTML where attribute values or tag bodies containing URLs might be defined on multiple lines, as in the following example:

```
document.write("<A HREF=\"\n");
document.write("http://www.iplanet.com\n");
document.write("\">link</A>\n");
```

Instead, make sure that the attribute's URL value appears immediately after the attribute in the same line. This makes it possible for the Rewriter to handle URLs contained in DHTML.

- Try to maintain well-formed HTML where quotes match up and are the same type. Avoid nested quotes where possible, and use consistency across tag definitions, as in the following example:

```
document.write("<IMG SRC='" + theSrc + "' HEIGHT=80
WIDTH='80'>");
```

If the SRC JavaScript variable has already been rewritten, this can result in the image URL being rewritten twice causing it not to be displayed correctly.

- Specify URLs with prepended path information whenever possible. Having prepended path information makes it easier for the Gateway to figure out address completion. The following is an example:

```
<IMG SRC="../../images/button.gif">
```

This avoids potential problems with BASE tag HREF attribute values that might not contain a path represented as a slash following the port number.

- Do not use uppercase or mixed-case protocol identifiers in your URLs, as in the following:

> 🚫 `<A HREF="HTTP://content-server.iplanet.com">`

In earlier versions of the portal server, mixed-case protocols were skipped, resulting in URLs not being rewritten. The suggestion remains as a good programming practice.

- Do not attempt to mimic the Rewriter behavior by adding the Gateway name to the URL prior to passing the content through the Gateway, as in the following:

> 🚫 ```
> var myRewrittenURL =
> https://gw.sun.com/http://cms.int.sun.com;
> ```

While this may work, it would be better to add the variable name to the ruleset. Using already rewritten URLs can be difficult to maintain in the source code, the page might not work when accessed directly, and it might not work properly in future versions of portal server.

- Avoid setting attribute values to null if a rule has been added to rewrite the attribute value. This again refers to limitations in earlier versions of the portal server, but it is good practice to make sure that attribute values that are URLs are non-empty. The following is an example of what you should avoid if possible:

> 🚫 ```
> <FRAMESET cols="20%, 80%">
>   <FRAMESET rows="100, 200">
>   <FRAME src="">
>   <FRAME src="page2.html">
>   </FRAMESET>
>   <FRAME src="page3.html">
> </FRAMESET>
> ```


Note – This is usually done so that JavaScript write methods can later be called to create the actual frame source. The alternative is to create a `page1.html` file that contains all of the necessary client-side JavaScript to create its own content.

- Avoid using the STYLE attribute with a background URL in HTML tags, as in the following example:

```
<BODY STYLE="background-
image:url(../../img/background.jpg);
background-repeat:repeat;width:770px">
```

The URL method of CSS is rewritten correctly, but rather than using it in an inline style sheet, it is better to define it inside a STYLE tag in the document HEAD. It is also a good idea to stick to strict CSS syntax when writing CSS that passes through the Gateway, to ensure that the URLs are rewriting correctly.

- Avoid using a SCRIPT tag with a language attribute other than JavaScript, as in the following example:

```
<SCRIPT Language="VBScript">
```

There is currently no functionality in the Rewriter to handle scripted languages other than JavaScript. So this requirement is not just for the language attribute value itself, but also for any contents within a SCRIPT element. JScript has JavaScript-like syntax and might work. JScript event handlers and built-in variables are not rewritten out-of-box except for those in common with its JavaScript counterpart. VBScript does not work at all, and you should port it to JavaScript even if it does not contain URL handling or modification.

- Do not pass gzipped HTML through the Gateway to be displayed by the client. This HTML might contain URLs that cannot be rewritten because the content is in a compressed format when it passes through the Gateway. The Rewriter initially determines which pages are passed in using the MIME type of the content. For a content-type of `application/x-zip-compressed` or `application/x-compress`, the Rewriter ignores it and sends it on its way to be decompressed by the browser or a helper application. Any HTML data contained in the compressed file is not rewritten. Beginning with portal server 6.1 software, the `accept-content: gzip` header is stripped from the request, so the content server should never send gzipped content.

- If you are using portal server 6.0 and have content that has only a # (hash) in the HREF attribute value, you must install a patch or upgrade to a later version of portal server 6, such as 6.1 or 6.2. Example:

```
<A HREF="#" onClick="launchWindow();">
```

This example is not rewritten correctly by portal server 6.0, and prevents this event handler from firing because it is rewritten to something similar to the following:

```
<A HREF="https://gw.sun.com/http://app.int.sun.com/" onClick=
"launchWindow();">
```

Note that the hash is mistakenly removed and the HREF attribute is rewritten rather than leaving the hash as is.

Rewriting Form Content

The FORM tag ACTION attribute is rewritten by the Gateway out-of-box. So the only things to be concerned about when rewriting form data are the INPUT and SELECT tag value attributes and any JavaScript event handlers if they are being used.

There are eight INPUT types that have supporting attributes that can contain URLs, in addition to the OPTION tag values that can have URLs as well. One of these INPUT types, image, also has a supporting SRC attribute that is rewritten by default out-of-the-box. Although the syntax for rewriting FORM INPUT values is different from most other content, the basic premise is the same. Only those values that contain URLs need to be considered. For example, it is unlikely that the value of a form INPUT TYPE of PASSWORD would ever be a URL. However, a drop-down menu used as a navigation tool could very well contain one or more URLs.

The general syntax for a rule used to rewrite form data is that it must contain at least three entries:

- Page or object identifier called *source*

  This is the actual name of the object, including any prepended path information that directly follows the protocol, Web server name, and port number in the URL. For example, the URL `http://www.iplanet.com/forms/signup.html` page identifier including the path is: `/forms/signup.html`.

- Form name, identified simply as *name*

  This is the name of the form defined using the NAME attribute in the opening FORM tag, as in the following example:

  ```
  <FORM NAME="menuForm">
  ```

- INPUT or OPTION tag NAME attribute, referred to as *field*

  This is the name of the INPUT or OPTION tag given using the NAME attribute, as in the following example:

  ```
  <OPTION NAME="destination1" VALUE="http://www.sun.com">
  ```

A fourth option, *valuePatterns*, can be used to pick out and rewrite URLs that might be buried in other data in the form values such as:

```
<INPUT TYPE="CHECKBOX" NAME="check" VALUE="0|http://www.sun.com">
```

These three or four rule attributes provide a more granular method to control how the Gateway rewrites form INPUT and OPTION data. Each rule attribute can also have wildcards for more general application. It is usually best to be as specific as possible when generating FORM input rules so that FORM data from other pages is not unexpectedly rewritten. Consider the following example:

```
<FORM>
This is a pulldown menu:<br>
<SELECT>
  <OPTION VALUE="___" selected>Select Destination</OPTION>
  <OPTION VALUE="http://www.sun.com">Sun Home Page</OPTION>
  <OPTION VALUE="http://www.sun.com/solaris">Solaris
Information</OPTION>
  <OPTION VALUE="http://www.sun.com/blueprints">Sun
BluePrints</OPTION>
</SELECT>
</FORM>
```

When accessed using the URL
`http://news.int.sun.com/forms/signup.html`, the FORM INPUT data is
rewritten by using the document name with its path (`/forms/signup.html`) in the
first field of the rule, and wildcards for the remaining two, making the
corresponding rule look like this:

```
<Form source="*/forms/signup.html" name="*" field="*"/>
```

The limitation here should be obvious—the rule is too generalized. However, if the
FORM has a name, the control of what data is to be rewritten can be increased
substantially as in this case:

```
<FORM NAME="menuForm">
This is a pulldown menu:<br>
<SELECT>
  <OPTION VALUE="___" selected>Select Destination</OPTION>
  <OPTION VALUE="http://www.sun.com">Sun Home Page</OPTION>
  <OPTION VALUE="http://www.sun.com/solaris">Solaris
Information</OPTION>
  <OPTION VALUE="http://www.sun.com.com/blueprints">Sun
BluePrints Home Page</OPTION>
</SELECT>
</FORM>
```

In this case, the rule is changed slightly to:

```
<Form source="*/forms/signup.html" name="menuForm" field="*"/>
```

The option tags can be given names as well to specialize the rule, so that only one
particular form and one particular value is rewritten. Be careful to order the rules so
that the most specific ones appear first and the most generalized ones appear later.
When accessing the above example, you see that the option values are rewritten. You
might have to make special concessions for the first option that is not a URL,
because it is still rewritten. There might be a CGI script that handles the form, or
there might be a JavaScript form handler that checks the current selected value
against "____". This value becomes
"`https://gw.sun.com/http://forms.int.sun.com/forms/signup.html__`
__" and the code check fails. To circumvent this problem, the form validation script
can look for a substring match for "_____", or the FORM rule can be removed, and
the form itself changed to something like the following:

```
<FORM NAME="menuForm">
This is a pulldown menu:<br>
<SELECT onChange="document.location.href=
this[selectedIndex].value";>
  <OPTION VALUE="___" selected>Select Destination</OPTION>
  <OPTION VALUE="http://www.sun.com">Sun Home Page</OPTION>
  <OPTION VALUE="http://www.sun.com/solaris">Solaris
Information</OPTION>
  <OPTION VALUE="http://www.iplanet.com">iPlanet Home
Page</OPTION>
</SELECT>
</FORM>
```

By adding the following rule, the form options are rewritten at runtime, and the current selected value is "_____".

```
<Variable type="EXPRESSION"> document.location.href </Variable>
```

One other thing to be aware of when specifying rules that are too generalized is that other form control values might be mistakenly rewritten. Consider an earlier example, plus a few additional input controls:

```
<FORM NAME="menuForm">
This is a pulldown menu:<br>
<SELECT NAME="navOptions">
  <OPTION VALUE="___" selected>Select Destination</OPTION>
  <OPTION VALUE="http://www.sun.com">Sun Home Page</OPTION>
  <OPTION VALUE="http://www.sun.com/solaris">Solaris
Information</OPTION>
  <OPTION VALUE="http://www.sun.com.com/blueprints">Sun
BluePrints Home Page</OPTION>
</SELECT>
<INPUT TYPE="HIDDEN" NAME="hidden_code" VALUE="00019283">
<INPUT TYPE="TEXT" NAME="url_field" VALUE="Enter a URL" SIZE="20">
<INPUT TYPE="SUBMIT" VALUE="Go!">
</FORM>
```

A rule that looks like the following example forces the input controls to be rewritten. This is easily identifiable when the label for the Submit button reads something like `https://gw.int.sun.com/http://membership.int.sun.com/forms/Go!` instead of just `Go!`.

```
<Form source="*" name="menuForm" field="*"/>
```

The rule should instead look like this:

```
<Form source="*" name="menuForm" field="navOptions"/>
```

Many FORM actions point to CGI scripts that parse the query string and evaluate the FORM data. Sometimes hidden field FORM elements are used to temporarily hold data to be sent to the CGI program that might contain a mixture of data in its value, part of which might include a URL. The following is an example:

```
<FORM NAME="menuForm">
This is a pulldown menu:<br>
<SELECT NAME="mySelect"
onChange="document.location.href=this[selectedIndex].value";>
<OPTION VALUE="___" selected>Select Destination</OPTION>
<OPTION VALUE="http://www.sun.com">Sun Home Page</OPTION>
<OPTION VALUE="http://www.sun.com/solaris">Solaris
Information</OPTION>
<OPTION VALUE="http://www.sun.com/blueprints">Sun BluePrints Home
Page</OPTION>
</SELECT>
<INPUT TYPE="HIDDEN" NAME="hidden_code" VALUE="00019283|http://
www.sun.com|898239">
<INPUT TYPE="TEXT" NAME="url_field" VALUE="Enter a URL" SIZE="20">
<INPUT TYPE="SUBMIT" VALUE="Go!">
</FORM>
```

The only thing that has changed in this example from the previous one is that the value of the hidden INPUT field named `hidden_code` now has pipe-separated data values that include a URL. Rewriting the second data element in the value requires a URL pattern to be used in the rule syntax. Thus, to rewrite this particular URL, a rule must be added that looks like the following example:

```
<Form source="*" name="menuForm" field="hidden_code"
valuePatterns="*|"/>
```

The `*|` pattern indicates to the Rewriter that the raw URL begins after the first pipe symbol in the value of the VALUE attribute. The use of non-white space separators is recommended so that rule creation is made possible.

Best Practices—HTML FORM Generation Programming for Use Through the Gateway

Following are rough guidelines for content developers to follow when creating original content to be accessed through the Gateway or in implementing content-based workarounds for corner cases that are difficult to address through configuration of the Rewriter. You should use the following HTML FORM generation best practices:

- Name all FORM and FORM-related tags that contain URLs.

  This gives you better control from the Rewriter as to which FORM data needs to be rewritten, as in the following example:

```
<FORM NAME="myForm">
  <INPUT TYPE="HIDDEN" NAME="myURL" VALUE="http://www.sun.com">
</FORM>
```

  Even if it seems superfluous at the time, it can't hurt to add names to all of your form elements, and to establish a unified naming strategy for URLs that can help in reducing the number of rules that have to be created to rewrite all of the form content.

- Avoid mixing contexts within the same SELECT tag.

  In other words, do not make some options URLs while others are bare strings, as in the following example:

```
<FORM NAME="myForm">
<SELECT NAME="mySelect">
  <OPTION VALUE="Destination1"
selected>Destination1</OPTION>
  <OPTION VALUE="http://www.sun.com">Sun Home
Page</OPTION>
  <OPTION VALUE="Destination2">Destination2</OPTION>
  <OPTION VALUE="http://www.sun.com/blueprints">Sun
BluePrints Home Page</OPTION>
</SELECT>
</FORM>
```

This is an unlikely scenario, but it points out that the URLs and the destination string values are both rewritten.

- Avoid the use of white space separators in `FORM` data whose `VALUE` attribute contains multiple elements, as in the following example:

```
<INPUT TYPE="HIDDEN" NAME="hidden_code"
VALUE="The URL is http://www.sun.com">
```

In this case, it is more difficult to specify a value pattern that will only rewrite the URL portion of the string. Specifying a valuePatterns of `*` is not allowed because the entire string would be matched. It may be possible to specify a value pattern of `*http://` in this particular case, but that is not a recommended approach.

- Avoid using generalized rules that might unintentionally rewrite other FORM data. For instance, you should avoid using a rule like the following:

```
<Form source="*" name="*" field="*"/>
```

While this might seem to be the lazy administrative approach to rewriting form data, you are likely to be inundated by users complaining that their forms are not working, or that the form labels contain URLs.

- Do not define FORM tag elements on multiple lines dynamically using JavaScript, as in the following example:

```
document.write("<INPUT TYPE=\"HIDDEN\" ");
document.write("NAME=\"hidden_code\" ");
document.write("VALUE=\"http://www.sun.com\">");
```

The Rewriter interprets each `document.write` statement individually, and makes no assumption as to the relevance to a previous or following `document.write` statement. All of the FORM content should be in a single `document.write` statement, or the URL value contained in the form should be extracted to a JavaScript variable that can be rewritten independently of the FORM content.

- Avoid generating entire FORM data from within a SCRIPT element using multiple string concatenations, as in the following example:

```
html+='<form name="myForm" target="myFrame" ';
html+='action="http://www.sun.com/cgi-bin/send_form.pl"
method="post">';
html+='<input type="hidden" value=
"http://www.sun.com"></form>';
```

For a similar reason, as the `document.write` approach, it is better to extract the URL from the HTML variable concatenation so that it can be rewritten aside from the form content itself.

- Avoid duplicate FORM element names, except when referring to a URL. This reduces the number of rules required for FORM data, as in the following example of what to avoid:

```
<FORM>
<INPUT TYPE="HIDDEN" NAME="field1" VALUE=
"http://www.sun.com">
</FORM>
...
<FORM>
<INPUT TYPE="HIDDEN" NAME="field1" VALUE="9899898">
</FORM>
```

When the content appears on the same page and the FORM elements are not named, there is no way for the Rewriter to differentiate one field from the next if they contain the same name.

- Avoid using JavaScript content to change FORM element data where a URL is a JavaScript variable, as in the following example:

```
<FORM TARGET="_self"
ACTION="http://www.sun.com/cgi-bin/gen_mail.pl"
onSubmit="this.MSG.value=top.homePageURL;">
<INPUT TYPE="HIDDEN" NAME="MSG" VALUE=
"http://www.sun.com">
</FORM>
```

You must be vigilant with JavaScript manipulating form values containing URLs so that the new URL overwriting the preceding one is rewritten correctly in addition to the initial value being rewritten. Some URLs should not be rewritten at all because they are provided only for an internal application parsing the form data for which to post the results.

- Try to handle URLs in scripted buttons in the JavaScript function body if the function parameter is not a raw URL, as in the following example:

```
<SCRIPT>
function openPage(url) {
tmpURL = url;
}
</SCRIPT>
...
<INPUT TYPE="BUTTON" NAME="Next" VALUE="-->>Next"
onClick="openPage(document.protocol + '://' + document.hostname
+
document.port + '/page2.html');">
```

Note – In this case, a rule needs to be created for the assignment to tmpURL so that other scripts requiring the value of `tmpURL` will get the already-rewritten value. A rule could be created to rewrite the first openPage function parameter too, but for readability reasons, if possible, it is better to rewrite it inside the function definition. With practice and familiarity with the code, and by following the recommendations in this book, you can determine where the best point of rewriting may be for the application to work correctly.

- Do not create dynamic paths for the page containing the FORM if you want to match FORM data using the URL object as one of the specified fields in the rule definition. The following is an example of what to avoid:

 `http://www.sun.com/cgi-bin/forms/988923/form.html`

In this example, part of the path itself is a random number (the session ID of `988923`) that is used internally by the form handling script. A value pattern of `*/forms/*/form.html` works, as long as you want to rewrite every dynamically created form.

Rewriting JavaScript and JScript Content

Because JavaScript is a programming language, there are any number of ways to represent the same functional result. The trick is that if the result contains a URL, the Gateway needs to understand that fact. The reasoning is exactly the same as the reason for rewriting HTML: If there is some URL handling performed using JavaScript content, then the request still needs to be sent back to the Gateway component rather than attempting to directly contact the internal Web application server.

For many portal server Gateway administrators, rewriting JavaScript content is the most difficult task in deploying and maintaining a secure portal server installation. The randomness at which URLs can occur throughout scripted code contributes to the difficulty. New methods and variables used with JavaScript to interact directly with the DOM, and the fact that JavaScript content is intertwined with HTML SPEC 4.01, add to the challenge.

Areas where JavaScript content might need to be rewritten include the obvious SCRIPT elements, event handlers within HTML tags, and imported JavaScript content. Specific things to look for are references to window and document object methods, events, and properties that might affect or refer to URLs. Within the JavaScript code itself, obvious areas might include variable assignments, function parameters, and JavaScript object arrays.

Having a good understanding of how to write JavaScript content is very helpful when trying to mine out URLs contained in it. While details about JavaScript content are beyond the scope of this book, the JavaScript objects and methods that you need to be concerned with, as they relate to the Rewriter, are covered in detail. The browser implementation of the document object model is different for different browsers, and each browser offers JavaScript content its own set of capabilities. With the advent of .NET, Internet Explorer has continued to use proprietary tags, attributes, and protocol extensions. Methods and objects that are common between the Internet Explorer and Netscape™ Navigator browsers are covered in detail. Known third-party product integrations that depend on proprietary technology are also discussed.

Web Browser Document Object Properties

Document object properties are generally manipulated through a JavaScript assignment statement. In most cases, the full object path is on the left side of the assignment operator, and a raw URL is on the right side of the assignment operator.

With that known, you can differentiate what rule type to specify when creating a rule that rewrites the assignment. Generally speaking, when the right side of a variable assignment is a raw URL, and the left side is a document object property, the full object path should be used as the variable name in the rule, and the rule's type should be URL. If there is any doubt as to whether the assignment will always be a raw URL, the type can also be set to EXPRESSION with the same results for an assignment that looks like the following:

```
document.location.href = "http://www.sun.com";
```

The right side is clearly a raw URL, so the rule to add to the appropriate ruleset looks like this:

```
<Variable type="URL"> document.location.href </Variable>
```

One of the enhancements made in portal server version 6 over portal server version 3 is that EXPRESSION rule types are first interpreted as URL types. This avoids being pigeonholed into deciding one over the other, because the EXPRESSION type is all-inclusive. In portal server 3, there were two separate profile sections for JavaScript variables, and you had to choose whether you wanted the Gateway to translate the URL before emitting the code to the client, or whether you wanted the Gateway to add logic so that the client would rewrite the URL at runtime. For images used in mouseovers, rewriting the URL at runtime might cause a pause while the appropriate URL for the image to display is figured out and then fetched. If the image is not cached, this continues to repeat itself, and can diminish the usability of the application.

Consider the following assignment:

```
document.location.href=newURL;
```

Because the RHS of the assignment is not a raw URL, the rule type must be EXPRESSION if your intention is to rewrite the built-in JavaScript variable. Alternately, newURL might also be rewritten elsewhere such as at its point of initialization. A rule that handles this particular assignment might look like this:

```
<Variable type="EXPRESSION"> *.location.href </Variable>
```

This matches parent.location.href, top.location.href, and so on. But it is not so generalized as to rewrite a variable called myhref unintentionally as the following rule would:

 `<Variable type="EXPRESSION"> *href </Variable>`

The value of newURL is not determined until runtime, so there is no way for the Gateway to accurately determine its value. Thus, when the preceding example is accessed through the Gateway, the assignment is modified to look like this:

```
document.location.href=
psSRAPRewriter_convert_expression(newURL);
```

The `convert_expression` function evaluates its single parameter and returns a rewritten URL using the browser's JavaScript engine. The function body and its helpers are also inserted into the page, if they have not already been defined. This results in some page bloat, but it is necessary to give enough context for the URL to be rewritten. In earlier versions of portal server 3, the `convert_function` definition was inserted after the point of reference, and even inside of HTML tags that contained JavaScript event handlers. The problems are far in the past, and the previous rule also takes care of the following assignment:

```
<BODY onLoad="document.location.href=newURL;">
```

The following are some browser object properties that can contain URLs:

- `document.location.href` – Used to change the URL for the current page
- `document.location.path` – Used as part of a relative URL
- `document.location.protocol` – Used to form a URL
- `document.location.host` – Used to form a URL
- `document.referrer` – Used for the URL of the document that referred to the current one
- `document.URL` – Used for the URL of the current document

Because of the JavaScript object scoping, each of the proceeding properties can also have `window` prepended to the full property path. The window object also has several event handlers that can contain additional JavaScript content. A few of the more well-used window object events are onLoad, onResize, and onUnload. Window events are often located in the BODY tag of the HTML document and they execute when the page is first rendered (as in the case of the onLoad event). Frames also often make use of the same such events.

As alluded to earlier, when referring to specific frames or other objects in the DOM hierarchy, the object path may differ, which requires either an additional rule or a wildcard rule, if possible. Neither `window.location.href` nor `parent.location.href` is matched by a rule value of `location.href`. However, by wildcarding the rule, you can take care of both instances.

Web Browser Document Object Methods

There is no one specific way to rewrite browser document object method calls that contain URLs. The rule syntax and appropriate section to be considered in the Gateway profile depends on the method parameters and semantics. For example, the `window.open` method takes several parameters, but they must be in a specific order, and all of them start with a URL as the first parameter. If the URL is a raw URL, then the function type can be URL. Otherwise, the function type should be specified as EXPRESSION.

The syntax for a rule that rewrites document object methods includes the function name, the type, and a pattern that indicates which method parameters must be rewritten. The pattern is a string of y's and commas, where a comma is used to signify multiple parameters and a y is used to tell the Gateway that a particular parameter requires rewriting. This might be easier to understand in practice. Consider a call to window.open in the following example:

```
<HTML>
<HEAD>
<SCRIPT>
function myWin() {
window.open('/channels/stocks_channel.html','Stocks',
'width=300,height=250,directories=no,location=no,menubar=no,
scrollbars=yes,status=no,toolbar=no,resizable=yes');
}
</SCRIPT>
</HEAD>
<BODY onLoad="myWin()";
</BODY>
</HTML>
```

After this document loads, another window with stock information automatically opens. The RHS of the onLoad assignment does not contain a URL in this instance, so it is of little consequence whether it has been removed from the ruleset, or if it was ever added at all. If the myWin function had a parameter that required rewriting, then a rule for onLoad would have to exist for the URL to be considered. In this particular example, the only URL to worry about is the one in the first parameter of the window.open method. Because window.open is so widely used in such a variety of ways, it should always be defined as an EXPRESSION type. Therefore, to rewrite the window.open document object method, you want a rule that looks like this:

```
<Function type="EXPRESSION" name="window.open" paramPatterns=
"y"/>
```

There are no commas displayed because there aren't any other parameters besides the first one in this particular case. If the URL instead occurred as the second parameter, the corresponding paramPatters value would look like y.

A rule for the window.open method has already been added to the Gateway profile, out-of-box. However, it is highly recommended to change its type to EXPRESSION. That way, if the first parameter is a raw URL, its value is translated by the Gateway, but if it is a variable, it is instead wrapped in the convert_function and rewritten at runtime. If the type is left as URL, and the parameter is a variable, it is ignored and might result in a connection failure preventing the contents from being displayed in the newly opened window.

Consider the example:

```
<HTML>
<HEAD>
<SCRIPT>
function myWin() {
myURL = '/channels/stocks_channel.html';
window.open(myURL,'Stocks',
 'width=300,height=250,directories=no,location=no,
menubar=no,scrollbars=yes,status=no,toolbar=no,resizable=yes'); }
</SCRIPT>
</HEAD>
<BODY onLoad="myWin()";>
</BODY>
</HTML>
```

This page works out-of-box once the window.open rule type is changed to EXPRESSION. The opposite recommendation was made in portal server 3 because window.open was so often called from JavaScript event handlers in HTML code, and there was a problem where the dynamic Rewriter function body would be inserted into the HTML element definition creating a syntactically incorrect result. The example included here shows you that there is more than one way to get the job done. If, for instance, the window.open type had to stay as URL for some reason, you could add a rule for the myURL variable, which means that the first parameter in the window.open method call would already be rewritten, and not need to be rewritten again.

The following are some other browser object methods that can contain URLs:

- document.assign – Sets the document.location.href property value.
- document.write – Used for dynamically creating content using client computing resources.
- document.writeln – Used in the same manner as document.write with the added benefit of a line break.
- window.open – Used for multiwindowed applications.

JavaScript Object Arrays

One other way JavaScript code is frequently used to manipulate URLs is through the use of JavaScript object arrays. These arrays provide accessory functionality to the JavaScript content so that attribute values can be changed dynamically after the page is rendered in the browser. Object arrays can be used in a variety of ways, including mouseovers for image buttons, preloading content such as images that are used in a JavaScript animation, or FORM field changes or checks. Most of the arrays containing URLs that you might need to address are anchors, applets, forms, frames, images, and links. The syntax of the JavaScript object array references includes the full object path, array name, index value, and attribute to change.

The following is an example:

```
<HTML>
<HEAD>
<SCRIPT>

function createImages() {
   for (var i=0; i<imgArr.length; i++) {
      document.writeln("<IMG SRC='" + imgArr[i].src + "' BORDER=
0><BR>");
   }
}
function preLoadImages() {
   imgArr = new Array();
   imgArr[0] = new Image();
   imgArr[0].src = "images/card_front.gif";
   imgArr[1] = new Image();
   imgArr[1].src = "images/card_back.gif";
   createImages();
}
if (document.images) {
   preLoadImages();
}

</SCRIPT>
</HEAD>
<BODY BGCOLOR="#FFFFFF" TEXT="#000000">
</BODY>
</HTML>
```

This example might force the page to take a bit longer to download because all of the images are fetched first, even if they are not initially displayed. This is common practice for mouseover events or animations where the usability of the page depends on quick retrieval (in this case, from the browser cache) of the images. The result of this code running is that the imgArr array is populated and can be accessed using the image src property. Once populated, the image HTML is dynamically generated using the values of the array indices. When rewriting arrays, it is important to note that because the Rewriter operates using regular expressions, brackets have special meaning and cannot be used in the rule entries. So, the correct rule is wildcarded and looks something like this:

```
<Variable type="URL">imgArr*.src</Variable>
```

The image constructors are dutifully ignored, and only the actual image URLs are rewritten. To demonstrate the flexibility of the portal server 6.x Rewriter, changing the rule type to EXPRESSION, and changing the example above just slightly so that the preloadImages function body looks like this:

```
function preLoadImages() {
   imgURL = "images/card_front.gif";
   imgArr = new Array();
   imgArr[0] = new Image();
   imgArr[0].src = imgURL;
   imgArr[1] = new Image();
   imgArr[1].src = "images/card_back.gif";
   createImages();
}
```

This yields very interesting results that look like the following:

```
function preLoadImages() {
   imgURL = "images/card_front.gif";
   imgArr = new Array();
   imgArr[0] = new Image();
   imgArr[0].src =psSRAPRewriter_convert_expression( imgURL);
   imgArr[1] = new Image();
   imgArr[1].src =
"https://gw.sun.comcom/http://content.int.sun.com/test_cases/boo
k/images/card_back.gif";
   createImages();
}
```

The image constructors continue to be ignored, the raw URL is rewritten directly, and the convert_function wraps the JavaScript variable imgURL. If the rule was accidentally created without the src extension, the example still works, though quite a bit slower, as every assignment containing imgArr would have to execute the convert function. This could be taxing on the client compute resources for larger arrays.

Similar to the preceding example, a rule can also be created that rewrites an array index of a built-in JavaScript array as in the following example:

```
.
.
.
function depress(imgNum){
  if (imgNum == 1) {
    document.images["IMG"+imgNum].src = "../../img/Back_lit.gif";
    liftUp(2);
  }
.
.
.
```

Here again, the only rule required to rewrite the JavaScript images array reference is:

```
<Variable type="URL">document.images*.src</Variable>
```

The wildcard *.src can also be used to reduce rule clutter and maintain performance by limiting the number of rules that the Gateway has to compare when rewriting JavaScript content. It is best, however, to keep the rules as detailed as possible—particularly if the ruleset is being generated only for a particular application or group of applications. Sometimes more generalized rules are required if the ruleset is mapped to an entire domain or subdomain. The leading period is still included to avoid accidentally rewriting of other assignments whose left side ends in src. Using a wildcard here, as in most cases, can be just as dangerous as it is beneficial. A rule of thumb is that specificity limits unintended consequence at the expense of flexibility.

Specialized JavaScript Variables

There are a few built-in JavaScript variables for which a relative URL is required, and therefore, should not be translated into an absolute URL. location.pathname, for instance, should only specify the path portion of a URL. Normally, if a page containing location.pathname is accessed through the Gateway, its value would incorrectly contain redirect/, in addition to the protocol and server where the content originated from instead of just the relative path.

There is a special variable type designation called system that handles the pathname usage. Similar to how the convert function is used, `location.pathname` is wrapped in a function that parses out the correct expected value. Out-of-box, there is a rule that looks like this:

```
<Variable type="SYSTEM">window.location.pathname</Variable>
```

In portal server 6.0 and 6.1, there is no way to specify additional system variables like `location.protocol` and `location.host`. Portal server 6.2 contains the appropriate wrapper functions that also handle these cases.

The following is an example of how `location.pathname` can be used:

```
<HTML>
<HEAD>
<TITLE>JavaScript Test</TITLE>
<SCRIPT LANGUAGE="JAVASCRIPT">
var pathname = window.location.pathname
</SCRIPT>
</HEAD>
<BODY>
<P>This page tests the windows.location.pathname system
variable.</P>
</BODY>
</HTML>
```

Out-of-box, the preceding example is rewritten as:

```
<HTML>
<HEAD>
<TITLE>JavaScript Test</TITLE>
<SCRIPT>
<!--

function psSRAPRewriter_convert_pathname(aPSPath)
{
    var lPSPath = aPSPath.substr( aPSPath.indexOf( "/",
            aPSPath.lastIndexOf("://") + 3 ) );
    return lPSPath;
}//psSRAPRewriter_convert_pathname()

//-->
</SCRIPT>
<SCRIPT LANGUAGE="JAVASCRIPT">
var pathname =
psSRAPRewriter_convert_pathname(window.location.pathname)
</SCRIPT>
</HEAD>
<BODY>
<P>This page tests the windows.location.pathname system
variable.</P>
</BODY>
</HTML>
```

The following is an example of how the built-in pathname variable can be used:

```
<HTML>
<HEAD>
<SCRIPT>
function aFunc(myPage){
  var URL=myPage.location.pathname; // contains full URL w/o
protocol
  var lowerURL =
  URL.substring(0,URL.toLowerCase().indexOf(".html")) +".html";
  return lowerURL;
}
var newURL = aFunc(self) + "/cgi-bin/aCGI?val1=foo&val2=bar";
</SCRIPT>
</HEAD>
<BODY BGCOLOR="#FFFFFF" TEXT="#000000">
</BODY>
</HTML>
```

In this case, `myPage.location.pathname` must be added as a system-type rule for the expected behavior to occur. The appropriate rule would look like this:

```
<Variable type="SYSTEM">myPage.location.pathname</Variable>
```

Nested JavaScript Code

Nesting JavaScript code makes the mining out of URLs a bit more difficult, and adding the correct rules a bit more challenging. For instance, the `window.object` method setTimeout takes an expression as a first parameter that can itself be a JavaScript function call.

The following is an example:

```
<HTML>
<HEAD>
<SCRIPT>
function statusMsg(msgURL) {
  window.status = msgURL;
}
</SCRIPT>
</HEAD>
<BODY BGCOLOR="#FFFFFF" TEXT="#000000">
<SCRIPT>
window.setTimeout("statusMsg('http://www.sun.com')", 1000);
</SCRIPT>
</BODY>
</HTML>
```

Assume that you could not work around this by rewriting the `window.status` assignment in the `statusMsg` function body. Instead, you are able only to rewrite the `window.setTimeout` statement for the application to work correctly.

In this case, two things must be done. First, the Rewriter needs to know that the first parameter of the `window.setTimeout` function call contains JavaScript content. So, the following rule is added to the JSRules section of the appropriate ruleset:

```
<Function type="DJS" name="window.setTimeout" paramPatterns="y"/>
```

DJS is a special type that tells the Rewriter the value specified by paramPatterns is to be interpreted as JavaScript content. The second thing that needs to be done to correctly rewrite this example is for the Rewriter to know that the first parameter of the statusMsg function is a raw URL. To do this, add the following rule to the appropriate ruleset:

```
<Function type="URL" name="statusMsg" paramPatterns="y"/>
```

If the first parameter sent to the statusMsg function was not a raw URL, the type must be set to EXPRESSION. Nested JavaScript can occur in variable assignments as well. To handle these particular cases, you need a DJS type rule to identify the JavaScript code, and an additional rule to rewrite it.

Consider the following example:

```
jsCode = "var curURL = 'http://www.sun.com'";
```

To identify the JavaScript code, use the following rule:

```
<Variable type="DJS">jsCode</Variable>
```

To rewrite the value of curURL, add the additional rule:

```
<Variable type="URL">curURL</Variable>
```

Nested JavaScript is often used in recursion and other kinds of computation, and used less for URL string handling.

Event Handlers

Event handlers are a special kind of HTML tag attribute whose value can contain JavaScript content. By convention, most event handlers begin with the letters on preceding the event name. The handlers tell the browser what to do if a particular event occurs, such as by user actions, like mouse events or keyboard activity. Many event handlers have already been added to the default rulesets, and they are located under the HTMLRules section. JSToken rules added must be valid HTML attributes whose value contains JavaScript code. By adding a JSToken rule you are essentially telling the Gateway to interpret its value as JavaScript, and to check if that JavaScript contains any URLs. The JSToken rules can be wildcarded with a relatively high level of confidence as long as there aren't other HTML attributes that begin with on. An example of short-handing the JSTokens:

```
<JSToken>on*</JSToken>
```

Imported JavaScript Files

Rewriting imported JavaScript files follows the same basic principles as rewriting inline JavaScript content, except that relative URLs might not be handled correctly. Specifically, Netscape 4.x browsers do not send an HTTP referrer header when requesting imported JavaScript content, so there is no way for the Rewriter to determine the exact URL to use as the base from the HTTP header in which to resolve the relative URLs.

Consider the following HTML source:

```
<HTML>
<HEAD>
<SCRIPT SRC="scripts/test.js"></SCRIPT>
</HEAD>
<BODY BGCOLOR="#FFFFFF" TEXT="#000000">
</BODY>
</HTML>
```

Here is the JavaScript source:

```
imgsrc = "images/test.jpg";
window.open(imgsrc,'test');
```

In portal server 3, using a Netscape 4.x browser, if the page was accessed using http://cms.int.sun.com/importedjs.html, and if imgsrc had already been added as a rule, then the imgsrc value would be rewritten as follows:

```
https://gw.sun.com/http://cms.int.sun.com/scripts/images/test.jpg
```

Instead of:

```
https://gw.sun.com/http://cms.int.sun.com/images/test.jpg
```

The reason for this is that the SCRIPT SRC attribute value is rewritten to `https://gw.sun.com/http://cms.int.sun.com/scripts/test.js`.

Without having a referrer header, this value is used to resolve the relative links in the imported JavaScript file. There is currently no fix for this limitation from AOL for the 4.x or 6.x Netscape Navigator browser, so portal server 6.x, adds a feature where the SRC attribute of imported JavaScript has a query string appended to it. This query string supersedes the browser behavior and provides the portal with a referrer of its own to use to rewrite the imported JavaScript contents. For example, after being rewritten, the SRC attribute for the preceding example might look like this:

```
https://gw.sun.com/http://cms.int.sun.com/scripts/test.js?script
Referrer=http://cms.int.sun.com/">
```

The added benefit of using its own referrer functionality is that there is no longer a browser incompatibility from the perspective of rewriting imported content.

Imported JavaScript content is used by many Web applications to make the page source cleaner, and as a way to hide intellectual property contained in the JavaScript content. URLs are not always contained in imported JavaScript content, but it is still a good idea to check. One way to view the imported JavaScript source, without having to dig through the browser cache, is to create your own Web page with links that point to the remote JavaScript file.

The following is an example:

```
<HTML>
<BODY>
<A HREF="http://cms.int.sun.com/scripts/test.js">test.js</A>
</BODY>
</HTML>
```

To access this page using the Netscape Navigator browser, right-click over the link, and choose Save As. The Internet Explorer equivalent requires you to right-click over the link and select Save Target As. After you have the JavaScript file saved, you can determine what, if anything, must be rewritten for the application to work correctly through the Gateway. If this is not possible, you can also set the log level to message as described in "Rewriter Logging" on page 292. After accessing the page, you can get the imported XML source from the `psSRAPRewriter_recordPage.`*default* file, where *default* is the appropriate Gateway instance name. For performance and security reasons, do not keep the log level set to message for an extended period of time in a production environment.

Dynamically Created HTML Blocks

One of the features that makes JavaScript programming language so attractive to Web application developers is its ability to manipulate multiple windows and frames dynamically using the client JavaScript engine. The functionality is used for navigation purposes, site maps, form handling, menus, and ad generation, to name just a few.

Consider the following example:

```
<HTML>
<HEAD>
<TITLE>Tests rewriting of dynamically created HTML blocks</
TITLE>
</HEAD>
<BODY BGCOLOR="#FFFFFF" TEXT="#000000">
<SCRIPT>
myWindow = window.open("","myWindow");
mySrc = "<HTML>" +
"<BODY BGCOLOR=#FFFFFF TEXT=#000000>" +
"<IMG SRC='/images/logo.gif'>" +
"</BODY></HTML>";
self.myWindow.document.write(mySrc);
self.myWindow.document.close();
</SCRIPT>
</BODY>
</HTML>
```

This example demonstrates opening a new window and then creating the source necessary for an image to be displayed in the new window. What sets this example apart from other JavaScript rewriting examples given so far is that the IMG SRC attribute is created dynamically by the client rather than being exposed as HTML passing through the Gateway, which would normally translate the SRC attribute value automatically. So, the Rewriter needs to know that the JavaScript variable mySrc contains HTML content that must be rewritten accordingly.

To do this, the following rule must be added to the JSRules section of the appropriate ruleset:

```
<Variable type="DHTML">mySrc</Variable>
```

It is important in this case not to confuse the DJS type with the DHTML type. It might seem that because the RHS of the assignment contains string concatenations that the type should be DJS. However, in this case, if a DJS type is used, after rewriting, the resulting page looks something like the following:

```
<HTML>
<HEAD>
<TITLE>Tests rewriting of dynamically created HTML
blocks</TITLE>
</HEAD>
<BODY BGCOLOR="#FFFFFF" TEXT="#000000">
<SCRIPT>
myWindow = window.open("","myWindow");
mySrc = "https://gw.sun.com/http://cms.int.sun.com/<HTML>"
+
"<BODY BGCOLOR=#FFFFFF TEXT=#000000>" +
"<IMG SRC='/images/logo.gif'>" +
"https://gw.ing.sun.com/http://cms.int.sun.com/</BODY></HTM
L>";
self.myWindow.document.write(mySrc);
self.myWindow.document.close();
</SCRIPT>
</BODY>
</HTML>
```

Not only does the IMG SRC attribute not get rewritten, but other page discrepancies are also introduced. There are a variety of ways that a JavaScript variable can be assigned a string value across multiple lines. The preceding example uses multiple string concatenations. Another practice is that of adding a delimiter at the end of each line similar to the following:

```
var html = '\
        <table width="100%" border="0" cellspacing="0" cellpadding=
"0">\
            <tr> \
              <td class="item-title-bar" nowrap >\
                <table border="0" cellspacing="0" cellpadding="0">\
                  <tr>\
                    <td class="item-title-bar"><img src=
"/images/iplanet.gif" alt="iplanet.gif"></td>\
                    <td class="item-title-bar">' + title + '</td>\
                  </tr>\
                </table>\
              </td>\
              <td class="item-title-bar" nowrap align="right"> \
                <table border="0" cellspacing="0" cellpadding="0">\
                  <tr> \
                    <td class="item-title-bar" nowrap>' + swoop +
'</td>\
                    <td class="item-title-menu">' + replyLink + '</td>\
                  </tr>\
                </table>\
              </td>\
            </tr> \
            <tr> \
              <td class="item-title-menu" colspan="2"><img src=
"/images/pixel.gif" width="1" height="1" alt="" border="0"></td>\
            </tr>\
          </table>';

document.write(html);
```

This is a similar example except that the entire RHS of the assignment is enclosed in single quotes with each line containing an escape character at the end indicating a line continuation. While it passes through the parser unaffected, portal server 6.0 and 6.1 do not rewrite it correctly. You should contact Sun if you find that you need this functionality in either of these releases. The JavaScript engine in the browser actually removes the delimiter upon assignment, and portal server 6.2 does the same before passing the message body back to the browser. Both the delimeters and the line feeds are removed, and the block is treated like a single string. For this example to work in portal server 6.2 software, you must add the following rule:

```
<Variable type="DHTML">html</Variable>
```

If pop-up windows in your Web application are not working correctly, or simply coming up blank, it might be due to the fact that there is an HTML block created dynamically using JavaScript code that is not being rewritten correctly.

JavaScript Code Used to Create JavaScript Content

Rare cases to be aware of when rewriting JavaScript content are statements where the RHS of the variable assignments themselves contain variable initializations that might have a their own RHS that is a URL literal string object.

The following is an example:

```
<HTML>
<HEAD>
<SCRIPT>
tmpURL = "var address = 'http://www.sun.com'";
</SCRIPT>
</HEAD>
<BODY BGCOLOR="#FFFFFF" TEXT="#000000">
</BODY>
</HTML>
```

In this particular case, tmpURL becomes a string object that contains `var address = 'http://www.sun.com'`. This syntax is useful in multiwindowing applications where JavaScript content in the parent is responsible for writing JavaScript content in the child window as a result of user events. This situation is discussed in further detail in "Nested JavaScript Code" on page 250. There are two rules required to rewrite this example. The first is to identify the JavaScript code using the following rule:

```
<Variable type="DJS">tmpURL</Variable>
```

The second step is to tell the Rewriter that the address variable contains a URL that needs to be rewritten. The address variable value is a raw URL, so the following rule should suffice:

```
<Variable type="URL">address</Variable>
```

A more frequently used application of JavaScript variables being assigned to JavaScript code is to create window handles in multiwindowed JavaScript applications. For example:

```
myWindow = window.open("http://stocks.int.sun.com","myWindow");
```

Because the RHS is identifiable as a function that has an associated rule, you do not need to add another rule for the myWindow variable for this example to be rewritten correctly. This may seem counterintuitive, but it reduces the number of rules you need to create for common JavaScript coding practices such as this.

JavaScript Code Obfuscation

Obfuscation can come in many forms, including scramblers, optimizers, and full-on obfuscation, whose only purpose is to make it difficult for another person to pick off publicly available JavaScript source embedded in pages. Usage of JavaScript code obfuscation site wide in an application server page (ASP) environment, a business-to-business model, or in a variety of other scenarios, can make rewriting difficult, if not impossible, depending on the nature of the JavaScript code and how the code obfuscator works. If the obfuscation is done dynamically, then it probably is not possible to create static Rewriter rules that predictably rewrite embedded URLs.

Different obfuscators contain different features, but to effectively obfuscate the JavaScript code, function names and variables are typically altered. The same code altered twice may contain different names, while other altered code may contain the same names.

The following is an example of the source for page A:

```
<SCRIPT>
text = "hi there";
</SCRIPT>
```

The following is the source for page B:

```
<SCRIPT>
url = "http://www.sun.com";
</SCRIPT>
```

After being run through JavaScript code obfuscator, both JavaScript variables could be translated to the same value.

```
<SCRIPT>x002323="hi there";</SCRIPT>
<SCRIPT>x002323="http://www.sun.com";</SCRIPT>
```

If JavaScript code obfuscation is a requirement, then URL references must be extracted from the code for obfuscation and handled a different way. Inserting them in a top-level frame or importing the raw JavaScript content containing the URL variables might work. You can use an obfuscator with configurable code generation in which variables and function names can be mapped.

The following is an example of an obfuscator that maps variables to three-letter codes:

```
url -> scf
```

Knowing that the obfuscated variable name remains the same, you can then add a rule to handle scf in the appropriate context.

Best Practices – JavaScript Programming for Use Through the Gateway

This section provides rough guidelines for content developers to follow when creating original content to be accessed through the Gateway or in implementing content-based workarounds for corner cases that are difficult to address through configuration of the Rewriter. You should use the following best practices:

- Avoid deeply nested JavaScript content.

  The more difficult and spaghettilike the code is, the harder it is to get it to work through the Gateway.

- Use absolute URLs or URLs relative to the content server root in imported JavaScript files.

  This recommendation is made mostly for older versions of portal server 3 that do not support the use of a script referrer added to the SCRIPT src URL.

- Avoid mixing JavaScript variables with HTML blocks that are created dynamically, as in the following example:

```
<HTML>
<HEAD>
<TITLE>Tests rewriting of dynamically created HTML
blocks</TITLE>
</HEAD>
<BODY BGCOLOR="#FFFFFF" TEXT="#000000">
<SCRIPT>
var myURL = "http://www.sun.com";
myWindow = window.open("","myWindow");
mySrc = "<HTML>" +
"<BODY BGCOLOR=#FFFFFF TEXT=#000000>" +
"<A HREF='" + myURL + "'>link</A>";
self.myWindow.document.write(mySrc);
self.myWindow.document.close();
</SCRIPT>
</BODY>
</HTML>
```

- Avoid defining URLs using multiple string concatenations or in different locations in the code, as in the following example:

```
<SCRIPT>
url = "http://www.iplanet.com";
url += "/scripts/gen_form.pl";
url += "?var1=foo&var2=bar";
url2 = url + ;"&var3=baz";
</SCIPT>
```

Avoiding this kind of scenario helps prevent URLs from being rewritten multiple times. In the example above, the correct rewriting approach is to rewrite the url2 variable rather than having a rule or url1.

- Avoid making assumptions about what a URL should look like.

More specifically, do not assume that in the JavaScript code a particular URL will be relative in nature. Things to be aware of include parsing using substring matches on the javascript.location.href variable.

- Avoid variables being used in src and href attributes in DHTML content, as in the following example:

```
<HTML>
<HEAD><TITLE>Test Case for rewriting src tags
twice</TITLE></HEAD>
<SCRIPT LANGUAGE="JavaScript">
lnk = "http://www.sun.com";
document.write('<img border="0" src=
"'+lnk+'/images/logo.jpg"
alt="ALT"></A><BR>\n')
document.write('<img border="0" src="/images/logo.jpg"
alt="ALT"></A>')
</SCRIPT>
<BODY>
</BODY>
</HTML>
```

- Avoid using JavaScript code obfuscation. If variables are obfuscated on-the-fly, there is no way to predictably rewrite the end result.
- Use standardized naming conventions for URLs throughout the code, and use them in the same context. Notice the inconsistent naming conventions in the following two examples.

The following is in the source for example page C.:

```
<SCRIPT>
url = "http://www.sun.com"
</SCRIPT>
```

The following is in the source for example page D.:

```
<SCRIPT>
tmpURL = "http://www.sun.com";
url = "The URL is" + tmpURL;
</SCRIPT>
```

- Do not overgeneralize when specifying wildcards in rules, as in the following examples:

```
<Variable type="EXPRESSION">*location</Variable>
<Variable type="EXPRESSION">*src</Variable>
```

Note – The `*location` wildcard is more generalized than the `*.location` wildcard and matches any variable that ends in `location`, resulting in undesired string objects being rewritten.

- Do not attempt to overload JavaScript function parameter rules. If there are different applications that have defined the functions differently, then they must each have their own ruleset mapped with the fully qualified host name on which the application resides.

The following is an example of what to avoid:

```
<Function type="EXPRESSION" NAME="openMyWin"
paramPatterns=",y"/>
<Function type="EXPRESSION" NAME="openMyWin"
paramPatterns="y,,y/>
<Function type="EXPRESSION" NAME="openMyWin"
pramPatterns="y"/>
```

Also avoid similar content that looks like this:

```
menu.addItem(
new NavBarMenuItem("Info",
"JavaScript:top.location='http://www.sun.com'"));
menu.addItem(
new NavBarMenuItem("Info","http://www.sun.com"));
```

Note – Only the first rule is matched. The individual function definition should determine how many parameters are passed using the `length` method, instead of defining multiple functions with the same name in different pages. This also eliminates the problem with the argument type and the order.

- Avoid mixing and matching comment types.

  To hide JavaScript from browsers that support it, comments are frequently added just following the opening SCRIPT tag and just prior to the closing SCRIPT tag. The closing comment should be preceded by the C++ style comment '//' so that the remaining --> is not interpreted by the JavaScript engine. Examples of what to avoid:

```
<SCRIPT>
<!--

-->
</SCRIPT>
<SCRIPT>
<!-- -->
var foo="bar";
</SCRIPT>
<SCRIPT>
/*<!--

*/
//-->
</SCRIPT>
```

- Do not dynamically create BASE tags. Doing so prevents the correct functioning of the BASE tag from being applied to other relative URLs that are also dynamically created. Example of what to avoid:

```
<SCRIPT  Language="javascript" >
var baseHref="http://cms.int.sun.com";
document.write('<BASE HREF="' + baseHref + '/apps/">');
</SCRIPT>
```

Rewriting Applet Parameters

As with creating dynamic Web applications which generate content on the server-side, it is good practice not to hard code fully qualified URLs in variables, or function parameters in Java applets either. One mechanism to provide the applet with the location to resources or values required for the applet to run is to use applet parameters that appear as a part of the APPLET or OBJECT element using PARAM tags.

The APPLET and OBJECT tags have two attributes related to Java applets that are rewritten out-of-box. The first attribute, ARCHIVE, contains a location to a Java JAR archive. The second, CODEBASE, is used in conjunction with the CODE attribute to determine where the executable Java byte code resides. The CODEBASE attribute is also used when the Java `getCodeBase()` method is called from the applet. Portal server 6.0 also rewrites the CODE attribute out-of-box, so if it is specified as an HTML attribute type in your ruleset, you should remove it if you expect applets and other embedded objects to work correctly. The reason for this is that the CODE attribute value is literally pasted to the CODEBASE attribute when a class file is downloaded. The resulting URL would be rewritten twice, and thus, the class file download would fail.

Note – If an HTML BASE tag is included in the page, then the APPLET or OBJECT tag should contain a CODEBASE attribute. Otherwise, one is inserted because the BASE tag is commented out as part of the page rewriting. Dynamically created APPLET and OBJECT tags should always contain a CODEBASE tag to avoid one being inserted out of context.

The applet parameters can be rewritten using rules similar in syntax to FORM data. The rules allow wildcards so that patterns can be appropriately matched. The general syntax for a rule added to the Rewrite Form Input Tags List section of the Gateway profile contains at least three entries:

- Page or object identifier

  Similar to `FORM` data, this entry can include prepended path information, or only the object itself. The URL `http://java.sun.com/applets/welcome.html` page identifier can be: `*/welcome.html`, `*/applets/welcome.html` or `*/applets/*`.

- Class name, including its extension

  This is the value of the CODE attribute, as in the following example:

  ```
  <APPLET CODEBASE="http://java.sun.com/applets/"
  CODE="myClass.class">
  ```

- Parameter name

  This is the name of the PARAM tag given using the NAME attribute, as in the following example:

  ```
  <PARAM NAME="headergraphic" value="/applets/images/banner.gif">
  ```

An optional fourth entry can be used to pattern match on the parameter value if required.

- A URL valuePattern if the right side of the value attribute assignment is not a raw URL, as in the following example:

```
<PARAM NAME="headergraphic" value=
"98234|/applets/images/banner.gif">
```

The following is an example of an APPLET tag with supporting PARAM values:

```
<HTML>
<BODY>
<APPLET CODEBASE="http://java.sun.com/applets/" CODE=
"hello.class">
<PARAM NAME="borderWidth" value="2px">
<PARAM NAME="leftImg" value="20px|/images/leftImg.gif">
<PARAM NAME="rightImg" value="20px|/images/rightImg.gif">
</APPLET>
</BODY>
</HTML>
```

If the page was accessed from `http://java.sun.com/welcome.html`, then the two rules added to the appropriate ruleset would be:

```
<Applet source="*/welcome.html" code="hello.class" param=
"leftImg" valuePatterns="20px|"/>
<Applet source="*/welcome.html code="hello.class" param=
"rightImg" valuePatterns="20px|"/>
```

With the entourage of Java Plug-ins and VMs products available, the successful loading of applets might depend on the correct rewriting of the PARAM values in the Applet or object tag. There are also a varied number of suggestions floating about as to the best practices for launching client-side Java code. Both the EMBED and the APPLET tags have been deprecated in favor of the more generic OBJECT tag, and the use of the OBJECT tag is the recommended way to load applets to run in the Sun Java Plug-in software.

It is probably no surprise that the implementation on the browser side differs slightly between Internet Explorer and Netscape or Mozilla. To load a Citrix ICA applet into Internet Explorer 6.0, for example, you might try something like the following:

```
<HTML>
<BGCOLOR="#FFFFFF" TEXT="#000000>
<OBJECT classid="8AD9C840-044E-11D1-B3E9-00805F499D93"
  WIDTH=600
  HEIGHT=800
  ALIGN="BASELINE"
  CODEBASE="http://java.sun.com/products/plugin/1.4/jinstall-14-
win32.cab#Version=1,4,2,mn">
<PARAM NAME="java_code" VALUE="com.citrix.JICA.class">
<PARAM NAME="java_codebase" VALUE=
"http://portal.int.sun.com/third_party"
<PARAM NAME="java_type" VALUE="application/x-java-applet;jpi-
version=1.4.2">
<PARAM NAME="scriptable" VALUE="true">
<PARAM NAME="cabbase" VALUE="JICAEngM.cab">
<PARAM NAME="address" VALUE="citrix-server.int.sun.com">
<PARAM NAME="ICAPortNumber" VALUE=1494>
</OBJECT>
</BODY>
</HTML>
```

The Netscape equivalent looks something like this:

```
<HTML>
<BGCOLOR="#FFFFFF" TEXT="#000000>
<OBJECT classid="java:com.citrix.JICA.class"
  codetype="application/java"
  WIDTH=600
  HEIGHT=800
  ALIGN="BASELINE"
  CODEBASE="http://java.sun.com/products/plugin/1.4/jinstall-14-
win32.cab#Version=1,4,2,mn">
<PARAM NAME="java_code" VALUE="com.citrix.JICA.class">
<PARAM NAME="java_codebase" VALUE=
"http://portal.int.sun.com/third_party"
<PARAM NAME="java_type" VALUE="application/x-java-applet;jpi-
version=1.4.2">
<PARAM NAME="scriptable" VALUE="true">
<PARAM NAME="cabbase" VALUE="JICAEngM.cab">
<PARAM NAME="address" VALUE="citrix-server.int.sun.com">
<PARAM NAME="ICAPortNumber" VALUE=1494>
</OBJECT>
</BODY>
</HTML>
```

The codebase attribute no longer reflects a value that needs to be rewritten (unless direct access to java.sun.com is not allowed due to security restrictions), so you still must rewrite the codebase attribute that the applet will be making use of that is now passed in as a parameter whose name is java_codebase. Because object elements do not contain code attributes, that entry in the Rewriter rule should be wildcarded, making the rule look something like this:

```
<Applet source="*" code="*" param="java_codebase"/>
```

Sun has a program that you can download from java.sun.com called HTML converter. This program helps you take pages containing APPLET tags and translates them into their cross-browser OBJECT-using equivalents. A good resource on the subject is located at
http://java.sun.com/j2se/1.4.1/docs/guide/plugin/developer_guide
/using_tags.html.

Best Practices – Java Programming for Use Through the Gateway

This section provides guidelines for content developers to follow when creating Java applets that will be accessed through the Gateway or in implementing content-based workarounds for corner cases that are difficult to address through configuration of the Rewriter.

- Always use a CODEBASE attribute with an APPLET or OBJECT tag.

  To avoid any potential problems with attributes or parameter values that depend on the implied CODEBASE, it is better to simply make it explicit, especially on pages where there is a BASE tag.

- Use prepended path information for PARAM tag values that contain URLs. The following is an example of what to avoid:

```
<HTML>
<BODY>
<APPLET CODEBASE="http://java.sun.com/applets" CODE=
"hello.class">
<PARAM NAME="headergraphic" value="images/banner.gif">
</APPLET>
</BODY>
</HTML>
```

  Prepended path information helps to ensure that parameter values are resolved to the correct fully qualified URLs.

- Do not add a rule for the CODE HTML attribute to any rulesets that might be used to also rewrite content containing APPLETS and OBJECTS.

  This results in the applet not loading properly because the browser cannot find the Java byte code, as explained earlier.

- Do not make network connections to hard-coded URLs.

  Instead, they should be passed through as applet and object parameters. The following is an example of what to avoid:

```
URLConnection myConn =
(new URL('http://java.sun.com')).openConnection();
```

- Do not allow users to specify their own URLs in the applet user interface.

  If this is required for the application to function, then you should consider running it using the Netlet instead of accessing it directly through the Gateway component.

- Use PARAM names when specifying Rewriter rules to avoid unintentionally rewriting other APPLET PARAM values. You should avoid using rules that are too generalized, such as:

```
<Applet source="*" code="*" param="*"/>
```

- Define the APPLET or OBJECT opening tag on a single line.

  The following is an example of what to avoid:

```
<APPLET code=foo.class
codebase="/foo/foo2">
<PARAM NAME=url VALUE="/somedir/some.html">
</APPLET>
```

- Do not split the APPLET or OBJECT tag definitions, or you might have to rewrite the PARAM values as HTML attributes instead. Example of what to avoid:

```
    _html += "" +
            "\n<PARAM NAME=\"java_code\" VALUE=\
"com.citrix.JICA.class\"> " +
            "\n<PARAM NAME=\"java_codebase\" VALUE=\
"http://portal.int.sun.com/third_party/\"> " +
            "\n<PARAM NAME=\"java_archive\" VALUE=\
"JICAEngJ.jar\"> " +
            "\n<PARAM NAME=\"java_type\" VALUE=\
"application/x-java-applet;jpi-version=1.4.2\"> " +
        "\n<PARAM NAME=\"scriptable\" VALUE=\"true\"> " +
        "\n<PARAM NAME=\"cabbase\" VALUE=\"JICAEngM.cab\
"> " +
            "\n<PARAM NAME=\"address\" VALUE=\
"braze.red.iplanet.com\"> " +
            "\n<PARAM NAME=\"ICAPortNumber\" VALUE=1494>";
    document.writeln(_html);
```

It is difficult to rewrite the java_codebase parameter in the context of the object element. If this code block needs to be generated dynamically, extract the codebase value out and create a variable assignment instead.

Rewriting Cascading Style Sheets

As of CSS2, there is only one way to specify URLs—using the URL( ) designator as in the following example:

```
<STYLE>
  BODY { background: url=("http://www.sun.com/im/sun_logo.gif") }
</STYLE>
```

In addition to internal sheets, the URL designator can also be used in an inline fashion like this:

```
<HTML>
<BODY STYLE="background:
url('http://www.sun.com/im/sun_logo.gif')">
</BODY>
</HTML>
```

Imported CSS is not supported by default in portal server 6.0. There is a patch available for portal server 6.0, and the feature is carried forward in later versions of portal server 6.x including portal server 6.1 and 6.2 versions. See "Patching the Portal Server Software" on page 10 for information on how to download the patch for version 6.2 of the portal server.

In addition to having the correct install level, the CSS MIME type must also be added to the MIME mappings section of the appropriate Gateway instance's profile. Imported CSS is given using an SRC attribute, so the URL is rewritten by the Gateway using the out-of-box ruleset that contains the rule <Attribute name= "src"/>.

Microsoft.NET adds another URL type to CSS called a behavior URL. A behavior URL is specified similar to an inline background URL like this:

```
<HTML>
<BODY>
<DIV id="idMsgViewer"
  class="msgViewer"
  acceptLang="en-us"
  rowsPerPage="25"
  style="behavior:url(/exchweb/controls/ctrl_View20.htc)"
  url="/exchange/uid/Inbox/"
  onReady = "onViewReady()"
  onRefresh = "onViewRefresh()"
  onkeydown = "onViewKeyDown()"
  onkeypress = "onViewKeyPress()"
  viewDescriptor = "xmlDefaultView"
  onChangeSort = "persostSortOrder()"
  onError = "onViewError()"
  onNavigate = "onViewNavigation()"
  onSelectionChange = "updatePreviewPane()">
</DIV>
</BODY>
</HTML>
```

The preceding example is extracted from Microsoft Outlook Web Access, and it shows how behavior URLs are specified. The HTML Component File (.htc) is a Microsoft implementation used to attach event handlers to individual HTML elements.

Rewriting XML

Most modern browsers ship with an XML parser that is typically used in conjunction with JavaScript to create HTML content on-the-fly and then insert it directly into the DOM. What this means from a rewriting perspective is that there might be URLs contained in the XML data that are used to fetch content such as images. These URLs must be rewritten. There are two types of data to be concerned about when rewriting XML: the PCDATA or text data, and the attribute values. For example, part of a DAV response body received by from Microsoft Outlook Web Access might look like the following:

```
<?xml version="1.0"><a:multistatus...
<prop2>http://ex-server://exchweb/img/icon-report-
ndr.gif</prop2>...</xml>
```

The prop2 value might be used in an XSL transform where its value directly translates to the URL specified in the IMG SRC attribute of the resulting HTML. Rewriting it as it comes across in XML form reduces the likelihood that you'll end up with broken image icons when the application is accessed through the Gateway.

Rewriting XML Tag Attributes

As with HTML attributes, XML attribute values can contain URLs. To rewrite XML attribute values, a rule containing the attribute name needs to be created in the appropriate ruleset. The following is an example:

```
<?xml version="1.0"?>
  <mytag desc="Sun Home Page"/>
  <mytag myAttr="http://www.sun.com"/>
</xml>
```

In this example, a rule must be added for the URL attribute under the XMLRules section of the appropriate ruleset. The rule looks like this:

```
<Attribute name="myAttr"/>
```

Sometimes an attribute becomes ambiguous with another tag, as shown in the following example:

```
<?xml version="1.0"?>
  <mytag myAttr="Sun Home Page"/>
  <yourtag myAttr="http://www.sun.com"/>
</xml>
```

To differentiate the attribute, the rule can be altered to only rewrite a particular attribute of a particular tag. This rule might look like the following:

```
<Attribute name="myAttr" tag="yourtag"/>
```

The notion of pattern matching exists for PCDATA rules as well, and can be used to rewrite only the portion of an attribute value that might contain the URL. The same technique should be followed when specifying valuePatterns for XML attributes as you would when specifying valuePatterns for form data. Portal server 6.2 adds an additional source rule attribute to help disambiguate similar tags and attributes so that only the one originating from a specific source is rewritten.

Rewriting XML PCDATA

PCDATA is essentially the text between the XML tags. It is defined as #PCDATA in the DTD. To rewrite PCDATA, create a TagText rule under the XMLRules section of the appropriate ruleset. The following is an example:

```
<xml>
  <mytag>
    http://www.sun.com
  </mytag>
</xml>
```

To rewrite this URL, use the following rule:

```
<TagText tag="mytag"/>
```

There might be cases where the PCDATA is dependent on the tag attribute values. In these cases, you can use the attributePatterns identifier. The following is an example:

```
<xml>
  <mytag myattr1="desc">
    Sun Home Page
  </mytag>
  <mytag myattr2="href">
    http://www.sun.com
  </mytag>
</xml>
```

To rewrite only the second occurrence of mytag, use a rule like this:

```
<TagText tag="mytag" attributePatterns="myattr2=href">
```

To rewrite any PCDATA where an attribute is included with the tag, the attributePatterns must be added to the rule. As with rewriting form data, it pays to be more specific rather than more generalized when rewriting XML content.

Best Practices – XML Programming for Use Through the Gateway

This section provides rough guidelines for content developers to follow when creating original content to be accessed through the Gateway or in implementing content-based workarounds for corner cases that are difficult to address through configuration of the Rewriter.

- Try to use unique attribute names specific to URLs.

  You should be sure they are all used in the same context. The following is an example of what to avoid:

```
<xml>
  <myTag>
    <tag1 url="The URL is:">myValue</tag1>
    <tag2 url="http://www.sun.com">myValue</tag2>
    <tag3 url="http://www.java.com">myValue</tag3>
  </myTag>
</xml>
```

  Creating ambiguity in the attributes or the tags can prevent the application from working or appearing correctly. For example, Microsoft Outlook Web Access provided with Exchange 2000 SP3 uses an ambiguous XML tag prop2 that sometimes contains a URL and often times does not. When the prop2 attribute is not rewritten, image expansion icons don't show up in the OWA interface. When it is rewritten, the labels on the address book page are prepended with the Gateway and the server address.

- Do not generate XML content containing URLs dynamically using JavaScript content. The following is an example of what to avoid:

```
<SCRIPT>
  document.write('<mytag url="http://www.sun.com"/>\n');
</SCRIPT>
```

  The Rewriter automatically assumes that this content is DHTML and none of the XML rules apply. Sometimes you can get XML attributes rewritten using HTML attribute rules when XML is embedded in the same page or identified by a nonstandard namespace identifier in an HTML document. This is not a recommended practice because the behavior is subject to change in future versions of the portal server product.

- Perform user-agent checks to ensure that the browser supports XML before emitting XML code to be rendered by the browser. This is just simply good programming practice.

Rewriting HTC

HTML component files are syntactically similar to HTML and thus can be parsed by the Gateway as such when the appropriate MIME type of *text/x-component* has been added to the MIME mappings, or the Web server sets the Content-Type header for the HTC file as *text/html*. HTC files create a data abstraction layer for individual page elements by defining and attaching events, and associating properties and property values with the individual element.

The composition of an HTC file includes HTML-like markup that is really closer to XML because none of the tags are defined in the HTML specification, and a script is used for the event-handling implementation. The script can be imported or inline. Because Internet Explorer fetches HTC files with a referrer header, the imported JavaScript should be rewritten correctly, even it contains relative URLs that would normally be resolved by the browser itself.

Only the script portion of HTC files usually requires rewriting. Follow the best practices outlined in "Rewriting JavaScript and JScript Content" on page 239 for tips on how to correctly handle it.

Rewriting XSL Transforms

The somewhat free-form syntax of extensible style sheets (XSL), widely varying implementations and standard practices, tag ambiguities, and lack of context surroundings possible URLs, are a few of the reasons XSL is not currently rewritten by the Gateway. The easiest way to handle XSL transforms in portal server 6.2 is by rewriting the XML message contents, or by inserting a temporary variable assignment that can be inserted into the DOM after the transform occurs. This is no easy task, and you must have a thorough understanding of how the application works before making these kinds of changes.In cases where the XSL must be rewritten, follow the same guidelines used for rewriting XML and be sure that text/XSL is added to the MIME mappings field.

The content-based workarounds to get XSL transforms to work as anticipated can be as easy as inserting an intermediary variable for the Rewriter to hook into, or by writing a complex script to manipulate the DOM directly following the transform. The following shows an example of creating an intermediary variable:

```
imgURL = m_szFolderURL;
m_szFolderURL = imgURL;
```

m_szFolderURL is a variable used throughout many of the controls files that ship with Microsoft Exchange 2000 SP3. There is no way to rewrite m_szFolderURL globally because of its ambiguous usage. The result is to add an assignment that the Gateway can easily identify. In this case, the new variable added is imgURL, and is needed to have an associated rule added to the appropriate ruleset for this instance of m_szFolderURL to be rewritten. A more complicated content-based workaround involves trolling the DOM and updating the URLs.

This particular example modifies the image URLs used for the folder icons and expansion status in Microsoft Exchange 2000 SP3, using an already-rewritten value m_szImagePath:

```
var curIMG;
for (var x=0; x<objChildContainer.children.length; x++) {
  curIMG =
objChildContainer.children(x).children("expIndicator").src;
  curIMG = curIMG.substring(curIMG.lastIndexOf("/")+1);
  curIMG = m_szImagePath + curIMG;
  objChildContainer.children(x).children("expIndicator").src =
curIMG;
  curIMG =
objChildContainer.children(x).children("folderIcon").src;
  curIMG = curIMG.substring(curIMG.lastIndexOf("/")+1);
  curIMG = m_szImagePath + curIMG;
  objChildContainer.children(x).children("folderIcon").src =
curIMG;
}
```

Both of these examples grab the object of the URL and append it to the value of m_szImagePath that has already been rewritten, and contains the same path information required to correctly retrieve the images. One thing to watch out for is that you don't rewrite a URL in one leaf while missing all of the others at the same level in the DOM tree. Sometimes, that can get programatically messy as the children seem to go on forever. It is better to be able to select a group of nodes and only operate on them rather than having a statement like this:

```
m_elDailyParentCont.children(0).children(0).children(0).chi
ldren(0).children(1).children(0).children(i).src = tmpURL;
```

Rewriting HTTP Headers

Rewriting HTTP headers is handled internally by the Gateway. HTTP 302 redirections, indicating content has temporarily moved, contain a location header that is rewritten by the Gateway so that the browser makes a follow-up request to the Gateway instead of directly to the content server. One way to see this activity is to write a CGI script that returns the redirection header:

```
#!/usr/bin/perl
print "Status: 302\n";
print "Location: http://www.int.sun.com\n\n";
```

When the above script is accessed through the Gateway, you eventually see that the browser's URL field displays `https://gw.sun.com/http://www.int.sun.com;` indicating that the HTTP header was rewritten correctly.

The Content-Length header may also be modified if the contents were rewritten. It is a good idea not to write any code that depends on a specific content length value, or you might wind up with truncated or corrupted content.

One other HTTP header that is very important to take into consideration is the content-type header. The Gateway makes copious use of this header to determine whether the content requires rewriting and what engine to use to rewrite it. If you are running Web services from an application server Web container, then it is vitally important to make sure those services set the appropriate content-type headers for data they emit. Because Web services can emit any kind of data, it is not possible to derive content types from file extensions or even the message bodies reliably. According to the HTTP specification, the default content-type is octet/stream, so don't assume that the default is text/html, or that creating a META tag in the message body that contains a content-type attribute indicating the type to be text/html. This becomes a classic chicken-before-the-egg dilemma, where the message body needs to be parsed as HTML to determine that the content-type is HTML. The 6.2 version of the portal server provides a bit more flexibility to associate content-types with URLs, but the appropriate place to make these changes, if possible, is in the application code itself. This is good programming practice, and carries a heavy recommendation in the HTTP specification that all HTTP responses that also contain a message body should contain the appropriate content-type header for the client intermediary proxies to correctly handle it.

Rewriting Cookies

Cookies must be rewritten for the browser to present them on follow-up requests to the Gateway that might be redirected to an Intranet Web application that requires a cookie for session handling or authentication purposes. Cookies are automatically rewritten once Enable Cookie Management is checked in the Gateway instance profile. You must also add the URL of the host setting the cookies to the Forward Cookie URLs list.

Cookies are rewritten by prepending the URLEncoded cookie domain and path to the original cookie name to make it unique. All of the original cookie data is packed together in a pipe-separated list so that the Gateway is able to determine whether or not it needs to forward cookies based on the destination of future requests.

One limitation to be aware of when cookies are being used for session handling is that browsers enforce the cookie limit per domain to approximately 20. Any more than that, and they are removed one by one in a FIFO manner. This means that a portal session might get eliminated unexpectedly. It is a better approach to use a single cookie for SSO purposes, rather than have each application maintain its own cookies for session and state.

A rewritten cookie might look similar to FIGURE 4-13.

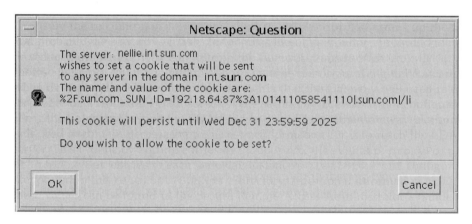

FIGURE 4-13 Rewritten Cookie

Rewriting Flash Content

Rewriting Flash content should be treated the same way as applets or other compiled applications embedded using the OBJECT tag. Only things that are exposed, such as the object parameters, can be rewritten. If the Flash content has hard-coded URLs, it is not possible for the Gateway to rewrite them, and the Flash content might fail to load or run correctly as a result.

Rewriting ActiveX

ActiveX is used by some .NET-enabled products to initiate XML over HTTP requests directly to a server from within a Web page. Generally speaking, you might worry more about the XML response bodies generated from an ActiveX request from a rewriting perspective than about the request for the content itself. One thing to make absolutely sure of, however, is that the URL of the server that the request is directed to is rewritten. For instance, consider the following example from Microsoft Outlook Web Access:

```
var objRequest = new requestFactory(szRootURL, "PROPFIND",
objContext, mfcb_AddHierarchy)
```

If the first parameter of the `requestFactory` function is not rewritten, the request fails because the host is unreachable outside of the firewall. A rule added to the JSRules section of the appropriate ruleset remedies this:

```
<Function type="EXPRESSION" name="requestFactory" paramPatterns=
"y"\>
```

Rewriting WebDav

WebDav extensions to HTTP1.1 are quickly becoming the de facto standard for distributed authoring and versioning of documents over the Web. In practice, rewriting WebDav mostly has to do with rewriting the XML response bodies that might contain URLs. The Gateway does not fully comply with the WebDav published standard, but it does not explicitly block WebDav requests, as many other full reverse proxies do. The result is that an authenticated portal SRA user can usually get most WebDav requests to work, and some Microsoft proprietary WebDav extensions such as those used in Exchange 2000 Service Pack 3 also work. It is an unlikely prospect to expect that a CMS system based entirely on WebDav will work with the portal by default. It is worth testing your WebDav-enabled application to see if it works through the Gateway, rather than assuming it will.

Not all XML response body contents generated as a result of DAV requests that are URLs need to be rewritten. In the case of Microsoft Outlook Web Access, some URLs are used by ActiveX code in future requests to the datastore, and a rewritten URL would prevent the data from being retrieved successfully. In these cases, an intimate knowledge of the application internals is required before you can fully ascertain if it can be successfully integrated with the Gateway.

Rewriter Deployment Scenarios

There are many uses for portal server SRA software, and the number of applications and content that may be requested through the Gateway is even more varied. The purpose of this section is to provide Gateway deployment scenarios for some of the most commonly used applications. These are exceptional applications in terms of the complexity of the content that they generate. Also included in this section are logical descriptions and explanations about why rules are needed and how to make the best-educated choice if there are multiple places where rewriting can occur. Some third-party integrations through the Rewriter are also provided in Appendix A.

What to Do About the Portal Server Desktop

The portal server 6.x desktop is treated like any other application that passes through the Gateway in that there are rules contained in the ruleset that specifically apply to the portal server desktop and applications that can be launched from it. Like other applications, the desktop URLs are fully qualified, compared with the Proxies for Domains and Subdomains list, and rewritten according to the rules specified by the ruleset associated with the domain or host of origin. The Gateway installs by default with an entry in the Proxies for Domains and Subdomains list for the portal node's DNS value, and the `default _gateway_ruleset` is associated with that domain as well. Assuming that the demo portal has been installed, there are rules contained in the `default_gateway_ruleset` that specifically apply to the portal server desktop. As you add portlets and channels to the desktop, you may find that you need to add additional rules in order for the content to work when accessed through the Gateway.

Adding Rules for New Channels

If you have a JSP channel that imports content fetched from a file system or remote location using a custom JSP tag, it might be necessary to add rules for that content. Consider the following example of `customtag.jsp` that includes a local file:

```
<%@ page import="java.util.Enumeration" %>
<%@ page import="java.io.*" %>

<%@ taglib uri="/tld/jx.tld" prefix="jx" %>
<%@ taglib uri="/tld/desktop.tld" prefix="dt" %>
<%@ taglib uri="/tld/desktopProviderContext.tld" prefix="dtpc" %>
<%@ taglib uri="/tld/frag.tld" prefix="dtfrag" %>

<dt:obtainChannel channel="$JSPProvider">
  <dtpc:providerContext>
  <dtpc:getStringProperty key="contentPage" id="contentPage"/>
  <jx:declare id="contentPage" type="java.lang.String"/>

<%
  String absPath = application.getRealPath(contentPage);
  String location =
absPath.substring(0,absPath.lastIndexOf("/")+1) + "frag.html";
%>


<dtfrag:frag type="file" loc="<%= location %>"/>

  </dtpc:providerContext>
</dt:obtainChannel>
```

The following example shows the source for `includeChannelFrag.java`, the custom tag implementation that is compiled and stored in `/etc/opt/SUNWps/desktop/classes/com/sun/jspapp`:

```
/* Custom tag implementation for frag tag */

package com.sun.jspapp;

import java.io.*;
import javax.servlet.jsp.*;
import javax.servlet.jsp.tagext.*;

public class includeChannelFrag extends TagSupport {
  String fragtype = "file";
  String location;

  public void setType (String type) { fragtype = type; }
  public void setLoc (String loc) { location = loc; }

  public int doEndTag() {
    JspWriter out = pageContext.getOut();
    if (fragtype == "file") {
      try {
      File stocksChannel = new File(location);
FileReader fr = new FileReader(stocksChannel);
      BufferedReader br = new BufferedReader(fr);
      String line="";
      while (line != null) {
        out.println(line);
        line = br.readLine();
      }
      br.close();
      }
      catch (Exception e) {
        try {
        out.println("Could not open file: " + location);
        }
        catch (Exception f) {}
      }
    }
    else {
      try {
      out.println("Type " + fragtype + " not understood...");
      }
      catch (Exception f) {}
    }
  return EVAL_PAGE;
  }
}
```

The following is the contents of `frag.html` specified in the custom tag in the JSP code:

```
<HTML>
<BODY BGCOLOR="#FFFFFF" TEXT="#000000">
<SCRIPT>
folderIMG = "http://imap.int.sun.com/images/folder.gif";
folderLabel = "Shared Folders";
document.writeln("<TABLE><TR><TD>");
document.writeln("<IMG SRC=\"" + folderIMG + "\"></TD>");
document.writeln("<TD>" + folderLabel + "</TD>");
</SCRIPT>
</BODY>
</HTML>
```

The following code is the `frag.tld` custom tag library definition stored at `/etc/opt/SUNWps/desktop/default/tld`:

```
<taglib>
  <tlibversion>1.0</tlibversion>
  <jspversion>1.1</jspversion>

  <tag>
    <name>frag</name>
    <tagclass>com.sun.jspapp.includeChannelFrag</tagclass>
    <bodycontent>empty</bodycontent>
    <attribute>
      <name>type</name>
      <rtexprvalue>true</rtexprvalue>
    </attribute>
    <attribute>
      <name>loc</name>
      <rtexprvalue>true</rtexprvalue>
    </attribute>
  </tag>
</taglib>
```

In this particular case, the JSP emits the contents of `frag.html` given in the custom tag reference:

```
<dtfrag:frag type="file" loc="<%= location %>"/>
```

While this example only uses one file that contains a JavaScript variable (`folderIMG` that will have to be rewritten), it is a good idea to also look at the other `frag.html` tags. It is useful to see this from the JSP code if it was developed in house, in case there is logic where the dynamic location is actually different under different circumstances. Otherwise, you must specify your Rewriter rules by looking at the source code of the entire desktop and you might unintentionally miss other code fragments given in different cases in the JSP.

Rewriting the Demo Portal Server Desktop

The first set of rules specified in the `default_gateway_ruleset` are used to rewrite the Netmail Applet parameters. The APPLET tag that launches the NetMail application looks like this:

```
<applet code=NetMail.class codebase=/portal/netmail archive=
nmui.jar height=2 width=1 mayscript>
<param name=cabbase value=nmui.cab>
<param name=servletURL value=/portal/NetMailServlet>
<param name=sessionId value=4297796>
<param name=exitURL value=/portal/NetMailServlet?nsid=
newAppletSession&exit=yes>
<param name=resourcesURL value=/portal/NetMailServlet?nsid=
4297796&loadResources=yes>
<param name=helpURL value=/portal/docs/en_US/netmail/topics.htm>
</applet>
```

Note – The sample desktop used throughout this subsection assumes a DEPLOY_URI of /portal.

The codebase attribute is rewritten by the following rule in the HTMLRules section of the ruleset:

```
<Attribute name="codebase"/>
```

Code, archive, and cabbase are all handled relative to the codebase, so rules are not required. If a rule is added for the code attribute, the applet cannot load correctly because its rewritten value will be appended to the rewritten codebase value, resulting in the incorrect URL to fetch the class file.

The other parameters containing URLs that must be rewritten are servletURL, exitURL, resourcesURL, and helpURL. These rules can be consolidated into the following:

```
<Applet source="*/NetMailServlet" code="NetMail.class" param=
"*URL" />
```

The Netmail installer additionally has a helpFilesURL parameter that needs to be rewritten, so the rule could be consolidated to:

```
<Applet source="*/NetMailServlet" code="*" param="*URL" />
```

Note the wildcard for the code value so that the installer applet will be rewritten using the same rule as the Netmail applet.

NetFile1 applet launch code looks like this:

```
<applet code=rp.class codebase=/portal/netfile archive=
nfuijava1.jar height=2 width=1 MAYSCRIPT>
<param name=cabbase value="/portal/netfile/nfuijava1.cab">
<param name=nfid value="e=mc2">
<param name=agent value="Mozilla/4.0 (compatible; MSIE 5.5;
Windows 98)">
<param name=uploadURL value=/portal/NetFileUploadServlet>
<param name=NetFileURL value=/portal/NetFileServlet>
<param name=InitURL value=/portal/NetFileServlet>
<param name=exitURL value=/portal/NetFileApplet?exitP=exit>
<param name=OpenFileURL value=/portal/NetFileOpenFileServlet>
</applet>
```

The cabbase contains a path that originates from the server root, so you must have a rule for it. Otherwise, it will be resolved incorrectly, using the codebase attribute value. A unified naming scheme helps condense the rules required to rewrite the Netfile 1 applet launch code to:

```
<Applet source="*/NetFileApplet" code="rp.class"
param="cabbase" />
<Applet source="*/NetFileApplet" code="rp.class"
param="*URL" />
```

Combined with the NetFile2 requirements, all of the NetFile applet parameters can be specified with the following rules:

```
<Applet source="*/NetFileApplet" code="rp.class" param=
"cabbase"/>
<Applet source="*/NetFileApplet" code="*" param="*URL"/>
```

The Netlet launch code looks like this:

```
<applet codebase="/portal/netlet" archive="netlet.jar" code=
"SServer.class" width=1 height=1 MAYSCRIPT>
<param name="cabbase" value="netlet.cab">
<param name="cookiename" value="iPlanetDirectoryPro">
<param name="configURL" value="/portal/NetletConfig">
<param name="resourcesURL" value="/portal/NetletConfig?func=
loadResources">
. . .
<param name=sessionId value=e=mc2>
<param name=numParms value=9>
<param name=doPortWarning value=false>
<param name=doReauth value=false>
<param name=showPortWarnCheckbox value=false>
<param name=defaultCipher value=Rijndael>
<param name=defaultKeyLen value=192>
<param name=proxytype value=DIRECT>
<param name=proxyhost value=>
<param name=proxyport value=0>
<param name=proxyoverride value=>
</applet>
```

Similar to NetFile and NetMail, the rules can be consolidated to:

```
<Applet source="*/NetLetConfig" code="SServer.class" param=
"*URL"/>
```

All of the JSToken entries can be consolidated to:

```
<JSToken>on*</JSToken>
```

Or, alternately, in portal server 6.2, they can be specified as HTML attributes with DJS types. For example:

```
<Attribute name="on*" type="DJS"/>
```

The `window.open` method is used on the portal server desktop to open help windows, detach channels, and display content from bookmark links once selected, among other things. Out-of-box, the type for the `window.open` rules is specified as URL, but it is recommended that the type instead be altered to EXPRESSION because a great deal of JavaScript code opens up new windows using a variable as the first parameter to `window.open` rather than a raw URL. The rule then overrides the existing one in the JSRules section of the ruleset, and it looks like this:

```
<Function type="EXPRESSION" name="window.open" paramPatterns=
"y"/>
```

One example of `window.open` being used on the desktop is to open help URLs similar to the following:

```
<a href="/portal/docs/en_US/desktop/usedesk.htm" onMouseOver=
"over('banner_help')" onMouseOut="out('banner_help')" onClick=
"javascript: var helpWin=
window.open('/portal/docs/en_US/desktop/usedesk.htm', 'wthelp',
'width=600,height=400,hotkeys=no,status=no,resizable=
yes,scrollbars=yes,toolbar=yes'); helpWin.focus();return false;">
```

In addition to Netlet requiring applet parameters to be rewritten, the Netlet also makes use of JavaScript for launching the Netlet pop-up window, and thus requires a few JavaScript rules as follows:

```
<Function type="URL" name="netletConfigOpen" paramPatterns=
"y,y"/>
<Function type="URL" name="netletWinOpen" paramPatterns="y"/>
<Function type="URL" name="netletActionOpen" paramPatterns="y"/>
```

One example of the context in which these rules are used is to launch the pop-up window if any static Netlet rules have been defined for the end user. A JavaScript example:

```
<script language="JavaScript">
netletWinOpen("/portal/NetletConfig?func=makepage", true );
</script>
```

The Bookmark provider uses two functions containing variables that require rewriting. Out-of-box, the variable names are rewritten, but instead, you can rewrite the function parameters of the two functions where they are referenced. For example:

```
<Function type="EXPRESSION" name="*_openURL" paramPatterns="y"/>
<Function type="EXPRESSION" name="*_findURL" paramPatterns="y"/>
```

The application of these rules supersedes the rules for location and surf_form_URL. All of the window handlers are handled by the EXPRESSION type rule for the window.open function. For example:

```
var appWin = window.open(url, name );
```

In this case, a dedicated rule does not need to be created for the appWin variable because the Rewriter can identify the function call on the RHS of the assignment without any administrative intervention.

Sun ONE Calendar Server Deployment

Portal server 6.0 software requires a patch for some of the edit links to work. The HREF attribute values fail URL validation in the Gateway, and therefore aren't rewritten even if an EXPRESSION-type rule is added to the ruleset. For example, the edit link on the Calendars page looks like this:

```
href="javascript:var x=
window.open('http://cal.int.sun.com/command.shtml?view=
new_cal&#38;id=b5qs6e8ws3hl0b8v&#38;crc=1188233024&#38;date=
20030729T224152&#38;newCalCalID=rlbaker&#38;tzid=&#38;freebusy=
1&#38;tab=1&#38;prevView=overview&#38;calid=
rlbaker&#38;security=1','','height=550,width=650');"
```

The Gateway incorrectly attempts to perform URL validation on the query string and gets confused by the & characters. There is a fix for this problem in portal server 6.0. See "Patching the Portal Server Software" on page 10. This is not a problem in portal server 6.1 and portal server 6.2.

One other Calendar client quirk to be aware of is that `window.open` method invocations are not caught by the Rewriter using a rule like this:

```
<Function type="EXPRESSION" name="window.open" paramPatterns=
"y"/>
or
<Function type="URL" name="window.open" paramPatterns="y"/>
```

The reason for this is that in the process of removing extraneous (human-readable) white space, JavaScript variable initializations containing white space are URL encoded. For example, consider the source code for the help link:

```
<a onMouseOver="over('documentation')" onMouseOut=
"out('documentation')" href="javascript:var%20newWindow=
window.open('http://cal.int.sun.com/en/chview.htm');"><img name=
"documentation" src=
"http://cal.int.sun.com/imx/white_bannerdot.gif" width="13"
height="9" border="0"></a></td><td><a onMouseOver=
"over('documentation')" onMouseOut="out('documentation')" href=
"javascript:var%20newWindow=
window.open('http://cal.int.sun/en/chview.htm');"><span class=
"banner-links"><FONT size="2" face="PrimaSans BT,Verdana,sans-
serif">help</FONT></span></a>
```

The only way to correctly rewrite the numerous `window.open` calls throughout the client application is to map a calendar-specific ruleset to the Calendar host that includes the following rule in place of `window.open`:

```
<Function type="EXPRESSION" name="*open" paramPatterns="y"/>
```

It is not recommended to add this rule to a default ruleset like `default_gateway_ruleset` because it will negatively impact the functionality of the portal desktop.

By mapping the ruleset to the Calendar server, you can be fairly certain that wildcarded rules that reduce the number of rules used for the application will not have any unanticipated side effects for other applications. The default_gateway_ruleset that ships with portal server 6.0 can be used for Calendar Server 5.1.1, but an application-specific ruleset can be used instead that looks like this:

```xml
<?xml version="1.0" encoding="UTF-8"?>
<!--
    s1calendar_ruleset contains all the rules needed for ICS 5.1.1
to work through the Gateway
-->
<!DOCTYPE RuleSet SYSTEM
"jar://rewriter.jar/resources/RuleSet.dtd">
<RuleSet type="GROUPED" id="s1calendar_ruleset">
<HTMLRules>
  <Attribute name="href"/>
  <Attribute name="src"/>
  <Attribute name="action"/>
  <Attribute name="background"/>
  <Attribute name="style"/>
  <JSToken>on*</JSToken>
</HTMLRules>
<JSRules>
  <Variable type="EXPRESSION"> *.location.href </Variable>
  <Variable type="EXPRESSION"> *location </Variable>
  <Variable type="EXPRESSION"> *.src</Variable>
  <Variable type="SYSTEM"> *location.pathname </Variable>
  <Function type="EXPRESSION" name="*open" paramPatterns="y"/>
  <Function type="EXPRESSION" name="*location.replace"
paramPatterns="y"/>
    </JSRules>
</RuleSet>
```

If you have two applications on the same machine, rewriting the Calendar application is a bit more challenging in portal server 6.0. However, portal server 6.2 enables you to map to individual URLs, which eliminates this problem.

Here are a few content examples taken from Calendar and shown for informational purposes only. They don't need to be applied to the ruleset for the integration to work.

Without the *open rule, for example, to prevent the logout link from redirecting back to the Calendar server itself (instead of the Gateway), the following rule would have to be added to the ruleset:

```xml
<Variable type="EXPRESSION">urlstring</Variable>
```

This would handle the full string concatenation in the following piece of code:

```
var urlstring = jmain.gCommandBaseURL + '/command.shtml?view=' +
escape(newView) + '&id=' + escape(gID) + '&crc=' + escape(gCRC) +
'&date=' + (newdate != '' ? escape(newdate) : escape(gDate)) +
'&prevView=' + escape(gOldView) + (navto_group != '' ? '&group='+
escape(navto_group) : '') + (navto_group != '' ? '&isAllGrou
p=false' : '') + (tzid != '' ? '&tzid=' + tzid : '') + "&security1";
```

Alternately, you could create a rule for gCommandBaseURL that would be rewritten in the main frame document and used as the base URL here.

Sun ONE Messaging Server Deployment

Although, the portal server ships with an HTML-based mail application called Netmail Lite, often Messaging Express, the HTML mail interface provided with the Sun ONE Messaging Server, is used instead.

Sun ONE Messaging Server 5.2 integration works out-of-box using the default_gateway_ruleset with portal server versions 6.0, 6.1, and 6.2. To have HTML links contained in the email messages for internal domains rewritten, add the following rule:

```
<Function type="DHTML" name="partObj" paramPatterns=",,,,,,,,,y"/>
```

Making this change prevents end users from having to copy the link address to the Bookmark provider on the portal server desktop to view the link contents. The message body text code might look something like the following after being rewritten:

```
part[1]=new partObj(1,null,'text/plain',35,true,0,null,hdr[1],'<A
HREF="https://gw.sun.com/http://cms.int.sun.com" target=
"1">http://cms.int.sun.com</A>',true)
```

One feature in Messaging Express that does not work through portal server 6.0 is subscribing to folders.

Rewriter Logging

At some point you might want to enable debug logging so that you can see what's going on in the Rewriter. The log you'll probably care most about from a content perspective is called psSRAP_Rewriter_recordURI.*default* (*default* represents the Gateway instance name). This log contains the exact URL used to fetch content at an exact failure point. This URL can then be used to examine other Rewriter logs to root out the source of the failure.

▼ To Enable Debug Logging for the Rewriter

1. **Open the** *install_dir*/SUNWam/AMConfig.properties **file with an editor.**

2. **Change the value of** com.iplanet.services.debug.level **from** error **to** message **and save the file.**

3. **If you are using version 6.0 of the portal server software, perform the following substeps, otherwise continue with Step 4.**

   a. **Change to the** /var/opt/SUNWam **directory.**

   ```
   # cd /var/opt/SUNWam/debug
   ```

   b. **Create debug files to avoid having to give world write permissions to the directory.**

   ```
   # touch amJSS amSession psSRAPRewriter_recordPage.default
   psSRAPRewriter_recordURI.default
   ```

   c. **Use the** touch **command to create any additional files needed for Gateway instances besides the default.**

   d. **Set file ownership to the Gateway user.**

   One approach with the Gateway running is as follows:

   ```
   # ps -ef | grep java | cut -d '' -f1 | head -n 1
   noaccess
   # chown noaccess amJSS amSession psSRAPRewriter_recordPage.default
   psSRAPRewriter_recordURI.default
   ```

4. Restart the Gateway.

```
# /etc/init.d/gateway -n default start
```

5. Log in to the Gateway as an end user, and verify that the logging is taking place.

```
# tail -f /var/opt/SUNWam/debug/psSRAPRewriter_recordPage.default
```

Ten Tips From the Trenches

This section presents ten of the most frequent Rewriter problems, and offers tips for solving each problem.

Problem: I'm having trouble mining out potential URLs from the logs because the formatting, line breaks, and unnecessary white space has been removed.

Tip: Parse out the page contents to a separate file. Use an HTML editor such as the editor available in StarOffice™ software to open the file. Select view HTML source, and you have beautifully formatted text that is easier to read and digest. This is a useful technique for debugging problems in Sun™ ONE Calendar Server software and Lotus iNotes.

Problem: I'm trying to administrate the BEA Weblogic Web container through the Gateway, but many URLs are not being rewritten.

Tip: The application server might not be sending a content-type header back with its responses as recommended by the HTTP specification. Refer to the BEA product for steps necessary to enable the appropriate HTTP headers.

Problem: When I disable client-side caching on the Gateway, I can no longer load data into helper applications using Internet Explorer.

Tip: This is due to a deficiency in how Internet Explorer handles no-caching headers. Internet Explorer decrypts SSL data to the cache before sending it to the helper applications. Selecting the Internet Explorer Advanced options "Do not save encrypted pages to disk" simply cleans up the file from the cache after it was decrypted. Microsoft has a fix for this browser limitation available at http://support.microsoft.com/default.aspx?scid=kb;en-us;323308.

Problem: Portal server 6.0 URL validation is preventing the following URL from being rewritten:

```
href="javascript:var
  x=window.open('http://gw.sun.com:82/command.shtml?view=
new_cal&#38;id=be8u2pu6p02mu98u8v&#38;
crc=1298682692&#38;date=20030306T194812&#38;newCalCalID=
enrolled&#38;tzid=&#38;freebusy=1&#38;tab=1&#38;prevView=
overview&#38;calid=enrolled&#38;security=1','','height=
550,width=650');
```

Tip: URL validation of the query string is removed in portal server 6.1 and portal server 6.2.

There is also a patch for portal server 6.0 (see "Patching the Portal Server Software" on page 10). Changing the default `window.open` rule to an EXPRESSION type does not help. However, if the `&#38;` characters are changed to ampersands, the `window.open` parameter is rewritten correctly.

Problem: My application won't work with the `default_gateway_ruleset` because the wildcarded rules incorrectly rewrite string literals which are not URLs. However, I can't figure out what specific rules I need to use instead.

Tip: By referring to the Rewriter debug log `psSRAPRewriter`.*default* with wildcarded rules still added to the application ruleset, you can determine what matches are made. Additionally, the format of these matches will be the exact rules that you can use to rewrite the data. Example of a wildcarded rule:

```
<Variable type="EXPRESSION"> *location </Variable>
```

If you already have a rule for *location.href, you can ignore that and just look for other rules that require location. Here's an example using the `grep` command:

```
# grep "location" psSRAPRewriter.default | grep -v "href"
 Rule was:<Function type="EXPRESSION" name="*location"
paramPatterns="y"
 />
Mache Object: <Function type="URL" name="window.location"
paramPatterns="" />
Rule was:<Function type="EXPRESSION" name="*location"
paramPatterns="y"
 />
Mache Object: <Function type="EXPRESSION" name="myLocation"
paramPatterns="" />
```

The rules that must be added for a match to continue to be made are specified following the "Mache Object:" statement. This enables you to narrow your search, because the psSRAPRewriter_recordPage.*default* log (where *default* is the name of the Gateway instance) will contain the assignment being matched that looks like this:

```
curLoc= "Santa Clara"
myLocation=myLoc
```

Remove the wildcarded rule *location and add a rule for `window.location` in its place. If multiple matches are made for `window.location` with differing types, then an EXPRESSION type should be used in the final rule that you add to the ruleset.

Problem: I am trying to rewrite an application that emits an HTML frameset. Inside one of the frames is a form, but I can't determine what source value to use for the rule required to rewrite the form data.

Tip: The Netscape browser can be used to view the page info for applications that can be accessed using either user-agent type. The view page option is located under the View menu heading. The page info indicates what the frame sources are.

In portal server 6.0, if the frame source URL contains a query string, you should wildcard the entire source value. Otherwise, add the rule as you normally would to rewrite form contents. For example, consider the page information for Sun ONE Calendar Express:

```
Sun ONE Calendar Express has the following structure:

      http://cal.int.sun.com/command.shtml?view=overview&id=
q62n8u8vben3bp3&calid=rlbaker
          Frame:
          http://cal.int.sun.com/command.shtml?view=
overview:toolbar&id=q62n8u8vben3bp3&crc=1974625198&date=
&prevView=overview&calid=rlbaker&id=q62n8u8vben3bp3&view=
overview&security=1
                Form 1:
                    Action URL: http://cal.int.sun.com/
                    Encoding: application/x-www-form-urlencoded
(default)
                        Method: Get
                Image: ...
          Frame:
          http://cal.int.sun.com/command.shtml?view=
overview:main&id=q62n8u8vben3bp3&crc=1974625198&date=&prevView=
overview&calid=rlbaker&id=q62n8u8vben3bp3&view=
overview&security=1
                Background Image:
http://cal.int.sun.com/imx/ltgrey.gifForm 1:
                    Action URL: http://cal.int.sun.com/
                    Encoding: application/x-www-form-urlencoded
(default)
                        Method: Get
                Image: ...
```

In the case of Calendar Server, if the data from Form 1 needs to be rewritten, the frame source URL is used as the source value in the rule. A limitation in the current versions of portal server 6 requires the use of a wildcard. The Gateway is not able to match based on the source because it is comparing to `http://cal.int.sun.com` instead of the full URL including the path. If you want to rewrite the following form:

```
<form name="form">
...
<input type="hidden" name="action" value=
"http://cal.int.sun.com/command.shtml"></input>
...
</form>
```

Don't use this specific rule:

```
<Form source="*/command.html*" name="form" fields="action"/>
```

Use this ruleset:

```
<Form source="*" name="form" fields="action"/>
```

The form source should be more specific to keep the Rewriter from unnecessarily looking at form data that it doesn't need to.

Problem: I want to get authentication URLs to work through the Gateway directly or through the BookmarkProvider.

Tip: The Gateway does not parse out authentication URLs. If a direct connection is attempted to an authentication URL through the Gateway, an error response is returned after the connection times out indicating that the Gateway was unable to connect to the host. The following is an example of the error response:

```
Unable to connect to host - uid@host.int.sun.com.

Contact administrator
```

If HTTP Basic Authentication is enabled, a one-time authentication URL can be used with the credentials prepended to the Gateway host name. An example of the direct URL is:

```
https://uid@passwd:gw.sun.com/http://cms.int.sun.com/login
```

After this, the authentication credentials are cached and no longer need to be specified with the URL. If Basic Authentication caching is not enabled, this URL format must be used any time an authentication URL is used. If the links are stored as bookmarks, then the bookmark provider must be modified to identify these URLs. After they are rewritten, the bookmark provider must prepend the UID and password to the Gateway hostport address as though the URL were being typed in the browser's URL field. To do this, the bookmark display template must be changed in /opt/SUNWps/desktop/[template_dir]/BookmarkProvider/display.template.

CODE EXAMPLE 4-16 shows a snippet of code that you can use to make stored bookmark authentication URLs work through the Gateway. This code is available for download. See "Obtaining Downloadable Files for This Book" on page xxi.

CODE EXAMPLE 4-16 Bookmark Provider `display.template`

```
.
.
.
function [tag:channelName]_openURL( url ){
    if (url.charAt(0) != '/') {
    var re = /:\\/\\//;
    var found = url.search(re);
    var urlAuth = false;
    var theQueryString, theProtocol, theHostAndPath, userName,
    passWord = null;
    if (found == -1) {
      url = "http://" + url;
    }
    tmpURL = url;
    re = /\\?/;
    if (tmpURL.search(re) > -1) {
      tmpArr=tmpURL.split("?"); // drop query string
      theQueryString = "?" + tmpARR[1];
      tmpURL = tmpArr[0];
    }
    tmpARR=tmpURL.split("//"); // drop protocol
    theProtocol = tmpARR[0] + "//";
    tmpURL=tmpARR[1];
    re = /\\@/;
    if (tmpURL.search(re) > -1) {
      tmpARR=tmpURL.split("@"); // drop host
      theHostAndPath = tmpARR[1];
      tmpURL=tmpARR[0];
      tmpARR=tmpURL.split(":"); // sep username:passwd
      userName = tmpARR[0];
      passWord = tmpARR[1];
      urlAuth = true;
      url = theProtocol;
      if (theHostAndPath != null) {
        url += theHostAndPath;
      }
      if (theQueryString != null) {
       url += theQueryString;
      }
    }
  }

  var surf_form_URL = url;
```

```
  if (urlAuth) {
    tmpArr=surf_form_URL.split("//");
    new_form_URL = tmpArr[0] + "//" + userName + ":" + passWord +
@" + tmpArr[1] + "//" + tmpArr[2];
  }
  counter++;
  var urlWin;
  var windowID = "";

  var windowOption = "[tag:windowOption]";
  if( windowOption == "all_new" ){
    windowID = "Webtop_url_number"+counter;
    if(urlAuth){urlWin=window.open(new_form_URL,windowID);}
    else { urlWin = window.open (surf_form_URL, windowID); }
    urlWin.focus();
  }
  else if( windowOption == "one_new" ){
    windowID = "Webtop_urls";
    if(urlAuth){urlWin=window.open(new_form_URL,windowID);}
    else { urlWin = window.open (surf_form_URL, windowID); }
    urlWin.focus();
   }
  else if( windowOption == "same" ){
    if (parentWindow != "undefined" && parentWindow != null) {
    if (urlAuth) {parentWindow.location=new_form_URL;}
    else {parentWindow.location = url}
      parentWindow.focus();
    } else {
      location = url;
    }
  }
}
 .
 .
 .
```

Problem: I am trying to determine rules for imported JavaScript by viewing the rewritten source using the browser.

Tip: Create an HTML page with links to the JavaScript files. Access the page and select Save As or Save Target As by right-clicking over the links. For example, generate a page that looks like this:

```
<HTML>
<BODY BGCOLOR="#FFFFFF" TEXT="#000000">
<A HREF=
"https://gw.sun.com/http://cms.int.sun.com/scripts/script1.js">
Script 1
</A>
</HTML>
```

By saving the file locally, you can look at the rewritten contents. Imported script content is additionally logged to the Rewriter debug logs in portal server 6.x.

Problem: I am using Internet Explorer and am accessing an application through the Gateway resulting in a SCRIPT error. How do I debug the problem?

Tip: Internet Explorer on Microsoft Windows 2000 has a script debugger that you can use to step through debugging to determine where the error is originating and determine why it is only failing when being accessed through the Gateway.

Problem: I'm having trouble with XSL transforms. Content in the XSL file is being rewritten incorrectly, or is resulting in data corruption.

Tip: The portal server 6.0 and 6.1 Rewriter does not handle XSL content. Check to be sure that the content-type of the XSL file being returned is not text/XML and that there is not an XML root element in the XSL file that is confusing the Gateway so that it is treating the entire file as XML content. Portal server 6.2 treats XSL files the same as XML files, and XSL rewriting should be administered as though the content were XML.

New Rewriter Technology in the Java Enterprise System

Portal server 6.2 embodies much of what you might expect to find in a future Rewriter. In addition to easing administrative burdens, there are additions to logging, increased security, and a smarter Gateway. Here are a few descriptions of what you can expect to find in a future Rewriter.

- Ruleset extension – One or more base rulesets can now be defined and others can extend or overload rules specified in that ruleset much like subclassing in Java. This furthers the notion of application-specific rulesets. Now, only rules that are unique to the application itself can be specified for the associated ruleset rather than having to define basic elements like HTML tag attributes that are applicable to all content passing through the Gateway.

- Logging enhancements – Additional log files have been added which make it easier for portal administrators to determine what the data being accessed looks like, and how to root out possible Rewriter misconfigurations or oversights. For example, an additional debug log is available for pages that were not rewritten, and that could raise suspicions about whether something that should have been rewritten actually wasn't. Additionally, two separate logs are kept that indicate what the page contents look like before rewriting and what they look like after rewriting.

- Obfuscation of Intranet URLs – When URLs are rewritten now, the path portion of the Gateway URL is obfuscated, making it more difficult to determine Intranet host addresses. This is particularly useful if caching of SSL content is enabled in the Web browser, or to add additional security against prying eyes where Intranet URLs might have been previously exposed in the location field of the browser.

- JSToken deprecation – JSToken rule values are simply HTML attributes containing JavaScript, so the tag is deprecated in favor of adding a DJS type to HTML Attribute rules. For example, the wildcarded JSToken rule can now be written as:

```
<Attribute type="DJS" name="on*"/>
```

- Simplified rule syntax – Rules are easier to administer and have common attributes for each of the ruleset content sections. Rules no longer need a separate closing tag for each of the entries, and the rule semantics are handled within each tag representing a rule.

## CHAPTER 5

Gateway: Gluing It All Together

This chapter discusses the Gateway technology in the SRA software. The Gateway is a portal server component that is used to direct traffic from remote users to the other portal server components and internal resources.

This chapter contains the following sections:

Note – In this book, the term *portal server* refers to Sun's portal server software with the SRA software unless specified otherwise. *Portal server node* and *portal platform node* refer to the portal server core product.

What is the Gateway?

The term *gateway* has a variety of meanings in the computer industry. Sometimes the term gateway is used in a broader context to indicate the piece of infrastructure used as the first jump point to route IP traffic to its next destination point. Gateways are generally used as single points of entrance to a local area network from the Internet protected by one or more firewalls, depending on the network topology and location of the gateway.

In the context of the Sun's portal server software, the term Gateway is frequently used interchangeably with the Rewriter. This is inaccurate because the Rewriter is actually a shared component between both the Gateway and the portal URL scraper.

The portal Gateway is really a partially implemented reverse proxy. Functionally, the Gateway differs from reverse proxies in several ways. To begin with, the Gateway does not contain a Web cache. Besides session information, the Gateway does not maintain any data that it retrieves. Secondly, the Gateway does not operate using static maps of internal and external URLs. Reverse proxies are sometimes used as virtual servers to protect internal resources by mapping internal URLs to external URLs and overriding certain HTTP headers, such as those resulting from errors, that may contain internal information. Alternately, the Gateway performs policy enforcement to decide whether or not external users are able to view internal content, and if so, the Gateway changes internal URLs to include the Gateway address in a process referred to as URL rewriting. In the portal server 6.2 software, internal URLs can be obfuscated so as to not expose them to remote users.

In addition to its normal proxying duties, the Gateway has a few other tricks up its sleeve. The Gateway differentiates between Netlet traffic and Web traffic, and can off-load either or both to proxies providing greater security by lessening the number of holes that need to be opened on a secondary firewall. The Gateway also makes sure that users have a valid session and the appropriate access policy when fetching internal data. Additionally, the Gateway manages HTTP message headers, rewriting them where appropriate, and tagging responses with no-caching headers when so configured. Unlike many other fully implemented reverse proxies, the Gateway allows pass-through of headers it does not understand. Without other security in place, this would normally be considered a bad practice, though it is required by many .NET applications that make use of proprietary HTTP protocol and WebDAV extensions. The benefit here is that many internal applications that may not work through other proxies will work through the portal Gateway as a result of this HTTP header pass-through.

Why Do I Need the Gateway?

The Gateway is the primary means for making remote access secure. Without the Gateway in place, internal systems and data would otherwise be left exposed to untrusted users. Here are ten reasons why it's not just nice to have a portal Gateway, but also why you really need it.

- Reason 1 – Ability to remove systems from the DMZ.
  Allowing mission-critical, Web-based systems to be moved behind a secondary firewall (out of the DMZ) is one of the most frequent reasons for using the Gateway. This prevents direct attacks by evildoers on systems that would otherwise have to sit with one side exposed. Numerous CERT advisories warn against protocol-level attacks such as buffer overflows that could result in a system being crippled or taken over altogether. Tucking critical systems away in the corporate intranet is a much better approach to securing these systems than security through obscurity or some other complex wizardry.

- Reason 2 – Cookie Rewriting
  The Gateway can be configured to rewrite cookies so that internal Web applications requiring cookie-based session handling will work well for remote users. If cookies are not rewritten, the browser does not resend them in future requests because the cookie domain would not match the DNS domain of the Gateway. By rewriting the cookie, all of the original cookie data is preserved, and it is left up to the Gateway whether or not to forward the cookies to specific internal hosts based on the cookie domain once the cookie has been unpacked (had the unnecessary, rewritten portion removed). Cookie rewriting can be turned off for flat network topologies where only one DNS domain is shared, or to explicitly prevent the use of cookies in other network topologies.

- Reason 3 – Location Header Rewriting
  Some Web servers can be configured to automatically redirect user requests for specific URLs. This is sometimes done by the Web server returning a location header field in the HTTP response. The Gateway ensures that this header is rewritten, so that the follow-up request is made through the Gateway instead of directly to the content server specified by the Location header value. Location header rewriting is governed by the same set of rules for domains and subdomains used by the Gateway instance when rewriting other kinds of content, so that redirections to publicly accessible content will not be rewritten, and the follow-up browser request will be made directly to the content server. This feature prevents the Gateway from being used to unnecessarily proxy traffic outside of the corporate intranet. Other techniques used for page redirection like the META tag are handled by out-of-box rulesets specifying HTML attribute values that require rewriting.

- Reason 4 – Encryption
  While the Gateway can be configured to run in HTTP mode (with no encryption), it is most frequently deployed in HTTPS mode (encrypted), reserving HTTP mode only to debug difficult problems that may require snooping network traffic on the Gateway machine's NICs. The advantage of running the Gateway in HTTPS mode is that all internal content retrieved by remote users will be encrypted. That prevents each host that would normally be accessed by remote users from having to be configured to run SSL, and having to purchase costly (expiring) server certificates for each of those systems to have users be able to access them seamlessly. The Gateway can be configured to use a self-signed certificate, but it is recommended to import a server certificate from a trusted CA in production environments. The cost benefit should be fairly obvious, however: One Gateway with one certificate can be used to access countless machines, instead of requiring many certificates for many machines all running in a bloated DMZ.

- Reason 5 – Load Balancing
  The Gateway can be configured to load balance using a round robin algorithm to a pool of platform servers when users initially log in. Because links on the portal server desktop would be rewritten using that platform node host name, the user session would be sticky until the user has logged out of the portal. This helps distribute the load of Gateway users to a set of platform instances for secure remote access purposes. Also, the Gateway itself can be preceded by a third-party load balancer with limited restrictions to create redundancy and increase scalability.

- Reason 6 – Authentication Enforcement
  Combined with other powerful features inherited from the Identity Server, the Gateway can also present authentication type and level enforcing, authentication chaining, and client certificate authentication. Certificate authentication is not as mobile, and therefore not as widely used for SRA deployments that require more flexibility than security. Authentication types may be different for users coming in through the Gateway than for users accessing the portal directly, or an additional authentication step might be added to the chain to provide added security for remote user access.

- Reason 7 – User Access Policies
  In addition to providing a variety of authentication options, the Gateway also maintains a list of allowable and denied resources. Enforcement is handled in a manner similar to a packet filtering firewall ruleset. The access list is an ideal means of exposing only a portion of the internal network to remote users, for such things as B2B ventures, partnering, and developer relations. The portions of the internal network available for these types of users do not need to be quarantined because the Gateway will deny user requests outside of allowed hosts or applications.

- Reason 8 – Reduce Complexity of Security Implementation
  By recommending multiple layers and reducing complexity, best practices security precautions always seem to be at odds with flexibility and usability. Generally, more layers imply more complexity. The more complex things are, the more unruly and unusable they tend to be. The Gateway itself does not single-handedly guarantee a secure network, but when used in conjunction with best practices network security methodologies, the Gateway offers additional layers of security. In doing so, it also allows a surprising amount of flexibility, while reducing complexity.

- Reason 9 – Scalability and Flexibility
  There is no doubt that the Gateway can be a predominant bottleneck in a secure remote access environment. The severity and magnitude of its impact can be mitigated by scaling both horizontally and vertically. Horizontal scaling can be achieved by running multiple Gateway instances on the same or multiple boxes, while vertical scaling is typically achieved through the addition of CPUs on a single box. Some horizontal scaling can also be achieved by off-loading tasks to specialized proxies and devices. Portal server 6.2 takes additional advantage of on-board SSL accelerator cards such as the Sun™ Crypto accelerator cards, and some off-board accelerators available from other vendors. Crypto cards make better use of CPU utilization that may be otherwise gobbled up by encryption and decryption tasks. Flexibility is further exemplified by the mobility of the solution. No client footprint is required besides a standards-compliant Web browser.

- Reason 10 – no-cache HTTP Headers
  The Gateway can be configured to add no-cache HTTP headers to responses adding an additional layer of security by making sure that sensitive internal content is not unintentionally cached on untrusted machines. The portal server desktop already contains these necessary headers, mostly because the content is expected to be dynamic in nature and should not be cached. By configuring the Gateway to add these headers, however, all content redirected through the Gateway will be tagged as well.

- Bonus Reason – Lots of other companies have one.
  If the first ten reasons aren't convincing enough, you might take comfort in knowing that there are many other companies using the Gateway. Sun uses the Gateway for its own employee secure remote access purposes. Dozens of other companies have used it for a single application integration to push servers out of the DMZ and back into the corporate intranet fold. Still others have used it to replace specialized proxies loosely put in place for B2B environments, and a significant number of companies have found the Gateway just as useful for employee remote access purposes as it is for a specialized partnering solution.

How Does the Gateway Work?

The first time a user logs in to the Gateway, the request is redirected either to the authentication page for the default organization, or to the organization defined by the path portion of the URL used to contact the Gateway.

For example, a URL like `https://gw.sun.com/suntone` can be used for a remote user logging in to an organization called Suntone that is set up for partnering purposes. The redirected URL and embedded page contents must be listed in the Gateway Service Non-authenticated URLs list, or the permission to access the resources will be denied and no users will be able to log in at all.

When the redirected request reaches the Identity Server, it verifies that the organization exists and creates an invalid user session. The Identity Server then sends a session cookie along with the response. Once the user successfully authenticates from the login page, the session ID contained in the cookie becomes valid, and end users have access to all internal content except what is explicitly forbidden by the Gateway profile's access list.

The Gateway is the single point of entry and exit for remote users. Both Web requests and Netlet traffic funnel through the same Gateway instance. The Gateway sorts and separates the different traffic types and handles them according to how the Gateway has been configured. For example, Web traffic might be decrypted by the Gateway and sent directly to a content server or Web proxy, or it might be encrypted again and then sent to the Rewriter proxy. The Rewriter proxy would then make the request directly to the internal content server.

In addition to funneling traffic, the Gateway handles some important protocol interactions. These include modifying HTTP headers including the location, cookie, and content length; the Gateway can be configured to add no-caching headers as well.

Finally, the Gateway can act as a relatively independent SRA device that requires very little interaction with the portal node if it is deployed to front existing Web applications and internal portals. This can be achieved by changing the redirection URL after successful login to point to another URL besides the portal server desktop.

How Do I Deploy the Gateway?

Because of the Gateway's placement in the network environment, usually no additional work is necessary to ensure security. The Gateway typically sits behind an external firewall with just one required opened port. If you use port 443, which is the default SSL protocol port, you don't need to include the port number in the URL. This port is usually already open on the external firewall. FIGURE 5-1 illustrates this side of the network topology for a simple SRA deployment.

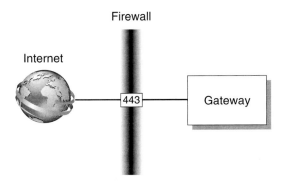

FIGURE 5-1   SRA Proof of Concept Network Topology

This simple network topology is usually inadequate for most environments because it implies that there is only one firewall between the Intranet and the rest of the world, and that the Gateway shares the same network as all of the application and content servers. A more realistic view puts the Gateway in a DMZ with a secondary firewall immediately following it. When no proxies are configured, the Gateway communicates directly with application and content servers. This may require the adjustment of packet filtering rules to allow for specific protocols and hosts. If users will be remotely accessing a wide variety of internal content located on independent servers and networks, the packet filtering rules on the secondary firewall may have to be quite generalized. FIGURE 5-2 shows a network topology where the Gateway is in the DMZ.

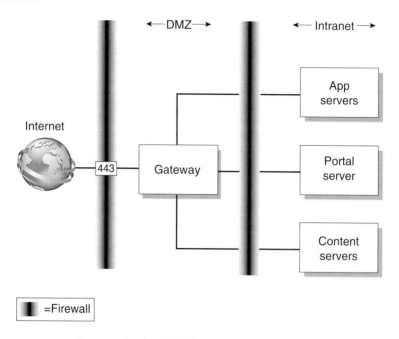

FIGURE 5-2 Gateway in the DMZ Network Topology

You probably don't want to have a lot of holes in your secondary firewall. Holes can be reduced dramatically by configuring the Gateway to use a Web proxy. FIGURE 5-3 shows a network topology with a Web proxy. One important thing to be aware of when deploying the Gateway in this manner is that the Gateway will need to fetch its profile data from the LDAP server. If the secondary firewall is not configured to allow the Gateway to reach the LDAP server directly, then the Gateway platform file will need to contain necessary proxy server information for it to reach the LDAP server. This is done by adding entries for `http.proxyHost`, `http.proxyPort`, and `http.proxySet` entries to each Gateway instance's `platform.conf` configuration file located in the `/etc/opt/SUNWps/` directory. Additional information about these values can be found in the Secure Remote Access Administrator's Guide.

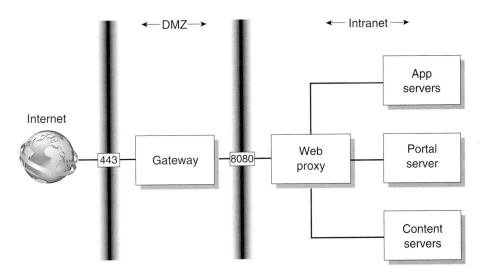

FIGURE 5-3 Web Proxy SRA Network Topology

The Gateway can be configured to make use of specialized proxies which communicate directly with internal content and application servers. The rewriter proxies' usage is similar to a Web proxy configured to run in SSL mode, with the exception being that the Rewriter proxy performs URL rewriting in addition to encrypting the content prior to sending it back to the Gateway. The Rewriter proxy provides a lightweight alternative to a Web proxy. The Netlet proxy can be used to tunnel Netlet traffic to an isolated network consisting of the backend Web applications. The portal server 6.2 version enables these proxies to be on independent machines, while earlier versions of portal server 6 require at least the Rewriter proxy be located on the portal server or platform node.

Note – Do not put proxies on a single-tier SRA installation because the `platform.conf` file will be wiped out and the Gateway will not function correctly. While it may be tempting to install "the works" for a single tier PoC environment, it is not sensible to install the portal proxies on the Gateway host because the very idea of using the proxies is to reduce the number of ports that need to be opened on a firewall. Having the proxies on the same host as the Gateway would obviously not help in this instance because the same number of ports would have to be opened between the Gateway and content servers as when the proxies were not installed at all.

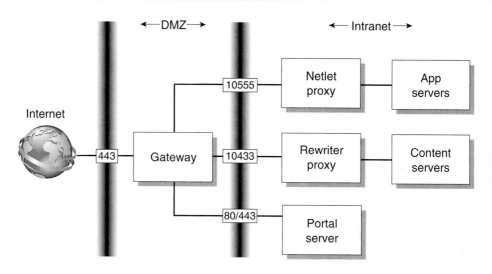

FIGURE 5-4   Portal Proxy SRA Network Topology

As previously mentioned, another approach to handling the front-end load is to precede the Gateway with a load balancer such as Resonate's Central Dispatch or Cisco's newer CSS product, or the older product, Local Director. The load balancer can be configured to balance multiple Gateway instances, and multiple Gateway nodes as shown in FIGURE 5-5.

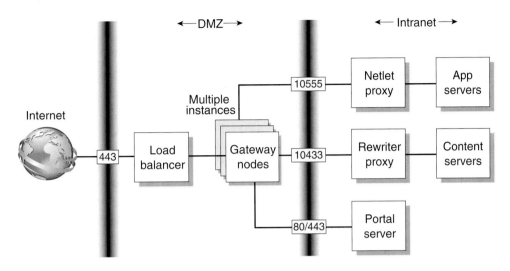

FIGURE 5-5 Load-Balanced Gateway SRA Network Topology

In addition to the Gateway running multiple instances, the portal server can have multiple platform nodes as well. There is a portal server limitation in having multiple, full software installations on the same node. To make the best utilization of larger hardware (big iron), you can use hardware domains that are available in many of the newer Sun systems. This feature enables multiple systems to operate independently of one another in the same physical box. FIGURE 5-6 shows multiple platform nodes.

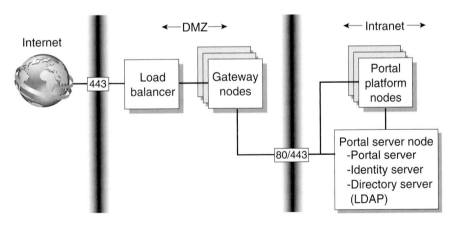

FIGURE 5-6 Multiplatform SRA Network Topology

If multiple platforms nodes are used, then it is advisable to remove the portal server node from the list of platforms the Gateway load balances. Some additional tricks can be done to maximize scalability and uptime for high-traffic deployment scenarios. The LDAP server remains the single point of failure. One approach to remove this limitation is to create an LDAP server cluster fronted by a directory proxy. This moves the single point of failure to the directory proxy instead of the directory itself, however, this requires at least one additional load balancer. A more reasonable approach is to configure at least two LDAP servers to run in a master/master or master/consumer relationship. The specific details for accomplishing this are beyond the scope of this book, but there are many other resources available to help accomplish this particular deployment scenario. Refer to the *Sun ONE Portal Server 6.0 Deployment Guide*, "No Single Point of Failure Scenario" section for more information.

Configuring the Gateway

The Gateway is configured through a combination of service modifications and platform configurations. Service modifications are made using the Identity Server Administration Console, while platform configurations are done by manually changing configuration files and properties files on the Gateway node.

The service modifications that affect the installation, manageability, runtime, and performance of the Gateway are discussed in the following sections.

Platform configurations are discussed in"Platform Configuration" on page 330.

Service Configuration

You use the Identity Server Administration Console to create and manage individual Gateway profiles. Each profile contains information pertinent to runtime characteristics of a Gateway running in single instance or multi-instance mode.

In portal server 6.1 and 6.2, the Gateway service is configured from the Service Configuration tab in the Identity Server Administration Console. Once this tab is selected, select the link next to Gateway in the SRAP Configuration subheading in the left panel. From there, the right panel provides you with the Gateway Service Configuration panel with checkboxes and fields for configuring the Gateway service. This panel is long, so the following sections describe logical parts of the version 6.1 panel using ten figures (FIGURE 5-7 through FIGURE 5-16).

FIGURE 5-7 shows what ports the Gateway instances listen on, whether or not portal proxies are used, and what ports are used to communicate with the proxies. The options are better organized in the portal server 6.2 administration screen with some additional options, including a list of Rewriter proxies since that version no longer requires the Rewriter proxy to be installed on the portal server node. For all deployments, except for internal proof-of-concept deployments, the Gateway should run over HTTPS, or else data transmission between the Gateway and the client will not be encrypted. The only exception to this is when the encryption is handled by an off-board encryption device.

The Gateway can also run simultaneously in HTTP mode and HTTPS mode, but this configuration should be reserved for debugging purposes only. Use the default protocol ports if users will be contacting the Gateway directly. If a load balancer is interposed between the client and the Gateway, the port number is not as important, and could be changed to a nonprivileged value. The proxies should be installed and running before you enable them in the Gateway Service Configuration panel. Otherwise, client connections will fail outright or appear to hang while the Gateway attempts to locate and communicate with a nonexistent or nonrunning proxy.

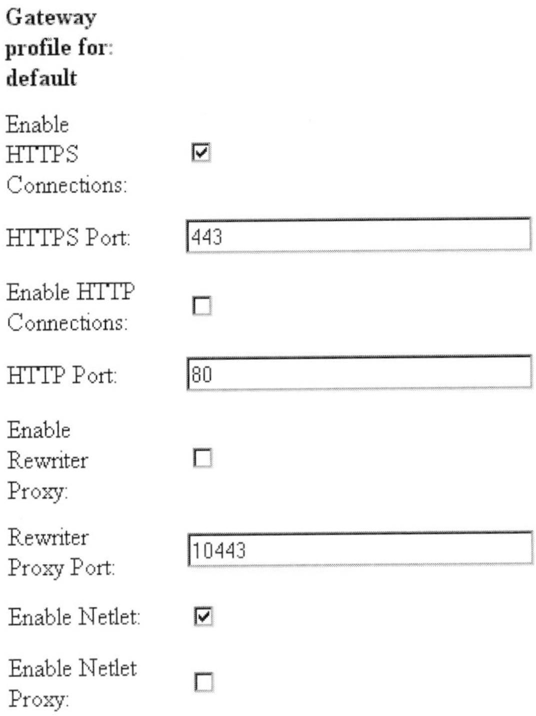

Gateway profile for:
default

Enable HTTPS Connections:	☑
HTTPS Port:	443
Enable HTTP Connections:	☐
HTTP Port:	80
Enable Rewriter Proxy:	☐
Rewriter Proxy Port:	10443
Enable Netlet:	☑
Enable Netlet Proxy:	☐

FIGURE 5-7 Gateway Service Configuration Panel (*1 of 10*)

The checkbox for Use Proxy (FIGURE 5-8) enables the Gateway to communicate using a Web proxy. This refers to traditional Web proxy servers and not to the Rewriter proxy, which is enabled with the Enable Rewriter Proxy checkbox. The Use Proxy option is helpful if the Gateway is deployed in an existing DMZ that already has a proxy in place that communicates directly with content servers and applications servers. It also simplifies secondary firewall rule management. The Use Web Proxy URLs field enables the Gateway to choose whether or not to use the Web proxy when accessing specific hosts. This field is only valid when the Use Web Proxy option is not selected. A wildcard in this field directs the Gateway to use the Web proxy for all URLs requested by clients.

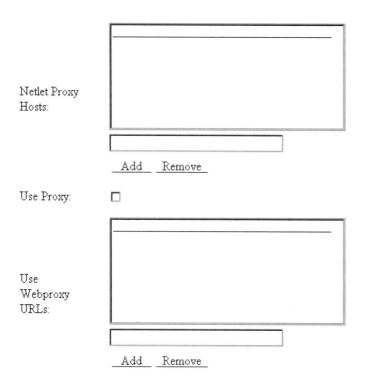

FIGURE 5-8   Gateway Service Configuration Panel (*2 of 10*)

The Do Not Use Webproxy URLs field (FIGURE 5-9) is used to explicitly deny the use of a Web proxy to access specific hosts. This field is only valid when the Use Web Proxy option is enabled.

The Proxies for Domains and Subdomains field (FIGURE 5-9) is very important for Rewriter functionality because this field indicates what domains are only accessible through the Gateway (internal addresses). The values in this field indicate whether URLs pointing to those domains need to be rewritten or not. Publicly accessible domains should not be added to this field unless there is a specific reason to do so—such as keeping a record of all content accessed by remote users. If you add publicly accessible domains to this field:

- The Gateway must be able to directly access the domain or know which Web proxy to use.
- Unnecessary load is placed on the Gateway retrieving content that would otherwise be fetched directly from the client browser. This counteracts one of the major benefits using portal server SRA capabilities instead of traditional VPNs.

The Proxies for Domains and Subdomains list is used to specify what proxy to use to access a server on a specific domain. For example, If Use Proxy is selected and the URL is not in the Do Not Use Web Proxy URL list, then the Web proxy specified in the Proxies for Domains and Subdomains list is used for requests to the specified domain. Alternately, if Use Proxy is not selected, the proxy in the Proxies for Domains and Subdomains is not used unless the URL is specified in the Use Webproxy URL list.

The contents of the Proxies For Domains And Subdomains field (FIGURE 5-9) is also used when rewriting content to determine individual URLs that might need to be rewritten, and for redirect types of URLs. Redirect URLs are used frequently when the rewriting of content must be done at runtime by the client browser. For example, if the URL `http://www.yahoo.com` is typed into the Bookmark provider on the portal server desktop, it is rewritten as `https://gw.sun.com/redirect/http://www.yahoo.com`. When the browser requests the URL, the Gateway checks to see if `yahoo.com` is listed in the Proxies for Domains and Subdomains field. If it is not, the Gateway sends a redirection back to the browser telling it to go directly to `www.yahoo.com`. If `yahoo.com` is in the list, the Gateway fetches the contents on the user's behalf and returns the contents (after being rewritten) to the client.

The domain of the portal server should always be listed in the Proxies For Domains And Subdomains field for the portal server desktop to function correctly through the Gateway. This is how the field is configured by default, but you should check the setting if the Gateway and portal server are located in different subdomains.

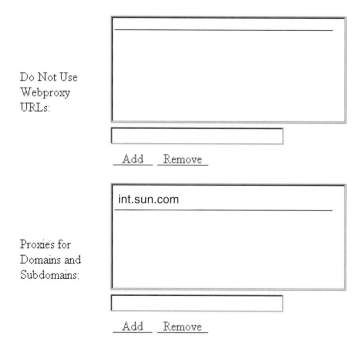

Do Not Use
Webproxy
URLs:

Add   Remove

int.sun.com

Proxies for
Domains and
Subdomains:

Add   Remove

FIGURE 5-9   Gateway Service Configuration Panel (*3 of 10*)

Specify proxy passwords in the Proxy Password List (FIGURE 5-10) if you have
proxies that require authentication between the Gateway and content or application
servers that the Gateway communicates with. Each entry should correspond to a
proxy listed in the Proxies for Domains and Subdomains list and the entry is
specified in the form *proxyname* | *username* | *password*. There can only be one entry per
unique proxy name in this list. Duplicate entries will be ignored in favor of the first
instance.

Enable Cookie Management (FIGURE 5-10) is a very important feature. It rewrites
cookies to use the Gateway's domain so that cookies set by applications make it back
to those same applications on future browser requests. The cookie is rewritten using
a two-way encoding process so that the original cookie contents remain unchanged.

One issue to be aware of is the 20-cookie-per-domain limit imposed by the cookie
specification. This can become a problem if too many disparate applications are
aggregated through the portal server desktop. Each have their own cookies for
session handling, rather than using a shared single-sign-on (SSO) token or some
other means of shared session management. The 20 cookie limit is enforced in a
FIFO manner, so the first cookie to get ejected is usually the portal server session
cookie. This means the client cannot continue using the portal server until they re-

authenticate. Some third-party applications such as SAP can be configured to use a multitude of cookies, or one master cookie. In this case, it would be better to use one cookie for SSO to the individual applications.

The Enable HTTP Basic Authentication option (FIGURE 5-10), when checked, is used to store authentication credentials for applications that make use of HTTP Basic Authentication. After authenticating for the first time, the credentials are stored along with the user's profile in the directory server and sent automatically during future requests to the same application. This feature can provide SSO capabilities for applications and content servers that rely on HTTP Basic Authentication for initial login. Portal server 6.0 can store only one credential per user, while portal server 6.1 and 6.2 allow multiple credentials to be stored for unique URLs and hosts. This feature does not cache credentials for other authentication protocols, including the proprietary NTLM authentication protocol. Applications that make use of this protocol will not work properly when accessed through the Gateway. The reason being that NTLM authentication is connection oriented and cannot be proxied. NTLM is not an optimal choice to make for authentication to external hosts anyway, since it was originally designed to work in an environment where the client and server are on the same NT domain. Such applications should be configured to use HTTP Basic Authentication, or some other solution that implements the authentication protocol, and exposes it as a shared SSO token or something similar. One thing to be aware of when using Basic Authentication is that HTTP Basic Authentication only encodes the user ID and password, so it might be subject to spoofing. This risk is mitigated by the fact that only authenticated users can proxy requests through the Gateway unless the resource has been added to the Gateway's Non-authenticated URLs list.

The Enable Persistent HTTP Connections option (FIGURE 5-10) is useful to gain performance when much of the content accessed through the Gateway is small in size. This option, when checked, enables HTTP 1.1 keep-alive connections between the Gateway and the backend server. The Gateway is not fully HTTP 1.1 compliant, however. Other advanced HTTP 1.1 features and specification extensions may not work correctly (such as WebDAV and other work-in-progress extensions) to the specification. For example, the destination HTTP header used by WebDAV for move and copy requests requires a patch for portal server version 6.2.

The Maximum Number of Requests per Persistent Connection field (FIGURE 5-10) only takes effect when Enable Persistent HTTP Connections is enabled. Consider the value for this field carefully. Set too low, the feature has very little benefit because the request pool is too small. Set too high, available sockets might become very sparse in high-traffic deployments. This is a result of waiting for the sockets to either time out if the maximum connection value is not reached, or waiting until the maximum value is attained.

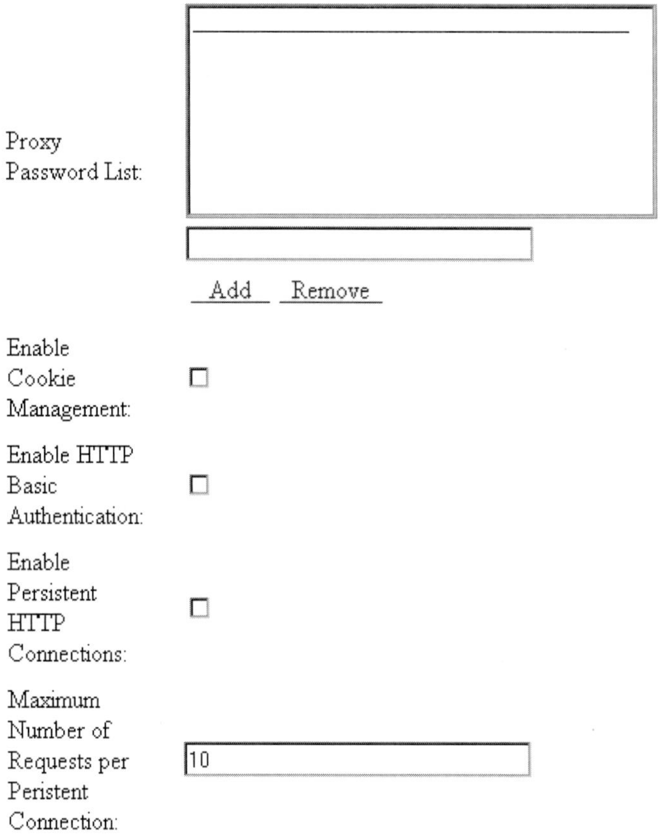

Proxy
Password List:

Add   Remove

Enable
Cookie
Management:

Enable HTTP
Basic
Authentication:

Enable
Persistent
HTTP
Connections:

Maximum
Number of
Requests per   10
Peristent
Connection:

FIGURE 5-10 Gateway Service Configuration Panel (*4 of 10*)

Both of the socket timeouts (the Timeout after which Persistent Socket gets Closed and Grace Timeout to Account for Turnaround Time fields, shown in FIGURE 5-11) are used to provide a granular way to control the Gateway's connection traffic. The Grace Timeout is used to make sure that the socket is not closed prematurely before getting a response from the back-end application. Both values are specified in seconds, and should be treated with an equal vigilance as the value for the Maximum Number of Requests per Connection. A high timeout value might appear to users as a hang condition if the connection pool is depleted, and the default connection timeouts may have to be cleaned up by the underlying OS. If the timeout is set too low, it may not be possible to get the maximum number of requests in during the time allotted, which would reduce the effectiveness of having persistent connections to begin with.

The Forward Cookie URLs list (FIGURE 5-11) is used by the Gateway to determine which cookies sent in a browser request should be forwarded to back-end applications. The portal server URL is added to this field by default to make sure that the portal user session cookie remains intact. Most applications on the portal server desktop require this cookie to be present to operate. If there are other applications that also need the cookies to be sent back to the respective applications, their URLs should be added to this list, or a wildcard should be used instead to indicate that all cookies should be forwarded based on rules established by the cookie specification.

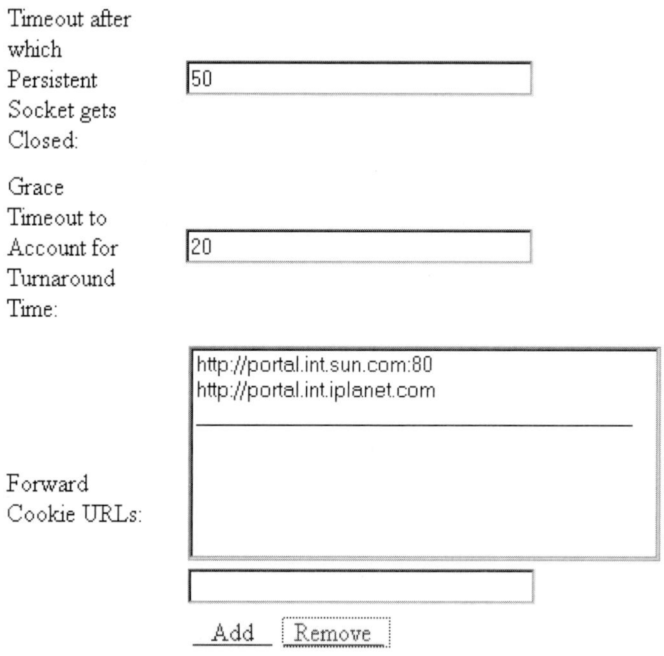

Timeout after which Persistent Socket gets Closed:

> 50

Grace Timeout to Account for Turnaround Time:

> 20

Forward Cookie URLs:

> http://portal.int.sun.com:80
> http://portal.int.iplanet.com

Add   Remove

FIGURE 5-11 Gateway Service Configuration Panel (*5 of 10*)

The Non-authenticated URLs list (FIGURE 5-12) enables internal URLs to be fetched requiring no prior authentication to the Identity Server. In rare cases, you might add URLs necessary to get the authlessanonomous desktop to be visible through the Gateway without having to first authenticate to the portal server. This enables the benefit of an open portal being used for general purposes, but once authenticated, reaps all the additional benefits that the Gateway provides.

More practically, the Non-authenticated URLs list serves to solve the chicken-and-egg dilemma where the Gateway does not fetch internal content until a user has been authenticated, but there is content on the authentication page itself that the Gateway must fetch prior to a user being authenticated. This explains why most of the prepopulated list contains URLs for login specifics. Additionally, if the anonymous portal is going to be allowed through the Gateway, *DEPLOY_URI*/dt must be added to this list. If delegated administration is not going to be allowed through the Gateway, then the /amconsole specific URLs should be removed from the list as a security precaution. This prevents password guessing on the amadmin user account. Otherwise, you can use an authentication chaining scheme to bolster additional levels of security.

The Maximum Connection Queue Length field (FIGURE 5-12) is used to define the total number of concurrent connections allowed by the Gateway instance. The default value is usually sufficient in most cases. Larger values could cause a flood of requests following a long garbage collection that would result in a long delay in service end-user requests. The need for a larger value probably indicates a bottleneck elsewhere in the system, and tuning would be better applied to remove that bottleneck instead of changing the Maximum Connection Queue Length.

The Gateway Timeout value (FIGURE 5-12) is used to reduce the susceptibility to denial of service attacks and hang conditions associated with the underlying system resources being consumed. Notice that the value is specified in milliseconds. By default, the Sun Web server times out idle connections after 60 seconds, so you might consider changing this value to 60,000 for higher load deployments, or for smaller sized configurations.

The Maximum Thread Pool Size field (FIGURE 5-12) allocates a number of threads to the Gateway process. If the logs indicate a large number of threads in a wait state, this value should be tuned higher than the default of 200. Multiple soak test runs with a higher-than-normal level of load help you determine what an adequate value may be for specific deployment purposes. The default value is adequate for most applications.

The Cached Socket Timeout label (FIGURE 5-12) is a bit misleading. It basically defines the timeout value on the other end of the connection. That would be the portal server, portal platform, or a content or application server. The value should be set reasonably high for total turnaround time of a request to one of these other servers. The value is less important than the timeout on the external-facing NIC. The default may be adequate except for an extremely slow network connection, or an internal server that is unable to service incoming requests in a reasonable amount of time.

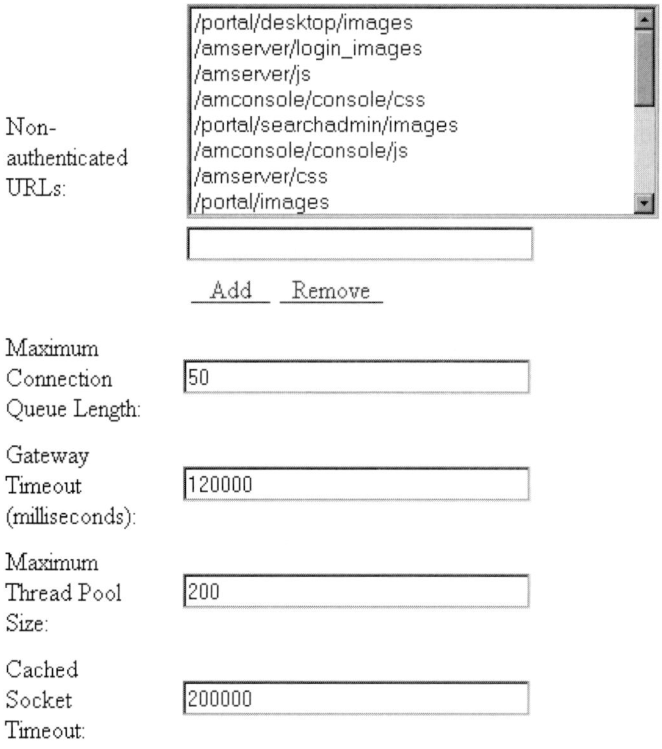

Non-authenticated URLs:

```
/portal/desktop/images
/amserver/login_images
/amserver/js
/amconsole/console/css
/portal/searchadmin/images
/amconsole/console/js
/amserver/css
/portal/images
```

Add   Remove

Maximum Connection Queue Length: `50`

Gateway Timeout (milliseconds): `120000`

Maximum Thread Pool Size: `200`

Cached Socket Timeout: `200000`

FIGURE 5-12 Gateway Service Configuration Panel (*6 of 10*)

The Certificate Enabled Gateway hosts list (FIGURE 5-13) contains those Gateway hosts that are able to participate in personal digital certificate (PDC) authentication of remote users. PDC might be a good solution as an authentication chain addition for remote administrators such as amadmin. The Gateway does not pass through certificates to internal systems that require PDC authentication because it is used solely in consideration for initial authentication purposes in conjunction with the Identity Server. In addition to the Gateway being listed here, additional steps must be followed. Refer to the product documentation for instructions on setting up the Gateway to allow PDC authentication.

The Allow 40-bit Browser checkbox (FIGURE 5-13) enables the Gateway to step down to handle requests from older browsers or SSL devices that do not support higher encryption levels. This feature is included for backward compatibility purposes and should be unchecked in most production environments. The labeling here is a bit misleading. When deselected, only 128-bit an higher ciphers are allowed. So 56-bit and 64-bit (previously export-grade encryption levels allowed by U.S. export law) connections are also disallowed. Export encryption requirements by the U.S.

government have been relaxed a bit, so almost all SSL connections now involve at least 128-bit ciphers, and newer cipher suites supporting SSL level 2 ship with all modern browsers.

Enable SSL Version 2.0 (FIGURE 5-13) should be checked to take advantage of new improvements made to the SSL protocol. In the portal server 6.2, SSL Version 3.0 ciphers are available as well.

If you have a requirement for a specific cipher, you can select one from the SSL2 Ciphers list (FIGURE 5-13). You also need to select Enable SSL Cipher Selection (FIGURE 5-13) in this case. Otherwise, the strongest shared cipher between the browser and Gateway is used. If a cipher selected from the list is not available on the client, the connection fails, so it is usually better to let the Gateway negotiate the cipher usage. The only exception to this is when you want 1024-bit Transport Layer Security (TLS) ciphers used explicitly. To do this, check the Enable SSL Cipher Selection checkbox, deselect the SSL2 ciphers, and select one of the TLS ciphers (FIGURE 5-14). The TLS cipher must be supported by the browser, or the connection fails. Also remember that performance degrades as encryption levels increase, due to the increased computational overhead associated with encryption and decryption.

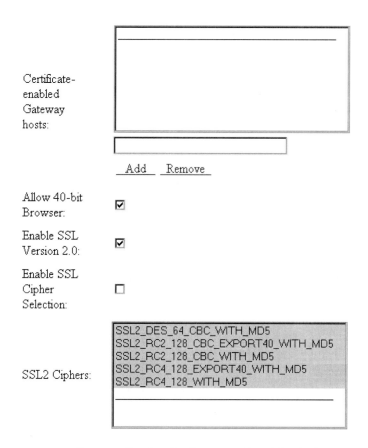

Certificate-
enabled
Gateway
hosts:

Add   Remove

Allow 40-bit
Browser:

Enable SSL
Version 2.0:

Enable SSL
Cipher
Selection:

SSL2 Ciphers:

SSL2_DES_64_CBC_WITH_MD5
SSL2_RC2_128_CBC_EXPORT40_WITH_MD5
SSL2_RC2_128_CBC_WITH_MD5
SSL2_RC4_128_EXPORT40_WITH_MD5
SSL2_RC4_128_WITH_MD5

FIGURE 5-13 Gateway Service Configuration Panel (*7 of 10*)

When the Rewrite all URLs checkbox (FIGURE 5-14) is checked, the contents of the Proxies for Domains and Subdomains list (FIGURE 5-9) is superseded, and all content is rewritten regardless of the location of origin. This option is useful for a network that fronts a wide variety of domains and subdomains, and where the Gateway is used to audit traffic flow for remote users. Selecting this option may unnecessarily burden the Gateway to make requests to publicly accessible content, and might require additional configuration for the Gateway to make those requests from within the DMZ. It is usually better to err on the conservative side and add domains to the Proxies for Domains and Subdomains list instead of enabling this option. An exception is specific deployment scenarios such as those that have unknown domains and subdomains that the Gateway will be required to rewrite.

The Domain-based Rulesets field (FIGURE 5-14) is used to determine what rules to apply to specific content. This granularity reduces the likelihood of rule trumping by associating a specific ruleset to a particular DNS domain or fully qualified host name. This enables the creation of application-based rulesets. The order of entries in this field does not matter because the most specific identifier's associated ruleset is used when rewriting. For more specific entries about how the Rewriter makes use of rulesets, refer to Chapter 4 "Rewriter: Secure Remote Access to Internal Web-Based Applications."

Portal server 6.2 has added a few additional useful options to this Gateway configuration screen. The Domain-based Rulesets field has gained the ability to map individual URLs to rulesets so that hosts serving differing applications can have multiple rulesets associated with them. Additionally, rulesets can be merged, allowing for a very generalized base ruleset to be merged with a more context-specific application ruleset to build upon. An Enable Obfuscation checkbox has been added that will obfuscate internal URLs and resource names in the path portion of the Gateway addresses. Also, an option to make the Gateway protocol match the original URI protocol can be used to offload the decryption and encryption to specialized devices while maintaining the benefits of URL rewriting.

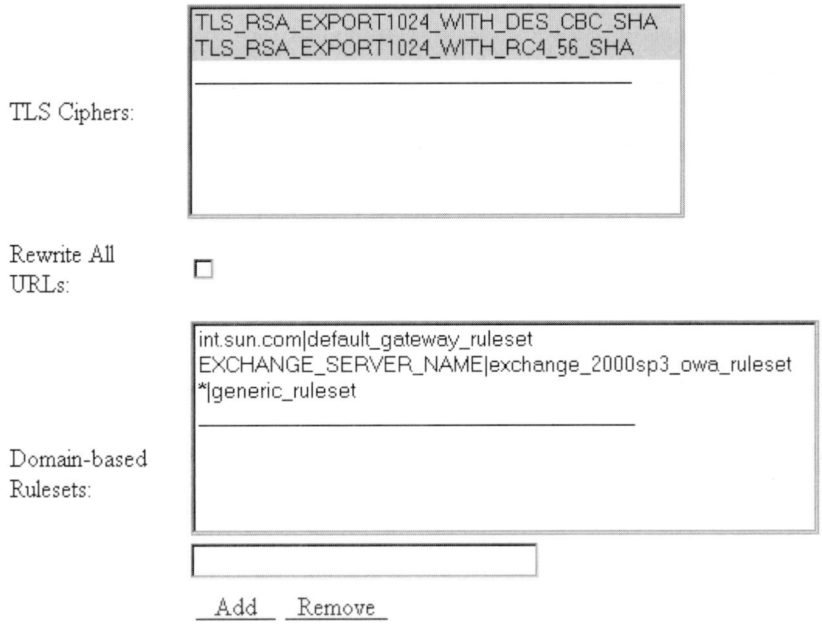

```
TLS_RSA_EXPORT1024_WITH_DES_CBC_SHA
TLS_RSA_EXPORT1024_WITH_RC4_56_SHA
```

TLS Ciphers:

Rewrite All
URLs: ☐

```
int.sun.com|default_gateway_ruleset
EXCHANGE_SERVER_NAME|exchange_2000sp3_owa_ruleset
*|generic_ruleset
```

Domain-based
Rulesets:

Add   Remove

FIGURE 5-14 Gateway Service Configuration Panel (*8 of 10*)

Use the MIME mappings list (FIGURE 5-15) to determine what Rewriter engines should be used for particular content types. Arbitrary Rewriter engines cannot be added, but you might want to remove the XML=test/xml entry. If no specific rules have been created to rewrite XML content, it is better to remove this line from the list to avoid possible problems as a result of the XML content being parsed by an XML parser. For instance, earlier versions of the portal server software translate specialized characters in XML when the content is parsed during rewriting. This results in syntax problems when the browser's XML parser works on the same code. There is a reverse mapping now for known specialized XML entities including &, <, and >. So if there are no rewriting requirements on behalf of the XML content that will be accessible through the Gateway, it is prudent to simply remove this line from the MIME mappings. See Chapter 4 "Rewriter: Secure Remote Access to Internal Web-Based Applications" for more information regarding the rewriting of specific content types.

The Default Domain Subdomain value (FIGURE 5-15) is used for URL expansion if the domain cannot be determined by other means such as a Referrer header, or the HTTP Host field of the HTTP Get request. The default is set to the domain in which the portal server node is installed, because that is usually in the local Intranet. This value probably won't need to be changed unless the servers are moved to a different DNS configuration, or most of the content and application servers reside in a different domain from the portal server node.

The Portal Server List (FIGURE 5-15) is used by the Gateway to load balance authentication and portal service requests to multiple portal platforms. By default, the list is prepopulated with the portal server node URL. If multiple platforms are being used, the portal server node URL can be removed, and the Platform Node URLs added instead. If the LDAP server is installed on a dedicated machine rather than the portal server node, then this change is not necessary. Otherwise, this change will help distribute the load more evenly across the platforms and not put extra load on the LDAP server which may be the single point of failure, depending on how it has ben deployed.

The Server Retry Interval (FIGURE 5-15) is the time in minutes the Gateway waits before seeing if the portal server is available. If the connection between the Gateway and Server is severed, users may perceive hang conditions or experience connection failures. In this case, the server is removed from the list of available servers for a minimum duration equal to the server retry interval. The Gateway attempts to refresh its own session in the event it was lost as a result of a server restart or some other similar situation.

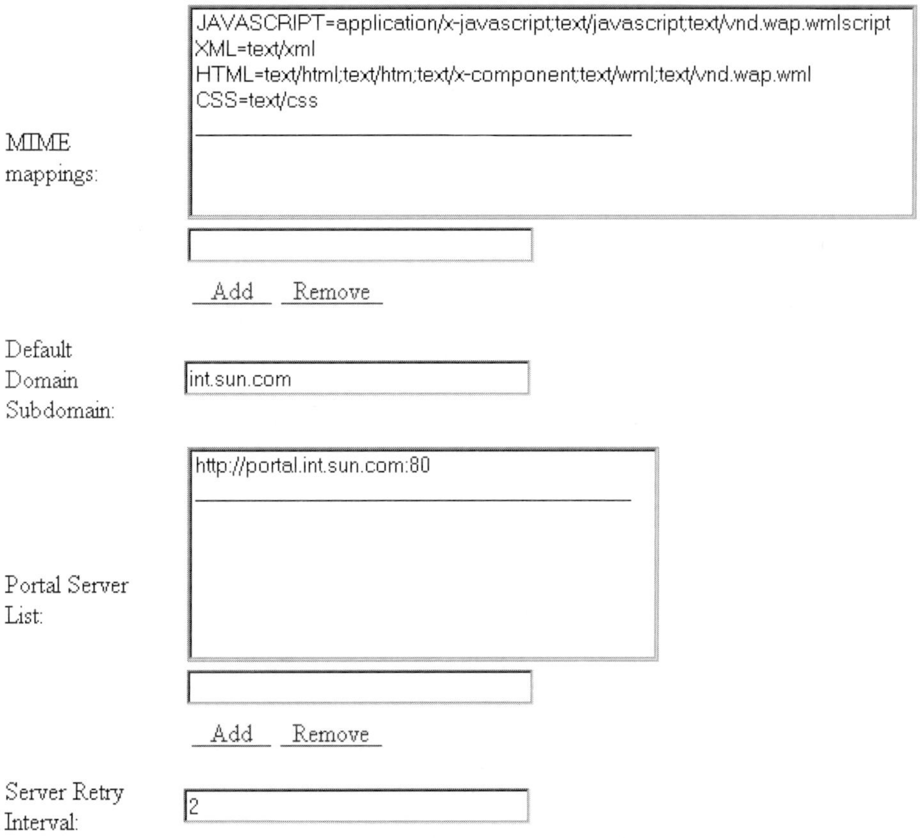

JAVASCRIPT=application/x-javascript;text/javascript;text/vnd.wap.wmlscript
XML=text/xml
HTML=text/html;text/htm;text/x-component;text/wml;text/vnd.wap.wml
CSS=text/css

MIME
mappings:

Add   Remove

Default
Domain
Subdomain:

int.sun.com

http://portal.int.sun.com:80

Portal Server
List:

Add   Remove

Server Retry
Interval:

2

FIGURE 5-15 Gateway Service Configuration Panel (*9 of 10*)

The remaining checkboxes in the Gateway configuration panel (FIGURE 5-16) control some of the additional logging aspects of the Gateway. Logging can affect performance, so only those logs needed for auditing or potential problem analysis should be enabled in a production environment. The logs you choose to enable are deployment specific. The per Session Logging option enables per thread views of user interactions. The Detailed per Session Logging option provides additional detail for each interaction. For more information about the Gateway and Netlet logging see "Logging" on page 352.

Netlet logging is not as useful as output that comes from the Java™ runtime environment (JRE) console on the client, but it can be useful to determine that the Netlet rules and ACLs are functioning appropriately during testing.

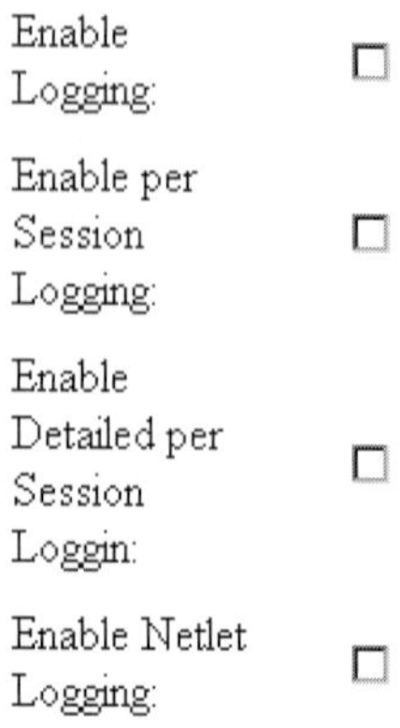

Enable
Logging: ☐

Enable per
Session   ☐
Logging:

Enable
Detailed per
Session   ☐
Loggin:

Enable Netlet ☐
Logging:

FIGURE 5-16 Gateway Service Configuration Panel (*10 of 10*)

Note – After making any modifications to a Gateway profile, those Gateway instances assigned to that profile must be restarted. This can be done by specifying the instance name as one of the Gateway start script command-line parameters.

Platform Configuration

Besides the Gateway Service Configuration, some flat files on the Gateway node might need to be changed. The `platform.conf` file is the primary place where changes are made on the Gateway. There are also some additional properties files that control look and feel, and logging characteristics.

CODE EXAMPLE 1 shows what the `platform.conf` might look like for a 6.1PC1 portal Gateway node. Line numbers have been added for readability and reference.

CODE EXAMPLE 1 `platform.conf.default` Configuration File

```
 1  #
 2  # Copyright 11/28/00 Sun Microsystems, Inc. All Rights
Reserved.
 3  # "@(#)platform.conf    1.38 00/11/28 Sun Microsystems"
 4  #
 5  gateway.user=noaccess
 6  gateway.jdk.dir=/usr/java1.3.1_06
 7  gateway.dsame.agent=
http://portal.int.sun.com:80/portal/RemoteConfigServlet
 8  portal.server.protocol=http
 9  portal.server.host=portal.int.sun.com
10  portal.server.port=80
11  gateway.protocol=https
12  gateway.host=gw.sun.com
13  gateway.port=443
14  gateway.trust_all_server_certs=true
15  gateway.trust_all_server_cert_domains=true
16  gateway.virtualhost=gw.sun.com 10.10.10.220
17  gateway.notification.url=/notification
18  gateway.retries=6
19  gateway.locale=en_US
20  gateway.debug=error
21  gateway.debug.dir=/var/opt/SUNWps/debug
22  gateway.logdelimiter=&&
23  gateway.external.ip=10.10.10.220
24  gateway.certdir=/etc/opt/SUNWps/cert/default
25  gateway.allow.client.caching=true
26  gateway.userProfile.cacheSize=1024
27  gateway.userProfile.cacheSleepTime=60000
28  gateway.userProfile.cacheCleanupTime=300000
29  gateway.bindipaddress=10.10.10.220
30  gateway.sockretries=3
31  gateway.min_auth_level=0
32  gateway.rewriter.ignorecl=false
```

The name value pairs defined in the `platform.conf` file determine many runtime characteristics of the Gateway process. When multiple instances are defined, each instance has an associated platform file named `platform.conf.`*instance_name*. Many of the values are the same between instances. Unique values between instances include the bind address, virtual host, Gateway host name, and external IP address.

The `gateway.user` defined on line 5 should be something other than `root`. This is an important and well-respected approach to Internet servers running in UNIX, which limits the damage possible in the unlikely occurrence of the process being hijacked. The Gateway uses a built-in user account called `noaccess` to run. If the `/etc/passwd` and `/etc/shadow` files on the Gateway system have been hardened and had this account removed, you should either add it back, or specify another non-privileged user in the `platform.conf` file.

The `gateway.jdk.dir` value (line 6) must point to the JDK that ships with the portal product. In certain cases, other JDKs may be used, but do not replace the portal JDK without first consulting Sun support on whether the configuration will remain supported and whether the portal will continue functioning with a newer JDK. The Java Enterprise System release takes some of the guesswork and speculation out of what versions of shared components can be mixed and matched with one another.

You only need to change the `gateway.dsame.agent` address (line 7) if the portal server node's DNS address changes, or the portal service is redeployed to a different URI than `/portal`.

Similarly, the `portal.server.protocol` and `portal.server.host` values (lines 8 and 9) are created at install time, and only need to change if the communication protocol between the portal and server changes. Changing the protocol from HTTPS and HTTP has additional implications on the `gateway.trust_all_server_certs` and `gateway.trust_all_server_cert_domains` (lines 14 and 15). By default, these are both set to `true` to reduce the administrative task of getting a working Gateway up and running. When the Gateway `trust_all_server_certs` is set to true, the Gateway will trust all valid SSL server certificates, irrespective of whether the CA certificate is in the Gateway certificate database or not. It is not recommended to set this value to true in a production environment.

There is some redundancy between the Gateway service configuration and the platform configuration with regard to lines 11 and 13 that deal with the Gateway protocol and port number. The values for `gateway.protocol` and `gateway.port` in the `platform.conf` file are used to construct the notification URL so that the Gateway is able to get session updates from the Identity Server. The equivalent values in the service configuration are used to determine the port and protocol the Gateway process runs on.

The `gateway.host` (line 12) doesn't necessarily need to be unique if multiple Gateway instances are listening on different ports on the same machine. The `gateway.bindipaddress` entry should be used if multiple Gateway instances are bound to separate NICs or logical interfaces, so the port and host name can remain the same. A load balancer would then be configured to balance load between the individual IP addresses, and would present a single external host name to clients. FIGURE 5-17 shows some detail for this deployment scenario.

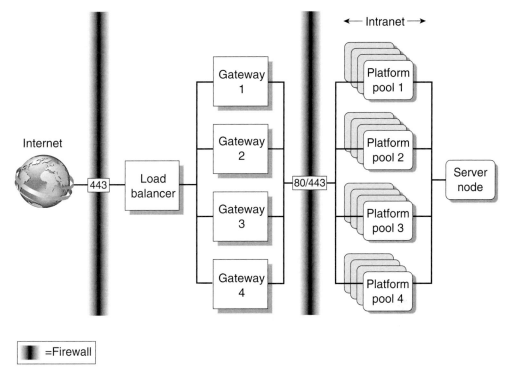

FIGURE 5-17 Using a Load Balancer in Front of Multiple Gateway Instances

What isn't obvious from the picture is that there can be four unique Gateway profiles, each with a set of platforms that they load balance by populating the Portal Server Instances field from the Gateway service configuration panel.

The `gateway.retries` value (line 18) is used to specify the maximum number of attempts the Gateway should make trying to contact the portal server as soon as the Gateway starts up. This is mostly useful in cases where the Gateway was mistakenly started before the portal server and the Gateway process would spin indefinitely until the process was killed, or the portal server was started. It should be set to a reasonably low value, and the default of 3 is probably sufficient.

The `gateway.locale` value (line 19) is used to determine the default character set for the Gateway. The actual string and character encoding is handled by the underlying JVM.

If additional Gateway process debugging is required, the `gateway.debug` value (line 20) can be changed from `error` to a more verbose value like `message`. This should be done only during problem isolation. Any changes made to the Gateway configuration files require a restart of the Gateway in order to make use of the modified values. The additional logging will create a performance bottleneck as well as unnecessary disk utilization, so it is not recommended to run in this mode for extended durations or during periods of peak usage. Additional details about this value are discussed in "Logging" on page 352.

The `gateway.debug.dir` value (line 21) should not be changed from the default location unless you have disk space limitations. Do not specify a directory location on the root partition to prevent disk full problems. Do not specify an NFS-mounted directory for performance reasons.

While the `gateway.log.delimiter` value (line 22) alone does not provide a significant means for easy parsing of the Gateway logs, it is somewhat helpful and can be changed if two ampersands are not satisfactory.

The `gateway.certdir` value (line 24) is the directory location where the Gateway certificate database is stored. The default value is `/etc/opt/SUNWps/cert/`*instance*, where `default` is usually the initial instance name. Unless there is a good reason to move the certificate directory, the default should be used. It is worth checking that the permissions on the directory and database files are restrictive.

The `gateway.allow.client.caching` value (line 25) is used to inform the Gateway that it should add necessary no-cache HTTP headers to all HTTP responses so that User-Agents do not cache the data locally. While disabling client-side caching means a bigger hit to the Gateway for repeat requests for the same content, it ensures a greater level of security by making sure that sensitive data isn't mistakenly stored on untrusted machines. 5.x versions of Internet Explorer had a limitation with caching SSL content where the data could not be handed off to helper applications if the HTTP response contained no-caching headers. In this case, each browser would have to be configured to not cache SSL pages, and the `gateway.allow.client.caching` option would have to be set to `true`. This limitation should be fixed in more recent versions of the IE browsers, and a patch is available from Microsoft for 5.5 versions of Internet Explorer.

The three caching options listed in lines 26-30 are used to keep local user profile entries cached to reduce the amount of requests that have to be made to the portal server. The `gateway.userProfile.cacheSize` value represents the total number of profile entries (not memory footprint) that can be cached, and it should be tuned to the total number of users accessing the Gateway instance. A smaller number means more frequent cache cleanups. This can be costly in terms of CPU utilization. The `gateway.userProfile.cacheSleepTime` defines the intervals between cache cleanups. The `gateway.userProfile.cacheCleanupTime` specifies the maximum duration that a cleanup can take. Both of the time values for the cache options are specified in milliseconds.

The `gateway.sockretries` value (line 30) specifies the number of times the Gateway should attempt to refresh its application session when the refresh interval is reached. If the Gateway is unable to validate its session, it might create a hang condition, so this value should be greater than one—particularly if the portal server is very busy. There is a 60-second timeout between each retry.

The `gateway.min_auth_level` (line 31) is currently only available in portal server 6.1 PC1. The option uses the Identity Server notion of authentication levels to define a minimum authentication level by which users must log in to the Gateway. So if a login screen is offered with multiple authentication options, including LDAP and UNIX authentication, only an authentication method with a matching or higher level than that specified by the `gateway.min_auth_level` (line 32) can be used to authenticate through the Gateway. This may be used as an alternative to chained authentication to provide an additional level of security for remotely authenticated users. Later version of the portal server software may include this feature as either a platform or profile option.

The `gateway.rewriter.ignorecl` option (line 32) is also only available in portal server 6.1PC1 and is used when content and application servers send a content-length header back that is greater than the actual message length. This is a corner case, so this value can usually be left alone with a default of `false`.

A `gateway.virtualhost` entry can also be added to present VIPs for a load balancer deployed in front of the Gateway to make use of. The VIP associates the address and hostname of the externally facing interfaces that the load balancer will communicate with. Refer to the Gateway administrator's guide for the exact syntax of this entry.

When One Gateway Instance Just Isn't Enough

Determining the ideal number of Gateways or Gateway instances to deploy depends on many things, including requirements pertaining to high availability (HA). See "Baselining Gateway Performance" on page 338 for information about how to accomplish this.

A script called `gwmultiinstance` is installed with the portal Gateway. This script is used to create an additional `platform.conf` file that is used for a new Gateway instance. The default profile can be used by multiple Gateway instances, or each instance can have its own profile. Multiple instances can be created on a single machine by binding to different IP addresses, or on different physical machines. Refer to the product documentation for additional details about how to install and configure multiple Gateway instances.

Proxies Proxies Everywhere

Proxies are an important part of any network topology. They limit the number of entry and exit points between networks. They can also be used to audit traffic passing to and from the networks. The portal proxies allow the reduction of open holes in the secondary firewall—similar to using a Web proxy. Portal server 6.2 allows fully independent, specialized systems to handle the proxying of Web traffic, while earlier versions of the product depend on the platform nodes.

In a production-level environment, use of proxies may be required to traverse internal subdomains between where the Gateway resides and where the portal server and other applications reside.

▼ To Configure the Gateway to Use a Rewriter Proxy

A Rewriter proxy can be used any time after initial installation of the portal server. For portal server 6.0 and 6.1, the Rewriter proxy must be installed on the portal server node or portal platform node. The Rewriter proxy should not be installed on the Gateway node or on a single-tier SRA installation because it will corrupt the Gateway's `platform.conf` file. The benefit of the Rewriter proxy is that the Gateway does not attempt to directly contact application or content servers, thereby reducing administrative requirements on the secondary firewall. The steps to configure the Gateway to use a Rewriter proxy in portal server 6.1 are described in the following procedure.

1. **Install the Rewriter proxy on the portal or platform node.**

   The Rewriter proxy can be installed from the SRA product distribution by running the `pssetup` command on the portal platform node.

2. **Configure the Gateway instance to use the Rewriter proxy.**

   Using the Identity Server administration console, modify the appropriate Gateway profile under the Gateway Service Configuration panel to make use of the Rewriter proxy. Enable Rewriter proxy needs to be checked, and the Rewriter proxy Port number should be specified (or the default port 10443 is used).

3. **Start the Rewriter proxy.**

   The Rewriter proxy can be started from the *install_dir*/SUNWps/bin directory by specifying the appropriate Gateway profile to use. For example:

   ```
   # /opt/SUNWps/bin/rwproxyd -n default start
   ```

4. **Restart the Gateway instance.**

   The Gateway must be restarted so it rereads the application profile information and starts making use of the Rewriter proxy.

5. **Connect to the Gateway and verify that the Rewriter proxy is being used.**

After accessing the Gateway using a browser, check that the Rewriter proxy is bound to the appropriate port. For example, type the following from the portal node:

```
# netstat | grep 10443
clk.red.iplanet.com.10443 exige.61988          24820     0 24820
0 LISTEN
```

All Web requests coming into the Gateway are now proxied through the Rewriter proxy listening on port 10443 of the portal server.

▼ To Configure the Gateway to Use a Netlet Proxy

A Netlet proxy can also be used any time after initial installation of the portal server. The Netlet proxy can be installed on either the portal server node or a separate system for any portal server 6.x versions. The Netlet proxy should not be installed on the Gateway node or on a single-tier SRA installation because it will corrupt the Gateway's `platform.conf` file. The benefit of the Netlet proxy is that the Gateway does not attempt to directly contact application or content servers, thereby reducing administrative requirements on the secondary firewall. The steps to configure the Gateway to use a Netlet proxy on a portal server node using portal server 6.1 are described in the following procedure.

1. **Install the Netlet Proxy on the portal or platform node.**

The Netlet proxy can be installed from the SRA product distribution by running the `pssetup` command on the portal or platform node. Choose the appropriate option to continue with the installation rather than mistakenly removing the existing installation by incorrectly typing the wrong value.

2. **Configure the Gateway instance to use the Netlet proxy.**

Using the Identity Server administration console, modify the appropriate Gateway profile under the Gateway Service Configuration panel to make use of the Netlet proxy. Enable Netlet must be checked, as well as Enable Netlet Proxy. Then the Netlet proxy port specified during Step 1 is used once when the Netlet proxy is started (10555 by default). The Netlet Proxy Hosts list should be populated with those hosts for which the Netlet proxy should be used to communicate. See the SRA product documentation for additional details about this field.

3. **Start the Netlet Proxy.**

The Netlet proxy can be started from the *install_dir*/SUNWps/bin directory by specifying the appropriate Gateway profile to use. For example:

```
# /opt/SUNWps/bin/netletd -n default start
```

4. **Restart the Gateway instance.**

The Gateway must be restarted so it rereads the application profile information and starts making use of the Netlet proxy.

5. **Connect to the Gateway and verify that the Netlet proxy is being used.**

After logging in to the Gateway, launch a dynamic Netlet session such as `Telnet` and check whether the process is bound to the port. For example, type the following from the portal node:

```
# netstat | grep 10555
portal.int.sun.com.34155 portal.int.sun.com.10555 32768      0
32768     0 TIME_WAIT
```

All incoming Netlet traffic is now proxied from the Gateway to the Netlet proxy listening on port 10555.

Baselining Gateway Performance

Gateway sizing is often an afterthought or ignored altogether. While specific sizing recommendations are outside the scope of this book, best practices for determining load-handling capabilities for individual Gateway nodes are discussed here. Once a baseline is established, it is easy to see how making different deployment decisions affects the overall performance of the system. For example, after a baseline is established using several soak tests, a Rewriter proxy can be added to determine how the overall performance changes, and how the individual system resource utilization changes.

Gateway and portal server testing indicates that the main limiting performance factor is the rate of authentications possible (logins per second). When the portal server is subjected to a tremendous amount of user activity that pushes the logins per second beyond a certain threshold, end users will experience unacceptable delays.

A second key performance factor is the Java heap size. Each user session occupies a given footprint in memory. After so many users have logged in and established sessions, the heap will begin to fill up, increasing the need for more frequent Java garbage collections (CGs). Beyond a certain point, GCs become so frequent that performance suffers.

Two things usually need to be baselined. The first is the maximum load the Gateway can handle, and the second is the duration of sustained load. Maximum load testing requires ramping up a huge number of users very quickly until service degradation surpasses a pre-established threshold. A duration of sustained load (including a fixed number of users and repetitive tasks) involves a fixed load for a pre-established period of time.

The load can be generated using a variety of third-party and freeware applications. Load-generation applications used by Sun for performance and benchmarking purposes include WebLoad, LoadRunner, and SLAMD.

The important thing to keep in mind is that there is no magic formula to performance sizing. A general rule of thumb states that you should have two Gateway nodes for each platform server, but experimentation after establishing a baseline is really the best way to size the Gateway for your own particular needs.

Maximum Load Testing

To model a load that will stress the system allowing it to reach its peak login rate, a script can be used that continually ramps up and then sustains user sessions. This test should be CPU bound, so system resources should be periodically checked throughout the test. As the system approaches its peak login rate, the time to authenticate will begin to degrade below an acceptable limit. A commonly used limit is one second. At the moment this occurs, the optimum sustained login rate has been reached. This usually affects the portal more than the Gateway, but the Gateway caches the user sessions and proxies the authentication traffic, so it is not a pass-through test by any means.

An example of a stress test is to rapidly log in users, allowing the test script to cycle through users without any delay or hindrances. As the test increases from one user to about 1,000 users, an exponential growth of sessions occurs, rapidly saturating the system. In an ideally tuned system, the CPU will be the primary bottleneck and approach maximum usage. However, other limitations could occur first, such as a threadpool reaching capacity, or LDAP connection restrictions to the directory. An undersized heap compared to the machine's CPU power will cause frequent GCs and throttle the throughput as well. The full file listing for the corresponding Webload script for this example is available as a downloadable file. The file is called `login-only.js`. See "Obtaining Downloadable Files for This Book" on page xxi.

CODE EXAMPLE 5-1   Maximum Load Test Script – Main Loop

```
     .
     .
     .
// Get Login Page. Add think time so iDS is not inundated
// Random think time between 0 and 2 min.

SetTimer(timerNameLoginPage)
wlHttp.Get(hanaServer + loginLink)
SendTimer(timerNameLoginPage)
```

```
if (wlHtml.GetStatusNumber() != 200) {
    ErrorMessage("Start page failed. Status: " +
wlHtml.GetStatusNumber())
}

if (titleNameLoginPage != document.title) {
    ErrorMessage("Login Page Title: " + document.title)
}

UserArr = GetLine(filename)
userId = UserArr[1]

// Login using the selected uid
wlHttp.ContentType = "application/x-www-form-urlencoded"
wlHttp.FormData["Login.Token0"] = "$WL$EMPTY$STRING$"
wlHttp.FormData["Login.Token1"] = userId
wlHttp.FormData["Login.Token2"] = userId
wlHttp.FormData["Login.ButtonLogin"] = "Submit"
wlHttp.FormData["gx_charset"] = "UTF-8"
wlHttp.SetCurrentHiddenValues()

// Time the initial reload
SetTimer(timerNameInitialDesktop)
wlHttp.Post(hanaServer + loginLink)
SendTimer(timerNameInitialDesktop)

statusNumber = wlHtml.GetStatusNumber()
if (statusNumber != 200) {
    ErrorMessage("Desktop load failed: status " + statusNumber)
}

if (titleNameInitialDesktop != document.title) {
    ErrorMessage("Desktop load failed. Title: " + document.title)
}
    .
    .
    .
```

This code snippet performs the individual login requests in a burst mode using prepopulated UIDs stored in helper files. The first helper file contains the information about the Gateway and server including the name, protocol, and port address, while the second helper file contains user names and passwords for test users. Think time is included, so that the portal performance can be adequately measured by reducing the directory server as a significant bottleneck.

Maximum Load Test Graphs

FIGURE 5-18 and FIGURE 5-19 show the Webload application displaying rapid bulk loading of user logins to determine at what point serious service degradation occurs. In this case, there are 1000 total users, but users randomly continue to log in as indicated by the Maximum Test Load script. In this case, some users' sessions are cached, gaining some enhancement in response time, while others are fetched from the directory, resulting in a negative impact on performance. According to FIGURE 5-18, CPU utilization remains constant once users have initially ramped up. CPU utilization is just a bit higher when the Gateway is running in HTTPS mode than when it is configured to run in HTTP mode.

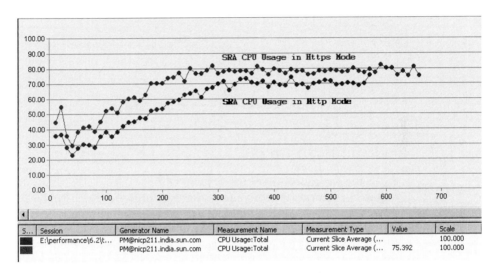

FIGURE 5-18 CPU Utilization During Maximum Load Test Run

According to FIGURE 5-19, service degradation occurs slightly earlier when the Gateway is running in HTTP mode versus HTTPS mode. As expected, total throughput is increased when run in HTTP mode as compared with running in HTTPS mode. During this specific test, the virtual users do not log out and their session does not time out automatically as a result of the idle timeout being reached.

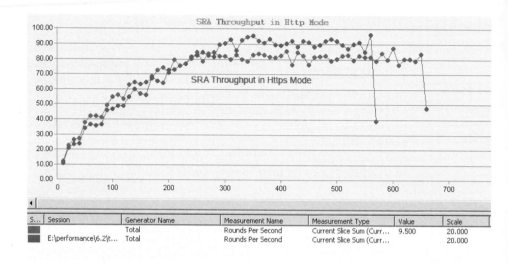

S...	Session	Generator Name	Measurement Name	Measurement Type	Value	Scale
▪		Total	Rounds Per Second	Current Slice Sum (Curr...	9.500	20.000
▪	E:\performance\6.2\t...	Total	Rounds Per Second	Current Slice Sum (Curr...		20.000

FIGURE 5-19 Total Throughput During Maximum Load Test Run

Reliability Testing

To ensure the reliability of the system, you can use a script that ramps up the users and then performs repetitive tasks for each of these users. This test should include think time to realistically mimic users, and the test should run successfully for a specific period of time. For example, one reliability test might include 10,000 users that first authenticate and then perform repetitive activity (such as desktop reloads) for a specified period of time. The user number can be adjusted to the point where service degradation begins at a set period of time. The maximum user session time must be equal to, or greater than, this set period of time.

CODE EXAMPLE 5-2 shows an example of a load generation script to use for reliability testing. The full script is available for download. See "Obtaining Downloadable Files for This Book" on page xxi. CODE EXAMPLE 5-2 shows the user activity following a successful authentication. In this example, the portal server desktop is being reloaded continuously by the virtual user.

CODE EXAMPLE 5-2 Reliability Load Test Script – Main Loop

```
.
.
.
while(elapsed_time < session_duration)
{
    theDate = new Date()
    idleTime = 0
    before = theDate.getTime()
```

```
    // Set a timer for the desktop reload
    // InfoMessage(userId + " reload the desktop")

    wlHttp.Header["Accept-language"] = "en_US"

    //Desktop Reload
    SetTimer(timerNameReloadDesktop)
    wlHttp.Get(hanaServer + desktopLink)
    SendTimer(timerNameReloadDesktop)

    if (wlHtml.GetStatusNumber() != 200)
    {
            ErrorMessage(userId + " desktop reload failed: status
" + wlHtml.GetStatusNumber() + " at " + TimeNow() )
    }

    ThisTitle=document.title
    if (ThisTitle != DesktopTitle)
    {
            ErrorMessage(userId + "Desktop Page download failed.
Title: " + ThisTitle + " - " +  TimeNow() )
    }

    //End Desktop Reload

    // Idle time between desktop reloads
    Sleep(GetRandomNumber(IdleMin, IdleMax))

    var nextDate=new Date()
    after=nextDate.getTime()
    elapsed_time += (after-before)
    // InfoMessage(elapsed_time + "   " + session_duration)
}
.
.
.
```

Reliability Load Test Graphs

In the graphs shown in FIGURE 5-20 and FIGURE 5-21, the spikes represent Java garbage collections (CGs) occurring on the portal server. The time duration from the left side of the graph to the right side represents the passage of one hour. The healthy graph shows approximately six GC runs, while the unhealthy graph indicates many more GCs piling up, and a larger time differentiation for the GCs to complete. In the reliability test, the load is constant once all of the users have logged in, which is represented by the flat line at the top of the graph (user load).

Each dot (on the lower line in each graph) indicates the amount of time it takes for a user to authenticate to the portal, and the vertical scale is set with a maximum value of 20 seconds. If the threshold determined to be adequate for reliability purposes is 20 seconds, and the graphs continued in a similar manner to how they appear for this hour duration, the first run would pass (FIGURE 5-20), while the second one (FIGURE 5-21) would fail because there are peaks that exceed 20 seconds (100 on the vertical scale).

Both runs would fail if a maximum threshold of 10 seconds is required for the portal deployment, and some additional sizing and tuning would be necessary to reach that goal. It is important to note that the horizontal scale is the sampling period, and the peaks would be less slanted for a shorter sampling period while the process is garbage collecting.

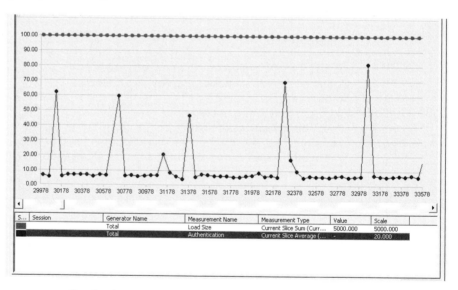

FIGURE 5-20 Graph of a Healthy Reliability Test Run

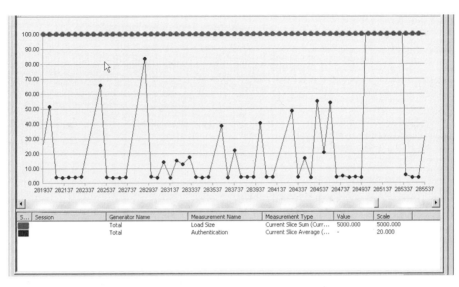

Below the graph is a data table:

S...	Session	Generator Name	Measurement Name	Measurement Type	Value	Scale
		Total	Load Size	Current Slice Sum (Curr...	5000.000	5000.000
		Total	Authentication	Current Slice Average (...	-	20.000

FIGURE 5-21 An Unhealthy Reliability Test Run

Additional Gateway Sizing Recommendations

Using the Java garbage collection logs is a useful way to size the system because the baseline of the memory utilization is higher and GCs occur more often. This is a long-standing conundrum with JVM sizing: Increase the heap size to reduce the frequency of GCs at the expense of GC duration, or decrease the heap size to reduce the duration of GC runs at the expense of frequency. GC logs can also be useful in assisting to locate memory leaks over long durations of time.

In FIGURE 5-22, the graphical representation of the `gclog` shows the heap size is a constant 2 Gbytes, represented by the flat line at the top of the graph. The sawtooth lines (two of them superimposed on each other) represent the memory utilization before and after GC. The slight uptick over time implies that there may be a small memory leak caused by one of the applications running in the JVM. JVM profiling techniques can be used to determine if this is the case, and can even help to isolate and eliminate the problem. Moreover, the GC logs can help assist in sizing for reliability when memory boundness can be a real problem. For example, if the GC logs indicate a trend that the system is running out of memory in three days at a constant load, and the reliability test indicates that the system must be able to maintain equal load for a full week, then additional tuning and sizing may be required to achieve this goal—especially if the memory utilization is simply a trend and not a leak.

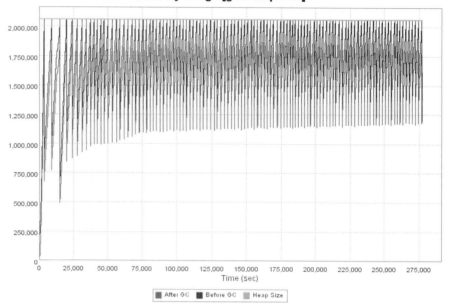

FIGURE 5-22 Possible Memory Leak Extended Over an Extended Period of Time

In FIGURE 5-23, the memory footprint remains almost flat during the entire remaining duration that load is applied to the system. This helps guarantee reliability at a given load. The heap size may need to be tuned. This depends on other factors, including CPU utilization and authentication times, that are evident in the load generation logs and by checking the system resources using the `iostat` command or other useful command-line utilities.

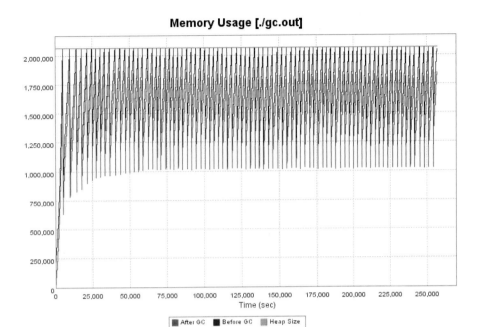

Memory Usage [./gc.out]

FIGURE 5-23 Stable Memory Utilization Over a Period of Consistent Load

The Gateway at Rush Hour: Balancing the Load

Load balancers such as those provided by Resonate or Cisco can be used to distribute the load to multiple Gateway instances while presenting a single external-facing address to remote users. If you are using Cisco's CSS as a load balancer, then use a later version of portal server 6.x than 6.0, or the CSS periodic health check feature should be turned off as a result of networking problems related to reset packets. As mentioned previously, Gateways are often initially sized to two Gateways per platform server. So the network topology looks something like a bell curve with one load balancer leading to many Gateways, to less platforms, to one server node. While the number of boxes may decrease on the back end, there have been many efforts made in the portal server 6.x version to reduce traffic that would otherwise go to a single point of failure. An example of this is creating local profile caches on each of the platform nodes to keep LDAP reads to a minimum.

Load balancers are useful with the Gateway because their agents can detect CPU activity and redirect load accordingly. This prevents too many requests from being queued up while bulk data is being encrypted and decrypted on a single Gateway instance.

Running SSL Between the Portal Server and Gateway Nodes

Running SSL between the portal server and the Gateway nodes provides an additional layer of security by preventing intruders from snooping on the Gateway's internal NIC for any unencrypted transmissions between the Gateway and portal server. Configuring SSL between the two is a bit more tricky with self-signed-certificates because the two servers need to be configured to trust one another. The Gateway `platform.conf` option for `trust_all_server_certs` is set to `true` by default so this is not a problem initially, but in production, a certificate from a trusted CA that is installed on both the portal node and the Gateway node should be used instead and the `trust_all_server_certs` value should be changed to `false`. The easiest way to get SSL to work between the Gateway and the portal server is to install the portal server and the SRA software in that manner to begin with.

After installing a two-tier installation configured to use SSL between the portal server and the Gateway, do the following to get the configuration to work correctly in a proof-of-concept environment when the portal server is deployed to the Sun Web server Web container.

▼ To Configure a Self-Signed Certificate on the Portal Server

1. **Install the Rewriter proxy on the portal server node.**

   This enables a certificate database to be created using the local fully qualified server address.

2. **Copy the self-signed certificate database used by the Rewriter proxy to the Web server alias directory.**

   Example:

   ```
   # cp /etc/opt/SUNWps/cert/profile_name/*.db
   install_dir/SUNWam/servers/alias/
   ```

3. **Change the names of the certificate database files to match the Web server instance running the portal Web application.**

   Example:

   ```
   # cd install_dir/SUNWam/servers/alias
   # cp cert7.db https-portal.int.sun.com-portal-cert7.db
   # cp key3.db https-portal.int.sun.com-portal-key3.db
   ```

4. **Modify the case of the certificate alias so that the Web server is able to locate the self-signed certificate created from certadmin.**

   The file that needs to be edited is *install_dir*/SUNWam/servers/https-portal.int.sun.com/config/server.xml

   Change the servercertnickname attribute value from Server-Cert to server-cert in the SSLPARAMS tag so that the Web server can find it when it is changed to SSL mode.

   ```
   <SSLPARAMS servercertnickname="server-cert" .../>
   ```

5. **Modify the default listen socket for the instance.**

   Do this by changing the values for ip, port, and security attributes in the LS tag of the server.xml file.

   ```
   <LS id="ls1" ip="10.10.10.220" port="443" security="on" .../>
   ```

6. **On the portal node, in the** *install_dir*/SUNWam/lib/AMConfig.properties **file, change** com.iplanet.am.jssproxy.trustALLServerCerts **to** true.

7. **On the Gateway node, in the** *install_dir*/SUNWam/lib/AMConfig.properties **file, change** com.iplanet.am.jssproxy.trustALLServerCerts **to** true.

8. **Restart the portal server.**

   ```
   # /etc/init.d/amserver startall
   ```

9. **Log in to the portal server to verify that SSL is functioning correctly.**

   You should see the normal warning indicating that you are using an untrusted certificate (self-signed), but you should be able to successfully log in the portal server desktop now using SSL.

10. **Start the Gateway node.**

   ```
   # /etc/init.d/gateway -n default start
   ```

Deployment Scenarios

Rather than concentrating on SRA deployment types categorized by size, this section addresses them by functional purpose, and describes the advantages and disadvantages of each.

Gateway Only

In actuality, this is not really a Gateway-only installation, because the Gateway cannot exist without a portal server node. However, it is called Gateway only because in this deployment scenario virtually all portal-specific features are ignored in favor of simply providing secure remote access services.

There are two primary reasons why you might choose a Gateway-only deployment. The first is to simply provide secure remote access to existing internal resources, which may include internally built or third-party portal servers. The Gateway access list is then used to define what the specific resources are that will be made available to remote users. The redirection to the internal sites can be changed from the portal server desktop default by configuring the success URL in the user's profile, or in the Authentication module being used.

The second reason you might want a Gateway-only deployment is to provide secure remote access capabilities to screen-scraping and remote terminal services applications through the Netlet. This helps to expose applications on Windows boxes in a more secure and controlled fashion. For example, an HR application that runs on Windows can be deployed using a business-to-business SRA portal for partnering companies without having to put the Windows machine in the DMZ where it could be susceptible to attacks. In these cases, a very basic portal server desktop is used with a single link to launch the Netlet. To spice this environment up a bit, refer to "Netlet: Secure Remote Access Through On-Demand VPNs" on page 17" to see how portal features and screen-scraping applications like Citrix can be combined on a single-channel branded portal server desktop.

Employee Remote Access

Employee remote access SRA deployment types tend to be a bit less restrictive than most others, depending on the level of sophistication of employees. Employees may want access to their own desktop machines and wide variety of applications and content that the portal administrator may be completely unaware of.

Because of the high level of flexibility required by many employees to be productive when working remotely, dynamic protocol types of targets are usually set up so that employees can tunnel email to their favorite email application, and the Gateway access list is frequently open-ended in terms of what internal content can be accessed remotely. Exceptions to this rule are usually few and far between, and can be added explicitly to the deny list of the Gateway profile.

HTTP Basic Authentication is also useful when enabled for employee access deployments because it provides SSO-like functionality to many of the user's frequently used internal applications. Once they have already authenticated to the portal server; it is of little value to require additional authentication requirements unless there is precedent to do so.

Most employee access portals also aggregate widely used applications into portlets or channels that summarize important information and provide jump points to native applications so workflow is not constrained inside a little box on the portal server desktop.

Executive

Executive-level SRA deployments typically provide an unprecedented amount of access and powers to a small number of people. These deployments are used solely for critical-path nomadic individuals who need to be in touch with their internal network and applications regardless of their point of presence.

These types of deployments can also be useful for sales and marketing people who use demos installed on internal systems to show customers without the risk of having to move the demo site to an off-LAN location or carry around bulky equipment to perform the demo locally.

A specialized example of an executive SRA deployment is a CEO accessing a global internal application from the convenience of a satellite uplink on his boat. Such deployments are easy to size and set up, but a great deal of attention has to be paid to making sure that they are very secure—especially when authenticated users have full run of SSO to very important business-critical applications.

Business-to-Business

Business-to-business SRA deployments vary from hosting solutions for application service providers to exposing portions of internal networks to partner ventures and the like. Business-to-business deployments usually make use of portal features including branding and identity management. The Gateway access lists also provide a nice feature for partnering companies to be able to use internal applications without having the full run of the internal network.

Some business-to-business SRA deployments also use very few portal-specific features, choosing instead to rely on the portal server only for authentication and access control purposes for applications running over TCP/IP using screen-scraping technologies.

Logging

Process-specific logging can be enabled by changing the `gateway.logging` option in the `platform.conf` file from `error` to `message` (or to `debug` for less verbosity). Each Gateway instance has it's own debug log stored on the Gateway node in the `/var/opt/SUNWps/debug` directory. Unless there is a specific problem that needs to be diagnosed, it is best to leave this value set to the default value of `error`.

In addition to Gateway logging on the Gateway node itself, there are some additional Gateway logging options that can be configured through the Identity Server Administration Console. These logs are stored on the Identity node because it is the centralized logging mechanism used for registered services. The specific log names, syntax, and contents vary across all of the portal server 6.x releases.

As with the Gateway process logging, the Gateway service logging should be used with discretion due to the I/O boundness of logging large quantities of data and transactions. See "Rewriter Logging" on page 292 for details on enabling debug logging to diagnose Rewriter integration problems—the most common reason for using this Gateway logging feature.

Another useful logging option added to version 6.2 of the portal server software is user access logging. Although the Gateway access logs are not presented in CLF format in 6.2, enabling the Detailed per Session Logging feature in the Gateway profile results in the creation of a log that contains a parsable file that can be manipulated and plugged into several popular logging analyzer programs.

The following procedure describes how you can start the Gateway to run in debug mode. This may help to root out process problems and communication issues.

▼ To Start the Gateway in Debug Mode

● **On your Gateway system, type the following command:**

```
# /etc/init.d/gateway -n default start debug
Stopping gateway... done.
Gateway debugging on
Starting gateway... done.
```

Additional Gateway logging information is available in the product documentation for your specific version of the portal server software

Ten Tips From the Trenches

This section presents ten of the most frequent Gateway-related problems, and offers tips for solving each problem.

Problem: Every time the shell window that started the Gateway process is closed, the Gateway process dies (SIGHUP).

Tip: This problem is shell related and can be worked around by changing the default root shell from the Bourne shell to something else like the Korn shell. Even though the Gateway process is started in nohup mode, it still dies upon exiting the terminal.

Problem: The Gateway is not able to download embedded desktop content in a NAT environment.

Tip: Network Address Translation can be a bit tricky between the Gateway and the portal server, especially when the Gateway attempts to fetch embedded content like images using a rewritten external address instead of the actual NAT internal address. This is an application for a Web proxy. Assuming that the Gateway is deployed to the DMZ, and the portal and content servers are sitting in the NAT intranet, do the following:

1. Log in to the Administration Console.

2. Select the Gateway Service.

3. Select the appropriate Gateway profile.

4. Select the Use Web Proxy checkbox.

5. Add the NAT addresses to the Proxies for Domains and Subdomains list.

   For example, if the Web Proxy was configured on `10.10.10.9` and the `sun.com` domain was translated to an internal address as well, the associated entry in the Proxies for Domains and Subdomains list might look like:

   `*.sun.com 10.10.10.9:8080`

Problem: No debug logs are being created after setting the debug level to `message`.

Tip: Portal server 6.0 and 6.1 software may require touching the debug files as the file owner before the logs can be written. Steps to perform this are explained in "Rewriter Logging" on page 292.

Problem: Applications requiring NTLM authentication are not working through the Gateway.

Tip: The Gateway does not support the NTLM authentication scheme. NTLM is sometimes configured as an authentication protocol for applications running on Microsoft Internet Information Server (IIS) Servers. Change the authentication from NTLM to Basic Authentication on the IIS Server. This way, the applications will work through the portal Gateway, and the authentication credentials can be stored with individual user profiles to provide SSO-like characteristics to the backend applications when they are accessed through the Gateway. Changing the IIS authentication scheme is discussed in Appendix A, "Application Integrations for the Rewriter," and Basic Auth Caching is discussed in detail in "Platform Configuration" on page 330."

Problem: Users have to log in to the portal and then again to applications that use Basic Authentication.

Tip: Enable HTTP Basic Authentication is disabled by default on the Gateway. Once enabled by checking the option in the Gateway profile, Basic Authentication credentials are stored following the first successful authentication attempt to the Basic Auth-enabled resource. If the same user requires different user and password combinations to the Basic Auth-enabled resource, it is recommended that you do not enable this feature. Portal server 6.0 limited the number of credentials that could be stored per user. That limitation has since been lifted in portal server 6.1 and 6.2 software.

Problem: Content passing through the Gateway is being truncated.

Tip: The root cause of this problem may be that multiple Content-Length headers are sent from the content server back to the Gateway. If the first Content-Length header is shorter than the last, then the content may be truncated. Be sure that content being emitted from internal sources is HTTP compliant. Some concession has been made in the Gateway to use the last header instead of the first, but it is better to simply make sure there is only one to begin with.

Problem: Users cannot log in through the Gateway without enabling cookies in the browser.

Tip: The Gateway requires user session information stored in a cookie to be sure that the session is valid before proxying requests. There is a feature added for Mobile Access that allows this session information to be postpended to the URL field and obfuscated. This is required by Wireless Application Protocol (WAP) Gateways that do not support cookies, and for handsets and other devices that do not support cookies. Typically, Web browsers have cookies enabled because of the large number of sites that use them. By default, the portal session cookie is not persistent, so no meaningful artifact will be left on a client machine that will allow another user to log in using the previous user's session information (assuming that the previous user either logged out or idled out of their session).

Problem: The portal session is destroyed immediately after logging in to the portal desktop.

Tip: This is likely due to the cookie domain limitation imposed by the cookie specification. The Gateway is handling cookies on behalf of other servers, so the Gateway DNS domain is used to set the cookies in the browser. When more than 20 unique cookies are set, the first cookie, often the portal session cookie, is ejected. This limitation is discussed in greater detail in "Service Configuration" on page 314.

Problem: Gateway sends numerous redirections for internal content to the Identity Server. Response keeps asking if they want to log in to another organization.

Tip: This is usually a sign that the rewriter has not been properly configured or the browser is using a stale cookie. Restarting the browser will take care of the latter problem. The former is a bit more tricky because it may indicate that an end user is accessing content that the generic gateway rewriter ruleset is not able to handle. There is also some contention between the rewriter and the reverse proxy because any path values that do not contain protocol identifiers are typically considered to be organizations. So, a user might type `https://gw.domain.com/myorg` to initially log in to their organization. Then they might surf using the Bookmark provider to a page that contained a JavaScript variable that represented a URL like `var myURL = '/path/object'`. Depending on how this variable is used, it might resolve using the browser's URL field, which would create a request that looks something like this:

```
Session: Request:
GET /path/object HTTP/1.0
Host: gw.domain.com
Accept: */*
Accept-Language: sv
Accept-Encoding: gzip, deflate
User-Agent: Mozilla/4.0 (compatible; MSIE 5.01; Windows NT)
Connection: Keep-Alive
Cookie: WEBTRENDS_ID=10.36.32.102-1962752080.29373270
```

The Gateway takes `/path/object` and forwards it to the Identity Server as a login request. The debug files can be very useful in mining out these kinds of occurrences. In this case, the logs would indicate that `myURL` should be added to the Rewriter ruleset.

Problem: PDC authentication to internal sites does not work when accessed through the Gateway.

Tip: PDC authentication should only be used for initial authentication purposes, and not by internal content servers. Authentication chaining can be used as a way of increasing security, but the PDC credentials are stripped of any requests by the Gateway prior to proxying them on to backend applications. Basic Authentication may be a viable alternative to requiring PDCs.

New Gateway Technology in the Java Enterprise System

The latest Gateway technology makes better use of crypto cards, otherwise known as SSL accelerators. These seek to bolster the Gateway's scalability, and reduce cost associated with having to size multi-CPU systems to manage the computational challenges associated with bulk encryption and decryption.

Application Integrations for the Rewriter

This appendix provides instructions on how to integrate Microsoft Exchange and Lotus iNotes with the portal server software.

This appendix contains the following sections:

- "Microsoft Exchange Integrations" on page 360
- "Lotus iNotes Integration" on page 391

Microsoft Exchange Integrations

Use the procedures described in this section to integrate Microsoft Exchange 2000 SP3 with portal server 6.x software. See Chapter 2 for information about integration steps and limitations for Exchange access through the Netlet.

Originally, Exchange integration could only be accomplished using the Netlet and the Microsoft Outlook fat client. Later, when Microsoft provided Outlook Web Access (OWA) in Exchange 5.5, Exchange could be accessed using a Web browser with a few caveats and configuration changes to the portal server Gateway profile. OWA was not as fully featured as its Outlook counterpart, but provided a nice remote access solution for Exchange messaging. Exchange 2000 OWA increased complexity significantly when accessed with an Internet Explorer user-agent, and the Rewriter had to be extended to rewrite XML content.

The default OWA ruleset was first included in the Sun ONE Portal Server 3.0 Service Pack 3 Hot Patch 1 (SP3HP1) software. Exchange 2000 SP2 and SP3 add technologies that alienate reverse proxies and middleware and adversely affect the manageability of URL rewriting technology. As a result, the complexity of the integration has increased. You must make decisions on which method of integration best suits your business needs.

At the time of this writing, only OWA5.5, Exchange 2000, Exchange 2000 SP3, and Exchange 2003 can be integrated for use with the Rewriter. The work involved with each is as follows:

- OWA 5.5 – requires additional Rewriter rules when localized.
- Exchange 2000 – requires XML rewriting, disabling of NTLM authentication, portal server version 6.2PC4 or 6.3, and Rewriter rules.
- Exchange 2000 SP3 – requires XML rewriting, disabling of NTLM authentication, portal server version 6.2PC4 or 6.3, and Rewriter rules.
- modifications to the OWA controls scripts, and Rewriter rules.
- Exchange 2003 – requires a custom ruleset and a 6.2 portal patch.

Obtain the Required Patches

If you are integrating Exchange 2000 SP3, contact Sun for a patch containing fixes required by the application integration. Specifically, for the Sun ONE Secure Portal Server 6.0 software, you must have patch ID 115156-01 (called 6.0SRAExchangeFixes) installed on the portal sever. Most portal patches are not yet available through the SunSolve Web site, so you must open a support case to get it. See "Patching the Portal Server Software" on page 10. Patch 11516 fixes and enhancements are carried forward from portal server 6.1.

Downloadable Scripts and Files For This Integration

Before you attempt to perform any of the procedures in this section, you should download the scripts that are available for this integration. See "Obtaining Downloadable Files for This Book" on page xxi.

The downloadable files for this book are provided in a zipped file. Once you unzip the file, you will have the following items in the `./817-5024-SDLC1/exchange2ksp3-int` subdirectory:

- `./modfiles.ksh` - Script that performs inline editing of uploaded Exchange 2000 files and `ed` scripts to manipulate those files.

- `./iwtBookmarkProvider/display.template` – Display template used for integration of portal server 3 and Exchange using the Netlet.

- `./iwtBookmarkProvider/edit.template` – The same template that is supplied with the Sun ONE Secure Portal Server 3 software.

- `./scripts/ctrl_FormatBar20.htc.script` – ed script

- `./scripts/ctrl_FreeBusy20.htc.script` – ed script

- `./scripts/ctrl_Poll20.js.script` – ed script

- `./scripts/ctrl_Tree20.js.script` – ed script

- `./scripts/ctrl_reminder20.htc.script` – ed script

- `./scripts/util_View20.js.script` – ed script

- `./scripts/ctrl_Tree20.xsl.script` – ed script

- `./owa_sp3_ruleset.xml` – Portal server 6 Rewriter ruleset that included rules for OWA 2000 SP3.

- `./owa_2003_ruleset.xml` – The portal server 6.2PC4 ruleset that includes rules for OWA 2003.

Summary of Integration

Client

This integration was tested using Internet Explorer 5.5SP2 + December 2002 Security update. Other IE browsers should work as well, but you should test them before deploying the application through the Gateway. The OWA user interface look, feel, and feature set differs based on the user-agent used to access the Exchange server. Most of the integration challenges specifically involve the IE user-agent. Netscape browsers often work to access OWA out-of-box through the Gateway.

Exchange 2000 SP3

- Disable NTLM authentication
- Eight modifications to `exchweb` scripts and HTML component files
- Works with portal server 6.0 with 6.0SRAExchangeFixes, 6.1, or 6.2 versions
- Use the Exchange-specific ruleset (`owa_sp3_ruleset.xml`)

Exchange 2003

- Disable NTLM authentication
- Works with portal server 6.2PC4, or 6.3 versions
- Use the Exchange-specific ruleset (`owa_2003_ruleset.xml`)

Advantages

- No specialized client required for access.
- Exposes native Exchange functionality to the Web browser.
- No client configuration required.
- Encryption/Decryption performed using SSL.
- User interface is the same when accessed from within or outside the internal corporate network.
- Takes advantage of new portal server 6 architecture where an individual ruleset can be mapped to the Exchange server so that there is no rule interaction between rules needed for OWA and more generalized rules used for other applications.

Disadvantages

- Exchange 2000 SP3 integration requires changes to Exchange server exposed scripts and component files, in addition to configuration changes and fixes for the portal server software.
- Integration is fragile in the sense that rules and modifications are inflexible and must be followed strictly or functionality will fail.

Exchange 2000 SP3 Feature Completeness (~99% Compatibility)

The following list describes various Exchange features, lists what functions are available, and describes known problems or limitations that you can expect in Exchange after the integration.

- Inbox – shelf view, message-to-message navigation, page-to-page navigation, composition, reply, reply all, Forward, explicit check for new messages, message polling, new message notification, delete, move, address book, all seven panel views, message status icons, message expansion and collapse, message ordering, message status icons, search.

- Message Composition – send, rich text editing, address book (GAL) access to receiver fields, attachments, online help, options, save as draft, importance tagging. Print not tested. Check Names does not appear to do anything useful (but doesn't appear to be broken).

- Calendaring – daily view, weekly view, monthly view, month-to-month navigation, appointment view and detail mouseover, day selection from calendar, today view, address book, new appointment, check for messages. Alert polling, notification, and Print untested.

- Calendar Appointments – save/close, send, attachments, priority, recurrence, invite using address book, availability, reminder, start time, end time, all day event, show time, and appointment icons.

- Alerts – alert polling, reminder pop-ups.

- Contacts – new contact, check for new messages, six contact views, expansion and collapse under supported views, address book (search only), person-to-person navigation, page-to-page navigation, delete.

- Contact Creation – All fields work. Directions points to an Internet link and thus is not rewritten. Send works as well as address book (which still doesn't do anything useful). Save/Close and online help work as well. Print untested.

- Options – All form fields. Password change requires Exchange code modification so that it does not use browser built-in variables to dynamically build the URL.

- View Items and recover deleted items untested. Selecting close goes to an empty unnamed folder. The password change might require resetting user's basic authentication to connect again to Exchange.

- Folder View – All folders, URLs, icons, expansion and collapse, all shortcuts, all right mouse-click submenu functionality including update, open, move, copy and delete.

- Journal, Notes, Tasks – All features complete, except for search and empty deleted items folder.

Known Problems With Microsoft Exchange 2000 SP3 and Portal Server 6 Integration

Problem 1: Rich Text Editing in Email Composition Does Not Work

This feature operates from an ActiveX control that does not appear in the menu bar when the OWA interface is accessed through the Gateway. Workaround: In the `ctrl_FormatBar20.htc` file, add quotation marks to the following line:

```
<attach event=ondocumentready handler=onDocumentReady />
```

The line should look like the following:

```
<attach event="ondocumentready" handler="onDocumentReady" />
```

Problem 2: Submenu Does Not Display Correctly From Folder View

This submenu is opened by right-clicking over a folder name when in the folder view of OWA. The menu is not displayed correctly because a necessary event (ondocumentReady) never fires for the handler in `ctrl_DropMenu20.htc` to create the DHTML necessary for the menu contents.

Workaround: In the `ctrl_DropMenu20.htc` file, add quotation marks to the following line:

```
<attach event=ondocumentready handler=dOnReady />
```

Once modified, the line looks like the following:

```
<attach event="ondocumentready" handler="dOnReady" />
```

What

You must perform the following actions (detailed instructions follow):

1. Set up a test environment for the integration.

2. Create a new Rewriter ruleset for Exchange.

3. Install the appropriate portal server 6 patch containing Exchange-related fixes.

4. Change the Authentication Scheme for Microsoft Exchange.

5. If integrating Exchange 2000 SP3, make necessary modifications to Exchange controls files.

6. Enable Rewriting of CSS content.

Note – Any change made to the Outlook Web Access source .htc, .js, or .xsl files that exist in the Exchweb folder is unsupported by Microsoft. Any customization changes that affect these files that have already been made may affect or prevent a successful integration using these procedures. Future minor and major releases of Exchange from Microsoft may overwrite these changes, and make other modifications that break the integration through the Rewriter. Upgrading to new releases of either product should be made carefully in a controlled manner in a test environment.[1]

See "Why" on page 380 for explanations for each integration action.

Setting Up a Test Environment For the Integration

Set up a two-tier portal installation, preferably with a packet-filtering firewall between the client and the portal Gateway. The firewall should have two ports open:

1. For the Gateway running in HTTP mode for debugging purposes.

2. For the Gateway running in HTTPS mode.

Using a firewall in a test environment is the best way to avoid network and configuration problems that might show up in production. A separate Exchange box, prepopulated with a few test accounts and data should also be used in the test environment.

▼ To Create a New Rewriter Ruleset for Exchange

The steps in this procedure assume that you are using portal server version 6.0. Steps may differ on versions 6.1 and 6.2 because of differences in the Identity Server UI.

---

1. From the Microsoft Exchange 2000; Server Customizing Microsoft Outlook Web Access White Paper, pg. 13.

1. **Copy the Exchange-specific ruleset file to the** *install_dir*/SUNWps/export **directory of the profile server.**

   Use one of the following files you downloaded according to the integration you are performing:

   - Exchange 2000 SP3 – owa_sp3_ruleset.xml
   - Exchange 2003 – owa_2003_ruleset.xml

2. **Using** rwadmin, **store the new ruleset in the LDAP server.**

   ```
   # install_dir/SUNWps/bin/rwadmin store --runasdn "uid=amAdmin,ou=
   People,o=sun.com,o=isp" --password "test"
   install_dir/SUNWps/export/owa_sp3_ruleset.xml
   SUCCESS
   # install_dir/SUNWps/bin/rwadmin list --runasdn ="uid=amAdmin,ou=
   People,o=sun.com,o=isp" --password "test" | grep owa
   owa_sp3_ruleset
   ```

3. **Log in to the Administration Console.**

4. **Select View: Service Management.**

5. **Select the Gateway link under the SRAP Configuration section in the left panel.**

6. **Select the Edit link for the profile that will be used by the Gateway node accessing the Exchange server.**

7. **Under the Domain-Based Rulesets section in the right panel, add the fully qualified host name for the Exchange server.**

   Example:

   ```
   ex-server.domain.com|owa_sp3_ruleset
   ```

   Portal server 6.2 allows the exact URL to be mapped to the ruleset. In this case, your entry might look like:

   ```
   *://ex-server.domain.com*|owa_2003_ruleset
   ```

8. **Select Save.**

9. **Restart the Gateway nodes to reread the new profile information.**

▼ To Install Portal Server 6.0 Patch Containing Exchange-Related Fixes

For information about how to obtain portal server patches, see "Patching the Portal Server Software" on page 10.

The patch you need for this procedure is called `6.0SRAExchangeFixes` (patch ID 115156-01).

1. **If you have added or changed files in the portal `web-apps` directory, back them up in case the changes are overwritten or lost when the service is redeployed.**

```
# cp -R install_dir/SUNWps/web_apps
install_dir/SUNWps/web_apps_pre6.0SRAExchangeFixes
```

2. **Uncompress and untar the patch contents.**

```
# gunzip 6.0SRAExchangeFixes.tar.gz
# tar -xvf 6.0SRAExchangeFixes.tar
```

3. **Install the patch using the Solaris `patchadd` command, first on the profile and platform nodes, and then on the Gateway node.**

```
# patchadd 115156-01
```

▼ To Install the Portal Server 6.2 Patch Containing Exchange-Related Fixes

1. **Log in to `sunsolve.sun.com` and download patch `1116856-04` (or later).**

2. **Unzip or untar the patch contents:**

```
# unzip 116856-04.zip
```

3. **Install the patch using the Solaris patchadd command:**

```
# patchadd 116856-04
```

▼ To Change the Authentication Scheme for Microsoft Exchange 2000 SP3

1. Launch the Exchange System Manager.

2. Expand Servers.

3. Expand the Exchange server instance.

4. Expand Protocols.

5. Expand HTTP.

6. Expand Exchange Virtual Server.

7. Right-click over Exchange and select Properties.

8. From the Properties window, select the Access tab.

9. Choose the Authentication button from Authentication Settings.

10. Uncheck Integrated Windows Authentication.

11. Enter \ (the default), or specify the realm authentication identifier for your configuration as the domain for Basic Authentication.

Note – Make sure that the realm is the same for all end-user Web-accessible Exchange components.

---

12. Select OK.

13. From the Control Panel, select Administrative Tools.

14. Select Internet Services Manager.

15. Expand the Web site icon representing the server instance that Exchange is using.

16. Expand Default Web Site.

17. Right-click over the Exchange folder and select Properties.

18. Choose Directory Security Tab.

19. Under the Anonymous Access and Authentication Control tab, choose Edit.

20. Select Edit next to Basic Authentication.

21. Select Use Default and then OK.

22. Deselect Integrated Windows Authentication.

23. Select OK.

24. **Right-click over Exchweb and make the same properties change.**

25. **Verify that the scheme has changed by directing an Internet Explorer browser instance to the OWA login page.**

There are now two user-modifiable fields rather than three. The third field in NTLM is for the domain being authenticated against.

Note – The configuration change is necessary from the Exchange System Manager as well as from Internet Information Services (IIS), so that NTLM is not enabled once the system is rebooted. The configuration should be rechecked after a system reboot to make sure NTLM has not been automatically re-enabled.

▼ To Change the Authentication Scheme for Microsoft Exchange 2003

1. **Launch the Microsoft Exchange System Manager.**

2. **In the left pane, expand Servers.**

3. **Expand the virtual server that Exchange was deployed to.**

4. **Expand Protocols ➤ HTTP ➤ Exchange Virtual Server.**

5. **Right select Exchange and choose Properties.**

6. **Select the Access tap in the Exchange Properties window.**

7. **Select the Authentication button.**

8. **In the Authentication methods window, be sure that Basic Authentication is selected and NTLM Authentication is not selected.**

9. **Select OK.**

10. **Select Apply and OK.**

▼ To Make Necessary Modifications to Exchange Controls Files for Exchange 2000 SP3 Integration

Perform these steps only if you are integrating Exchange 2000 SP3. These steps are not necessary for Exchange 2000 or Exchange 2003.

The following procedures require downloaded scripts and tools. See "Obtaining Downloadable Files for This Book" on page xxi.

1. **Determine the best approach for updating your Exchange files:**

a. If the following files in *ex_server_install*/exchweb/controls **have not been modified, you can run the** modfiles.ksh **script to update your Exchange files automatically (where** *ex_server_install* **is the full path to the Exchange installation, such as** D:\Exchange**).**

The files that the script modifies are:
- ctrl_Tree20.xsl
- ctrl_FormatBar20.htc
- ctrl_Poll20.js
- ctrl_Tree20.js
- util_View20.js
- ctrl_reminder20.htc
- ctrl_FreeBusy20.htc

To run the modfiles.ksh script, go to Step 2.

b. **If any of these files have been modified in any way, you must manually update the files, otherwise the script will overwrite any customizations that you have made. Refer to the following manual procedures:**
- "To Remove the XML Namespace Identifier From ctrl_Tree20.xsl" on page 372
- "To Change Tree State Image Manipulation in ctrl_FormatBar20.htc" on page 372
- "To Insert an Interim Variable in the mf_Poll() Function of ctrl_Poll20.js" on page 374
- "To Modify Expindicator URLs After XSLT Transform in ctrl_Tree20.js" on page 375
- "To Modify Icon Image URLs When Folders Are Expanded in ctrl_Tree20.js" on page 376
- "To Strip the Portal Gateway Hostport Off the Deleted Items in util_View20.js" on page 377
- "To Create an Interim Variable in the mf_RemindersXML() Function of ctrl_reminder20.htc" on page 378
- "To Add an Already Rewritten Interim Variable to the IMG SRC Attribute Value in ctrl_FreeBusy20.htc" on page 379

2. **Go to the** *ex_server_install*/Exchweb **directory of the Exchange server.**

3. **Right-select the controls folder and choose Save as controls.zip.**

4. **Make a copy of the** controls.zip **file and name it** orig_controls.zip**.**

5. **Use the** ftp **command to copy the** controls.zip **file to the directory containing the portal integration tools that you have downloaded.**

6. **Run the** `modfiles.ksh` **script as shown.**

```
# ./modfiles.ksh
Found contols.zip...unzipping...
Archive: controls.zip
  inflating: controls/ctrl_FormatBar20.htc
  inflating: controls/ctrl_FreeBusy20.htc
  inflating: controls/ctrl_Poll20.js
  inflating: controls/ctrl_reminder20.htc
  inflating: controls/ctrl_Tree20.js
  inflating: controls/ctrl_Tree20.xsl
  inflating: controls/util_View20.js
Backing up original file as controls_orig.zip...
Creating diffs directory for modified files at diffs/...
Modifying ctrl_FormatBar20.htc ...
Created diffs/ ctrl_FormatBar20.htc .diff...
Modifying ctrl_FreeBusy20.htc ...
Created diffs/ ctrl_FreeBusy20.htc .diff...
Modifying ctrl_Poll20.js ...
Created diffs/ ctrl_Poll20.js .diff...
Modifying ctrl_Tree20.js ...
Created diffs/ ctrl_Tree20.js .diff...
Modifying ctrl_Tree20.xsl ...
Created diffs/ ctrl_Tree20.xsl .diff...
Modifying ctrl_reminder20.htc ...
Created diffs/ ctrl_reminder20.htc .diff...
Modifying util_View20.js ...
Created diffs/ util_View20.js .diff...
Zipping new file contents in to controls.zip...
  adding: controls/ctrl_FormatBar20.htc (deflated 74%)
  adding: controls/ctrl_FreeBusy20.htc (deflated 76%)
  adding: controls/ctrl_Poll20.js (deflated 70%)
  adding: controls/ctrl_reminder20.htc (deflated 66%)
  adding: controls/ctrl_Tree20.js (deflated 76%)
  adding: controls/ctrl_Tree20.xsl (deflated 73%)
  adding: controls/util_View20.js (deflated 70%)
Done.#
```

7. **Use the** `ftp` **command to copy the new** `controls.zip` **file back to the** *ex_server_install*/exchweb **directory of the Exchange server.**

8. **Unzip the new** `controls.zip` **file so that it overwrites the current contents.**

9. **Test Exchange connectivity without going through the Gateway.**

10. **If anything doesn't work, the modifications can be backed out by unzipping** `orig_controls.zip` **over the** `controls` **directory.**

    If this is the case, consider the following:

    - You may be using a different version of Exchange other than what the `modfiles.ksh` script operates on. Refer back to "Summary of Integration" on page 361 for version specifications.

    - Your files might have been modified prior to performing this procedure. In this case, you must perform the file modifications manually using the following procedure.

Manually Updating Controls Files

The following eight procedures explain how to update the controls files manually. You only perform these procedures if you decide not to run the `modfiles.ksh` script.

▼ To Remove the XML Namespace Identifier From `ctrl_Tree20.xsl`

1. **In the** `Exchsvr\Exchweb\Controls` **directory on the Exchange server, make a backup copy of the** `ctrl_Tree20.xsl` **file.**

2. **Edit** `ctrl_Tree20.xsl` **and remove the root node:**

   `<?xml version="1.0"?>`

3. **Save the file and close it.**

▼ To Change Tree State Image Manipulation in `ctrl_FormatBar20.htc`

- **Make the following changes to the** `onDocumentReady()` **function body of** `ctrl_FormatBar20.htc` **file:**

The following example uses the `diff` command to display the changes that you need to make in the `ctrl_FormatBar20.htc` file.

```
# diff -c ctrl_FormatBar20bak.htc ctrl_FormatBar20.htc
*** ctrl_FormatBar20bak.htc     Fri Feb  7 14:27:50 2003
--- ctrl_FormatBar20.htc        Fri Feb  7 15:56:44 2003
***************
*** 307,313 ****
                var obj = m_eFormatbar.children[szButton];
                if( null != obj )
                {
!                       obj.innerHTML = szVal;
                }
        }
        if (null != this.dhtmlEdit)
--- 307,332 ----
                var obj = m_eFormatbar.children[szButton];
                if( null != obj )
                {
!                       ///////////////////////////////////////
!                       // Workaround for SunONE Portal
!                       // The img tag has already been stripped
!                       // off here so we need only replace the
!                       // src attr value with an already
!                       // rewritten one
!
!                       //alert ("Image tag before: " + szVal);
!                       var imgre = /src=/;
!                       var imgTag = szVal;
!                       var imgStartIndex = imgTag.search(imgre) + 5;
!                       var tmpImgTxt = imgTag.substr(imgStartIndex);
!                       var imgStopIndex = tmpImgTxt.lastIndexOf("'") +
imgStartIndex;
!                       tmpImgTxt = imgTag.substring(imgStartIndex,
imgStopIndex);
!                       var imgObj =
tmpImgTxt.substr(tmpImgTxt.lastIndexOf("/"));
!               imgTag = imgTag.substring(0, imgStartIndex) + imagePath
+ imgObj + imgTag.substr(imgStopIndex);
!                       obj.innerHTML = imgTag;
!                       //alert (Image tag after: " + obj.HTML);
!                       ////obj.innerHTML = szVal;
!                       ///////////////////////////////////////
                }
        }
        if (null != this.dhtmlEdit)
```

▼ To Insert an Interim Variable in the `mf_Poll()` Function of `ctrl_Poll20.js`

● **Make the following change to the** `mf_Poll()` **function body of the** `ctrl_Poll20.js` **file:**

```
# diff -c ctrl_Poll20bak.js ctrl_Poll20.js
*** ctrl_Poll20bak.js    Fri Feb  7 14:22:06 2003
--- ctrl_Poll20.js       Fri Feb  7 14:22:16 2003
***************
*** 247,252 ****
--- 247,259 ----
  // Check for notification by using stored subscription identifier
  function mf_Poll()
  {
+         ///////////////////////////////////
+         //  Added for SunONE Portal Server
+         //
+         imgURL = m_szFolderURL;
+         m_szFolderURL = imgURL;
+         //
+         ///////////////////////////////////
          if( !m_fEnabled )
          {
                  return;
```

▼ To Modify Expindicator URLs After XSLT Transform in `ctrl_Tree20.js`

- **Make the following change to the** `mfcb_AddHierarchy()` **function body of the** `ctrl_Tree20.js` **file:**

```
# diff -c ctrl_Tree20bak.js ctrl_Tree20.js
*** ctrl_Tree20bak.js    Fri Feb  7 14:22:33 2003
--- ctrl_Tree20.js       Fri Feb  7 14:30:36 2003
***************
*** 382,387 ****
--- 382,403 ----
                if(null != szDisplayName)
                {
                        var objFolder = objFolderTLH.children[0];
+                       /////////////////////////////////////////
+                       // Added for the SunONE Portal Server to
+                       // avoid unecessary redirects caused from
+                       // the image URL being fetched using the
+                       // Gateway host as the base.
+                  // EX: https://gw/exchweb/img/tree-splus20.gif
+
+                       //alert("objFolderTLH.innerHTML is: " +
objFolderTLH.innerHTML);
+                       var curIMG =
objFolder.children("expIndicator").src;
+                       //alert("curIMG is: " + curIMG);
+                       curIMG =
curIMG.substring(curIMG.lastIndexOf("/")+1);
+                       curIMG = m_szImagePath + curIMG;
+                       //alert("Final curIMG is: " + curIMG);
+                       objFolder.children("expIndicator").src =
curIMG;
+                  //alert("szDisplayName is: " + szDisplayName);
+                       /////////////////////////////////////////
                        if(null != objFolder)
                        {
                                var objAnchor =
objFolder.children(objFolder.url);
```

▼ To Modify Icon Image URLs When Folders Are Expanded in `ctrl_Tree20.js`

● **Make the following change to the** `mfcb_ExpandFolder()` **function body of the** `ctrl_Tree20.js` **file:**

```
# diff -c ctrl_Tree20bak.js ctrl_Tree20.js
***************
*** 1156,1161 ****
--- 1172,1196 ----
                  objChildContainer.innerHTML =
  objXML.transformNode(objXSL.documentElement);
                  if(objChildContainer.children.length > 0)
                  {
+                         ///////////////////////////////////////////
+                             // Added for the SunONE Portal Server so
+                         // that the icon images and expansion status
+                             // symbols inside subfolders will be
+                             // displayed correctly.
+                             var curIMG;
+                             for (var x=0;
  x<objChildContainer.children.length; x++) {
+                                 curIMG =
  objChildContainer.children(x).children("expIndicator").src;
+                                 //alert("curIMG is: " + curIMG);
+                                 curIMG =
  curIMG.substring(curIMG.lastIndexOf("/")+1);
+                                 curIMG = m_szImagePath + curIMG;
+                                 //alert("final curIMG is: " + curIMG);
+
  objChildContainer.children(x).children("expIndicator").src =
  curIMG;
+                                 curIMG =
  objChildContainer.children(x).children("folderIcon").src;
+                                 curIMG =
  curIMG.substring(curIMG.lastIndexOf("/")+1);
+                                 curIMG = m_szImagePath + curIMG;
+
  objChildContainer.children(x).children("folderIcon").src =
  curIMG;
+                             }
+                         ///////////////////////////////////////////
                          objChildContainer.style.display = "";
                          objFolder.children("expIndicator").src =
  m_szImagePath + m_szMinusIcon;
                          objFolder.expanded = "true";
```

▼ To Strip the Portal Gateway Hostport Off the Deleted Items in `util_View20.js`

- **Make the following change to the** `mfcb_AddHierarchy()` **function body of the** `util_View20.js` **file:**

```
# diff -c util_View20bak.js util_View20.js
*** util_View20bak.js    Fri Feb  7 14:24:45 2003
--- util_View20.js       Fri Feb  7 14:24:59 2003
***************
*** 64,69 ****
--- 64,81 ----
      szXMLBatchString = "<?xml version='1.0'?><D:" + szXMLCommand
+ " xmlns:D='DAV:'><D:target>";
          for(var i = 0; i < objItems.length; i++)
          {
+             /////////////////////////////////////////////
+             // Change required for SunONE Portal Server
+             // a:href nodes from the DAV response must
+             // be rewritten in order for the tree view
+             // folder URLs to be correct, but they cannot
+             // be rewritten for a BMOVE request for a
+             // batch delete to work on the backend.
+             tmpURL = objItems(i).text
+             tmpURL =
tmpURL.substring(tmpURL.lastIndexOf("http://"));
+             objItems(i).text = tmpURL;
+             /////////////////////////////////////////////
+
              szXMLBatchString += "<D:href>" + objItems(i).text
+ "</D:href>";
          }
      szXMLBatchString += "</D:target></D:" + szXMLCommand + ">";0
```

▼ To Create an Interim Variable in the mf_RemindersXML() Function of ctrl_reminder20.htc

- **Make the following change to the** mf_RemindersXML() **function body of the** ctrl_reminder20.htc **file:**

```
# diff -c ctrl_reminder20bak.htc ctrl_reminder20.htc
*** ctrl_reminder20bak.htc       Fri Feb  7 14:23:44 2003
--- ctrl_reminder20.htc Fri Feb  7 14:23:55 2003
***************
*** 86,91 ****
--- 86,97 ----
  // Search for reminders that should now be displayed
  function mf_RemindersXML()
  {
+       ////////////////////////////////////
+       //  Added for SunONE Portal Server
+       imgURL = m_szFolderURL;
+       m_szFolderURL = imgURL;
+       //
+       ////////////////////////////////////
        if( !m_fEnabled || (CONST_B_SEARCH == (m_fState &
CONST_B_SEARCH )) )
          {
                return;
```

▼ To Add an Already Rewritten Interim Variable to the IMG SRC Attribute Value in `ctrl_FreeBusy20.htc`

● **Make the following change to the** `ctrl_FreeBusy20.htc` **file:**

```
# diff -c ctrl_FreeBusy20bak.htc ctrl_FreeBusy20.htc
*** ctrl_FreeBusy20bak.htc Thu Feb 6 19:12:00 2003
--- ctrl_FreeBusy20.htc Thu Feb 6 21:27:08 2003
***************
*** 578,584 ****
    "<SPAN class='fbLegend2clr tentClr'> </SPAN><SPAN
class='fbLegend2txt'>"+m_szTentative+"</SPAN>"+
    "<SPAN class='fbLegend3clr busyClr'> </SPAN><SPAN
class='fbLegend3txt'>"+m_szBusy+"</SPAN>"+
    "<SPAN class='fbLegend4clr oofClr'> </SPAN><SPAN
class='fbLegend4txt'>"+m_szOof+"</SPAN>"+
!   "<SPAN class='fbLegend5clr unknownClr'><IMG src='/
exchweb/img/form-noinfo.gif'></SPAN><SPAN
class='fbLegend5txt'>"+m_szUnknown+"</SPAN>"+
    "</TD></TR></table>" +
    "<DIV id='_DIVFB' nowrap onselectstart='return(false)'
class='fbbody'>" +
    "<div id='DIVHIDESPLITTERS'
style='position:absolute;top:0px;width:"+m_iRecipWidth+"px;heig
ht:100%;background-color:#b0b0b0;z-index:0;'></div>" +
--- 578,586 ----
    "<SPAN class='fbLegend2clr tentClr'> </SPAN><SPAN
class='fbLegend2txt'>"+m_szTentative+"</SPAN>"+
    "<SPAN class='fbLegend3clr busyClr'> </SPAN><SPAN
class='fbLegend3txt'>"+m_szBusy+"</SPAN>"+
    "<SPAN class='fbLegend4clr oofClr'> </SPAN><SPAN
class='fbLegend4txt'>"+m_szOof+"</SPAN>"+
!   "<SPAN class='fbLegend5clr unknownClr'>" +
!   "<IMG src='" + g_szVirtualRoot + "/img/form-noinfo.gif'>"
+
!   "</SPAN><SPAN class='fbLegend5txt'>"+m_szUnknown+"</
SPAN>"+
    "</TD></TR></table>" +
    "<DIV id='_DIVFB' nowrap onselectstart='return(false)'
class='fbbody'>" +
    "<div id='DIVHIDESPLITTERS'
```

Why

This section describes why these changes are necessary.

Why Do I Need a Test Environment?

A test environment is useful for many reasons, including working out any kinks to avoid disrupting service to end users on a production system. A firewall is important for testing the Rewriter integration because there are many areas in Exchange where the IE browser initiates direct HTTP requests using ActiveX triggered from user-initiated events. Part of the Rewriter integration requires making sure that these ActiveX requests go back to the portal Gateway rather than directly to the Exchange Server.

Why Are Each Of the Rewriter Rules Necessary For the Integration to Work?

The ruleset was generated by meticulously tracking where and how URLs are used throughout the Exchange product when accessed with an Internet Explorer browser. The ruleset has been finely tuned to reduce or eliminate extraneous rules which might do more harm than good. The following tables provide descriptions and usage examples of the context in which the new rules are applied for Exchange 2000 SP3. Many of these rules also apply to Exchange 2003 and are present in the `owa_2003_ruleset` file.

TABLE A-1   Rules for Rewriting JavaScript Content

Rule	Reason	Usage Example
`<Variable type="URL">` `g_szUserBase </Variable>`	Variable is used throughout Exchange to fully qualify relative URLs with the Exchange server host port.	`util_View20.js:` `szDeletedItemsFolder =` `g_szUserBase +` `g_szDeletedItemsURL +` `"/";`
`<Variable type="URL">` `g_szVirtualRoot` `</Variable>`	Similar to g_szUserBase except g_szVirtualRoot points to /exchweb instead of /uid.	`vw_Calendar20.js:` `m_eCalendar.addBehavior(` `g_szVirtualRoot+"/contro` `ls/ctrl_Calendar20.htc")` `;`
`<Variable type="URL">` `this.viewClass` `</Variable>`	Loads the XSL required for a specific message view.	`ctrl_View20.js:` `this.viewClass =` `"/exchweb/controls/ctrl_` `View20.xsl";`

Rule	Reason	Usage Example
`<Variable type="URL">` `g_szBaseURL </Variable>`	Used as the base for dynamically building URLs for the Global Access List (GAL).	`dlg_GAL20.js:` `var szURL = g_szBaseURL +` `"/?Cmd=galfind" +` `m_szUrlParams;=`
`<Variable type="URL">` `g_szURL* </Variable>`	Used interchangeably with `szURL`.	`frm_ReadNote20.js:` `opener.idMsgViewer.seekU` `RL(g_szURL,-` `1,window.name);`
`<Variable type="URL">` `g_szNewMailWav` `</Variable>`	Used for new mail notification.	`vw_Navbar20.js:` `oSnd.src =` `g_szNewMailWav;`
`<Variable type="URL">` `g_szReminderWav` `</Variable>`	Used for audible notification of alerts.	`vw_Navbar20.js:` `rgParams["WavFile"] =` `g_szReminderWav;`
`<Variable type="URL">` `g_szPublicFolderUrl` `</Variable>`	Used for accessing and manipulating files in the public folder.	`m_szHttpFbServerUrl    =` `g_szPublicFolderUrl +` `"?Cmd=freebusy"#``
`<Variable type="URL">` `g_szExWebDir* </Variable>`	Duplicate of `g_szVirtualRoot`.	
`<Variable type="URL">` `m_szImagePath </Variable>`	Used to create relative URLs from the Exchange server root. Many image URLs created using this variable are for icons and status.	`ctrl_Tree20.js:` `objFolder.children("expI` `ndicator").src =` `m_szImagePath +` `m_szMinusIcon;`
`<Variable type="URL">` `eSpan.src </Variable>`	Used to set a status image in the Appt creation page.	`ctrl_FreeBusy20.htc:` `eSpan.src =` `"/exchweb/img/form-` `noinfo.gif";`
`<Variable type="URL">` `objIMG.src </Variable>`	Used ambiguously where the RHS of the assignment might or might not be a raw URL that might also not already be rewritten.	`ctrl_View20.js:` `objIMG.src =` `m_szImagePath + "view-` `minus.gif";` `...` `wfview.htc:` `objIMG.src =` `objIMG.checkedimage;`

Rule	Reason	Usage Example
`<Variable type="URL">` `m_objGroupIMG.src` `</Variable>`	Used in the same manner as `objIMG.src`.	`ctrl_View20.js:` `m_objGroupIMG.src =` `m_szImagePath + "view-` `minus.gif";`
`<Variable type="URL">` `imgURL </Variable>`	Intermediary variable created for the Gateway to leverage rewriting hooks in the Exchange code.	`imgURL = m_szFolderURL;` `m_szFolderURL = imgURL;` `...` `m_oXmlSearch.open(` `SEARCH', m_szFolderURL,` `true);`
`<Variable type="URL">` `szURL </Variable>`	A workhorse variable used throughout Exchange in various contexts.	`util_View20.js:` `var szURL =` `idMsgViewer.url + "?Cmd=` `getview&SortBy=...`

TABLE A-2   Rules for Rewriting JavaScript Function Parameters

Rule	Reason	Usage Example
`<Function type=` `"EXPRESSION" name=` `"objTree.addHierarchy"` `paramPatterns="y"/>`	Adds a new folder to the folder tree in the navigation bar. Some parameters may already be rewritten, in which case SP4HP3 has a fix where the runtime Rewriter function correctly handles already rewritten URLs.	`navbar.js:` `objTree.addHierarchy(szP` `ublicFolderUrl, false,` `g_szPublicFoldersDN)`

TABLE A-2   Rules for Rewriting JavaScript Function Parameters *(Continued)*

Rule	Reason	Usage Example
`<Function type="EXPRESSION" name="requestFactory" paramPatterns="y"/>`	Used to create WebDAV requests using ActiveX initiated by the IE client.	`ctrl_Tree20.js:` `var objRequest = new requestFactory(szRootURL, "PROPFIND", objContext, mfcb_AddHierarchy)`
`<Function type="EXPRESSION" name="mf_Subscribe" paramPatterns="y"/>`	Used to poll for new messages and alerts.	`ctrl_Poll20.js:` `mf_Subscribe(m_sFolderURL, m_szType);`
`<Function type="EXPRESSION" name="mf_setViewDescriptorNode" paramPatterns=",,y"/>`	The third parameter passed to this function in `wfview.js` is used to create the prepended relative URL path. This rule affects the images in the search results of the search view and the phone list order of the contacts view.	`wfview.js:` `mf_setViewDescriptorNode(objViewNode, "customimagepath", "/exchweb/img/", true);`

TABLE A-3   Rules for Rewriting XML Text Data

Rule	Reason	Usage Example
`<TagText tag="imagepath" attributePatterns=""/>`	DAV response artifact used in XSLT transformation for various images which have relative URLs defined in XSL files.	`<!-- Flag status col -->` `<xsl:when test="prop[. =` `...` `<xsl:value-of select="/view/imagepath"></xsl:value-of>view-flag.gif</xsl:attribute>` `...`
`<TagText="prop2" attributePatterns=""/>`	Another artifact used for message status image URLs.	`<?xml version="1.0">><a:multistatus...` `<prop2>http://ex-server://exchweb/img/icon-report-ndr.gif</prop2>...`

Rule	Reason	Usage Example
`<TagText tag="davhref" attributePatterns=""/>`	Artifact used in various transforms. May also return the initial message to be viewed on a DAV SEARCH response for the Inbox contents.	`<davhref>http://ex-server/exchange/Administrator/Inbox/Undeliverable:%20test.EML</davhref>`
`<TagText tag="e:smallicon" attributePatterns=""/>` `<TagText tag="d:inbox" attributePatterns=""/>` `<TagText tag="d:calendar" attributePatterns=""/>` `<TagText tag="d:sentitems" attributePatterns=""/>` `<TagText tag="d:deleteditems" attributePatterns=""/>` `<TagText tag="d:contacts" attributePatterns=""/>` `<TagText tag="d:drafts" attributePatterns=""/>` `<TagText tag="d:outbox" attributePatterns=""/>` `<TagText tag="d:sendmsg" attributePatterns=""/>` `<TagText tag="d:msgfolderroot" attributePatterns=""/>` `<TagText tag="URL" attributePatterns=""/>` `<TagText tag="Icon" attributePatterns=""/>` `<TagText tag="g:smallicon" attributePatterns=""/>` `<TagText tag="d:smallicon" attributePatterns=""/>`	Artifacts returned by a DAV PROPFIND request for the user's folder list.	`<?xml version="1.0"?><a:propfind xmlns:a="DAV:" xmlns:b="urn:schemas:httpmail:" xmlns:c="http://schemas.microsoft.com/exchange/"><a:prop><a:href/><a:displayname/><a:hassubs/><a:contentclass/><b:unreadcount/><c:smallicon/><b:inbox/><b:calendar/><b:sentitems/><b:deleteditems/><b:contacts/><b:drafts/><b:outbox/><b:sendmsg/><b:msgfolderroot/><a:contentclass/></></>`

Rule	Reason	Usage Example
`<TagText tag="a:href" attributePatterns=""/>`	Ambiguous artifact used for both request URLs and internal Exchange URLs to query the Microsoft datastore.	`ctrl_Tree20.js:` `szFolderURL = objXML.selectSingleNode( "transferdata/item/a:hre f").text;`

TABLE A-4   Rules for Rewriting HTML Attributes

Rule	Reason	Usage Example
`<Attribute name="url" tag="*" paramPatterns= ""/>`	Used as an attribute value for an HTML component so that it can be accessed directly using the DOM.	`<DIV id="idMsgViewer"` `...` `url = "http://ex- server/exchange/Administ rator/Inbox/"` `...`
`<Attribute name= "viewClass" tag="*" paramPatterns=""/>`	HTML component property used to keep track of the current view and of events which can operate on that view. Also referred to using the object path `this.viewClass`.	`view.htc:<property name= "viewClass"` `put="put_szViewClass" get="get_szViewClass" />`
`<Attribute name= "draftsURL" tag="*" paramPatterns=""/>`	HTML component property used to keep track of the URL for the drafts folder.	`composeappt.js:` `var vRetval = window.showModalDialog(o bjMessage.draftsURL+"/?C md=dialog&template= dlg_recurrence",...`
`<Attribute name= "imagePath" tag="*" paramPatterns=""/>`	HTML component property which stores the relative URL from the server root to the images directory.	`ctrl_View20.js:` `m_szImagePath` `=` `mf_chooseValue(m_objView Description.selectSingle Node("view/imagePath"),t his.imagePath,"/exchweb/ img/");`

Rule	Reason	Usage Example

`<Attribute name= "implementation" tag="*" paramPatterns=""/>`	XML tag attribute value used in attaching an HTML component file to a specific HTML element.	`<?IMPORT namespace="WM" implementation= "http://ex-server/exchweb/controls/ util_CalMessaging20.htc" >`
		`...`
		`<WM:CALMESSAGING id= "idCalMessaging" onDelete= "onDeleteAppointment();" .../>`

`<Attribute name= "folderUrl" tag="*" paramPatterns=""/>`	HTML component property used for storing a current folder URL.	`vw_Calendar20.js: m_eCalMessaging.openNewA ppointment(m_eCalViewer. folderUrl,m_eCalViewer.m sDailyDate)`
`<Attribute name="folder" tag="*" paramPatterns= ""/>`	HTML component property.	`ctrl_Notify20.htc: <PUBLIC:PROPERTY NAME= "folder" GET= "f_getFolder" PUT= "f_setFolder" />`
`<Attribute name="t:src" tag="*" paramPatterns= ""/>`	Used for audible event notification in the navbar.	`t:src="http://ex-server/exchweb/img/notif y.wav"`
`<Attribute name= "imageNextArrow" tag="*" paramPatterns=""/>`	Used for month-to-month navigation in the calendar view.	`ctrl_Calendar20.js: '<IMG border=0 height=10 width=5 src= "'+element.imageNextArro w+'" rightNavButton= "1">';`
`<Attribute name= "imagePrevArrow" tag="*" paramPatterns=""/>`	Used for month-to-month navigation in the calendar view.	`ctrl_Calendar20.js: '<IMG border=0 height=10 width=5 src= "'+element.imagePrevArro w+'" leftNavButton="1">';`

Why Do I Need to Change the Authentication Scheme in Microsoft Exchange?

Microsoft ships Exchange with NTLM authentication enabled by default. NTLM authentication is a Microsoft proprietary protocol which is not implemented in many reverse proxies, including the portal Gateway. There are arguments for and against NTLM being more or less secure than BASIC Authentication. Regardless, the NTLM authentication scheme should only be used in a Windows domain, so it should be disabled for customers accessing OWA from the Internet. This authentication type must be disabled for Microsoft Internet Explorer users accessing the Exchange Server through the portal Gateway to:

- Successfully authenticate to Exchange.
- Allow the Gateway to store the Basic Auth credentials so that Exchange access can be done using single sign on (SSO) to the portal server after the first login.

Why Must a Portal Server Patch Be Applied For the Integration to Work?

The following fixes are also required, and are included in the portal server 6.0/Exchange integration patch:

- BugID 4780863 – Gateway strips off XML declaration tag.

  Pages or response bodies that contain an XML namespace identifier that looks like `<?xml version="1.0" ?>` end up having the root tag dropped. The direct effect on Exchange is not clear unless something depends on this root element being present.

- BugID 4788050 – Rewriter should ignore comments which occur prior to opening XSL tag.

  Currently, Microsoft has a copyright statement in the Exchange XSL files which precedes the XSL root element. These comments should be ignored to avoid the Rewriter attempting to translate the XSL file and corrupting it before sending it on its way to the browser.

- BugID 4778676 – Gateway should not translate special characters (XML Entities) when rewriting XML.

- For example, when an email message is expanded, Exchange sends a DAV SEARCH request with the following message body:

```
<searchrequest xmlns="DAV:">
<sql>SELECT "http://schemas.microsoft.com/exchange/x-
prioritylong"
as prop1, "http://schemas.microso
ft.com/exchange/smallicon" as prop2, "http://
schemas.microsoft.com/mapi/proptag/x10900003" as prop3,
"urn:schemas:httpmail:hasattachment" as prop4,"http://
schemas.microsoft.com/mapi/subject" as prop5, "
urn:schemas:httpmail:datereceived" as prop6, "http://
schemas.microsoft.com/mapi/proptag/x0e080003" as
prop7,"urn:schemas:httpmail:read" as read, "http://
schemas.microsoft.com/exchange/outlookmessageclas
s" as messageclass, "DAV:href" as davhref FROM Scope('SHALLOW
TRAVERSAL OF "") WHERE "http://schemas
.microsoft.com/mapi/proptag/0x67aa000b" = false AND
"DAV:isfolder"
= false ORDER BY "http://schemas.m
icrosoft.com/mapi/sent_representing_name" ASC,
"urn:schemas:httpmail:datereceived" DESC</sql>
<range type="find" rows="1">WHERE "http://schemas.microsoft.com/
mapi/sent_representing_name
" >= CAST("System Administrator" AS "string")</range>
</searchrequest>
```

Relevant URL references are being rewritten correctly, but the > character is being translated by the Gateway XML parser. By the time it gets to the Exchange backend, the XML is no longer syntactically correct for the request to be serviced, and a multistatus response is sent with a 404 status in the response body.

- BugID 4781754 – Not rewriting the URLs in CSS Content.

CSS is used in many places through the OWA code. This is a fix for added functionality in portal server 6 software.

The following Exchange-related fixes pertain to the portal server 6.2 and Exchange 2003 integration.

- BugID 4981726 – The href attr of the XSL style sheet is not rewritten.

This prevents the importation of style sheets in the declaration section of XML files.

- BugID 4972535 – The Rewriter does not handle chunked Content-Coding.

Message bodies carrying a Chunked Content-Coding HTTP header can be truncated by the rewriter.

- BugID 4967552 – ERProxy does not handle Destination headers. This affects pages using HTTP redirections.

- BugID 5018351 – The Rewriter mishandles hex and decimal ASCII representations in SML content. Specialized character entities in hex or decimal format are incorrectly translated as HTML entities.

The following *why* statements address why certain file modifications are required for the Exchange 2000 SP3 integration.

Why Does the XML Namespace Identifier Have to be Removed From `ctrl_Tree20.xsl`?

Having an XML root node for an XSL file forces the Gateway to interpret the file as though it were XML and rewrite it as such. Because of the syntax of most of the XSL files, it's better not to attempt to rewrite the XSL content, and either rewrite the XML prior to the transform or rewrite the resulting URL once the transform is done. XSL content is rewritten by default and should not be changed.

Why is the Tree State Image Manipulation Necessary in `ctrl_FormatBar20.htc`?

In the message composition window, there is an HTML element with an ID of `idFormatbar` which contains an attribute called `buttonHTML`. This attribute value is assigned a chunk of data which is handled through regular expressions in the `ctrl_FormatBar20.htc` `onDocumentReady` function. The assignment looks something like this:

```
buttonHTML="FontDialog::<IMG border='1'
style='cursor:hand;border-color:buttonface' src='http://exserver/
exchweb/img/tool-font.gif'>"
```

The RHS is arbitrary in nature, so you are forced to make the change where the UI is rendered. The way it is being done in the code modification is to extract the image object out of the `IMG` tag, rewrite it, and then reinsert it. It is rewritten using a known `imagePath` attribute value which also exists for the `idFormatbar` element. The result is code that renders the UI the same whether the user is accessing Exchange directly or through the Gateway.

Why Must an Interim Variable be Inserted in the `mf_Poll()` Function of `ctrl_Poll20.js`?

The `mf_Poll()` function uses a variable `m_szFolderURL` that cannot be added to the Gateway profile without causing message polling to break. So before the value of `m_szFolderURL` is used to create a POLL request in `mf_Poll`, we insert a hook for the Gateway to rewrite it in a just-in-time (JIT) fashion within the function body. If the value is not rewritten, the POLL request attempts to be made directly to the Exchange server and fails (assuming the browser is unable to directly contact the Exchange server).

Why is it Necessary to Modify the expIndicator URLs After XSLT Transform in `ctrl_Tree20.js`?

`mfcb_AddHierarchy` is used to create the tree view in the navigation bar when the folders button is selected from the left frame. There are images used to determine folder state and whether or not the individual folders contain any children, such as subfolders or items. The tree is built dynamically, using the resulting message body contents returned from a DAV PROPFIND request. The XML contents of the message body are transformed, using a corresponding XSL file which determines the final image URLs used to fetch the individual icons. Prior to the Exchange portal patch, this fetch would result in a redirection to the portal server desktop login because the URL would look something like `https://GW/exchweb/img/m_szPlusIcon`. Either a 302 redirect or a 404 not found error message is returned to the browser instead. If a 404 is returned before the dynamic HTML is inserted into the DOM, we can rewrite the URLs so that the images can be fetched successfully. This is done with another JavaScript variable `m_szImagePath` that is initialized at the beginning of `ctrl_Tree20.js` already added to the Gateway profile.

Why is it Necessary to Modify Icon Image URLs When Folders are Expanded in `ctrl_Tree20.js`?

When `mfcb_ExpandFolder` is called, only the outer expIndicator images are handled correctly because they are assigned using `m_szImagePath` that is rewritten at the point it is initialized in `ctrl_Tree20.js`. Unfortunately, all of the other children in each folder tree have URLs which are not rewritten, so we must explicitly set those URLs with rewritten equivalent values. This is done by first extracting out the image object, which is either a folder icon or a folder status image, and then assigning the value back using direct DOM access. This is done for the expIndicator as well as for the `folderIcons`.

Why Must the Portal Gateway Hostport be Stripped Off the Deleted Items in `util_View20.js`?

`a:href` is an ambiguous artifact. In this case, it is used to generate a batch request to move the selected item or items to the deleted items folder. For the batch request to complete successfully, the individual message URLs which are already rewritten must have the portal Gateway information stripped off of them for their locations to match in the Microsoft datastore.

Why is it Necessary to Create an Interim Variable in the `mf_RemindersXML()` Function of `ctrl_reminder20.htc`?

For the same reason as in the `mf_Poll()` function, we cannot add `m_szFolderURL` to the Gateway profile, so we must rewrite it in a JIT fashion prior to the DAV search request being initiated. If this request fails, the individual folders cannot be polled for new messages.

Why Do I Need to Enable the Rewriting of CSS Content?

CSS content is used in various places throughout OWA. To keep the interface consistent with what a user would see accessing the Exchange server directly, it is necessary to enable the rewriting of CSS content.

Lotus iNotes Integration

Use the following information as a rule of thumb when integrating Lotus iNotes (now called Domino Web Access) with portal server 6.

Obtain the Required Patches

If you are integrating iNotes with portal server 6.0, you must contact Sun for a patch containing fixes required by the application integration. See "Patching the Portal Server Software" on page 10.

For the Sun ONE Portal Server 6.0 software, you must have patch ID 115156-01 (called 6.0SRAExchangeFixes) installed on the portal sever.

Note – The patch name contains the word *Exchange* and not *inotes*. This is a bit misleading because the patch fixes both Exchange and Lotus iNotes integrations.

This fix is required to enable the rewriting of CSS content used for themes and other style elements in iNotes. Portal server versions 6.1 and 6.2 already include the fix.

Summary of Integration

Lotus iNotes is a very difficult application to debug through the portal Gateway because its source code is obfuscated and the formatting is removed prior to it being emitted to the Web client. This section describes what is involved in this integration.

Client Browser

This integration was tested using Internet Explorer 5.5SP2 + December 2002 Security update. Other Internet Explorer 5.5 and 6.0 versions should work as well, but they need to be tested thoroughly as a part of the integration process. iNotes only works with Internet Explorer because it makes use of browser-specific technologies including ActiveX, XSLT, and HTML extensions. IBM offers another UI called the webmail UI that makes use of Java applets and is cross-browser compatible. If Notes users are configured to use this UI, you must create Rewriter rules, which are not discussed here.

Notes Server

The Notes Server version used is:

```
<!-- Domino Release 5.0.12 (Solaris Sparc) -->
```

The server version information can be found by viewing the document head of any of the iNotes pages. This is the latest release of Domino available at the time of writing.

Notes Client

The Notes Client version (iNotes) used is:

```
<!-- $HaikuForm - 567 -->
```

The client version information is also available from the document source and is mostly useful for any support tickets that may need to be opened with IBM.

Portal Server

Required Versions:

- Sun ONE Portal Server 6.0 + SRA + 6.0SRAExchangeFixes
- Sun ONE Portal Server 6.1 + SRA
- Sun ONE Portal Server 6.2
- New iNotes-specific ruleset (`inotes_ruleset.xml`)

Advantages

With this integration, the native user interface can be used to access Notes from inside or outside the corporate network.

- No client configuration required.
- Notes server does not have to reside in DMZ.
- Encryption/Decryption is performed using SSL.
- Can be used in conjunction with Lotus Notes portlets developed for portal server 6.
- Takes advantage of new portal server 6 architecture where an individual ruleset can be mapped to the Notes server so that there is no rule interaction between rules needed for iNotes and more generalized rules for other applications.

Disadvantages

- `Notes.ini` entry must be added to prevent portal session loss when iNotes users log out. This entry is not available on Notes server version 5.0.11.
- Cannot use out-of-box default ruleset.
- Portal server 6.0 integration must disable XML rewriting for Gateway instance used to access iNotes because of problems translating specialized characters like `&amp;`

Known Problems With iNotes Integration

There are no known problems with iNotes integrations.

What To Do

To integrate iNotes with the portal server software, you must perform the following procedures (detailed instructions follow):

1. Create a new Rewriter ruleset for the portal server desktop.

2. Create a new Rewriter ruleset for iNotes.

3. Associate new rulesets with the appropriate Gateway instance.

4. Create a proxies for domains and subdomains entry for iNotes server.

5. Install the portal server 6 patch containing Exchange-related fixes.

6. Enable Rewriting of CSS content.

7. Disable Rewriting of XML content.

8. Modify the `notes.ini` start file.

9. Modify Portlet URLs, if applicable.

10. Restart the portal components.

▼ To Create a New Ruleset for the Portal Server Desktop

1. **From the Administration console, select View: Service Management.**

2. **Select the Rewriter link under the Portal Server Configuration section of the left panel.**

3. **Under the Rules section, select New.**

4. **In the text field, change the RuleSet ID attribute value to desktop_ruleset:**

   <RuleSet id="desktop_ruleset">

5. **Create a ruleset that accounts for the portal server desktop contents that you have deployed.**

These contents may include URL scraped content if the ruleset is shared, the Bookmark provider, the Netlet provider, and so on.

The following ruleset is specific to the portal server 6.0 desktop.

```
<?xml version="1.0" encoding="UTF-8"?>
<!DOCTYPE RuleSet SYSTEM
"jar://rewriter.jar/resources/RuleSet.dtd">
<RuleSet type="GROUPED" id="desktop_ruleset">
<HTMLRules type="GROUPED" id="idshtmlrules">
<Applet source="*/NetMailServlet" code="NetMail.class" param=
"*URL" valuePatterns="" />
<Applet source="*/NetFileApplet" code="rp.class" param="*URL"
valuePatterns="" />
<Applet source="*/NetletConfig" code="SServer.class" param=
"configURL" valuePatterns="" />
<Attribute name="action" tag="*" valuePatterns="" />
<Attribute name="background" tag="*" valuePatterns="" />
<Attribute name="codebase" tag="*" valuePatterns="" />
<Attribute name="href" tag="*" valuePatterns="" />
<Attribute name="src" tag="*" valuePatterns="" />
<Attribute name="value" tag="*" valuePatterns="" />
<Attribute name="url" tag="*" valuePatterns="" />
<Attribute name="archive" tag="*" valuePatterns="" />
<Attribute name="style" tag="*" valuePatterns="" />
<JSToken>on*</JSToken>
</HTMLRules>
<JSRules type="GROUPED" id="idsjsrules">
<Variable type="URL">location.href</Variable>
<Variable type="URL">parent.location</Variable>
<Variable type="URL">self.location</Variable>
<Variable type="EXPRESSION">window.location</Variable>
<Variable type="EXPRESSION">location</Variable>
<Variable type="EXPRESSION">surf_form_URL</Variable>
<Variable type="SYSTEM">window.location.pathname</Variable>
<Function type="EXPRESSION" name="*findWindow" paramPatterns="y"
/>
<Function type="URL" name="openSavedBookmarkURL" paramPatterns=
"y" />
<Function type="URL" name="openURL" paramPatterns="y" />
<Function type="URL" name="openAppURL" paramPatterns="y" />
```

```
<Function type="URL" name="openNewWindow" paramPatterns="y" />
<Function type="URL" name="parent.openNewWindow" paramPatterns=
"y" />
<Function type="URL" name="window.open" paramPatterns="y" />
<Function type="URL" name="netletConfigOpen" paramPatterns="y,y"
/>
<Function type="URL" name="netletWinOpen" paramPatterns="y" />
<Function type="DHTML" name="document.write" paramPatterns="y" />
<Function type="DHTML" name="document.writeln" paramPatterns="y"
/>
</JSRules>
</RuleSet>
```

6. **Select Save.**

▼ To Create a New Rewriter Ruleset for iNotes

1. **From the Administration console, select View: Service Management.**

2. **Select the Rewriter link under the Portal Server Configuration section of the left panel.**

3. **Under the Rules section, select New.**

4. **In the text field, change the RuleSet ID attribute value to** `inotes_ruleset`:

   ```
   <RuleSet id="inotes_ruleset">
   ```

5. Create a bare-bones ruleset which looks something like this:

```xml
<?xml version="1.0" encoding="UTF-8"?>
<!DOCTYPE RuleSet SYSTEM
"jar://rewriter.jar/resources/RuleSet.dtd">
<RuleSet id="inotes_ruleset">
<!-- Rules for Rewriting HTML Source -->
<HTMLRules>
<!-- Rules for Rewriting HTML Attributes -->
<Attribute name="action" />
<Attribute name="background" />
<Attribute name="codebase" />
<Attribute name="code" />
<Attribute name="href" />
<Attribute name="src" />
<Attribute name="lowsrc" />
<Attribute name="style" />
<Attribute name="content" tag="meta" />
<!-- Rules for Rewriting HTML Attributes containing Java Script -->
<JSToken>on*</JSToken>
</HTMLRules>
<!-- Rules for Rewriting JavaScript Source -->
<JSRules>
<!-- Rules for Rewriting JavaScript variables in URLs -->
<!-- <Variable type="URL"> LayoutOption3 </Variable> -->
<Variable type="URL"> imgsrc </Variable>
<Variable type="URL"> *location.href </Variable>
<Variable type="URL"> parent.location </Variable>
<Variable type="URL"> self.location </Variable>
<Variable type="URL"> location.replace </Variable>
<Variable type="EXPRESSION"> src </Variable>
<!-- Rules for Rewriting JavaScript Function Parameters -->
<Function type="EXPRESSION" name="window.open" paramPatterns=
"y"/>
<Function type="DHTML" name="document.write" paramPatterns=
"y"/>
<Function type="DHTML" name="document.writeln" paramPatterns=
"y"/>
</JSRules>
</RuleSet>
```

6. Select Save.

▼ To Associate New Rulesets with the Appropriate Gateway Instance

1. From the Administration console, select View: Service Management.

2. Under the SRAP Configuration section in the left panel, select the link next to Gateway.

3. Select the Edit link next to the Gateway instance which will be used to connect to the Notes server.

4. Under the domain-based rulesets, do one of the following (listed in order of recommendation):

   a. **Create an entry for the fully qualified iNotes server.**

      This is the easiest and most manageable approach. The entry would look something like `inotes.int.sun.com|inotes_ruleset`, where `inotes` is the host name of the Notes server and `int.sun.com` is the internal domain in which the Notes server resides.

   b. **Create an entry for the iNotes server's DNS domain.**

      This is useful if the Notes server is in a separate subdomain from the portal server node so that the ruleset for the portal server desktop, URLScraper, Bookmark provider, and so forth, can be kept separate from the ruleset used for iNotes. The entry might look something like `int.sun.com|inotes_ruleset`.

   c. **Create an entry with a superset of the** `inotes_ruleset` **and the** `desktop_ruleset`.

      This option may be required if the portal and iNotes server are deployed on the same physical domain and host because a URL cannot yet be associated with a specific ruleset. To prevent unwanted rules from being applied to iNotes, or the portal server desktop being rewritten incorrectly, a dedicated Gateway instance might have to be used solely for users wishing access to iNotes. The entry might look something like `sun.com|sunwide_ruleset`.

5. **Select Add.**

6. **Also under the domain-based rulesets section, change the portal server node's domain ruleset from default, or** `gateway_default_ruleset` **to** `desktop_ruleset`.

7. **Select Add.**

8. **Select the previous rule entry for the portal server node's domain.**

9. **Select Remove.**

10. **Select Save.**

▼ To Create a Proxies for Domains and Subdomains Entry for iNotes Server

---

Note – This step is only necessary if the Notes server is on a different DNS subdomain from the portal server node.

---

1. **From the Administration console, select View: Service Management.**

2. **Under the SRAP Configuration section of the left panel, select the link next to Gateway.**

3. **Select the Edit link next to the Gateway instance which will be used to connect to the Notes server.**

4. **Add the DNS domain of the Notes server to the Proxies for Domains and Subdomains section.**

5. **Select Add.**

6. **Select Save.**

▼ To Install the Portal Server 6 Patch Containing Exchange-Related Fixes

---

Note – This patch installation is only required for portal server 6 versions earlier than 6.1.

---

1. **Obtain the required patch.**

   The patch you need is called `6.0SRAExchangeFixes` (patch ID 115156-01).

2. **If you have added or changed files in the portal** `web-apps` **directory, back it up in case the changes are overwritten or lost when the service is redeployed.**

   ```
   # cp install_dir/SUNWps/web_apps \
   install_dir/SUNWps/web_apps_pre6.0SRAExchangeFixes
   ```

3. **Uncompress and untar the patch contents.**

   ```
   # gunzip 6.0SRAExchangeFixes.tar.gz
   # tar -xvf 6.0SRAExchangeFixes.tar
   ```

4. Install the patch using the Solaris `patchadd` command—first on the profile and platform nodes, and then on the Gateway node.

```
# patchadd 115156-01
Checking installed patches...
Executing prepatch script...
Verifying sufficient filesystem capacity (dry run method)...
Installing patch packages...
Patch number 115156-01 has been successfully installed.
See /var/sadm/patch/115156-01/log for details
Executing postpatch script...
Checking for previous patch revisions...
Restarting SunONE Portal Server Gateway w/ original settings.
stopping gateway ... done.
starting gateway ...
done.
Gateway restarted. Please wait a moment before connecting to it.
Postpatch processing complete.
Patch packages installed:
SUNWpsgw
SUNWpsrw
```

▼ To Enable Rewriting of CSS Content

1. From the Administration console, select View: Service Management.

2. Under the SRAP Configuration section, select the link next to Gateway.

3. Select the Edit link next to the appropriate Gateway instance.

4. Add `CSS=text/css` to the Mime mappings section.

5. Select Add.

6. Select Save.

▼ To Disable Rewriting of XML Content

1. From the Administration console, select View: Service Management.

2. Under the SRAP Configuration section, select the link next to Gateway.

3. Select the Edit link next to the appropriate Gateway instance.

4. Select the `XML=text/xml` entry from the Mime mappings section.

5. Select Remove.

6. Select Save.

Note – XML rewriting does not have to be disabled for versions later than 6.1 PC1, or 6.2 later than PC4.

▼ To Modify the `notes.ini` Start File

1. **Make a backup of the existing `notes.ini` file.**

2. **Add the following line to the `notes.ini` file:**

   `iNotes_WA_SkipEndIESession=1`

3. **Restart the Notes server.**

▼ To Modify Portlet URLs, if Applicable.

- **Modify the creation scripts to the iNotes equivalent URLs**

  For example, to create a new task, the default URL used to load the webmail templates instead of the iNotes templates is:

  `http://notes.int.sun.com/mail/uid.nsf/Task?OpenForm&ui=webmail`

  The links need to be changed at the provider's source level. This might require professional services intervention if you do not have the provider source. One example of how this link would correctly load in iNotes is to change it to:

  `http://notes.int.sun.com/mail/uid.nsf/($ToDo)/$new`
  `/?EditDocument&Form=h_PageUI&PresetFields=`
  `h_EditAction;h_New,s_NotesForm;Task`

▼ To Restart the Portal Gateway Component

- **Restart the Gateway nodes.**

  Perform this by issuing the `/etc/init.d/gateway -n` *debug* `start` command where *debug* is the name of the Gateway instance being used to access iNotes.

Why

This section describes why these changes are necessary.

Why Do I Need to Create a New Rewriter Ruleset for the Portal Server Desktop?

Maintaining a separate ruleset for the desktop is useful to isolate only those rules which are absolutely necessary for the default portal providers to work. The custom ruleset for the desktop is less generalized than either of the default rulesets, which means there is less chance of things being rewritten improperly. One entry that is specifically added to the portal server desktop ruleset is:

```
<Function type="EXPRESSION" name="*findWindow" paramPatterns="y"
/>
```

This ensures that a link added to the Bookmark provider to launch iNotes with the rewritten URL does so. Depending on other rules, the link may appear to be rewritten by checking the browser status when performing a mouseover. This is a bit misleading because the HREF attribute value is rewritten, but the JavaScript onHandler is what actually loads the appropriate URL. For example:

```
<A HREF=
"https://gw.sun.com/http://notes.int.sun.com/mail/uid.nsf"
target="iNotes" onClick=
"javascript:Bookmark_findWindow('http://notes.int.sun.com/mail/u
id.nsf'); return false;">iNotes</A>
```

The rule is wildcarded because each bookmark channel that is defined for the container has its own `findWindow` function. The alternative would be to change the `window.open` function rule from a URL type to an expression type so that the bookmark URL passed to the `findWindow` function would be rewritten at runtime when the window was opened:

```
<Function type="EXPRESSION" name="window.open" paramPatterns="y"
/>
```

This correctly rewrites the URL reference in the function body:

```
function Bookmark_findWindow( url ){
  counter++;
  var urlWin;
  var windowID = "";
  var windowOption = "all_new";
  if( windowOption == "all_new" ){
   windowID = "Webtop_url_number"+counter;
   urlWin = window.open( url, windowID );
   urlWin.focus();
  }
 ...
}
```

If the link is not rewritten by one of the methods recommended above, the browser attempts to initiate a direct connection to the Notes server, which is likely to fail if the user is outside of the firewall.

Why Do I Need to Create a New Rewriter Ruleset for iNotes?

By creating a separate ruleset specifically for iNotes-related integration, the ruleset can be maintained and modified independently of other default rulesets to prevent rule trumping and to extend the ability to create a specific Gateway node. Notes users log in to access iNotes if required. The overzealous default rulesets provided with portal server 6 break most of the menu functionality including Save, Save & Close, and Edit functions. An additional entry was added:

```
<Variable type="EXPRESSION"> src </Variable>
```

This rewrites the dynamically created IFRAME source URL for the Web Page Panel type so it works. This addition is necessary because of the arbitrary variable name used for the layout panel, and the fact that the value specified for the Web page panel doesn't get rewritten correctly because of the encoded colon after the protocol identifier:

```
var LayoutOption3 =
'http%3A//stocks.int.sun.com/channels/stocks_channel.html';
```

The layout variables are loaded into an array, and the dynamically created IFRAME src is set in the following script block:

```
<script> function np(index){if
(theWelcomeFrameset.frames[index].mL().readyState !=
"complete"){setTimeout('np(' + index + ')', 3000);
return;}theWelcomeFrameset.frames[index].lj(true);}function
nq(index){theWelcomeFrameset.frames[index].lj(false);
document.body.onclick =
function(){theWelcomeFrameset.lj(true);};var
s="setTimeout('np(" + index + ")'," + 3000 + ")";
haiku.LB.add(s);}if
(h_ClientBrowser.isIE5()){nq(ht); var mg=
theForm.document.createElement("IFRAME"); with(mg){id=ld(); src=
LayoutOption[ht];style.display=
"none";}document.write(mg.outerHTML);}else{var s="<layer>nyi - "
+
LayoutOption[ht] + "<\/layer>";document.write(s);}}</script>
```

FIGURE A-1 shows the layout page to set the Web page panel type.

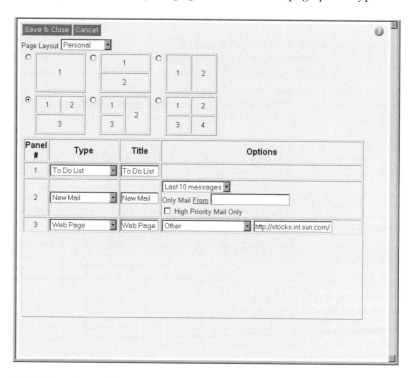

FIGURE A-1 Layout Page

The IFRAME for the third panel when loaded properly through the Rewriter ends up looking something like FIGURE A-2.

Web Page

Real-time ECN Quotes :Wed May 28 18:30:48 2003		
Symbol	**Price**	**Change**
SUNW	4.20	-0.02
AAPL	18.21	-0.67
AMZN	35.00	+0.15
AOL	14.80	-0.18
CSCO	16.08	-0.07
JNPR	13.82	-0.07
EBAY	100.95	-2.10
IBM	87.64	-0.05
ORCL	13.25	+0.60

FIGURE A-2 IFRAME for the Third Panel

If the src assignment is not rewritten correctly, the browser alerts the user about mixed secure and insecure content on the page when the IFRAME is attempted to be downloaded. Selecting No to load the page content anyway ends up displaying a NavigationCancelled error in the IFRAME, and answering Yes displays an IE 404 or 500 error if the browser is unable to initiate a direct connection with the iNotes server. This is one reason it is important to test the integration with the Gateway running in SSL mode, because it helps catch embedded objects which aren't being rewritten correctly.

Why Do I Need to Associate the New Ruleset With the Appropriate Gateway Instance?

To prevent the default ruleset from breaking the iNotes interface, ensure that iNotes launches from the Bookmark provider, and to get the Web page panel types to work in the customized iNotes layout, the rulesets must be associated with the proper FQHNs or DNS domains.

Why Do I Need to Create a Domains/Subdomains Entry for iNotes Server?

This is necessary if the Notes server is in a different DNS subdomain or domain than the portal server node. Adding an additional value to this section tells the Rewriter that any content originating from that domain must be rewritten according to the mapping laid out in the Domain-Based Rulesets section. The most appropriate entry in the Domain-Based Rulesets section is used to determine how to find URLs that require rewriting in content originating from that host name or domain.

Why Do I Need to Install a Portal Patch For iNotes to Work?

The iNotes integration requires a combination of configuration changes (the Rewriter ruleset) and fixes or enhancements in the portal server Gateway component. The portal patch contains the following fixes:

- BugID 4780863 – Gateway strips off XML declaration tag.

  Pages or response bodies that contain an XML namespace identifier that looks like `<?xml version="1.0" ?>` end up having the root tag dropped. The direct effect on third-party applications is not clear unless something depends on this root element being present.

- BugID 4788050 – Rewriter should ignore comments that occur prior to opening the XSL tag.

  If the opening XSL tag is preceded by anything else, the page is rewritten. The correct fix for this particular problem needs to be carefully considered because there might be times when the XSL code must be rewritten because it is used in a transform that controls URL values.

- BugID 4778676 – Gateway should not translate special characters (XML Entities) when rewriting XML.

  For example, when an email message is expanded, Exchange sends a DAV SEARCH request.

  All URL references that matter are being rewritten correctly, but the > character is being translated by the Gateway XML parser. By the time it gets to the Exchange backend, the XML is no longer syntactically correct for the request to be serviced and a multistatus response is sent with a 404 status in the response body.

- BugID 4781754 – Not rewriting the URLs in CSS Content.

  CSS is used in many third-party applications for look and feel purposes. This is a fix for functionality added in portal server 3 that has not yet been ported to the portal server 6 software.

Why Do I Need to Enable the Rewriting of CSS Content?

CSS content is used in various places throughout iNotes. Specifically, almost the entire skins implementation uses dynamically created CSS content to handle the look and feel of the primary interface.

Why Do I Need to Disable Rewriting of XML Content?

Disabling rewriting XML is used as a workaround for a corner case that still exists where specialized XML characters are still being translated by the Gateway. The visible result in Lotus iNotes is that if there are any of these characters contained in the email headers (such as error notifications), none of the other headers are fetched. By specifying the exact URL used to fetch the headers, the browser may display an error similar to the following:

```
The XML page cannot be displayed
Cannot view XML input using XSL style sheet. Please correct the
error and then click the Refresh button, or try again later.
--------------------------------------------------------------
----------------
Whitespace is not allowed at this location. Line 15, Position 139
<text>DELIVERY FAILURE: No route found to domain iplanet.com from
server SUN/SUN. Check Server, Connection and Domain documents in
Name & Address Book.</text></entrydata>
--------------------------------------------------------------
--------------------------------------------------------------
----------^
```

Note the translated ampersand. As the original XML indicates, the Gateway is translating the character as the XML passes through the Rewriter.

```
...
<entrydata columnnumber="5" name="$73">
<text>DELIVERY FAILURE: No route found to domain sun.com from
server
SUN/SUN.
Check Server, Connection and Domain documents in Name &amp; Address
Book.</text></entrydata>
...
```

Why Do I Need to the Modify `Notes.ini` Start file?

More recent versions of iNotes contain an ActiveX component that does session-related cleanup once the logout link is selected. The result of this ActiveX running is that the portal session is destroyed as well. This is not a Rewriter problem, as the behavior can be reproduced from a child browser by going directly to iNotes and logging out.

The modification to the `notes.ini` file circumvents the requirement to force the ActiveX not to run, or for ActiveX to be set to `prompt` instead of `run` in the browser security configuration. The following URL, when accessed through the portal Gateway, destroys the portal session:

```
/mail/uid.nsf/iNotes/Proxy/?OpenDocument&Form=
s_Logout&CacheResults&MaxExpires&TimeStamp=
20021223T190926,36Z&charset=ISO-8859-1&PresetFields=
s_UseActXUpload;1
```

If s_ActXUpload is set to `false`, logout works fine without destroying the portal session.

```
/mail/uid.nsf/iNotes/Proxy/?OpenDocument&Form=
s_Logout&CacheResults&MaxExpires&TimeStamp=
20021223T190926,36Z&charset=ISO-8859-1&PresetFields=
s_UseActXUpload;0
```

The code that runs this ActiveX looks something like this:

```
<script language="JavaScript"> if (s_UseActXUpload == "1"){var s=
'<div style="display:none">'; s+='<object id="UploadControl"
width=
"100%" height="20" ' + 'classid="clsid:1E2941E3-8E63-11D4-9D5A-
00902742D6E0" ' + 'codebase="' + getUploadAXCodebase() + '">' +
'<param name="General_Mode" value="' + 1 + '">' + '<param name=
"General_DrawButtons" value="0">' + '<param name="General_URL"
value=
"' + getNsfPath(self) + '/' + "0" + "/" + h_PageUnid + '">' +
'<param
name="General_ServerName" value="' + BTf () + '">' + '<param name=
"Attachment_Lengths" value="">' + '<param name="Attachment_Names"
value=""><param name="Attachment_Times" value="">'; s+=
'</object></div>'; document.write(s);}</script>
```

Note – If other applications require XML rewriting to be enabled to function correctly, a dedicated Gateway instance might have to be deployed specifically for iNotes users.

Why Do I Need to Modify Portlet URLs if Applicable?

The portlets now ship with links that launch the native cross-browser webmail interface provided by IBM for Web-based Notes accessibility. If the Notes user accounts are configured using the iNotes templates instead of the webmail templates, selecting any of the *creation* links from the upper-left corner of the individual portlets might result in the error shown in FIGURE A-3.

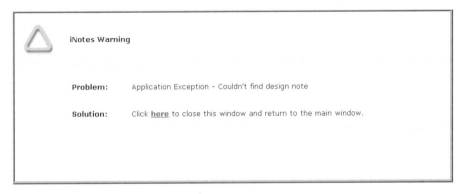

iNotes Warning	
Problem:	Application Exception – Couldn't find design note
Solution:	Click here to close this window and return to the main window.

FIGURE A-3 Error Received by Notes User

Why Do I Need to Restart the Portal Components?

The Gateway instance needs to be restarted to reread its profile to pick up the new Rewriter rulesets and domain mappings.

Risks and Workarounds for the `deploy` Command

This appendix provides information about the problems you might encounter using the `deploy` command, and offers suggestions for avoiding them.

The `deploy` command installs as a part of portal server software, and is used to deploy the portal Web service to the underlying Web container. The `deploy` command is not specifically related to SRA, but is important in the overall system, particularly when providing SRA to a customized portal desktop.

The `deploy` command manages the complexity of various web service deployments and non-default directory hierarchies. Portal server versions 6.1 and 6.2 have additional support for Web containers that are included in several popular application servers. This means that the `deploy` command provides a centralized way to manage the portal web services deployment to the additional Web containers.

The `deploy` command contains a subcommand called `redeploy` that is primarily used to push file modifications to the Web container in a hot-swapping manner. In the Sun ONE Portal Server 6.0 software, the `deploy` command is undocumented. The risks of using the `deploy` command in portal server 6.0 include wiping out your search instance and any customizations made to the portal instance's web-apps directory, including those not specifically identified by the DEPLOY_URI variable. This limitation is addressed in portal server 6.0 software instead by making changes to files in the web-src directory and manually coping them to the web-apps directory.

The `deploy` command is documented in portal server 6.1 software, and it no longer presents a risk to the search instance. This is because the `deploy` command has added another flag specific to search.

The `deploy` command was modified slightly in portal server 6.1 Patch Consolidation 1 (PC1) so it no longer removes the entire web-apps directory in each server instance. This prevents the `deploy` command from removing other Web applications that might be deployed to the same Web container. This was done for the purpose of sustaining the Sun ONE Portal Server 6.1 software, and to reduce the likelihood of patches overwriting customizations or permanently removing other Web applications that were deployed using the native Web container utilities.

The portal server 6.2 software offers the same limited information about the `deploy` command as portal server 6.1 software, and it should be used with equal caution if you have deployed other Web applications besides the portal server. To avoid problems with data loss or similar unpleasantries, the following sections provide recommendations for using the `deploy` command. The suggestions below assume that the Sun Web server is used as the portal Web container. Other Web containers can have their own deploy command-line interfaces that can be used as well.

Portal Server 6.0 Installations

Make changes to the `web-src` files and manually copy them to the server instances. This reduces the chance of the loss of your customizations due to a software patch or update internally running the `deploy` command. Also, avoid deploying additional Web applications to the portal Web server instances. Do not modify files directly in the `web-apps` directory or make different modifications in each Web container instance as a way to offer different content in each instance. Refer to the *Sun ONE Portal Server 6.0 Desktop Customization Guide* for alternative approaches to desktop branding, if this is the requirement for making different changes per instance.

Portal Server 6.1 Installations

Upgrade to Sun ONE Portal Server 6.1PC1 software or to a later patch consolidation. Continue to make changes to the `web-src` files, and use the `deploy` command to redeploy them. See CODE EXAMPLE B-1 for a scripted method to redeploy the portal Web services. Additional Web applications can be deployed to the Web container, and they will no longer be removed when the `deploy` command is run.

Portal Server 6.2 Installations

Modifications should be made to the `web-src` files only. The `deploy` command can be used in conjunction with the `redeploy` subcommand to propagate the changes. Caution is in order for Web applications deployed to the same Web server instances containing the portal Web application. Contact Sun Support if this deployment scenario describes your needs, to see if you need a patch for the `deploy` program to prevent it from blindly removing your other Web applications deployed to the same Web server instance.

Calling the `deploy` Command From a Script

CODE EXAMPLE B-1 shows how the `deploy` command can be called with the `redeploy` subcommand option in portal server 6.1PC1 and portal server 6.2 to push portal Web service changes to the live production environment.

CODE EXAMPLE B-1   `deploy` Command Script

```ksh
#!/bin/ksh
# redeploy.ksh

GREP=/usr/bin/grep
AWK=/usr/bin/awk

pkginfo -q SUNWps
if [ $? -eq 0 ]; then
  INSTALL_DIR=`$GREP "BASEDIR=" /var/sadm/pkg/SUNWps/pkginfo |
$GREP -v DEPLOY | $GREP -v IDSAME | $AWK ' BEGIN { FS="=" } { print
$2 }`
  DEPLOY_URI=`$GREP "DEPLOY_URI=" /var/sadm/pkg/SUNWps/pkginfo |
$AWK ' BEGIN { FS="=" } { print $2 }`
  DEPLOY_DOMAIN=`$GREP "DEPLOY_DOMAIN="
/var/sadm/pkg/SUNWps/pkginfo | $AWK ' BEGIN { FS="=" } { print $2
}`
  DEPLOY_INSTANCE=`$GREP "DEPLOY_INSTANCE="
/var/sadm/pkg/SUNWps/pkginfo | $AWK ' BEGIN { FS="=" } { print $2
}`
  DEPLOY_TYPE=`$GREP "DEPLOY_TYPE=" /var/sadm/pkg/SUNWps/pkginfo
| $AWK ' BEGIN { FS="=" } { print $2 }`
fi

redeploy() {
$ECHO "Backing up and redeploying Portal web service with updated
files..."
if [ $DEPLOY_TYPE = "IWS" ]; then
  for INSTANCE in `$LS $INSTALL_DIR/SUNWps/web-apps | $GREP https-
| $GREP -v pre`
  do
    $CP -R $INSTALL_DIR/SUNWps/web-apps/$INSTANCE
$INSTALL_DIR/SUNWps/web-apps/$INSTANCE.pre$PATCHID
  done
  DONE="n"
  if (($LOCAL_DIR)); then
    GUESS_FILE=$INSTALL_DIR/SUNWam/bin/ammultiserverinstall
    if [ -f $GUESS_FILE ]; then
      DIRBASE=`$GREP "DIRBASE"
$INSTALL_DIR/SUNWam/bin/ammultiserverinstall | cut -d "=" -f2 |
sed -e "s/\"//g"`
```

```
        GUESS=`$GREP "siepid:" $DIRBASE/admin-serv/config/adm.conf
| cut -d ":" -f2 | sed -e "s/ //g"`
        $INSTALL_DIR/SUNWps/bin/deploy redeploy -is_admin_password
"$GUESS"
 else
        while [ "$DONE" = "n" ]; do
        $ECHO
      $ECHO "Please enter Identity Server Administration Password: "
        $STTY -echo
        read ANSWER
        $STTY echo
        if [ "$ANSWER" != "" ]; then
          print "Again? $OMIT_CHAR"
          $STTY -echo
          read ANSWER_REPEAT
          $STTY echo
          print ""
          if [ "$ANSWER" != "$ANSWER_REPEAT" ]; then
            print "Password verification failed! $BELL_CHAR"
          else
            DONE="y"
          fi
        fi
    done
    $INSTALL_DIR/SUNWps/bin/deploy redeploy -is_admin_password
"$ANSWER"
    if [ $? != 0 ]; then
       $ECHO "Redeploy failed."
       $ECHO "You will need to run again manually using
$INSTALL_DIR/SUNWps/bin/deploy redeploy -is_admin_password
<password>"
    fi
    fi
  fi
elif [ $DEPLOY_TYPE = "SUNONE" ]; then
  $CP -R $DEPLOY_DOMAIN $DEPLOY_DOMAIN.pre$PATCHID
  DONE="n"
  while [ "$DONE" = "n" ]; do
    $ECHO
    $ECHO "Please enter Deploy Administration Password: "
    $STTY -echo
    read ANSWER
    $STTY echo
    if [ "$ANSWER" != "" ]; then
      print "Again? $OMIT_CHAR"
      $STTY -echo
      read ANSWER_REPEAT
```

CODE EXAMPLE B-1 `deploy` Command Script *(Continued)*

```
        $STTY echo
        print ""
        if [ "$ANSWER" != "$ANSWER_REPEAT" ]; then
          print "Password verification failed! $BELL_CHAR"

  else
          DONE="y"
        fi
    fi
  done
  $INSTALL_DIR/SUNWps/bin/deploy redeploy -deploy_admin_password
"$ANSWER"
else
  $ECHO "Unsupported or unknown DEPLOY TYPE: $DEPLOY_TYPE..."
fi

}

redeploy
```

Glossary

Access Client List (ACL) Used to describe a method by which access is controlled either by user name and password combinations, or other factors such as client IP address, or policy mappings in LDAP.

ACL See Access Client List (ACL).

Admin Console Refers to the Identity Server Administration Console; the primary UI for service configuration of the portal server software.

Automatic Proxy Configuration (PAC) file Used to determine which proxy servers to use to access specific URIs outside of the LAN.

authlessanonomous desktop An out-of-box desktop for the purpose of an information-only portal that does not require user authentication.

CA See Certificate Authority (CA).

Cascading style sheets (CSS) A style sheet format for HTML and XML documents used for styling purposes.

certificate Data that identifies a person, machine, or application.

Certificate Authority (CA) Trusted network entity that digitally signs a certificate containing information that identifies the user; such as the user's name, the issued certificate, and the certificate's expiration date.

CGI See Common Gateway Interface (CGI).

cipher suite Used in public key cryptography to determine a suitable key length and algorithm to use in secure communications.

clean install	A new installation with no remnants, such as packages and directories from a previous installation.
channel	A portlet that has been compiled using Sun-specific portal APIs.
Common Gateway Interface (CGI)	Programs executed by Web servers to provide Web clients more dynamic content.
Content aggregation	Describes the process of taking a significant amount of disparate content and assimilating it into a single interface.
cross-pollination	Describes the interaction problems between multiple Netlets using the same client/server port combinations or a single Netlet rule mapping one client port to multiple server ports.
CSS	See Cascading style sheets (CSS).
CWD	current working directory
deprecated	Describes a program or feature that is considered obsolete and in the process of being phased out, usually in favor of a replacement. Deprecated features often linger on for many years.
desktop, portal server	See portal server desktop.
Directory Server Access Management Edition (DSAME)	Marketing designation for what has become the Identity Server. DSAME initially shipped with the portal server 6.0 version.
DMZ	Demilitarized zone. In computer networking, used to refer to the area of the network nested between an outer and inner firewall.
Document type definition (DTD)	A document containing the declaration of tag names and attributes that can be used by an accompanying XML file.
DOM	See document object model (DOM).
document object model (DOM)	A specification for an API from the W3C that allows programs and scripts to update the content, structure and style of HTML and XML documents. DOMs are included in Web browsers, and provide a set of functions that let scripts access browser elements such as windows and history. Additional functions allow dynamic updating of HTML content.
DSAME	See Directory Server Access Management Edition (DSAME).
DTD	See Document type definition (DTD).

fat client	A client-side program that occupies memory and compute resources to perform non-rudimentary tasks that would typically be accomplished by a server instead.
firewall	An implementation through hardware, software, or both, that enforces network security policies to keep a network secure from intruders. Firewalls are widely used to give users secure access to the Internet as well as to separate a company's public Web server from its Intranet. Firewalls often perform some level of IP packet filtering based on a set of rules that either allow or deny the routing of packets.
forging	Describes the act of falsifying Netlets that have not been assigned to the user through policy.
FQHN	See Fully qualified host name (FQHN).
Fully qualified host name (FQHN)	Dotted path notation for the host name, subdomain if one exists, and the domain name.
Gateway	Similar to a reverse proxy, provides the interface and a level of security between remote user sessions originating from the Internet and the corporate intranet. The Gateway presents content securely from internal Web servers and application servers through a single interface to a remote user.
Gateway profile	Contains information pertinent to runtime characteristics of a Gateway running in single-instance or multi-instance mode.
hijacking	Term used to describe the act of a third party (virtual or physical) interacting with a port that the Netlet applet is actively listening on.
HTTP Basic Authentication (Basic Auth)	An authentication scheme used to protect Web-based resources by requiring a user name and password credentials before allowing user access.
identity	An extension to the user profile that can include more specific organizational data such as the user's role within the company, or the group or business unit to which the user belongs.
Identity Server	A software product from Sun that manages user sessions, service definitions and policies for the portal server.
IEAK	See Internet Explorer Administrator Kit (IEAK).
IIS	See Internet Information Services (IIS).
instance	A duplicate server process used to achieve horizontal scaling.

Internet Explorer Administrator Kit (IEAK)	Used to create customized versions of the Internet Explorer browser for the purpose of branding and to lock down options that would otherwise be changeable.
Internet Information Services (IIS)	The name of Microsoft's Web server product.
Internet Message Access Protocol (IMAP)	Allows remote access to mailboxes and folders. IMAP clients usually leave some or all messages and folders on the server, unlike POP, in which messages are downloaded to a client machine.
Java Development Kit (JDK)	Java software tools used to write Java applets or application programs.
Java runtime environment (JRE)	A subset of the Java Development Kit (JDK) for users and developers who want to redistribute the runtime environment. The Java runtime environment consists of the Java virtual machine (JVM), the Java core classes, and supporting files.
Java Server Pages (JSP)	An extension to the Java servlet technology that provides a programming mechanism for displaying dynamic content on a Web page. The JSP is an HTML page with embedded Java source code that is compiled and executed in the Web server or application server.
Java Virtual Machine (JVM)	The part of the Java runtime environment (JRE) responsible for interpreting byte codes.
JDK	See Java Development Kit (JDK).
JSP	See Java Server Pages (JSP).
LAN	See local area network (LAN).
Lightweight Directory Access Protocol (LDAP)	Used for storage and retrieval of information in a directory server. LDAP is optimized for read requests. The efficiency of informational protocols can be greatly improved by properly incorporating an LDAP server (directory server), and thus avoid some of the overhead imposed by a relational database.
LHS	Left-hand side, and indicates the left-most portion of the assignment operator ($=$).

load balancer	Presents a single, externally facing IP address to users and distributes equal load to multiple systems to attain maximum uptime and acceptable performance.
local area network (LAN)	A communications network that serves users within a set geographical area.
MCD	Mission Control Desktop. Netscape software application used to create customized versions of the Netscape Communicator browser.
MIME	Multipurpose Internet Mail Extensions. A method for transmitting non-text files through e-mail, which was originally designed for only ASCII text. MIME encodes the files using one of two encoding methods and decodes it back to its original format at the receiving end.
Mission Control Desktop (MCD)	A software administration package used to create customized Netscape Communicator browsers for corporate use.
NAT	Network Address Translation. Process of hiding internal network addresses by translating the source address when passing through the NAT router or NAT-enabled firewall.
NetApps	Portal SRA applications including Netlet and NetFile, and the portal server 6 NetMail application.
NetFile	One of the key components of the portal server secure remote access software, enables remote users to securely transfer files bidirectionally to back-end systems.
Netlet	One of the key components of the portal server secure remote access software, enables users to run common TCP/IP services securely over public networks.
Netlet applet	A Java applet that is the client portion of the Netlet component.
Netlet provider	The portal desktop portion of the Netlet provider that exposes user-specific and role-specific Netlet rules that have been configured through the Identity Server Administration console.
NFS	Network File System. A file system distributed by Sun Microsystems that enables a networked computers to access each others files in a transparent manner.
NTLM	NT Lan Manager. Microsoft Windows authentication scheme. Used for authentication purposes within a Microsoft LAN environment.
organization	An object that represents the top level of a hierarchical structure used by an enterprise to manage its departments and resources. Upon installation, the portal server software dynamically creates a top-level organization. Additional organizations can be created after installation to manage separate business units. All created organizations fall beneath the top-level organization.

out-of-box	A software configuration that has not been altered from the defaults or the state of the system just following installation with no customizations.
OWA	Outlook Web Access. Enables users to access their Exchange Server using a Web browser.
PAC	See Automatic Proxy Configuration (PAC) file.
packet filtering	Decision analysis to determine whether to route packets or not, and where to route them based on port numbers or IP traffic protocols.
PCDATA	XML content model where data characters are contained within the element tags.
personal digital certificate (PDC)	User certificate that can be used to identify and authenticate users to secured Web-based applications.
PKI	See Public Key Infrastructure (PKI).
port	The location (or socket) to which TCP/IP connections are made. The Netlet uses some special client ports to securely communicate with the Gateway.
portal	A single point of dynamic content aggregation.
portal server desktop	The presentation layer for aggregated content displayed as channels. The portal server desktop is the primary portal user interface.
portlet	(JSR168 specification) A Java technology-based Web component, managed by a portlet container that processes requests and generates dynamic content. Portlets are used by portals as pluggable user interface components that provide a presentation layer to information systems.
proxy	An intermediary program that makes and services requests on behalf of clients. Also see reverse proxy.
Public Key Infrastructure (PKI)	Encryption technology based on key (certificate) exchange and trust relationships.
push technologies	Web-based applications that refresh or stream content to a client application.
raw URL	Any string, string literal, or string object that is clearly identifiable from a syntax perspective as being a URL. Strings that begin with a protocol identifier or prepended path information are usually raw URLs.
reverse proxy	A proxy that fetches content on a user's behalf by mapping internal and external URLs so that internal network addresses and information are not exposed to external users.
Rewriter	A component of the portal server Gateway that is responsible for the translation of URLs so that all browser requests for Intranet content go through the Gateway, rather than attempting to contact Intranet content servers directly.

RHS	Right-hand side. Indicates the right-most portion of the assignment operator (=).
Rhino	The Mozilla open source JavaScript parser Java implementation.
ruleset	A logical grouping of Rewriter rules used for a specific application, host, or a group of Intranet servers on a particular domain or subdomain.
rule trumping	The inaccurate determination of a variable value to be rewritten by the Rewriter. This often occurs when one particular application requires a URL to be rewritten, while another application with the same variable name does not.
Samba	An open source program that exposes the proprietary SMB protocol for UNIX and UNIX-like clients such as Linux.
screen scraping	Acquiring data displayed on a screen by taking a snapshot of the desktop and sending the required information to recreate the desktop on another display.
section	The area of a ruleset where a particular rule should be placed according to the DTD.
Secure Remote Access (SRA)	When used in the context of Sun's portal server product, Secure Remote Access (SRA) provides additional functionality (policy engine, user and session management, and other features). Depending on the version of the portal server, the Secure Remote Access software may or may not be part of it. When used in the generic sense, secure remote access refers to making remote network access secure.
Secure Socket Layer (SSL)	A form of secure, low-level encryption used by many Web-based applications for encryption of data in transit, and to add additional security to HTTP Basic Authentication.
Server Message Block (SMB)	Used with Microsoft windows OS for user-level access to remote file systems.
Simple Object Access Protocol (SOAP)	A lightweight, XML-based protocol for exchange of information in a decentralized, distributed environment.
single-sign-on (SSO)	Used to describe scenarios where authentication is checked by one application and authentication to other applications is then made transparent, requiring no deliberate intervention on the user's behalf.
SOAP	See Simple Object Access Protocol (SOAP).
split DNS	An approach to deploying DNS so that internal addresses can be externally resolvable to specialized addresses like 127.0.0.1.

SRA	See Secure Remote Access SRA).
SRAP	iPlanet Portal Server Secure Remote Access Pack (SRAP).
SSL	See Secure Socket Layer (SSL).
SSO	See single-sign-on (SSO).
stickiness	Used to describe web sites that have enough interesting content to keep users at their site; satisfying advertisers, business partners, and end users alike.
takeover	Another Netlet, possibly from another user session, immediately binding to the `localhost` port as soon as a Netlet session is terminated.
tunneling	Process of encrypting an IP packet and wrapping it in another (unencrypted) IP packet. The source and destination addresses on the inner and outer packets can be different.
Uniform Resource Indicator (URI)	A standard notation for specifying the path and file name of a resource on a server. The server translates the URI into the native format for its operating system.
URL rewriting	When used in the context of deploying SRA, describes the process of translating URLs by first fully qualifying them and then prepending them with the Gateway address.
ULR scraper	A portal server provider that fetches content from other content servers and displays the content on the portal desktop.
VPN	Virtual private network. VPNs are a method whereby all network traffic is passed back and forth between a VPN server and client over a secure encrypted tunnel.
VPN-on-demand	Provides the same functionality as a VPN, but only traffic to and from the internal network is encrypted.
W3C	World Wide Web Consortium. The Internet standards governing body.
WebDAV	HTTP 1.1 extension for distributed authoring and versioning.
Web proxy	See reverse proxy.
wide open relay	Refers to a situation that arises when SMTP messages are not authenticated or properly filtered, which allows email spammers to use your email server as a point of origin and often results in the messaging server or entire DNS domain to be blacklisted. See `http://www.ordb.org`.
XML	Extensible Markup Language.

Index

appWin variable, 288
ARCHIVE attribute, 263
array index of JavaScript, 247
assigning encryption algorithms for Netlet, 28
associating URLs with Netlet rules, 29
attribute values, null, 229
attribute values, rules for, 182
authentication
    chaining scheme, 322–323
    credentials, 297, 354
    credentials for applications, 319
    credentials, Basic, 355
    enforcement, 306
    scheme for Microsoft Exchange, 368
authentication level, defining, 335
authentication page for the default
    organization, 308
authentication URLs, xxiii, 297–298
authentication URLs tip, 297
authlessannonymous page, user directed to, 179
authlessanonomous desktop, 321
autoconfiguration files for Netscape, 59
autoconfiguration URL, 22
auto-detect, NetFile, 142
auto-detection, 137
automated ruleset creation, 219
automatic proxy configuration files *see* PAC files
autoproxy application example, 42
availability, 5
Availability Services, 9
Available And Visible list, 95

B

backend Web applications, 311
background images, displaying, 184
BACKGROUND, rules for, 183
banner for FTP clients, adding a customized, 86
BASE HREF attribute, 179, 227
BASE tags, 179, 225, 263
baseling Gateway performance, 338
Basic authentication credentials, 355
BEA Weblogic Web container through the
    Gateway, 293

behavior URL, 271
bibliography, xxvi
BIND configuration file, 112
book organization, xix
bookmark authentication URLs tip, 298
`Bookmark` file, 114
Bookmark provider, 62, 98, 114, 116, 169, 173, 179,
    288, 291, 297, 317, 356, 395, 398, 402, 405
Bookmark provider display template, 298
bounding box, 188
Bourne shell, 353
brackets in rule entries, 246
branding section in an `ins` file, 58
branding with autoconfiguration files, 55
broken image icons, 188, 193
browser
    document object methods, 242
    document object properties, 240
    encryption key icons, 193
    JVM, 44
    JVM support, 60
    object methods, 244
    object properties, 242
    proxy settings, 21, 61
    security model, 60
    settings, configuring dynamically, 55
business to business portals, 2, 154, 351
business to consumer portals, 2
business to employee portals, 2
buttons, scripted, 239

C

cache cleanups, defining intervals between, 334
cached data, limiting, 171
Cached Socket Timeout label, 322
cached, portal desktop, 62
caching time, maximum, 36
caching, defining for the Gateway, 334
calendar content examples, 290
Calendar Server deployment, 288
Calendar Server form tip, 296
calendar-specific ruleset, mapping the, 289
cascading style sheets, rewriting, 270

case sensitive JavaScript functions, 59
certificate
    authority, 70
    database, 334
    database, defining the Gateway, 334
Certificate Enabled Gateway hosts list, 323
certificates, 73, 119, 306, 323, 332, 348
CGI for PAC applications, 41
CGI script for returning a redirection header, 277
CGI scripts that parse query strings, 235
chained authentication alternative, 335
channel action buttons, removing, 97
Channel and Container Management panel, 181
channel buttons, 67
channel properties, modifying, 96
channels, 2–4, 351
    adding rules for, 281
    definition of, 15
character set, defining for the Gateway, 333
chroot limitation, 84
cipher usage, 324
Cisco, 347
Cisco's CSS product, 312
Citrix, 5, 19, 21, 88
    configuring a Netlet rule for ICA, 90
    deployment considerations, 91
    ICA applet, 88, 266
    KeepAlive mechanisms, 79
citrix.jsp file, xxii
citrix_start.html file, 88
class names, 264
CLASSPATH variable, 50
clean.ins file, 56
client applications and Netlet, 38
client certificate authentication, 306
client footprint, 5
Client Port field, 31
client ports, 34
client-side
    disabling caching, 293
    disabling caching on the Gateway, 334
    footprint, 168
    Java code, 265
    XML transforms, 171
clipping, 4

CODE attribute, 263
    removing, 183
CODE HTML attributes, 268
code obfuscation, 206
CODEBASE attributes, 226, 263, 267–268, 284
CODEBASE principles, enabling, 70
code-signing certificates, obtaining, 73
Collaboration and Communication Services, 9
comment marks, 263
Common Hosts field, 138, 144
Communicator FTP client, using, 84
complex proxy environments, 19
components, portal server, 12
concurrent connections allowed by the
    Gateway, 322
config/mime.types file, 40
configuration files, automatic, 55
connection denied, Netlet, 37
connections failing, Netlet, 124
container directory, default, 68
content
    aggregation, 2–3
    containers, 15
    rewriting, 168
content handling enhancements, 215
content servers and the Gateway, 309
content types, 14, 172, 204, 214, 277, 327
    JavaScript, 173
    mixed, 197
Content-Length header, 53
content-type header, 277
control files, manually updating, 372
convert_expression function, 242
convert_function, 243, 246
convertps command, 221
cookies, 74
    enabling for Gateway, 355
    for SSO, 319
    iPlanetUserID, 54
    management, 305
    non-persistent, 62
    per-domain limit, 318, 355
    portal user session, 321
    rewriting, 278, 305, 318
    stale, 356

F

fat client, 34
field identifier, 232
file compression, 13
file extension (.pac), using, 41
file modification checkboxes, 139
file modification checkboxes (figure), 139
File Upload Limit and Search Directories Limit fields (figure), 140
File Upload Limit field, 139
FindProxyForURL function, 39–40
findWindow function, 402
firewall holes, reducing, 128
firewall timeouts, 63
firewalls
  and proxies, 63
  holes in, 310
  secondary, 304, 309
fixed-port applications, 13
  TCP/IP, 38
Flash content, rewriting, 278
flexibility and scalability, 307
forging Netlet rules, 37
forging static rules, 32
form content, rewriting, 231
FORM data, 197
FORM element names, duplicate, 238
FORM elements, hidden field, 235
FORM field changes, 245
FORM INPUT and OPTION data, 232
FORM INPUT tags, 177
form submission, 185
FORM tag ACTION attribute, 231
FORM tags, naming, 236
forms, 245
Forward Cookie URLs list, 278, 321
FQDN of the URL, 176
frag.html tags, 284
FRAME attributes, 69
frames, 245
frameset, Netlet, 66
FTP, 13, 21, 23
  active and passive, 81
  alternative, 128

  commands in Communicator, 84
  commands in IE, 85
  over a Netlet connection, 81
  port-host-port mapping, 82
  UID problem, 123
  URLs, 81
FTP clients, using other, 85
FTP Netlet rule, 34
  managing, 83
  setting up, 82
FTP rules
  dynamic, 81
  user name, defining, 29
FTP type, 142
ftpd, tips for administrating, 86
FTP-like command syntax, 153
ftpusers file, 86
fully qualified host name, 31
fully qualified URL, 173
fully qualified URL with no path, 178
function parameters, rules for, 182

G

Gateway, 12–13, 303–357
  access list, 350
  application and content servers, and, 309
  balancing the load, 347
  certificate database, defining, 334
  concurrent connections, 322
  configuration and cookies, 318
  configured to use a Netlet proxy, 337
  configured to use a Rewriter proxy, 336
  configuring the, 314
  connection traffic, controlling, 320
  debugging, configuring for additional, 333
  defining the user, 331
  deploying, 309
  deployment scenarios, 350
  description of, 304
  encryption, 306
  encryption control, 323
  fetching internal content, 321
  high availability (HA), and, 335
  horizontal and vertical scaling, 307
  how it works, 308

P

configurations, 21
passwords, 318
settings in autoconfiguration files, 55
transparency, 22
URL addresses, 40
PROXY entry, 22
Proxy Password List, 318
`pssetup` command, 220
`psSRAP_Rewriter_recordURI` log file, 292
public anonymous access, 29
public key, 119
purchasing portal server software, 9
push servers and the Netlet, 30

R

rate of authentications, 338
raw URLs, 172, 177, 240
raw URLs in JavaScript content, 177
RC4 cryptography, 64
RC5 algorithm, 21
`readpkcs` command, 72
reauthentication, 34
Reauthentication For Connections option, 35
`redeploy` subcommand, 67, 411
redirected requests, 308
redirection header, returning the, 277
redirection URLs, 317
reducing complexity, 307
referrer, portal, 253
registered services for the new organization (figure), 155
regular expression matching problems, 203
regular expressions, 246
relative prepended path, 178
relative URLs, 180–181
release notes, portal server, 10
reliability load test graphs, 344
reliability load test script, 342
reliability testing, 342
`reliability.js` file, xxiii
remote access employees, 18
Remote Access software, 7

remote access through browsers, 180
remote file systems, 147
remote point of presence, 21
remote terminal access, 117
remote users and the Gateway, 308
Remote X commands through an SSH session (figure), 121
Remote X tunneling, 117
remote-employee entry point, 37
removing nuisance log entries (example), 60
repopulating the PAC file URL, 59
request pool size, Gateway, 319
requests for internal URLs, enabling, 169
resolved proxy to use is null, 122
Resonate, 347
Resonate's Central Dispatch load balancer, 312
resourcesURL, 285
restarting the portal server, 68
reverse mapping, 327
reverse proxy, 304
mappings, 169
similarity to rewriting technology, 169
Rewrite all URLs checkbox, 173, 176, 326
Rewrite Form Input Tags list rules, 264
Rewriter, 12–13, 167–301
configuring, 191
configuring for application integration, 223
deploying, 181
deployment scenarios, 280
dynamically created HTML, 89
engines, configuring, 327
example, 173
how it works, 172
identifying misconfigurations, 213
improvements, 211
Java Enterprise System features, 301
logging, 292
Microsoft Exchange integrations, 359–391
proxies, 336
results, 174
rules for Exchange integration, 380
rules, adding and modifying, 207
tips from the trenches, 293
versus the browser, 180
versus the Netlet, 179
Rewriter proxies and the Gateway, 308, 311

Rewriter ruleset
    for Exchange, creating, 365
    for iNotes integration, creating, 396
    for the desktop, 402
rewriting
    ActiveX, 279
    APPLET parameters, 263
    array data, 215
    content, 168
    cookies, 278, 305, 318
    CSS content, 400
    Demo desktop, the, 284
    Flash content, 278
    HTC, 275
    HTML attributes, rules for, 385
    HTTP headers, 277
    indirectly, 179
    JavaScript content, rules for, 380
    JavaScript event handlers, 186
    JavaScript function parameters, rules for, 382
    JavaScript image object assignments, 187
    JavaScript methods, rules for, 182
    raw URLs with URL type, 214
    URLs, 311
    URLs dynamically at execution time, 173
    URLs in CSS content, 388
    variables or expressions with EXPRESSION
        type, 214
    WebDav, 279
    XML, 271
    XML attribute values, 191
    XML PCDATA, 273
    XML tag attributes, 272
    XML Text Data, rules for, 383
    XSL transforms, 275
Rhino, 22
    installation information (Note), 49
    jar file, 49
    JavaScript engine, 45
    and PAC files, 44
    parser missing, 48
rich text editing in email composition, 364
role-based portal, 125
root level, 23
root password and NetFile with NFS, 146
rule extraction methodology, 192
Rule Name entry, 27
rule trumping, reducing, 211

rules
    adding, 26
    attributes of, 232
    definition of, 14
    deleting, 26
    editing, 26
    Exchange integration, 380
    generalized, 234, 237
    individual, 183
    migration of, 216
    Netlet, 21
    order of, 233
    simplified syntax of, 301
    specified as XML tags, 214
rules and rulesets, adding Rewriter, 207
`rules.xml` file, 222
ruleset
    application example, default, 184
    associated with Gateway instances, 405
    comprised of XML, 172
    definition of, 14
    extensions, 301
    language, 214
    mapping per host/domain, 213
    multiple, 326
`RuleSet.dtd` DTD file, 182
rulesets that break menu functionality, 403
runtime characteristics, Gateway process, 331
runtime Rewriter function definitions, 215
`rwadmin` command, 208–209

S

Samba, 147
`samplecontent.jsp` file, 93
SampleJSP
    attributes, changing, 95
    channel properties, modifying, 96
    code, 93
SAP, 319
satellite connections, 169
scalability, 306
scalability and flexibility, 307
scoping, JavaScript object, 242
scramblers, 258
scraped content, rules for, 182

inform**IT**

YOUR GUIDE TO IT REFERENCE

Articles

Keep your edge with thousands of free articles, in-depth features, interviews, and IT reference recommendations – all written by experts you know and trust.

Online Books

Answers in an instant from **InformIT Online Book's** 600+ fully searchable on line books. Sign up now and get your first 14 days **free**.

POWERED BY

Catalog

Review online sample chapters, author biographies and customer rankings and choose exactly the right book from a selection of over 5,000 titles.

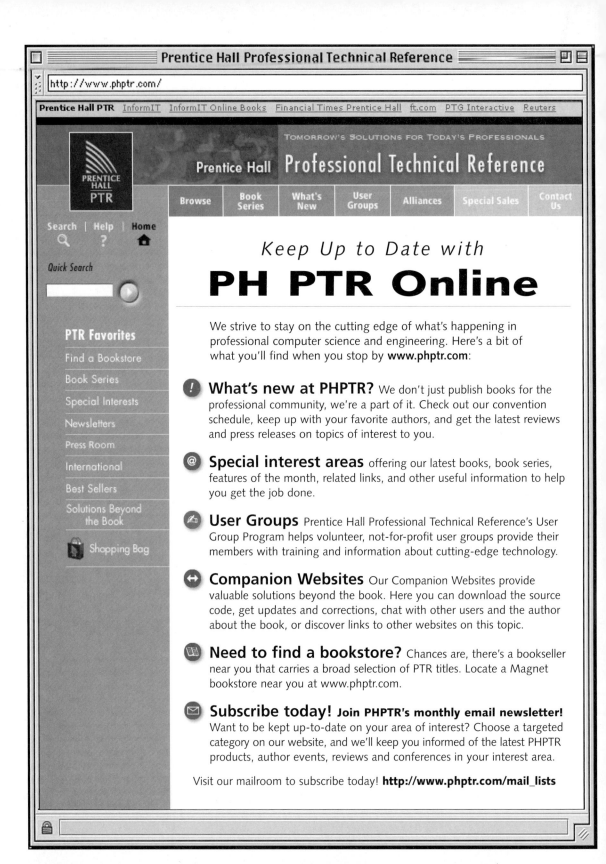

http://www.phptr.com/

Prentice Hall PTR   InformIT   InformIT Online Books   Financial Times Prentice Hall   ft.com   PTG Interactive   Reuters

PRENTICE HALL PTR

TOMORROW'S SOLUTIONS FOR TODAY'S PROFESSIONALS

Prentice Hall **Professional Technical Reference**

| Browse | Book Series | What's New | User Groups | Alliances | Special Sales | Contact Us |

Search | Help | Home

Quick Search

PTR Favorites

Find a Bookstore

Book Series

Special Interests

Newsletters

Press Room

International

Best Sellers

Solutions Beyond the Book

Shopping Bag

Keep Up to Date with
PH PTR Online

We strive to stay on the cutting edge of what's happening in professional computer science and engineering. Here's a bit of what you'll find when you stop by **www.phptr.com**:

(!) What's new at PHPTR? We don't just publish books for the professional community, we're a part of it. Check out our convention schedule, keep up with your favorite authors, and get the latest reviews and press releases on topics of interest to you.

(@) Special interest areas offering our latest books, book series, features of the month, related links, and other useful information to help you get the job done.

(⌂) User Groups Prentice Hall Professional Technical Reference's User Group Program helps volunteer, not-for-profit user groups provide their members with training and information about cutting-edge technology.

(↔) Companion Websites Our Companion Websites provide valuable solutions beyond the book. Here you can download the source code, get updates and corrections, chat with other users and the author about the book, or discover links to other websites on this topic.

(📖) Need to find a bookstore? Chances are, there's a bookseller near you that carries a broad selection of PTR titles. Locate a Magnet bookstore near you at www.phptr.com.

(✉) Subscribe today! Join PHPTR's monthly email newsletter! Want to be kept up-to-date on your area of interest? Choose a targeted category on our website, and we'll keep you informed of the latest PHPTR products, author events, reviews and conferences in your interest area.

Visit our mailroom to subscribe today! **http://www.phptr.com/mail_lists**